"... an elegant historical novel, written in the first person voice of the complicated British naval hero, takes readers from his beginnings to the moment of his death. Exhaustively researched, Tortorice's battle scenes are exciting ... he has ably created both the thunder of deck guns and the pounding of one man's heart."

—*Blueink Review*

"This novel succeeds in painting a rich portrait of Nelson, bringing him to life as a man who is as ardent in bed as he is in battle ... a well-researched and absorbing, sprawling novel that gives a real flavor of the man, the era, and the sea."

—*Kirkus Review*

"Alternately scholastic and romantic, the novel I, Horatio, incorporates historical documents into an imaginative, riveting, and often scandalous first-person account of trying times on the high seas.

Tortorice's research proves expansive, and excerpts from Nelson's correspondence, as well as from documents connected to those around him, add to the novel's realism. Horatio's personal arrogance is on full display, but his genius as a military leader shines through.

Nelson becomes a larger-than-life figure. I, Horatio, is a gripping and intelligent adventure story, peppered with intriguing social commentary."

—*Michelle Schingler, Clarion Review*

I, Horatio

A Novel of Historical Fiction

Donald A. Tortorice

authorHOUSE®

AuthorHouse™
1663 Liberty Drive
Bloomington, IN 47403
www.authorhouse.com
Phone: 1-800-839-8640

Cover design by Greg Bear/gbmediadesign

Published by AuthorHouse 01/30/2015

ISBN: 978-1-4969-3237-2 (sc)
ISBN: 978-1-4969-3238-9 (hc)
ISBN: 978-1-4969-3236-5 (e)

Library of Congress Control Number: 2014914021

Contents

For Nance, Coops, Wook, Tock, Arm, Ty, and Krinta.

Preface

This is a book of history and fiction. Its plot is taken from history. All of Nelson's assignments, missions, and engagements with the enemy are true. I have presented a chronology based upon a time line of events that actually happened. Letters, dispatches, and many historical quotes are taken from historical fact and are presented in italics. However, major elements of the book are fiction. One can never know exactly what Nelson may have been thinking and what he actually said during the various dramatic episodes of his life. I have simply tried, after decades of reading and thinking about the man, to present him as I think he would have acted during the events I describe. In so many ways he was an enigma. His chaplain aboard the HMS *Victory*, Alexander Scott, wrote of him, "Men are not always themselves and put on their behaviour with their clothes, but if you live with a man on board ship for years, if you are continually with him in his cabin, your mind will soon find out how to appreciate him. I could forever tell of the qualities of this beloved man, Horatio Nelson. I have not shed a tear before the 21st October, and since whenever I am alone, I am quite like a child." He also said that Nelson "possessed the wisdom of a serpent and the innocence of the dove." As Nelson's statue stands above the great illuminated column in Trafalgar Square, he is remembered as the savior of the British Isles, and the remembrance is fully justified.

As a naval commander, Nelson was unique - and magnificent. When a junior captain at the Battle of Cape St. Vincent, he took his small frigate out of line, arguably against orders, and fearlessly led the attacks that resulted in the capture of two enormously larger Spanish battleships. In the capture of Corsica, he lost the sight of his right eye, and in the attack on Tenerife in the Canary Islands, he lost his right arm. Undaunted, he continued to serve, and the Admiralty was wise enough to value his ability to command. At the Battle of the Nile, his tactical imagination in ordering the first sea battle at night and brilliantly exploiting the strategic vulnerability of an anchored enemy fleet was nothing less than genius. At the Battle of Copenhagen, when the issue of victory or defeat hung in the balance and his commanding officer signalled a withdrawal, he lifted his telescope to his blind eye and said, "I see no such signal," and continued the furious engagement until it resulted in victory and ultimately the end of Napoleon's armed alliance with the Baltic States. Finally at Trafalgar, he infused his captains, his band of brothers, with a sense of purpose and commitment that reflected his own, which then won him a victory, terminating permanently any ability of Napoleon to invade the British homeland. If one looks for a greater military commander, the search will be in vain.

I have been somewhat graphic in relating his various episodes with women, and the reason is because those relationships were without doubt very meaningful episodes in his experience. Unabashedly they are presented with the same inferential detail as presentations of his actions in battle or his interaction with superior officers, colleagues, or others with whom he had meaningful contact. All are portrayed in an attempt to present the full tapestry of his life. Those who are familiar with Nelson's life will know that his precipitous marriage to Fanny was troubled. In my reading I have been led to believe that there was probably some psychological or physiological condition that rendered Fanny to be less than an acceptable fit with Nelson's need for a woman, and her inability to conceive children with him was always profoundly troublesome. At the other end of his sexual spectrum, Emma Hamilton was perfect, and his adulation of her continued through his life, memorialized in the last words he wrote before he died. Along the way his affairs with an unnamed woman in London and the opera singer named Adelaide Coreglia are true. And of course, his relationship with Emma Hamilton was the central obsession of his life. However, the sexual elements of his recovery treatment in Jamaica, his brief episode with a woman named Juliana in Helsingor, one with Mary Moutray in Antigua, and his dalliance with Celeste in France are fiction. However, such occurrences quite likely happened one way or another, and presenting them as I have done is clearly within the scope of his proclivity.

This book has been in process for more than fifty years. As a first-year midshipman at the University of Texas at Austin, I read a memorable textbook titled *Sea Power* by E. B. Potter and Fleet Admiral Chester W. Nimitz, USN. The part of that text that fascinated – even mesmerized me – was the section on the Napoleonic wars and particularly the role played by Admiral Horatio Nelson in destroying French and Spanish fleets that would have been crucial to an attack on the only part of Western Europe Napoleon had not subjugated, the British homeland. By the time I left Austin, Nelson had become one of the iconic heroes of my life. I like to think that he would be pleased to know that his nature of total commitment to duty was a model for the enablement of a very young man halfway around the world in the middle of America to transcend from an average student to one who graduated with honours, commanded the battalion of midshipman at the university, and was granted the Nimitz sword as the top graduate of the naval officers' training class. Between then and now, I served as an officer in the US Navy, including the command of a swift boat in the Vietnam War, leaving the theatre of conflict with an individual Vietnamese Cross of Gallantry. I attended law school at the University of California at Berkeley, practiced law for more than twenty-six years as partner with a firm based in Philadelphia, Pennsylvania, and served as a professor at the Law School of the College of William and Mary for thirteen years before I retired to write in 2013. During all of that time I have been absorbed in readings concerning Nelson's life, his battles, the ships in which he served, the people around him, and the profound effect he had on the sweep of history. I always intended at some point to write this book, and now I have been able to make it a reality.

There are hundreds of truly excellent books on Nelson's life by authors who, with remarkable assiduity, have researched and written exhaustively – and excellently. Among them I salute Alfred Thayer Mahan, Edgar Vincent, Colin White, Christopher Hibbert, Peter Goodwin, Tom Pocock, Robert Southey, Robert Gardiner, Alan McGowan, John Harland, Marianne Czisnik, James Harrison, Nepean Longridge, Adam Nicolson, Joseph Callo, Pauline Blair, Terry Coleman, Andrew Lambert, Geoffrey Bennett, Nicholas Tracy, John Sugden, Roget Knight, Angus Konstam, Roy Adkins, Joel Hayward, Ernle Bradford, Stephanie Jones, J. T. McDaniel, Brian Lavery, Simon Worrall, Carola Oman, David Lyon, David Donachie, and John Webb. And even this rather extensive list is incomplete.

My objective has been to have Horatio Nelson tell his fearless, emotional, sensitive, sensual, triumphant, tragic, and robust story in a manner that is as close as I could achieve to the way in which I believe he would have told it. I hope I have succeeded.

Horatio Nelson was a man of unparalleled and fascinating measure. He was also mortal.

A Special Note Concerning Italics

This is a book of history and fiction. Its chronological plot is taken from history. All of Nelson's assignments, missions, and engagements with the enemy are true. I have tried to weave a tapestry of his life based upon major events that actually happened. However, there is a major element of fiction. As I present this entire account as being from Nelson himself (with the exception of letters, dispatches, and historical quotes), it is fiction, and those matters that are taken from historical letters, dispatches, and colloquy are presented in *italics*.

Chapter 1

I Remember

I, Horatio Nelson, was given by God a life that I was destined to live. It was given as a clear slate upon which I could write my destiny simply by the way I determined to live that life. I willed myself to do everything I undertook so that when the opportunity was met, executed, and exhausted, I could look back and say with truth that came from my heart and soul, "That was absolutely the best I could do." I believe that I was a man favoured by the Almighty with a nature of commitment and fury taken to the very end of every engagement. I knew no other way, and by the grace of God, I loved it. I absolutely loved it.

There is much I remember, much of both triumph and disaster. I remember that when dawn broke on the morning of 21 October 1805, the sea was calm, and a mild but ample wind blew from the west-north-west. As Admiral of the Fleet, I slowly paced the quarterdeck of HMS *Victory* and looked out upon a scene that was, to my eyes, a view of majestic beauty. Some twenty miles to the east lay Cape Trafalgar at the south-west corner of Spain. The wind filled the sails of two great fleets – mine and the combined fleet of the enemy. We were about to engage in a battle that would define dominance of the seas for the next century. Our intelligence sources had advised that the combined French and Spanish fleet of more than thirty warships had rested at anchor in the port of Cadiz under command of French Admiral Pierre de Villeneuve. It was the fleet Bonaparte needed to enable an invasion of Britain. Our task, my task, was to destroy that fleet. Two days earlier on 19 October, scouting frigates reported that the admiral had taken the entire fleet into open water. I suspected that he might dash to the Strait of Gibraltar without engagement, but we had intercepted him and his entire combined fleet. They would have no escape. What would become the Battle of Trafalgar was at hand.

I had fully explained the memorandum of my battle plan to the captains of each ship in my fleet, and they, each and every one of my valiant band of brothers, were under full sail and flying at the enemy. I believed victory to be a certainty. I knew my ships. I knew and had utmost confidence in every captain of every ship. I knew the British seamen and had not a trace of doubt that they would prevail, as they had so magnificently done when we destroyed the enemy fleets in the Battles of Cape St. Vincent, the Nile and Copenhagen. A great victory was about to unfold. I knew that it would be so, and the stream of praise and honours that had already been bestowed upon me would become a deluge of glory.

Before that morning at Trafalgar, my life had been very much like a river that ran swiftly in many twists and turns, winding fitfully, inexorably, wonderfully, and always to the sea.

There are many memories, very many, rich and clear.

A Boy Captain

Some twenty years before Trafalgar when I was a very young captain, there was a time when I truly feared that I would die. I had crossed the Atlantic in September 1780 to my first sea command in the Caribbean, but when I was brought home to Portsmouth, I was deathly ill. The surgeon of HMS *Lion*, the ship that had carried me during the voyage, often doubted that I would survive the crossing. I remember vividly the bouts of vomit, disorientation, chest pain, and consuming weakness, but I had survived to be gingerly carried and placed upon the dock in a canvas bed. I remember the many times during the transit when, burning with fever, I prayed fervently to God that He would spare me.

I had contracted malaria during a short campaign in Nicaragua, where the fury and temporary success in action against a Spanish garrison in the San Juan River was brief and insignificant compared with the disablement and ultimate defeat suffered by the expedition as a consequence of the swarming attacks of darting, buzzing, biting mosquitoes along the coast that would thereafter bear their name as the Mosquito Coast. I also suffered from dysentery after I drank water from an apparently clear pool over which branches of a manchineel tree had provided a seemingly benign shade. It was not realized that the shade of the tree's overhanging branches would be accompanied by a release of caustic sap that would impart a poison to the men of the entire expeditionary force who drank from the waters, including Colonel John Polson, commander of the expedition, who at first had called me "that thin and light-haired boy."

I was at the time 22 years old and commander of the twenty-eight-gun frigate, HMS *Hinchinbrook*. My orders had been to protect the troop convoy and to deliver its soldiers at the mouth of the San Juan River, which led to a Spanish garrison and fortress some forty miles upriver.

Capturing the fort was the objective of Polson's brigade. My task was simply to deliver and disembark the brigade and await its return. However, a significant action was about to take place, and I would then (as forever after) find it impossible to be passive. To me, passivity at a time when I could contribute was a mark of disservice. With the scent of action in the air, I had to be a part of it. Involuntarily I wanted to become a wolf within the pack, disregarding limitations and blind to obvious dangers, immune to impulses of reason or safety, and deaf to everything except the clamour of impending battle. Unable to stand aside and await the results of the expedition, I assembled a contingent of Hinchinbrook seamen and marines, and we joined Colonel Polson's force.

Age 22

The ascent to the Spanish positions was reported by our intelligence dispatches to be "open and dry, abounding in necessities of every kind." It was, however, anything but that. The river was brown and rapid, overturning many boats and swamping others, with provisions and men scattered in the racing water. Amidst an enthralling beauty overhead, complete with the music of spectacular songbirds, egrets, and parrots of every colour, the situation on the ground was despairing. Our force slowly slogged through muck and mud above our boots. We carried heavy packs and heavier guns, constantly swatting at mosquitoes, flies, and hideous looking spiders. One of the men walked into a snake dangling from a bush and was bitten near the eye. Within hours he was dead. Another who ventured off to relieve himself was mangled by a jaguar.

After weeks of ascent against the river through wet savannahs and deep, fetid jungle, the expedition came upon a Spanish battery guarding the approach to the fort. I assessed the situation and went to Polson with a plan. "Sir, the redoubt is limited, and I believe that I and my company of men can take it. If your forces proceed in silence up the bank of the river to block any retreat, I shall make a frontal attack with my seamen and marines. Their ramparts are earthen and can be scaled. With haste, it can be done without time for reinforcement from the fort."

Polson paused, walked about ten feet away, paused again in thought, and then turned and said to me, "It is a workable scheme. I should dispatch a company to make the assault."

That was, however, not my plan, and I replied, "With respect, sir, your total force is essential to protect the rear, and we have no knowledge of the size of reinforcements that may be coming from the fort. Your total complement will serve as a battle group to decide even a sizeable engagement with any new forces. That is crucially important. My men and I can take the garrison."

Polson replied, "But you must be sure that you can succeed. Are you confident that your group is large enough?"

I answered him with assurance, "Colonel, in the morning's light my men and I will be standing on the ramparts. I guarantee it." I looked at him directly with a complete faith in my ability to carry out the plan. I also believed that although he had been sceptical at the beginning of the mission about my abilities and temperament, throughout the entire and agonising trek up the river, I had made myself the most resolute officer in the campaign, never faltering in the daily misery or exigencies along the way. I constantly strove to be an example of the determination and resolve that Polson wanted in subordinates. I was confident that he now believed in me and trusted none of his subordinates more than myself. Perhaps he felt a reservation that I would die leading the assault, but such was the accepted risk of any young officer in battle. I was more than willing. I was eager to take that risk.

Polson paused and ordered, "Very well. Let us proceed thus."

Through the early morning Polson silently led his forces to the upstream rear of the garrison. He positioned his light cannons and soldiers to confront any retreat from the garrison or reinforcement from the fortress and watched for my assault with *Hinchinbrook* seamen and marines.

Once Polson had moved into position, I gathered my sailors and marines. I called them close, looked into their eyes, and spoke, "My good men, God, in his wisdom and grace, has given me the great privilege of commanding each of you in an action which we are about to undertake. It will be the fulfilment of a destiny God has given to us all, and I am deeply thankful that we few souls will together, on this day, go into battle for God, king, and country. So many of our countrymen will never have the divine calling we are about to have, and in our response to that calling we will define ourselves as the very best men of the empire. You and I will land on the island before us and take its garrison with the strength of our arms and the force of our will. Today we will do that which you will tell to your children and they will repeat to their children. The pride that will come from the telling of today will be a light within your soul, and the history of your name will be worth more than gold. Today each of you will be a great man, and we shall have a great victory. God is with us. Now let us go."

The men looked at each of the faces around them. I believed that from man to man, anxiety had been allayed, and what had been their individual fear was replaced with resolve of the group in a mission that together we would undertake. And I was resolved to be the very embodiment of a young Hotspur officer leading them.

It had been hoped that the Spaniards could be taken by surprise, but as our boats paddled furiously up the river current, a lookout either heard the splash of oars or saw us approach and cried an alarm that brought the full garrison to the rampart. As the boats reached the island, the Spaniards opened fire with muskets and cannon. The great volley of their fire blessedly whizzed over our heads or fell short in splats of mud in front of us. As my lead boat touched the island, I lifted my sword, and with the fullest voice I could muster, I cried, "Follow me!" I leapt to the ground, sinking almost to my knees in mud that sucked off my shoes. I paid no mind and slogged to firmer ground, circling my raised sword and shouting, "Follow me. Follow me." The sailors and marines dashed with me toward the rampart. Spanish guns fired in a roaring volley. Musket balls whistled through the air, but had no effect on our charge. With my sword held high, I and my gallant men ran toward to the rampart with nothing else but one firm and singular intent. We must engage the Spanish man-to-man. The rampart would be taken, or we would die in the effort.

Faced with the speed of the assault, the stern visages that could be seen on each assaulting face, and the evident determination of our charge, the Spanish commander called a retreat. As his force scrambled to the rear of the garrison, Polson's contingent opened fire. The Spanish captain stopped, and knowing that he would soon be isolated in crossfire, he dropped his rifle and raised his hands in surrender.

The victory was small and quick but exquisite. None of our assaulting force had been killed. Two marines had been wounded. I called my men together and then approached and knelt by the wounded men, shoeless and with mud splattered over my uniform. I placed my hands on their shoulders and spoke to them, "Know this. The wounds upon your skin will leave a scar, and it will be greater than any medal that could be given to you. It is witness to what you have done today and can never be taken away." I stood, turned to the assembled group, and told them, "What you have accomplished today is nothing less than valiant. I knew with certainty it would be so, and let it be testament to all that you ever shall do or become. My pride in you is surely small compared with the pride that must burn in your chests. What you did today in the face of fear and death must now be the pattern of your life." I smiled and looked into the eyes of all, turning from man to man. The spirit of the day and the morale of my gallant men glowed upon their faces.

The euphoria of the moment would, however, be short-lived. The balance of the expedition would be nothing less than disaster. I had encouraged an immediate attack upon the fortress itself, but Colonel Polson decided to wait for several weeks until promised reinforcements arrived with scaling ladders, more artillery, and fresh soldiers so that a full siege could be laid against the fort. But when the remnants of reinforcement arrived, they reported that all of their cannons, most of their ammunition and stores, along with many of their men had been lost to the river, now swollen with a furious current from the winter rains. Of far greater consequence, Polson's force almost in its entirety had been overcome with dysentery and fevers, the combined effects of malaria and manchineel poison. I was among the worst to be affected, bedridden and suffering from dizziness with only short periods of comatose sleep. The reinforcing party had also delivered orders that I had been appointed to command of the frigate HMS *Janus* and was to return to Jamaica. At first Polson thought me too ill to move but soon concluded that taking me to the coast was a better alternative to remaining in the miasma of the jungle, where I would probably perish. I was, therefore, sent downstream together with the remainder of my ship's seamen and marines.

When I arrived at the *Hinchinbrook*, my friend, Captain Cuthbert Collingwood, who had been appointed my successor in command of the ship, expressed shock by my emaciated condition – yellow in colour, almost inaudible in speech and hardly able to move. Collingwood's surgeon ordered me bathed, provided with fresh nourishment, and treated with quinine. The following voyage to Jamaica did not bring a material recovery, and assumption of command of the *Janus* became impossible.

Jamaica

In Jamaica, I came under the care of an old friend, Lord Captain William Cornwallis, commander of HMS *Lion* and younger brother to General Charles Cornwallis, soon to be discredited with loss of the American colonies at the Battle of Yorktown. The younger Will Cornwallis was a looming figure in Jamaica, a big, red-faced man who was direct and commanding, but circumspect in his treatment of others and held in high regard by both seniors and subordinates. His acumen and tact had also made him beloved in the islands and particularly successful in island business. He immediately decided not to send me to the local hospital, where so many of its patients had perished. Instead he brought me to his plantation home and entrusted my care to Cubah Cornwallis, an articulate and beautiful slave, freed by the bachelor Cornwallis for service as his housekeeper, nurse - and eventual mistress.

Cubah and her remedies of quinine, herbal teas, daily hot baths, vegetarian nourishment, and hand massages with engaging conversation had been particularly effective in treatment of island fevers, malaria, and dysentery. It would be so with me as well. On the first morning of her care I was given a bath almost too hot to stand followed by a meal of small pieces of banana, guava, and pot liquor of rosemary and collard greens with crumbled cornbread. She then laid me out, weak and passive on my bed, raised my head, and softly dried and combed my hair. She then placed my head on the softest pillow I had ever felt and covered my body with soft muslin, leaving only my head exposed.

Cubah looked at me and said, "Now, my beautiful young captain, I want you to think of nothing more than the man you are." Her fingers closed my eyes and began a rhythmic caressing of my forehead. After rubbing slowly for a while and whispering a soft and dulcet song, she continued, "Let me tell you this. You are simply the sum of all your parts, and we must heal every one of them before anything else can happen for you in this world." She took down the muslin to my waist and ran her hands over my shoulders and down my arms and then up and down again in repetitions that each seemed more vitalising than the last. She then moved to my chest and abdomen, tracing the muscles in repeating but smooth strokes. It was not a massage that pressed upon the muscles but a caressing outline of each and every inundation of my wasted torso. She then removed the coverlet entirely, and in a reflex of modesty I reached for my cover. Cubah laughed softly, placed her hand on my arm, and said, "Relax, my young captain. There is nothing here that I have not seen. Relax completely and think of the very best things you can remember." I relented and relaxed, exposed, vulnerable, and trusting of this woman whose touch became the best comfort I had ever known. Her soft magic drew me down and back into a perfect reverie of childhood games with my brothers and sisters on the field of the Burnham Thorpe green, near Norfolk. In a trance I could see so clearly the beautiful face of my young sister, Kate, whose blond hair was haloed by sunlight. Then came sleep, not fitful and dark, but for the first time in a month, it was deep, soft, and paced by the rhythm of peaceful breathing.

In the early evening I awoke, covered again with the loose muslin that allowed a soft trade wind breeze to cool my body. What I noticed first was the clarity of things about the room. I could now see the small folds of the window drapes slowly moving in the tropical wind and the features of pictures which before had simply been a blur. I could see through the window, and in the distance I saw a deep red and gold outline of the setting sun above the dark green Jamaica hills. For the first time I could sense the sweet azaleas surrounding the veranda as well as the musty coconut mulch that covered their roots. I tried to sit up but the exertion would not be tolerated by my unrecovered brain that showered stars before my eyes and sent a streaking pain into my head. I fell back on the bed and heard Cubah enter the room.

"No, no, my young captain, you must not hurry. It will take time to climb out of this deep hole. Just lie here and know that you are a little better but have a long way to climb. We will get you out, but you must be patient. The best and important things cannot be rushed. Lie still." She placed her hands on my chest and repeated softly, "Be still. Be still." Again she lowered the coverlet to my waist and began the same soft and beautiful song I could not understand, while she moved her fingertips over my forehead and face with a perfectly exquisite effect. I did not fall into a sleep, but I savoured every movement of her touch as her progression seemed to awaken every successive part of my body. She finally raised the coverlet to my shoulders, sat and looked at me, and placed her hand on the muslin covering my manhood. Her hand did not move but simply rested there. The touch was exciting, and no words were spoken. She paused, smiled, leaned over, lightly kissed my forehead, and said, "You will be fine my sweet young man. You will be fine." She then left the room.

For the next week Cubah continued her quinine and nutrition, adding mild goat broth and some sweet cane cakes. The base of fruits and greens, however, remained. She returned each morning and late afternoon to her song and touches, leaving me at the end of each session with a sense of relief and restoration, each session finishing with the sense of excitement and in each instance a termination of increased tumescence of my ever more sensitive manhood. Never before had I felt such a touch from a woman.

After a few days I was able to walk about, slowly rediscovering my balance and gingerly holding onto a chair and then a door and then a porch railing. I came to love the late-afternoon breezes, sitting on the chaises under shade of the palm and banana trees that outlined the veranda and circled the large Cornwallis estate house. In the late afternoon, tea and biscuits with bits of dried fig and raisins would be brought to me by Cubah or her daughter, Elsinore, a beautiful young woman with a bright smile and complexion like coffee with milk, suggesting strongly that her parentage surely had some English ingredient. As I so enjoyed my times on the veranda, my thoughts often returned to the San Juan expedition, and the more I recalled the chronology of action, the more anxious I became.

Would the final account of failure attach blame to me, and would Colonel Polson bring me and my actions within its orbit of disaster? I was keenly aware of how detailed the Admiralty would expect the account to be and how profound its effect would be on the possibility of future appointments. A nagging concern haunted me as a constant and dark companion I could not escape.

After a week I began having dinner with Lord Captain Cornwallis. They were lovely affairs. Warm delicacies were set upon pale china with silver service. I believed Lord Cornwallis enjoyed my company. He also spoke frequently of the praise my former commanders had paid to my prior service and the promise of my future service to the Crown. Those accounts buoyed my hopes and assuaged but did not erase my nagging doubts concerning the San Juan report. Frequently Lord Cornwallis would ask my opinion on the art of seamanship, such as close-haul tacking, reefing before the wind, or paralleling close hauled yards to the horizon. To each question, my answers seemed well received, and frequently Lord Cornwallis would laugh heartily and almost shout, "By God, lad, that's right on the point! I would do the same." The exchanges were enjoyed immensely by both of us, forming what I believed to be a bond that only those committed to sailing the open seas could understand.

In the fourth week of my stay at the Cornwallis house, news came that upon orders of Governor Parker, I would be transferred at the end of the week for convalescence at Cooper's Hill, the governor's manse at the top of Admiral's Mountain, and that my care would become the charge of Lady Parker and her staff. A letter transmitting the orders had stated that the governor sought information from me before he finalized his report on the San Juan expedition. His account would be the final and official report. I received the news with a conflicting sentiment. While I was relieved that I would be able to provide a direct commentary on the report, I nevertheless regretted deeply that my recuperation at the Cornwallis house would be ended. Nevertheless, I looked forward to seeing Governor Parker, with whom I had served as a lieutenant when he commanded HMS *Bristol*. As Cubah assisted me back to my bed following Cornwallis's announcement, she stated sombrely, "This is too early in your cure for you to leave, my young captain. We will have to rush things more than I would like, but I hope it will suffice. Elsinore will tend to you in the morning." I had no appreciation of her meaning.

I slept well through the night, and following my normal ablutions, I readied myself for what had been my relished morning ministrations. As Cubah had promised, Elsinore appeared with a broad smile.

"Mother has told me that I should tend to you this morning, my sweet captain, and it will be my pleasure to serve you."

"Why doesn't Cubah come?" I asked with true puzzlement.

"She believes it now best done by me," Elsinore answered. "I also asked her earlier if I could do the final treatments, and she agreed that it would be best. Just lie back and we shall see."

I did not understand but was captivated by the young woman I had watched and admired with a special intent as she moved about the house with a beauty and grace that would attract the gaze of any healthy young man. I lay back, covered by my muslin, and she began the pattern of Cubah's caressing, except that her hands were smaller though just as magical. To each progression, there was a combined but not conflicting relaxation and excitement. Her touch to my abdomen radiated a sensation down to the tips of my fingers, and when she drew her fingers across the bottom of my feet, the back of my scalp tingled. I lay throughout, transfixed and totally receptive. But instead of completing the ministration at my feet and resting her hand upon my covered manhood as Cubah had done, she began to ascend my legs, first with the ankles and then my calf and thighs, abdomen and shoulders a bit more quickly than before. She brought my arms up so that my hands were above my head and gently rubbed the inside of my forearm and upper arm. She moved her fingers through the light hair of my underarm, stroking in a way I never dreamed could be so sensitive and pleasurable. Surprised by the excitement of this new touching, I looked anxiously at her, and she said, "Don't move yet, my sweet captain. Relax and wait. Just wait." Her hands moved slowly to my chest and abdomen, while my excitement increased exquisitely with each touch and movement. By the time her progress down to my abdomen had reached the blond mane at the base of my now excited manhood, it was standing at erect attention. She moved her fingers upon it and said, "You have made great progress, my sweet captain. You have made great progress." As her fingers traced up and down its length, every part of my sinew came alive. She then raised her skirt and moved her body above me, straddled my loins, and then took me slowly into her. The sensation was so exquisite that I made a soft, guttural grunt and closed my eyes. She moved upon me with a slow and complete envelopment that sparked the intensity of my reaction to a quick point of release. She paused and then moved down upon me completely, and I felt the eternal ecstasy of an uncontrollable, pulsating springing of my seed. She continued her slow rocking motion as my hands clinched upon her legs, and I believe I made an involuntary, extended low moan that was almost a cry. She continued slowly, rhythmically drawing everything from me, and then stopped her movement, remaining fixed in a perfect coupling. After a while she bent forward, and kissing my lips, she whispered, "Thank you, my sweet captain. I believe you are well served, and although your cannon fired quickly, it fired well. You have made great progress." She raised herself and then moved from the bed.

"Oh my, must you go?" I asked.

"Ah yes, my sweet captain, there is a long-necked kettle that I must attend to so that there is no inconvenience that may result from this morning. You should sleep. I will see you again this afternoon." She smiled, bent, and again kissed me lightly, and then she left the room. I fell into a sleep that seemed a perfect resolution to the expression of a sexual union I had never before experienced.

In the early afternoon I awoke and did my ablutions with fervour at the large Chinese bowl in the corner of my room, delighted to have arisen and walked about with no falter or faint-headedness whatsoever. I still felt a mild glow of arousal from Elsinore's ministrations of the morning and could not help relishing an anticipation of the afternoon. Clean and refreshed, I took out my uniform, brushed away the lint, and put it on, and after I shaved, I regarded myself in the silver mirror above the Chinese bowl, rather liking what I saw. I combed my hair, brushed it back, and drew it into a Prussian pigtail, which I then tied with a black silk ribbon.

To pass some time, I carried Drake's *Instructions of Seamanship* to the veranda and began reading passages on studding sails in different points of a following wind, passages that I had read and reread many times before. After a while I confess that my ability at concentration was compromised as I glanced through the veranda doors to the room door where Elsinore would enter. I read and glanced, read and glanced. With a soft trade wind blowing through the banana trees, I reclined my head against the high back of the white rocking chair, and at total peace with the world I dozed.

A faint touch along my cheek woke me, and I saw Elsinore standing there with a perfect smile. I stood, and she said, "My sweet captain is the best-looking man in His Majesty's Navy."

I responded, "My dear, I do not know what to say about—"

She put a finger to my lips and said, "Do not speak, sweet captain. There are no words for this morning." She took me by the hand and led me into the room, closed the long-paned veranda doors, and pulled the drapes across the panes. Standing before me, she raised her blouse over her head, revealing herself as a light brown replication of the best figure that Titian had ever painted. Her head and face were beautiful under coal black hair pulled back and tied in a bun. Her breasts were somewhat small but perfectly rounded and firm with dark areoles and nipples that stood out, small but distinct. She loosened the tie around her skirt and let it fall to the floor. Her hips were slim but rounded and ample. Her legs were thin and her feet dainty.

"Elsinore, you are—" I started to say.

She again put her finger to my lips and said, "Please say nothing, sweet captain, and be what you are. Be what you must be." I started to remove my jacket, but she took my hands and placed them again at my side. Then she removed the jacket and placed it neatly on a chair. She loosened and removed the silk scarf around my neck and unbuttoned each of the ivory buttons down my shirt. When she removed the shirt, she placed it over the jacket. She stood before me, smiled, and placed her hands on my waist. Then she ran her fingers slowly up my abdomen and chest. She then held my face and kissed me. The scent of rosemary and mint, which she had added to her bathwater, went through my senses with a greater allure than could be affected by any French perfume. She held the kiss then and slowly broke it with a gentle pass of her tongue. Her hands went to my buckler. She unfastened it and undid the hooks of my leggings and pulled them along with the undergarment gently to the floor. Her sight of my loin made certain that I was as excited as a young man could possibly be. She rolled down my stockings and held the back of my shoes as I stepped out of them.

"It will be different this afternoon," she said and got into the bed. "Lie beside me, sweet captain." My heart was pounding, and my whole body seemed on the edge of explosion. "For now, just lie here with me, and let me put my head on your shoulder." I complied, and she pulled up the muslin to cover all but our heads. We lay together for a long while, and she said, "Now, my sweet captain, it is good that you should first explore." And she took my hand gently to her breast. I touched the nipple and circled my finger around the areole, first the left and then the right. From her breast I instinctively moved my hand to her face, turned it to mine, and kissed her deeply. Suddenly I was no longer overcome with excitement, but I became confident that what followed should be under my control. My hand ran down her abdomen and over the outside of her thigh and then down her leg as far as I could reach. The movement was repeated. Then I passed my hand down her thigh, across to the inside of her leg, and slowly up to the soft down that surrounded her wet slit. I touched it and caressed its moist fold up and down. I felt in complete, consuming control. I kissed her and moved myself between her legs. With her guiding hand, I entered her, and she encircled me with her legs, making a faint gasp. I hesitated, not wanting to hurt her. Then as she began her pelvic movement, I made my slow thrusts successively deeper. I was in charge and in the middle of a full and consuming assault upon the fortress of human passion. Our sounds were quiet and intense, and I moved my mouth time and again from her neck to her lips until I heard a shortening of her breathing and felt my approach. With my successive, intense pulses, I looked at her face and saw that she was wincing at the top of her own crisis.

Afterward we lay together silently for a long while. I brought her close to me and said, "You may not stop me from speaking now, for I must tell you that no other woman has—"

Disobediently she put her finger to my lips and said, "I know. I know, and it has been my great pleasure to be coupled with you, for you are my sweet captain." She kissed me again and whispered, "Now I must go and help with dinner after I tend to my kettle." She kissed me yet again, moved from the bed, put on her clothes, and left the room. At the door she looked back with a gentle smile that would never leave my memory.

The dinner that evening was sumptuous. Cubah's best pork roast was paired with fresh greens and fruits made up with shavings of coconut and papaya. I took a just a bit of wine but refused rum and tobacco. Anxiously I looked for Elsinore, as she usually had helped with service, but she never appeared. After dinner I asked Cubah the way to the kitchen, but she touched my arm and said, "You should not go to the kitchen, sir. There is nothing to be said there. You must go and talk with Lord Cornwallis." I complied.

Early the next morning Governor Parker's carriage arrived to take me to Admiral's Mountain. I was up and ready, eager to have my story of the San Juan failure told to the governor but regretful that I was leaving the house where I had regained and newly discovered so much of myself.

My baggage was packed, and I walked slowly but steadily from my room and across the veranda to say farewells to Lord Cornwallis.

"My lord, I cannot fully express my gratitude for all that you have done for me. Please know that my esteem for you and your household is the greatest that I can feel and I shall never forget it," I said as I touched my hat in salute.

He responded, "My boy – actually I should say my young and valiant captain – it has been our pleasure to do all we have done, and it is a gift to us that you are recovering so well."

I shook Cornwallis's hand and then embraced Cubah and told her, "You have been an angel of resurrection to me."

She answered, "We should have more time, but it cannot be. I have sent your treatments with your bags." I held the embrace as my eyes roamed the veranda for Elsinore. She was not there. I smiled and nodded my thanks to the rest of staff and then gingerly descended the veranda stairs to the carriage. As it pulled away, I saw Elsinore standing at the corner of the house. I raised my hand to her and craned my head to the window. She smiled and raised her hand in response. Then she was gone.

At Cooper's Hill on Admiral's Mountain, Governor Sir Peter Parker's estate was very much the same as Cornwallis's but larger with a sweeping view of the Caribbean and acres upon acres of planted banana trees, tobacco, and breadfruit fields. I was looking forward to renewing an acquaintance with the governor. It was Parker who had first recognized my seafaring and command abilities. He had placed me in command of the *Bristol's* brig, the HMS *Badger*. I responded with the fullest of effort, carrying out every order and manoeuvre with dispatch. And it was Parker's glowing recommendation that had led to my command of the *Hinchinbrook* ahead of many more senior officers.

Lady Marianne Parker, a young woman with dark brown tresses done up in the French fashion, was standing with her staff of servants on the steps of Cooper's Hill to greet me. "I am sorry Sir Peter cannot be here to greet you properly, but he will join us for dinner. Come. We have a sea-view room readied for your use. I think you will find it pleasant." It was indeed a marvellous room with a large canopied bed, leather furniture, oil paintings of English landscapes, and tall paned doors that framed a panorama of the Caribbean Sea. Lady Parker added, "Our house man, Moses, and his wife, Matilda, will be taking care of you, as they will remain at the house when Sir Peter and I have to go to our Kingston house next week."

Moses was a stern-looking man with a grey beard, and Matilda was a large woman whose unsmiling demeanour rather matched that of her husband. I asked if the treatment package sent by Cubah Cornwallis had been received, and I was told by Moses that it had been discarded as unusable. He added, "Those materials, sir, are considered to be part of ungodly witchcraft and are not suitable in a Christian household." It was the first indication to me that my treatment would be quite different than at Cooper's Hill.

Sir Peter arrived for dinner and invited me to join him for discussion beforehand. I wore my uniform to meet the governor, feeling still a bit wobbly as I walked to the pre-dinner service set on the veranda.

Sir Peter welcomed me, "My dear Captain Nelson, it is so good to see you again and to remember the excellent service you provided to me aboard the *Bristol*. I welcome you to Cooper's Hill, and regret that we must soon go to Kingston for convening of the government session. It demands all of my attention in a place that is not at all as pleasant as Cooper's Hill. But please be assured that you may stay here for your convalescence. By the way, instructions arrived today, and you are ordered back to England with Lord Captain Cornwallis, who will make the crossing in the *Lion*. It will sail in two weeks' time. In the meantime I desire very much to have your recollections regarding the San Juan matter, a very regrettable sacrifice of His Majesty's forces." He added, "Here, good man, have a cigar and some of our best rum."

"Thank you, sir, very much." I responded and took the long black cigar and glass of gold-tinged rum. "I am eager to give you all of the information you may need." Sir Peter nodded in acquiescence and lit his cigar and then mine.

"Governor, I am sure that Colonel Polson will tell you of my exertions at San Juan, how I left my ship and carried troops and provisions for leagues up a treacherous river. It should be known that I led the attack on the garrison and captured it with no loss of life in our force, that I made batteries to defend our position, and that I caused no failure in the expedition. When I became ill, it was my hope to remain for the attack on the fort, but Admiralty orders sent me down the river and on to Jamaica." I spoke, fervently hoping that this true account would blunt any criticism in the expedition's draft report.

Sir Peter took a long draw on his cigar, slowly released its grey smoke, smiled, and then answered, "Your account is quite consonant with the draft. In fact, my lad, Colonel Polson was very complimentary of your actions, even effusive. Let's see. Here it is. He says, '*The totalities of Captain Nelson's effort were exemplary. Words are hard to find that express what I owe to that young officer for his contributions to the expedition.*'[1] In fact, sir, you are not only blameless but are made to be rather heroic throughout it all. I would have expected no less."

Polson's account came over me with the effect of a total salutary bath, washing away the anxiety that had lingered in me for weeks. I remembered Polson, the stocky and seemingly unimaginative commander whose integrity in writing the hard truth had not only saved my reputation but became to me a sentinel of professional conduct. I would remember Polson for the rest of my days and value his example of keeping faith with a colleague and telling an honest truth.

"Did you know that the fort surrendered?" Sir Peter asked.

"No, I did not," I answered. "Then the expedition became a success?"

"I am afraid not," Sir Peter answered. "The fort surrendered because its cistern was depleted and they simply had no water. The expedition, however, ended there, and the objective of capturing the capital and establishing British rule in Nicaragua was lost. The pestilence of the jungle overcame the remainder of our force, which quit the expedition and retreated down the river. Two thousand of our men were buried in the jungle. None fell to the Spanish but, it seems, all to the eventual victor, the jungle itself."

"Two thousand men," I gasped. "My God, what a price for nothing gained."

Sir Peter gravely nodded, "Yes, quite so. An evaluation of making another effort has concluded that such effort would be unwise. The interests of the Crown have far greater needs elsewhere."

Our conversation turned to other matters, chiefly to the remembrance of our service together in the *Bristol*. Sir Peter asked if the accommodations suited me, and I replied that they were excellent, not mentioning my reservations regarding the disposal of Cubah's treatments

---

[1] As noted in the preface, letters, dispatches, colloquy, and other text taken from reported historical accounts shall be italicized.

out of fear of offending the Parker household. When Moses announced that dinner was ready, my head already had begun a slight spin in reaction to my intolerance of rum and the smoke of a strong cigar. I begged their forgiveness for lack of appetite and need of rest and then went directly to my room and puked up the rum and traces of my earlier lunch. I collapsed on my bed, still in uniform, and morphed my still-spinning uneasiness into a fitful sleep.

As dawn broke, I arose and removed my wrinkled jacket and leggings. Still nauseated from the last evening, I drank water from the nightstand only to have it soon come up again. I fumbled through my suit trunk and found the sleeping gown Cubah had provided. Then I stretched out on the bare mahogany floor, seeking its coolness next to my newly fevered body. When Matilda found me the next morning prostrate on the floor, she let out a scream, and a full household tumult ensued. Sir Peter had already departed for Kingston. Lady Parker took control, ordering that I be cooled with a wash of water from the deep well until my fever abated. Her attention was fully directed to me for the rest of the day, and I responded with a return of sentience and some reduction of fever.

"I must confess that we had a terrible fright when Matilda found you this morning," she said. "Poor Matilda thought you were dead, and seeing you there on the floor, I had the same thought."

"Worry not, my lady," I responded. "What Sir Peter told me last evening made everything right. I shall recover. Of that you can be assured. When must you go to Kingston?"

"Alas, tomorrow. However, Moses and Matilda will be here to care for you, and I am confident in their tending to your needs," she assured me. The next day Lady Parker and their staff with a carriage-load of bags and accoutrements left for the Kingston house after a brief good-bye to me, sitting on the veranda with a breakfast of fish, eggs, and potatoes untouched. I was slightly recovered from my bout with rum and tobacco, feeling somewhat hungry but not at all attracted to the cold dish brought to me by an unsmiling Matilda. Nevertheless, my spirits had been renewed by the positive accounts of my service that would be sent to the Admiralty.

For the next week I moved about my large room and ambled unsteadily about the veranda, enjoying the view and high mountain breezes. My fever came and went. I asked for fruit, and it was brought to me. I asked for boiled collards, and it was brought. There was, however, no quinine or conversation with anyone, and Moses or Matilda left me as quickly as they had come with nothing more than my specific request. I could not ask for visits from anyone at the Cornwallis estate in Port Royal because it was more than a half day's ride away, and I knew that the full activity of the Cornwallis estate was preparing for his departure to England. I wrote to my old friend, Captain Locker, "*What I would give to be at Port Royal with its wonderful people. Sir Peter and Lady Parker are not here, and the servants let me lay as a log, taking no notice.*" When finally the week had passed, I readied my belongings and boarded the carriage, which blessedly took me away from my sumptuous incarceration.

As I arrived at the dockside berth of HMS *Lion*, Captain Cornwallis received me on the quarterdeck. "My God, Horatio, you look a fright. What has happened, my boy?" I answered, "Nothing, my lord, that cannot be remedied by your good graces. I return to England, and that prospect alone revives me. It was the conditions of the mosquito jungle and treatment of the staff at Cooper's Hill, which did not measure up to the standards of your household, which has laid me low. Home, family, and the expectation of new assignment will restore me." Fearful of my emaciated condition and greyish complexion, Cornwallis ordered me berthed in his own command quarters with a gimballed bed. He ordered the ship's carpenter to build a wall between my quarters and the balance of the command berth, where the ship's officers would take their meals, and Cornwallis would sleep on a bunk the carpenter fashioned.

The crossing was a hellish three weeks. Although the ship rode the gulf current with excellent speed, the seas were perverse and constant with seldom a day when I could get out of my bed. I had been prone to seasickness in heavy weather from the time I was a young midshipman, and now my constitution was near the lowest point. Captain Cornwallis stayed constantly with me, venturing on deck only to ensure proper weather rigging and navigation. The officer corps of the *Lion* was most competent, allowing their captain to tend to the administration of quinine and nutrition as Cubah had instructed. However, even her regimen would often be rejected by my stomach, and my condition worsened throughout the transit. Frequently the ship's surgeon would lament the possibility of my not surviving the crossing, and several times Cornwallis would rise from his bed, doubting that he would find me still alive. Only a five-day stretch of good weather before we put into Portsmouth enabled me to retain medicine and food that made my survival possible.

Bath

At Portsmouth, the first orders given by Captain Cornwallis were that I be taken into fresh air and that a messenger be sent to my father to come with a doctor. Father, however, was not at the Burnham Thorpe home, so two of my brothers came to take me straight away to Bath, where my father was under treatment and taking the baths.

Before I allowed my cot to be placed athwart the carriage brought by my brothers, I called for Captain Cornwallis. "My good lord, I must say to you that you have saved my life. I am sure that providence will make my life a significant contribution to my king and country. Please know that no sun will rise on any day without my thoughts of gratitude to you."

Cornwallis responded, "Go, my young captain, and make your life. I know that it will become more than you can imagine. God bless and smile upon you."

My first days in Bath were buoyed by the presence of my father and family with a strengthening feeling simply that I was again home in my beloved England. I did worry that a condition of feebleness and convalescence might count against the Admiralty giving me another command. I wrote again to my colleague and mentor, Captain Locker, *"I have been so ill since I have been here that I have been obliged to be carried to and from bed with excruciating tortures … I am physicked three times a day, drink the water constantly, and have baths every other day, besides not drinking wine which is the worse torture of all … but I shall drink to your health with a drought of my physician's cordial."* With agonizing slowness, I did get better, and within the month I was able to venture out to the theatre.

In May 1781, I was well enough to present myself to the Admiralty. I felt a keen anxiety because at the time the first lord of the Admiralty was John Montague, the fourth Earl of Sandwich, a man known for his vanity, attention to political connections, and irascible demeanour that had followed the murder of his mistress, mother of most of his children, at the hands of a rival suitor. I had studied the nature of the earl and very much wanted to be received as a friend as much as a competent naval officer.

As I entered the earl's cavernous and ornate chamber at the Admiralty, my heart was racing, and my fingers somewhat trembled. Extending my hand, I began with an unauthorized greeting and a tribute that I had contrived to appeal to the first lord's well-known vanity. "My Lord, I bring the compliments of the governor of Jamaica, who asked that

I convey his high regards. Please also allow me to say that I am a great admirer of your contributions to the formation and design of the western squadron. It has been a profound check upon the extension of French influence in the Caribbean."

To my great relief, the earl's dour demeanour changed to a smile, and he responded, "Thank you, Captain. I am pleased to meet you." He shook my hand and asked me to sit. "I have reviewed your jacket and am pleased to say that it is replete with positives. It is a pity you were felled by the jungle fever but a blessing that it did not kill you. How is your health now?"

"Fit and ready," I lied. Since I had returned to London, my digestion was still irregular. My left arm would not respond normally, and I frequently lost sensation in my fingers.

The first lord said, "I am pleased to hear that. However, there are no ships ready for new appointments, but I will keep your readiness very much in mind. Tell me something. I believe that reports of His Majesty's officers should contain not only information regarding the action and fitness of the commander's ship but should extend to an appraisal of other ships in concerted action. Further, I believe it should also include commentary on the cohesiveness of all commanders as well as information regarding the committed allegiance of your colleagues to His Majesty's government. Will you fully report that?"

I knew very well that there was but one answer to the question. "Of course I will, my lord." The first lord nodded and again made a slight smile. "Good. Then I will send you on your way. Hopefully you will hear from us in near time." He stood, indicating that the audience was over. We shook hands, and I added, "I shall be eternally grateful to you, sir, and please know that I shall commit unswervingly to your service." As I left the room, I was satisfied that I had made a positive impression and hoped that I had not appeared obsequious. The fear of that, however, did not terribly bother me.

I returned to Burnham Thorpe and went straight away to the postal office, where I left instructions that my mail should be retained for my daily pickup. My digestion became much better, and the function of my arm became close to normal. Walks about the village were pleasurable. I visited my school and was informed of the whereabouts and activities of many of my schoolmates. I was eventually able to visit the pub for lunch and a pint of bitters. It was also a wonderful time spent with my father and family. I visited the grave of my mother and remembered the depth of her doting love before her death when I was nine years old.

It was a time of enriching renewal. I laughed with my brothers and sisters, particularly my favourite, Kate, and for the first time in a year I was filled with hope and enthusiasm. I brushed, washed and repaired my uniforms, and polished my buttons and sword. I slept well, and in the morning I would frequently recall the soothing song and touches of Cubah. I relived the sensations of exquisite ascendency with Elsinore to my first eruption into manhood. It was a time of regeneration, and at the end of the month orders came.

I was to report in seven days to command of the frigate HMS *Albemarle*, a twenty-eight-gun frigate dry-docked in Woolwich. With the prospect of a new command at sea, my spirit soared.

Chapter 2

Woolwich

I remember so clearly the day I departed Burnham Thorpe for HMS *Albemarle*'s dry dock at Woolwich, the very day after I received my orders, although I did not have to report until seven days later. I wanted to see her condition, observe close at hand the refitting work being done, and appraise her possibility as a combat ship. I simply could not wait either. The *Albemarle* was built as a French merchant vessel, *La Menagere*, and soon after she launched, she was captured by a British frigate and converted into a twenty-eight-gun British warship, albeit of lighter construction than true frigates of the line. At Woolwich, a new and longer mast was being installed as a measure to increase her speed. Copper strips were being laid to her bottom to lengthen its life and retard growth on the hull.

Upon arriving dockside, I looked upon the dismasted *Albemarle* in its final stages of restoration – ringed with scaffolds, boxes of copper laid all about, and workmen sawing, shaving, boring and nailing constantly. It was a scene of confusion, and to the normal eye, the shape of the vessel was unrecognisable as one of His Majesty's handsome frigates. But I viewed it as a father would look upon a new-born child – beautiful in its nascent promise and loving it for what I knew it would become. I introduced myself to the master shipwright and complimented him on the report that refitting was ahead of schedule. The shipwright was grateful for the compliment and offered to review the work underway. We toured the ship for most of the day, the shipwright explaining that the new mast would be stepped in place the next day and that increased shrouds would be necessary because of the mast's length. It would be necessary to shorten the foremast and mizzen yardarms. The sheathing and tarring of the new copper hull were almost completed. Surprisingly the gun mounts were not being changed, which was disappointing, because the scope of the running freeboard seemed adequate to allow for four more nine-pound or perhaps twelve-pound cannons on each side. I later learned that restructuring for additional guns would have taken more time and a greater budget than Admiralty plans allowed.

Near the end of the day after the refitting crew was dismissed, I walked the deck fore and aft, envisioning and relishing its operations in a few weeks' time. I then saw my old friend and mentor, Captain William Locker, approach, responding to my invitation to visit and tour the ship. Captain Locker had been in command of the thirty-two-gun frigate named HMS *Lowestoffe* when I passed the examination that elevated me from midshipman to lieutenant. My first assignment at 18 years of age was as a second lieutenant in the *Lowestoffe*, and a strong professional as well as personal relationship with Captain Locker began. At first I was simply one of several subordinate officers, but as what I believe to be my attention to duty and acumen in the ship's piloting, rigging, and gunnery became evident, Captain Locker paid special attention to me and thereafter would become not only a mentor but a confidant and friend as well. The bond of mutual respect and admiration would extend throughout our lives. Finding that Captain Locker would be near Woolwich, I had invited him to come and view the *Albemarle* in its restoration.

As he approached, I rushed to the dock, touching my cap in a joyful salute to my old commander and friend. Locker returned the salute and announced, "Horatio, my good man, how good it is to see you, so much better after that jungle matter. I have heard well of your actions and had anticipated no less."

The greeting pleased me immensely, and I replied. "Captain, nothing could prevent me from returning to England and its service. Welcome to my ship. I would love to have your thoughts on her."

Captain Locker

We walked each of the *Albemarle's* four decks, its bilge, forecastle, and quarterdeck. We discussed at length the problems to be encountered as a result of the merchant ship's rounded hull and the lengthened masts necessary to accommodate speeds required in formation sailing. "She will wallow, Horatio, because she does not have the depth of keel on most ships of the line. You will have to handle a great deal more rigging, and boatswain mates who have served on proper frigates will not know how to ride this bastard of a ship."

"I know, sir. She will be somewhat different," I agreed. "But given her tending to roll and yaw, it will require more bending of topsails in broad winds with less buntline loosening in fore winds. However, a few weeks under sail will give us what we need to know. The increased shrouds will help the sails handle tighter sheets in the wind, and we can bend headsails more often than other ships. Our riggers will be exercised, but we will make it work."

Captain Locker listened intently, and I liked to think that each of the major shortcomings of the ship had already been realised by myself, each problem not only anticipated but solved with a full understanding of the special seamanship demands posed by this unique ship. I concluded, "Captain, I will learn to handle her."

"I know you will, Horatio. I know you will," Locker responded.

On 22 August 1781, I hoisted my command pennant and welcomed the new company of officers. On the same day 150 of the ship's seamen reported back aboard, shy of its listed complement of 175. On 1 September, the ship was taken out of dry dock and lashed dockside for final outfitting. The mainmast had been delayed but was stepped into place within the week. When refinished fore and mizzens were added, the ship was ready for sailing at the beginning of October. With a true feeling of constant enthusiasm, I wrote to my brother, *"I have been busy getting my ship's company in order for service. They are, in my opinion, as good a set of men as ever I saw – indeed, I am perfectly satisfied with both, officers and ship's company. All of my marines are likewise old standers."*

Impressment

The insufficient number of seamen reporting to *Albemarle* had to be remedied, and I knew how the problem could be readily corrected. I would press into service seasoned sailors from ships called "Indiamen," merchant ships that plied the trade between England and India. Pressing sailors into naval service had begun under the reign of Queen Elizabeth in compliance with what was called the "Maintenance of the Navy Edict" and later refined by acts of Parliament, although the process was never closely administered. I spoke with the ship's purser, Ross Bear. "Tell me what yearly allowance we have for the shortage of men in our complement. My plan is to use the money to promote the pressing of the better men we shall find."

When *Albemarle* first set sail, our destination was the mouth of the Thames to look for merchant ships under the flag of any country of the empire. I did not have to wait for long. Before we reached the Thames, an Indiaman that was set low in the water with what had to be a full and valuable cargo was spotted and hailed to heave to and drop sail. She ignored the signal and changed course away from the *Albemarle*. Enraged at the impudence of a merchant captain ignoring the command of a warship of His Majesty's Navy, I ordered full sail and tight trim to overtake the scoundrel. As *Albemarle* approached, the merchant ship persisted in her course, and I ordered a blank shot fired from the forecastle gun. The merchant still did not respond. I ordered the marine drummer to beat to general quarters and shouted, "Master gunner, open the gun ports and run out the cannons. If need be, we shall load them with chain shot and strip this fool of his sails." The crew came to life, each man excited by our demonstrated willingness to press a fight.

Down the line I heard a chief gunnery mate say, "This lad is full of piss and vinegar, eh? It seems we have a terrier on the quarterdeck." The comment pleased me.

At the sight of the *Albemarle*'s guns run out, the Indiaman dropped its sails. I ordered the marine captain to assemble a platoon and be ready to board. I ordered the purser to follow me. *Albemarle* came alongside and was lashed to the drifting merchant. I leapt to her deck followed by the purser and the marine captain with his platoon carrying rifles cocked at ready arms.

As soon as the marines were on board, I shouted to the crew of the merchant, "No man is to move from his spot, and if anyone does, my lieutenant of marines will have him shot for an assumed act of insurrection." The full attention of the merchant crew became fixed on me. I then looked at the ship's captain and said, "Sir, a word with you in your quarters." The captain led me into his stateroom, followed by Mister Bear with his satchel. I looked with a full intensity at the captain and spoke, "My first impulse is to arrest you, clamp you in irons, and haul your fat and scruffy self onto my ship for an intentional breach of the Navigation Acts by failing to respond to an order of His Majesty's ship. My second impulse is to impound this cargo and to take it to Plymouth for escheat to His Majesty's treasury in consequence of your crime."

What had been a sullen demeanour of resistance on the captain's face disappeared, and I noticed that his hands had begun slightly to tremble. I continued, "Captain, I know that the masters of your shipping company are eagerly awaiting your arrival and are rubbing their hands together at the prospects of profits from your cargo. However, it will be impounded in Plymouth unless we can come to an accommodation. My intent, indeed my right under the Maintenance of the Navy Edict, is to acquire necessary seamen for His Majesty's Navy. This could have been a simple and commodious matter but for your contumacious and foolhardy resistance. However, I propose a solution. First you will assemble fifteen of your most experienced seamen, and you will pay them today all of their wages for this voyage. I will then welcome them into His Majesty's service. Then you will be permitted to proceed to London. My purser will write out a captain's agreement to this effect, and you will sign it. So tell me, Captain, where do you wish to go? To London under sail or to Plymouth in chains?"

The merchant captain, who was older than I was by probably two decades, replied, "To London, sir."

"We are agreed," I answered, and then I said to my purser, "Now, Mister Bear, please write out the captain's agreement, and when it is signed, gentlemen, please join me on deck."

When the fifteen sailors to be impressed were selected, I spoke to them, "Men, I have suggested, and your captain has agreed, that you will now be paid your full wages for this voyage. In addition, if you will volunteer to be welcomed into the Royal Navy, half of your yearly allowance will also be advanced to you today. Of course, if you do not volunteer, no advance will be paid, and you will be, under order, pressed into His Majesty's service. If you do not agree to impressment and glorious service in our navy, I will hang you from the yardarm this morning. Now all who have been selected and agree to volunteer, please take a step forward." The fifteen men stepped forward. They were paid their wages by the merchant captain and boarded their new ship.

Back on the *Albemarle* the new men were assigned to their billets, and I again assembled them. "Men, you have agreed to service in one of His Majesty's best ships. There are more pounds sterling in your pockets than you have held in many years. You will entrust it to the purser, Mister Bear, for security and he shall provide you portions of it for all good reasons when we reach ports of call. In this ship I venture to say that you will find glory and prize money that will give your life great happiness. If you do not serve with the best of your efforts, the result will be great unhappiness. I guarantee that. Now find your place and be content in a great future." The impressed men disbursed to their assignments with a sense of comfort rather than the fear and dread that had possessed them when the *Albemarle* first came alongside the Indiaman.

Mr. Bear later approached me as the ship continued back to Woolwich and said, "Sir, I have participated in many boarding parties for impressment and never realized that the laws authorise such actions as you described."

I paused and then responded with a slight shrug, "Mister Bear, I intended to carry out every threat that I spoke, and if the laws do not have the effects that I described, then they well should."

North Sea and Denmark

Back in Woolwich the ship was readied for active service and supplies were brought on board. I ordered that the top and gallant sails be double-stitched, being fearful that they would be subject to more than normal stress because of the *Albemarle's* extended mainmast. It didn't take long before orders were delivered as the officers sat down for evening dinner. Eager to be at sea again, I hurried in opening the double-sealed envelope. When I read the contents, I smiled broadly.

An officer asked, "Why does the captain smile?"

I answered, "We are to join a convoy of six merchantmen at Southampton and escort them through the channel and the North Sea to the Danish port of Helsingor, or as we English know it, Elsinore."

"Very good captain, but why does that make you smile?"

"It's a private matter, sir, a private matter," I responded as I looked out the window of my cabin in a brief reverie of rosemary and mint. I recovered and added, "Besides, it will give us a good test in the winds of the North Sea."

At Southampton we set out with the convoy, which I had ordered in a double-breast column with *Albemarle* on its starboard flank. The convoy passed through the channel in good winds and even seas. I was pleased at the competent ship-handling skills of the merchantmen in our convoy. The conditions also provided two days for my officers and boatswains to drill all hands in scaling aloft, laying out the yards, tracing up the booms, and working the sheets, bunts, and spring lines. In the first drill of going aloft it concerned me that the pace was too slow. So I ordered all hands down and told the first maintop starboard mate that I, the ship's captain, would scale the port ladder and meet him at the top. "Do not lag!" I ordered, and the two of us climbed to the maintop yard, with the mate arriving just before myself. I offered my hand to the mate and said, "That's better, my man. Well done." The crew looked at one another, probably incredulous that I could scale the ship's rigging almost as quickly as an experienced seaman.

Spontaneously they doffed their hats, waved them, and cheered us both. It was precisely the effect that I had wished my stunt to have.

At dusk on the second day in the channel I ordered an extra round of grog after dinner and passed the order that any man with a fiddle should play. In the gold and red hues of the setting sun, reels were played, and a number of old hands danced the sailors' trot and stomp. When the boatswain's pipe sounded the evening watch, all hands not on watch went below to what I hoped would be a welcomed sleep with tired bodies and contented spirits. We would enter the North Sea in the morning.

The North Sea

To sailors who have sailed the North Sea, it is an expanse of grey foreboding eminence never to be trusted. Frequently shrouded in dense fog banks with little wind, it can lure a captain into complacency with full sails set only to replace the fog with lashing rain and gale force winds in a matter of minutes. Even great ships can be heeled over with sails shredded before they can be hauled down or reefed. I had sailed the North Sea many times as a midshipman, and I was wary of its petulant moods. As the convoy sailed ahead in moderate seas, I signalled the merchant captains to secure their decks, rig lifelines, batten hatches, and have sea anchors at the ready. I ordered the *Albemarle's* gun ports to be locked tight and its cannons to be double-lashed. Loose cannons careening about on a tossing deck had injured or killed many a hapless sailor.

In the afternoon the winds came on strong, and the sea grew in anger. I signalled the convoy to strike all sails except the main on the foremast. As the gale increased into a howl and ships began taking water over their bows, I became concerned for the safety of the convoy under my direct orders and signalled that each ship should deploy such sail only as it deemed necessary to keep its head into the seas. I admit to being terrified by the prospect of a ship broaching in the heavy swells and perhaps sinking as a result of the heavy cargo it carried on board. The signal ran up the lanyard with the flags snapping furiously. I watched as each merchant ship deployed storm jibs forward and struck their mainsails. Some also hoisted high trysails to keep leverage against extreme rolling. I was relieved and quite impressed with the seamanship of the merchant captains. However, I was concerned that although *Albemarle's* own forward mainsail was secure, in large part because of her double stitching, I nevertheless knew that she would make better speed than the merchants and would likely lose contact with the convoy. I ordered a trysail hoisted on the foremast and the forward yards dropped with the mainsail half-reefed, hoping that the ship would keep its head into the ever-increasing waves.

The storm continued throughout the night without abatement. I stayed on the quarterdeck, facing windward with cold rain scouring my face like ice pellets. As the *Albemarle* pitched and dived into monstrous waves, I prayed that the merchantmen would manage. As I tried to make my way to my quarters, the ship lurched, and I grabbed at a stanchion, pulling a muscle in my back. The pain was intense. I repeated to myself, "Endure. Endure. These are testing times." Nothing was visible in the black of night, and the hours passed in a continuing slow ordeal of pitching and rolling in an unremitting, pounding sea.

At the first light of dawn the wind's intensity eased, and the seas morphed into long and gentle swells. I ordered a come-about tack and, with my officers, walked the length of the ship, looking for the scattered convoy. Calls rang out. "Ship sighted two points aft the port beam." "Three ships broad on the port beam." By midmorning the last of the merchants was found, and I ordered a flag signal for the convoy to reform. As the double column came into shape, my feeling was close to the ecstatic. The fear of catastrophe that had dogged me throughout the night was replaced with the cathartic relief of a full convoy sailing intact and in perfect order. I shouted, "Signal master, hoist the 'well done' signal to port. Then half up on the starboard line, signal to 'splice the main brace.'" It was a suggestion to the convoy that they issue an extra tot of rum to their crews. As the message was acknowledged by each ship, sailors crowded to their gunwales, cheering and waving their hats. We had come through the storm together.

Two days later *Albemarle* and its brood entered the port of Helsingor. I ordered the crew at deck parade with each man in a fresh uniform lining the starboard gunwale. It would be a formal show of respect to our host country, and when the Helsingor fort would fire its customary salute, *Albemarle* would respond with its own. I ordered the convoy to single-file column for entry into port, and I had the *Albemarle* stand off until each merchant entered the port. I then instructed the ship at full parade to pass the point and be ready to return the expected salute. We approached. No salute came. We passed the point. No salute came. As we entered the port, I seethed at the breach of courtesy and protocol which should be accorded to every visiting warship. I ordered the crew to break parade and set the docking watch and then spoke aloud, "Men, we were paraded in respect, and the ship has set into port after defeating a worthy storm of the North Sea. The *Albemarle* was due a formal salute, and I promise that such an affront will not be repeated. I authorize a general shore liberty until midnight and bid you have a good time of Danish food and moderate drink."

I retired to my quarters and awaited the welcoming port officer. Soon a young man in uniform appeared at the quarterdeck and was escorted to my cabin. Further angered that an officer was not sent to welcome the *Albemarle*, I asked the young man, "What is your name and rank?"

"I am Midshipman Kristofer Seglem, sir, and I have brought the portfolio of port instructions and a form for the ship's next sailing plan."

"What if I have a question regarding the anticipated currents and tides in this harbour? Have you, Midshipman, ever taken a ship to sea from this dock?"

"No, sir, I have not as yet."

"Mister Seglem, please go directly to the officer in command of this port and relate a message to him. First as observed in the established protocol of nations in time of peace and as an act of respect to your king and country, I formally paraded my crew when entering this port. Secondly my ship was ready to return the customary salute that was expected when a warship of His Britannic Majesty enters the port. But none came. I also expected to be welcomed by an officer of your navy who could interpret the sailing conditions of this port, and none has come. You have done as instructed, and I have no criticism of you. However, I have questions regarding the conditions of this port and request the presence of an officer who can answer them."

"I shall relay those things, Captain," responded the midshipman, who then saluted and left my quarters.

Within the hour the Helsingor harbourmaster appeared with profuse apologies. Not wanting to belabour a negative experience, I offered my hand and said that offence would not be taken. Issues of tide and current were discussed, and as the harbourmaster was ready to leave, I added, "Sir, we will depart on an ebbing tide the day after tomorrow. My ship will be ready to answer a salute from the fort." The harbourmaster fully understood my meaning and offered to host me and my officers at dinner that evening.

I appreciated the obvious gesture of rapprochement but refused, saying, "Unfortunately much of our time this evening will be taken with securing the repairs to our ship as a result of fighting our way through a gale on our trip to your port, but I thank you."

"Well, if you do go ashore for a solid meal and spirits, I recommend the Stollenmark public house, which is very close by," the harbourmaster replied with well-spoken English.

After review of the ship's damages and instructions given for necessary carpentry, repair of lines, and tightening of shrouds, I invited my first officer and gunnery lieutenant to join me for dinner ashore. The Stollenmark was an eating place and inn for sailors not unlike the pubs of Woolwich and Portsmouth. I was somewhat hesitant about eating with the crewmen of various ships in the harbour but was relieved when the innkeeper invited us to dine on the second level, reserved for officers. "The servers speak English, and I think you gentlemen will find the service and staff quite acceptable and accommodating." True to the promise, the beer was first rate although a bit light in the manner of continental lager, and the whitefish was well turned in butter and lime juice, with boiled beans and thin potatoes fried in fatback. Each of us declined sweets after our main meal. During and after dinner I reviewed with my officers the further repairs needed for *Albemarle* and discussed the replenishments that the first officer would order the next morning. After the discussion the other officers excused themselves to return to the ship. I was content to relax with some precious quiet time and ordered a glass of Lisbon port from the woman who had served the meal. She was somewhat older than I, but she had a pretty face with blond hair tied in the back with a red ribbon. She was also well-figured and not unattractive to the eye. I enjoyed very much watching the sway of her cadence as she walked away after she took my order.

When she returned with my wine, she remarked, "I see from your sleeve that you are the captain of a ship. That is impressive because I would say that you are very young."

"I am quite old enough, madam," I replied rather tartly.

She slightly raised her hands to me and replied, "Oh, I am sorry. I did not mean to offend you. It means that you must be very good at sailing a big ship, and I could tell that you were in charge by the way you spoke to the other men who dined with you." She then smiled and slightly tilted her head, inviting a response.

I was mollified by her compliment and relaxed. "What is your name, ma'am, if I may ask?"

"Juliana."

"Can you sit with me?"

"Yes, I can. All dinners have been taken away, and my time is free," she responded and took a seat next to me.

"Where are you from, Juliana?

"I am from Skagen. I came here with my husband two years ago. He was a fisherman who went to sea last year and did not return. Karl, the innkeeper, and his wife have been very kind to me by letting me work here and paying me enough to live. Where is your home, Captain?"

"I live at sea now, in my ship, the *Albemarle*, but I came from a small place near Norfolk called Burnham Thorpe," I replied. Our conversation continued with recounting of our home villages and reminiscences of family and growing up. She had taken English in school rather than the normal courses of French because she knew that in the section of Denmark where she lived there would be more English spoken than French. I was quite taken with the woman's warmth, quick smile, and interest in my stories of going to sea as a young lad as well as my adventures in voyages to the Arctic and the East Indies. She particularly laughed when I told the story of chasing after a polar bear in hopes of killing it and taking its hide back to my father. "I was, however, called back to the ship by a gun signal that may have saved me from becoming the bear's next meal," I confessed with a smile. She had been an intent listener, and our conversation continued, neither of us wanting to break it off until Karl approached and told us that he was closing the inn for the night. As I rose, I apparently winced from the pain of the back muscle that I had injured in riding out the gale.

"You have a pain, sir?" she asked and extended a hand to help.

"It's nothing that time and rest cannot cure," I answered.

"Well, if you like, Captain, I believe I can help. You see, I have rubbed out many muscles that have been pulled at sea. My little place is very near, and if you are comfortable with it, I can help your injury."

Completely taken with this woman and delighted that our time together would not be ended, I answered, "I would be quite comfortable with that, my dear lady."

I walked with Juliana, her arm in my own, down two streets from the inn and turned into a narrow side street and then climbed up a flight of stairs to her room. It was modestly furnished but neat and clean. A vase of yellow flowers sat on a table at the window. "I have no wine, Captain, but can I offer you a cup of tea?" she asked.

"Thank you, but it tends to disturb my rest if I take tea at a late hour."

"Well then, I suggest that you remove your jacket and shirt and sit in this chair with your chest against its back." She took my coat and shirt and laid them aside. "As you lean against the chair, let your arms hang free, and more than anything else, relax yourself as much as you can." She went to her cupboard and took a bottle of oil from which she poured a small amount onto a cloth. Then she wiped the cloth over the back of a large wooden spoon and then onto her hands. She moved a chair behind my exposed back and gently ran her hands slowly and smoothly down the muscles on each side of my spine. The sensation was wonderfully soothing until her fingers found knots of muscles near the small of my back. When she touched them, I winced and flinched with a stab of pain. "Ah, yes," she said, "there is the problem. Now relax, Captain, as best you can and try to enjoy the pain because it is a message of your recovery. Relax. Try to relax." She took the oiled spoon and placed it above the knots and then ran it down and over the knots slowly and gently at first but then with slightly increased pressure, up and down, down and up on both sides of the crease of my spine. After many minutes of tracing the spoon with each causing less pain than the time before, she set the spoon aside and rubbed the muscles gently with her hands, smoothing out the knots that had become much smaller, only slight elevations above the normal tissue. She then extended the scope of her massage to the surrounding muscles over the sides of my back and slowly up to my shoulders. I then noted with some amazement that as she gently worked my back, she hummed a tune, and I was transported to the vivid memory of other touching with soft murmurs of song, cool Caribbean breezes, and the scent of rosemary and mint.

Juliana washed the spoon and set it aside. She rubbed soap with warm water into cloth and slowly washed my back. Then she rinsed the cloth, poured some water with a lavender scent onto the cloth, and gently rinsed away the soap from my back. The rinsing ended at the nape of my neck, where she lingered, soothing the tense muscles of my neck. She spoke, "I can tell much from your back, Captain. You are intense, and you bear up well under pain. You are a good commander. And I could tell from your talk with the other officers at your table that you have authority and they respect you. Our conversations also reveal that you understand much and will reach great heights." Nothing could have been said that would have meant more to me.

I stood with no pain, turned to Juliana, and did not know what to say. The visage of this lovely and understanding woman slightly smiling with warm and bright eyes created an involuntary comfort and longing that pervaded my senses. "You are wonderful," were the words that involuntarily came from my mouth.

Juliana, hearing this, apparently did not know how to respond, but in time she spoke, "What can I say to this man before me with this young, chiselled face and bare chest? This moment is unlike any other I have known since the death of my husband. You are beautiful to me. You are strong, and I sense that your future will be rich in many ways. At this moment, you leaving so quickly saddens me." For a long moment she stood there, looking at me.

I moved the moment to do the only thing I could do, the thing I had to do. I bent forward and gently kissed her lips. The kiss apparently untied the knot of her restraint, and she put her arms around my neck, holding me tightly with a tremor she could not subside. I encircled her waist with my arms and kissed the side of her face and her neck, taking in the light scent of lavender. She took my face in her hands and kissed me with an intensity and release that brought tears to her eyes.

I had no other thought than to feel her next to me and prayed that she felt the same. I felt confident that I was the only man since the death of her husband whom she had touched so lovingly, and I fervently hoped she wanted to feel my touch as well. We moved to her bed and lay together. We did not speak. We kissed softly, passionately, and then softly again. I moved my hands over the contours of her body, relishing the softness of her breasts and the very femininity of her abdomen and thighs. She seemed to like the touch of my hands, and it seemed to bring visceral arousal that she probably had not known for more than a year. Her breathing and murmurs conveyed to me the pleasure she felt. When my constraint could no longer be withheld and when her breathing against my neck became quick and intense, I mounted and gently entered her. Our union became a symphony of rhythmic love rising to a crescendo of ecstasy, each of us feeling the intensity of giving of ourselves and the satisfaction of receiving the unrestrained passion of each other.

When the union was broken, Juliana lay with her head on my shoulder, softly moving her fingers on my chest. I kissed her forehead, tilted her face, and then kissed her lips. The sequence was repeated. I loved the quiet sound of her breathing. The silence of the room was broken only when I spoke again, "You are wonderful."

She kissed my chin and said, "I wish, Captain, that you were a Dane." But I was not. I had to go. I arose and dressed myself, held her gently once more at the door, kissed her again, and returned to my ship. I like to think that Juliana went back to her bed, still warm where we had been, and lay there, reliving what had happened. My last thought after I returned to the ship but before I fell asleep that night was that she never asked my name. The next day the *Albemarle* was a fit of activity. Carpenters' hammers and saws sounded throughout the day. New lines were hoisted. Sails were triple stitched at the corners. Stores were brought aboard. Water and grog casks were replenished. The ship was made ready to sail the next morning.

When the sound of eight bells set the evening watch, several officers asked if I would join them for dinner ashore. I paused and then declined, saying, "I've too much to do, but go ahead and enjoy a good supper with modest drink." I then went to my private store of provisions and filled a canvas bag with all of my cheeses, hams, dried beef, salted lamb, fruits, and sugared things. I wrote a message and, for the first time, sealed it with my captain's crest. I gave the bag to the messenger of the watch, instructing him to take it to the Stollenmark public house and deliver it to a server named Juliana. The messenger hoisted the heavy bag and carried it away. The messenger confirmed that Juliana was called and received the bag at the Stollenmark. He said that when she opened and read the sealed message, she smiled. It read, "It is with absolute pleasure that I share some of my things with someone so dear in my memory. My back is healed, and as I leave this land, my heart is heavy. You are wonderful. Capt. H. Nelson, HMS *Albemarle*."

Return Home

The next morning the *Albemarle* was made ready for departure on the midmorning ebb tide. I called the first officer, "Mr. Marshall, parade the crew and charge the salute cannon. We will leave with the respect and dignity accorded to our host port. Also, in the event we are not accorded the courtesy of a parting salute, order an eight-pounder ready to leave a mark on the wall of the fort. If we are not given a proper salute, that mark will be our parting message." The crew readied the cannons. Smiles were exchanged among the men who had come to a full understanding that I and my ship were not to be offended.

The *Albemarle* sailed out of Helsingor in a soft breeze under full sail. My sailors were lined on the port side in fresh uniforms. Both cannons were ready. As the ship passed abreast of the fort, a salute cannon was fired. In the distance I could see the harbourmaster on the top of the fort wall touching his hat in an additional salute to the parting ship. The *Albemarle* fired its return salute, and I faced the harbourmaster, touching my hat in recognition of his personal salute. We both smiled.

In the return transit to England, the North Sea offered perfect sailing. Moderate winds and waves provided an excellent opportunity to exercise my crew in making and reefing sails at sea. I drilled officers, midshipmen, and boatswains in handling the proper sheets to be loosened and tightened when the ship tacked in a following wind. I then ordered the ship to come about, and the same drills were executed in a headwind.

When a tack was not performed to my satisfaction, I would shout, "Men, these are fair winds, and we are not under fire! We must know exactly what to do and how to do it because there will be times when these same manoeuvres must be done in stout winds and under fire. If we will know how to do it well and the enemy does not, we will survive the day, and they will not. We must be better, much better, and there can be no question about it." The officers and senior petty officers became fully engaged in the mandate for proper ship handling, and the first two days under sail in perfect weather were not spent in leisurely sailing but in arduous schooling and under a chorus of orders and response.

"Man topgallant lines and secure the sheets, weather the braces!"

"Let go main clew lines, lee braces, jib downhaul. Let go the windward lines and fore braces."

"Haul and taut the boomvang aft! Sheet home and double fix! Hoist away topgallant and jib! Trim and secure!"

"Lay aloft and loose topsail. Man the weather braces and topsail sheets! Haul taut! Take sheets home to weather. Let go the buntlines!"

The first two days sent men aloft time and again. Sails were hoisted, reefed, and struck and then hoisted, reefed, and struck again but in a different direction and under a different wind. I and my officers were all about the ship, giving orders, correcting, and praising any action well taken. At the end of each day, knowing that the men were calloused and tired from more work than they had ever performed, I allowed a double ration of grog. Exhausted and enjoying the mild glow imparted by their watered rum, the men did not complain. Each knew that he had become a better seaman or a better officer.

The third day was particularly anticipated, as I planned it would be filled with gunnery drills, the very purpose and effect of a warship. I also knew from experience that the roar of gunfire excited and energized the crew as nothing else could. It was also a practice whose importance and dangers required expert teamwork. The propellant was gunpowder, whose explosiveness required that it be kept in a special storage area below deck. Powder monkeys, typically boys who were ten to fourteen years old, ran powder from the armoury up to the gun deck. Cannons were usually kept lashed behind gun ports during normal sailing. After the first round was fired, a wet swab was used to mop out the interior of the barrel, extinguishing embers which might set off the next charge of gunpowder prematurely. Gunpowder in a parchment cartridge was then loaded and "rammed home" with a gun rod. It was then pierced by a metal "pricker" through the firing hole. A cloth wad was rammed next to the powder cartridge. Next the shot was rammed followed by a wad to prevent the shot from rolling out of the barrel if the muzzle was depressed. The gun was run out by men heaving on the gun tackle until the barrel protruded from the gun port. This required exceptional effort by the gun crew, as the weight of cannon and its carriage could reach well over a thousand pounds.

The touch hole above the powder cartridge was primed with finer gunpowder and then ignited by a gunlock flint that was operated by the gun captain pulling a long lanyard. He stood behind the gun, well beyond its range of recoil. The gun captain gave orders to the gun crew to elevate or depress the gun using wooden wedges. When the ship was engaged at close quarters, the wedge was removed, and the gun was simply fired point blank as quickly as the crew could load, fire, and reload it. It was generally conceded that the English were the best at rapid fire, and it was the goal of every gun crew to fire, reload, and fire again within a minute's time.

I had the gunnery officer practice all twenty-eight of the gun crews repeatedly in dry drills throughout the morning, emphasizing the work of each individual member. The afternoon would consist of drills with actual firing. When the noon meal was called, I announced to the crew, "This afternoon, there shall be a contest. The four fastest gun crews in this afternoon's firing will receive double dinner rations and double grog!" Each crew assembled over their noon meal, gun captains instructing and encouraging their crews. Each would be keen to be the best in the afternoon. Wet cotton cloth was distributed to each man to be stuffed in his ears. Kerchiefs were distributed, and the new men were shown how to fold and wear them as masks against powder smoke. Sand was spread over the gun deck, and water was poured about to simulate the footing during battle when the decks would likely be wet with blood and tissue.

The balance of the day was filled with the flash and thunder booms of the *Albemarle* broadsides. Smoke filled the gun deck, and the first acrid smell of gunpowder filled the nostrils of young powder monkeys as they scurried repeatedly up and down from armoury to gun deck. Using a pendulum clock, times were called out as each gun crew finished its round. Cheers rang out from the observing deckhands. Backs were slapped. Stanchions were sometimes kicked in disappointment; however, the times in each round of competition were improved, and at the end of the afternoon every man had become familiar with the sound and intense focus of battle gunnery. At the end of the drills after guns were cleaned and the deck swabbed, I asked, "Chief boatswain, do you know a song?"

He answered, "I do, sir. I do."

I ordered, "Then sing it. Sing it loud!" The sound about the ship was that of wind softly whistling through the rigging, the chief boatswain belting out the lyrics and the entire ship – officers, petty officers, old salts and young boys – joining in the chorus,

> *Our anchor we'll weigh,*
> *And our sails we will set.*
> *Goodbye, fare-ye-well,*
> *Goodbye, fare-ye-well.*
> *The maidens we're leaving,*
> *We leave with regret,*
> *Hurrah, my boys, we're homeward bound.*
>
> *We're homeward bound,*
> *Oh joyful sound!*

> *Goodbye, fare-ye-well,*
> *Goodbye, fare-ye-well.*
> *Come rally the capstan,*
> *And run quick around.*
> *Hurrah, my boys, we're homeward bound.*
>
> *We're homeward bound*
> *We'd have you know*
> *Goodbye, fare-ye-well,*
> *Goodbye, fare-ye-well.*
> *And over the water*
> *To England must go,*
> *Hurrah, my boys, we're homeward bound.*

When the *Albemarle* sailed up the Thames and docked again at home, she was a very different ship from the one that had departed a month earlier.

Chapter 3

North America

I remember well the late summer of 1782 when *Albemarle* and I set sail for Quebec in company with an assisting frigate, the HMS *Daedalus*. I was given command of a convoy of forty merchant ships for resupply of British forces in Canada. *Albemarle* itself carried bullion worth £100,000 to pay the British Army. From the first day prevailing bad weather brought constant disorder and confusion to the convoy. Keeping it in any orderly formation was a constant challenge. I became furious when some merchants would negligently and repeatedly fall out of their assigned stations. With so many ships in the convoy spread out over great distances, one falling out of station could be lost over the horizon. Signal flags addressed to recalcitrant ships were hoisted hourly, and still certain ships would not properly respond. When my patience wore thin, I would order a shot fired across the bow of the lagging merchant and at times would hoist a signal that a fine worth 10 per cent of their cargo would be levied for impairing the speed of the convoy. I did not know whether such a fine was authorised, but I hoped the mere threat would have a curative effect. I confess that my overall temperament was further exacerbated by chronic seasickness in the ever-pounding seas. I also suffered a fever, perhaps the lingering effects of malaria. The transit took more than an agonising month to complete, but the convoy arrived intact.

After three weeks at sea and severely behind schedule, *Albemarle* had run out of fresh greens and citrus. Scurvy broke out among our crew, causing gums to become spongy and teeth to become loose. Worse of all, grog would sting the crew's mouths, requiring that they resort to the "long sea drink," a method of rolling the tongue so that a quaff of grog would go directly into the throat, touching gums or teeth as little as possible. When the convoy finally reached Quebec, the men suffering most were taken to hospital. Fresh provisions were ordered, and after a time, we recovered. My temperament was lifted by the exquisite beauty of an early autumn in Quebec. I had never before seen the beautiful spectacle of trees in an eruption of beautiful gold and red leaves, shimmering in the steady breezes of the early Canadian fall. Feeling the effects of its bracing weather, I wrote to father, "*The greatest of blessings is what I now have and what I never truly enjoyed until I saw fair Canada. The change it has wrought is wonderful.*"

The Harmony

After only enough time for the crew to recuperate, *Albemarle* set out for its first cruise at the North American station. Sailing off the coast of Massachusetts, we encountered and captured an American schooner, the *Harmony*, owned by a man named Nathaniel Carver. After we closed and hailed him, Carver struck his flag in submission. He was perceptive enough to know that if necessary, *Albemarle's* guns would be used. He was also a desperate man when he came aboard to speak with me.

"You have captured everything I and my family have, Captain. I entreat you please to take my cargo if you must, but please – I beg you – let me have my ship to provide for my family. I have no part in politics and have never taken up arms against the king."

Unmoved, I responded, "That is a convenient plea, sir. I do not know that what you say is true. And in any case you live in the company of Boston traitors, and I daresay that the trade you carry on will benefit them. It is the price you pay for living in the company of scoundrels who no longer want to be English."

I brought the *Harmony* crew aboard *Albemarle* and assigned one of my senior midshipmen with four of Carver's seamen to sail *Harmony* in our wake. Both ships soon became shrouded in a fog bank and drifted for hours. When the fog lifted, I was astounded to see that my ship was within shot range of four French warships, three large ships of the line, and the frigate *Iris*. *Albemarle* was immediately and severely in extreme danger, as the French would be able to bear more than two hundred guns against the *Albemarle's* twenty-eight. My only hope was to flee. However, as the *Albemarle* did not have the sailing lines of a proper frigate, the French began to close range to firing distance. Immediately I assessed my options – strike my colours or fight a hopeless battle and die with dignity, taking my crew with me. However, the Almighty provided that there was a saviour aboard in the person of Nathaniel Carver, who hurried to my side.

"*Captain, you are close to the shoals of the outer Saint Georges Bank, and I know them well. Your ship obviously has a rounded bottom and a shallower draft than the Frenchmen. I can show you where to go,*" Carver offered.

"*By the grace of God, man, show me!*" I cried out and called for general quarters, ordering the crew to battle stations with cannons loaded and run out.

Carver pointed to distant landmarks and described how to get to the deep channels which could not be seen but could be found only by reference to local sighting points. Seeing *Albemarle* veer toward the shore and out of concern for piloting in shallow water, the three larger French warships turned to open sea, leaving only the *Iris* to continue pursuit.

Carver advised, "If you go in straight toward that beacon for about a mile, you will find a lobster channel that is just beyond a very shallow bank, and if the Frenchman follows straight away, he will probably go aground."

At once it appeared to me that disaster could possibly be transformed into glory. A single ship action against the *Iris* was inviting to me under any conditions, but if the *Iris* went aground and became a stable target, I could manoeuvre the *Albemarle* broadside to her bow or stern and rake her mercilessly. The *Iris* would have to surrender. She would be ours! With Carver's piloting, we crossed into the lobster channel, backed our sails, put the helm over, and presented a broadside to the pursuing *Iris*, a direct invitation to the Frenchman to battle then and there. However, rather than accept the invitation, the *Iris* suddenly turned and set course for the open sea.

Seeing the *Iris* depart, with the larger French ships out of sight, I shouted, "Helmsman, heave to port and make directly for that ship. We do not need the advantage of shoals to take her." *Albemarle* crossed into open sea and headed for the Frenchman. The *Iris* did not turn but continued its course toward the horizon, and because of its ability to make greater speed, slowly and steadily increased its distance. With my combat juices in full flow and disappointed at the loss of an opportunity to fight the Frenchman ship upon ship, I ran to the mid-ship rail of the quarterdeck and shouted, "Run, you French bastard! Run, you coward. The *Albemarle* is here and ready to fight! Look, men. They are afraid of us! Look! They run from us! They run from the *Albemarle*!"

The fighting spirit that I wanted so fervently to exhibit became infectious to the crew who believed with me that our ship, small but fierce as a cornered badger, was without peer among any frigates on the sea. Savouring the adrenalin of the moment, the crew waved their hats with cheers and backslaps as the French ship faded and disappeared in the distance.

Our loaded cannons had to be relieved of their shot, and in the late-afternoon air a staccato of cannon fire echoed across the St. Georges Bank. I went to Carver and shook his hand and then ordered a second round of grog for the crew, whose excitement had been as fully engaged as my own throughout the incident. The glow of the evening would be defined not only by the golden fire of the setting sun reflected in thin stratified clouds over the green rolling hills of New England but within each member of the crew as they reflected on the events of a day that portended death and disaster in one moment followed by near glory in another. It was a day unlike any other.

Albemarle remained on station, looking for prizes that did not appear. Carver had become an invaluable piloting asset in and about the shallows of the New England coastline. Near the end of our station assignment I called my officers to conference, and after the conference I called for Carver.

"Mister Carver, you have been a godsend to my ship and its crew. You may take your schooner and go home." Carver removed his hat and looked at me for a long moment. Tears came to his eyes, and he said, *"Captain, you have given up the Harmony as a rightful prize. I know that. You and your officers must know that you have restored my life and that of my wife and children."* I also gave to Carver something else that I thought would be of great value – a certificate of gratitude which would protect him from capture by any other English ship. The decency of the act was suggested by me and approved by each and every one of my officers, all of whom relinquished shares in selling off the American schooner as a prize of war. Compared to the events of the day, it was a small price to pay.

Carver took the *Harmony* and sailed for home and family. The little schooner, however, appeared again on the next day, off the beacon point at Plymouth. As Carver brought *Harmony* abreast of *Albemarle*, he shouted to me, *"Captain, I have things for you."* Knowing that *Albemarle's* crew had been without fresh food for several weeks, Carver offloaded four sheep, a brace of poultry cages, and twenty sacks of fresh vegetables. As he pushed off and again sailed home, Carver looked to me and touched his hat. Standing together on the quarterdeck, I and my officers returned the salute. Minutes later as the *Harmony* made her way home, she heard in the distance three salute rounds fired from *Albemarle's* forecastle. What Carver had done for us had been monumental, and I would always remember his gift of piloting and how invaluable it could be to ships in close proximity to land.

Quebec

Albemarle was finally relieved on station by the *Daedalus* after we cruised for weeks without taking a prize, at least not one that we kept. As the ship sailed up the Saint Lawrence River and put into Quebec, the crew was content simply to be returning alive with memories of extreme danger, deliverance, frustrated glory, and a fulfilling act of human kindness.

In Quebec, I met and soon became friends with a man named Alexander Davison, a young merchant and contractor who in the coming years would become my confidant and agent. We met when Davison appeared one morning to inquire about contracts for replenishment. He related stories from members of Admiral Hood's staff concerning myself and their description of me as "an intense young captain" who had been assessed by the admiral as showing great promise. The description pleased my sense of pride and confirmed the committed tack of professional life I had chosen to follow. Davison also carried a letter of recommendation by my old friend, Captain Locker.

"Mister Davison, my good friend, Captain Locker, makes good mention of you as an honest agent who delivers goods in good condition and on time," I told him.

"I try to do just that, Captain, for I find it is the most advisable business a man can do. I understand that you had very little time when you first visited our city, and it would also be my pleasure to introduce you to Quebec. It was a trophy well worth the fight when we took Canada from the Frenchmen," Davison replied.

"In addition to the beauty of the city, are there pleasant diversions? I am tired from a long cruise off the colonies and would be quite relieved with pleasant things," I confessed.

"There are many, Captain. I know that you are preparing your ship to mark the anniversary of the King George's coronation, and your twenty-one-gun salute will be well noted. Tomorrow evening there will also be a ball at the governor's house, and I will be happy to introduce you to ladies and gentry of this city."

On the following afternoon the military parade ended with a formal governor's inspection of the troops and the traditional singing of

"God Save the King." The festivity was concluded when *Albemarle* fired its salute, with the crew formally paraded and signal flags rigged from bow to mainmast to stern. The ship never looked better. I wore my best formal uniform and was in the mood for a good time. Davison had come on board during the afternoon and supplied his carriage for transportation to the governor's ball.

The governor's house was more than just a house. It was a large white manse with a ballroom large enough to hold more than a hundred of the important English gentry, including wives, daughters, and associates. Davison guided me through the throng of the city's society, introducing me to the governor, army commanders, influential merchants, and older women who smiled and made the proper conventional remarks that would have been made had I been at any social gathering in London or Portsmouth. He then took me to a small gathering of army officers and gentlemen. In their midst was a young woman, the daughter of the provost marshal of the garrison in Quebec and the prettiest girl in the city.

Davison waited for a pause in conversation and spoke, "Miss Simpson, may I present Captain Horatio Nelson, commanding officer of the HMS *Albemarle*. Captain Nelson, I am pleased to present Miss Mary Simpson."

I was immediately thunderstruck by the visage of the young woman. She was probably not yet twenty but had a look of precocious beauty with light brown hair naturally combed without pretence, dark brown eyes, a narrow and delicate nose, thin but ample lips formed in a pleasant smile, and the fairest of skin.

"I am pleased to meet you, Captain, and have heard so much about your deeds in bringing the summer convoy through the ocean," she said, extending her hand.

"It was my honour, Miss Simpson," I answered. Then after an awkward moment I took her hand and lightly kissed it.

"Tell me, Captain. Is it easy to command a ship?" she asked.

"It is if you know and love the ship, ma'am. There is always much to do, and the attention to duty is a labour of great satisfaction."

She smiled broadly. "That is why you must be so attached to what you do, for Mister Davison says that you are very accomplished and that you were quite gallant in a place called Nicaragua."

The words were the most satisfying that I could hear at that moment, and I smiled back at the young woman. An infatuation of her seemed immediately to come over me. "Mister Davison does me great honour, ma'am."

The klatch of young men who surrounded Mary Simpson clearly resented her very genial exchange with a mere young naval officer in his striking blue coat with gold epaulets and sleeve stripes. They quickly renewed their discussion about plans for the forthcoming winter season. I listened to the rather vapid conversation, never taking my gaze from her face and noting with delight that from time to time, she would furtively but distinctly glance at me. With each glance my heart leapt. I was captivated.

The evening was filled with music and dancing, chiefly cotillion reels and minuets, all of which were unknown to me. I had no idea when to present a left or right arm or when to turn with a lady or parade with the line. I stayed on the periphery of the room, watching Mary Simpson as she glided across the room with one partner and then another. My sense of not truly belonging in this great formal ritual was relieved on several occasions by glances and smiles from the face of my newfound obsession.

As I rode back to *Albemarle* with Davison, I asked, "When can I see her again?"

"See whom?" Davison asked absentmindedly.

"Miss Simpson," I replied.

"Horatio, that young woman may as well be the only young woman in Canada, as every young man in or near this city sniffs around her constantly," Davison replied. "Besides, within the month the Saint Lawrence will be frozen, and you will have to take your ship away before it is locked in the ice."

My heart sank in recognition of the brutality of the truth contained in Davison's response. My return to *Albemarle* was filled with preparations for the unavoidable reassignment to the open sea and warmer waters. I met frequently with Davison to arrange the ship's outfitting and stores. My attention to duty was, however, broken frequently with memories of the face that had captured me, and each time it happened, I resisted in the knowledge that my duty made impossible any further advancement of my desire. I was, however, jolted into emotional turmoil within the week when a note was delivered. I was invited to tea on the next day – with Mary Simpson.

Teas with Mary

The Simpson home was a large white house in the French provincial style on the Chemin Saint-Louis, overlooking the Cathedral Montmartre Canadien and within an easy walk from *Albemarle's* dock on the Boulevard Champlain. I made the walk during the morning to determine the exact walking time, ensuring that I would arrive at the appointed hour. And at precisely three o'clock in the afternoon I presented myself in the same full-dress blue uniform I had worn to the ball.

Mary herself answered the door. "Welcome, Captain Nelson. I am pleased that my invitation was convenient for you." She led me into a small sitting room that was decorated in the English country manner without the crowded look of formal London convention. She asked me to sit, and an older woman entered with a silver tea service. I stood.

"Grandmother, I am pleased to present Captain Horatio Nelson. Captain, this is my grandmother, Mrs. Althea Simpson. She has been tending to the house and taking care of me while my mother and father are in England. I believe you will like her biscuits very much. They are made with ground almonds and cinnamon."

Mary's grandmother said, "Captain Nelson, I am very pleased to meet you. Mary has told me that you presented yourself very well at the Coronation Ball."

I replied, "I am honoured to meet you, ma'am, and pleased that Miss Simpson has spoken well of me."

Our conversation was spent in discussion of Miss Simpson's schooling in Switzerland, France, and London. I recounted family and adventures at sea. The elder Mrs. Simpson seemed particularly pleased that my father was a church rector. I could hardly take my eyes from Mary's face, and she returned my attention with smiles, subdued laughs, and directed attention that magnified my total captivation. The social convention of spending no more than thirty minutes at tea came and went. I would have stayed the entire afternoon.

Mrs. Simpson finally announced, "Captain, it has been a pleasure to have you, but I have many things that must be done before dinner."

"I will see the captain off, grandmother," Mary added quickly, and Mrs. Simpson left the room. At the door Mary said, "Captain—"

"Please call me Horatio," I interrupted.

"Thank you, Horatio, and thank you for coming. It has been a wonderful time. You are a very attractive and experienced man, quite different from those who live here in sedentary duty, waiting for the Americans to come. I very much look forward to seeing you again."

"Mary, I leave in two days," I said bluntly.

"Then you must come again tomorrow, at the same time if it is convenient," Mary responded.

My heart again leapt at the chance to be with her again, and I responded, "Nothing could prevent me from it."

I took her hand and kissed it. On the way back to *Albemarle*, I floated in a trance of emotion. Aboard ship, I was preoccupied with my total intoxication of the beautiful Mary. Reports of the ship's condition and readiness were approved without serious review or critique. The ship was managed by my competent officers as though I had not been present. The trance and anticipation of the next day possessed me.

When I returned to the Simpson house at the appointed hour for tea, Mary greeted me, "Grandmother is out, but I feel that we can have a pleasant time without her almond biscuits. Please come and sit with me. Where will you go from here?"

"I am ordered to convoy a fleet of transports to New York. Their provisions are sorely needed to quell the rebellion by the colonists," I answered.

As our conversation proceeded through question about my ship and what my career would be, I answered with exactness, impressing her with my professional acumen and serious devotion to my duties. She listened intently to all that I said, and then she said, "Captain—"

"Horatio, please call me Horatio," I blurted.

My demeanour became serious, and she offered a telling remark. "Yes, Horatio, you are a very impressive young man, accomplished well beyond your years, but you have a rather stern aspect. I feel that if you relax your temperament, your effect can be even more pleasing, and it will sacrifice nothing of what you have to say."

"I cannot doubt that it is true, my dear Mary. And for all time I would have you counsel me in the ways of social propriety. My greatest wish is to spend time with you, for I find you the most attractive woman I have ever known."

She blushed and looked down at her hands folded in her lap and said, "It is a pity that you must go so soon." She rose and said, "Sadly I can only wish you well in a future that will be bright with accomplishment."

We walked slowly to her door, my heart heavy with regret. We paused, and I looked at her with a regard of honest adoration. She said softly, "Bon voyage, my young captain," and she kissed my cheek. Without thinking and with disregard for the possibility of her objection, I bent forward and softly kissed her lips. To the delight of my entire being, she gently returned the kiss.

"Good-bye. Duty calls," I said, and left.

For the remainder of the day and night the image of Mary Simpson remained in my senses. The memory of the kiss possessed me. Her smile, her gentle laugh, and the way she looked at me – the totality of her – became foremost encouragement to my inner drive as a man besotted with a quest for ethereal love and driven by primordial instincts of a young man who had experienced the ecstasy of having enjoyed woman flesh. I wanted her with a passion I had never known.

The next morning *Albemarle* prepared to get underway. The docking detail was set, and sails that had become frozen to their yardarms were beaten free of ice, unfurled, and set. Lines were cast off, and the gentle eastern current of the Saint Lawrence pushed the ship away from the dock under a north-western breeze. Overcome with remorse, I watched the skyline of the city as the ship moved away, and before we had travelled a mile, I ordered my first officer to back the sails and anchor the ship on the southern shallows of the river. I then instructed that the dinghy be lowered.

"Is there a problem, Captain?" my first lieutenant asked, rather astonished. "The convoy is already proceeding down the river."

"There is something I must do," was my curt reply. The small boat was lowered, and I climbed down with a handling crew of three seamen. When the dinghy was tied to the Quebec dock, I leapt out and made my way toward the city when, by sheer happenstance, I encountered Alexander Davison.

"*Pray, Horatio, why are you here?*" Davison asked.

I answered, "*I have come back to speak with Miss Simpson. I find it utterly impossible to leave this place without laying myself and my fortunes at her feet. I desire that she become part of my future and my world.*"

"*Horatio, that would be your ruin, situated as you are,*" Davison responded.

"*Then let it follow, for I am resolved to do it,*" I declared.

"*And I positively declare that you shall not,*" Davison answered.

"*A life with her at my side will be worth whatever price must be paid,*" I responded.

"*No, Horatio, you do not understand the way things stand.*"

"*I understand only that I love her,*" I said.

"*You and a score of other men in Quebec,*" Davison replied. "*The young woman has attracted every young man of standing in the city, and all have become entranced by her beauty and her womanly attraction. There are suitors who would line up at her door who believe she is the perfect object of their future lives.*"

"*But, I must——*" I began.

"*Listen, Horatio,*" he interrupted, "*There are many, Horatio, many who seek her hand! And, know this – she is quite friendly, and has been for some time, with a Captain Matthews who has asked for her hand. And, she has confided that when he is promoted to Major, she will accept his engagement to marry.*"

Davison took me firmly by the shoulders, turned me toward my ship, and said, "*Horatio, look,*" and pointed to it. "*There is your future, my young, besotted friend. Do not abandon it.*"

I was struck to my core by Davison's words. My emotion of desire for Mary Simpson was suddenly overcome by the facts Davison had recited and the obvious truth and wisdom spoken by a wise friend.

Standing on the dock, reality descended over me. I paused and looked at Davison and said, "*Thank you. I believe you.*"

I returned to *Albemarle*, and it set out with full sail to escort the convoy. It was my assigned duty, and I could not deny it, whatever the personal cost. I did not look back.

New York

The transit to New York was uneventful with favourable seas and north-westerly winds that often prevailed in the fall season of North America. Convoy ships stayed in assigned stations, and I was able to spend time in further training of *Albemarle's* already very competent crew. It was tradition in the Royal Navy that the crew be exercised to ward off the lethargy that comes with hours upon hours of sailing in transit on a steady course in calm seas. Very often ship commanders ordered dancing to raise the crews' pulses, but I preferred practical exercise. As in the North Sea, gun crews would compete in firing drills, with the last rounds fired with live shot. I would change the ship's course so that tacking could be practiced by deck hands at different points of wind, or the yards could be jibed as an alternative to tacking. I would also change things about and have boatswains handle cannons while gunnery mates would handle yard lines in tacking the sails. I would even do "officer strings," in which the officers themselves would do loading drills at the cannons and would handle sheets in tacking against a fore wind. I would always place myself as a member of the officers' string. The crew would laugh and point with derision at the officers' ineptitude, but inside each of them they would have a feeling of respect for officers and their captain, who would get willingly and heartily into the heave and sweat of doing what the crew would do in battle. It was a simple act of respect and something that, so far as I knew, the ship's crew had never experienced on other ships. As well as keeping the men exercised, it served to heighten their spirits and to impart a sense of unity as well as a better understanding of ship functions.

In New York, I met Admiral Robert Digby, Commander of the North American Station. The war in the Americas was winding down as a result of the surrender and capture of our army at Yorktown, Virginia. And because the war had become a long and fruitless expenditure of British lives, money, and national patience, Parliament had passed a resolution to authorise no further offensive operations. The British stronghold in New York was the last. American forces were in essential control of the remainder of the colonies, and there was no real prospect for a British resurgence without a monumental effort that politicians at home had no will to authorise or stomach to carry out. The American uprising was over, and the Americans had, with crucial French support, effectively won the war for their independence. Having failed to quell the American rebellion, the British focus shifted to the Caribbean. It was there that major economic and political influence remained, and it was there that the French threat was most imminent.

I wanted to take *Albemarle* to the Caribbean, for I felt it was in that sea and among those islands where immediate issues with the French would be determined. Digby could not understand why I wanted to leave his North American assignment, as it seemed the most fruitful ground for attaining prize money. After all, ships left American ports regularly, and a formal state of rebellion continued with the colonies. As long as there was a state of conflict, any ship captured would be a prize of war, and the value of the ship, escorted to New York or England, would be serious revenue to the capturing ship's officers and crew.

"You have come to a fine station for making prize money," Digby told me on my arrival.

"Yes, sir," I replied. "But the West Indies are the station for honour."

"Is there no honour in taking prizes from rebellious colonies that are at war with the king?" Digby asked with some astonishment.

"I cannot gainsay your characterization, Admiral, but it seems that Parliament has neither further interest nor any real commitment to the fight," I answered. "And the French have moved to challenge control of our Caribbean islands."

With the French largely withdrawn from North American waters and concentrated in the Caribbean, I could not understand how a true captain of His Majesty's line could want to remain outside of the real theatre of conflict, and in hopes of gaining orders for *Albemarle* to sail to the Caribbean, I applied for an interview with Admiral Hood, commander of Caribbean Forces. When I arrived aboard Hood's flagship, it was happenstance that I would also meet someone who would be eventful in many aspects of my future life. That person was Prince William Henry, the third son of King George III. Prince William was sufficiently impressed with me to make a lengthy entry in his journal. It was later confided to me that he described me thusly:

His dress was worthy of attention ... his lank, un-powdered hair was tied in a stiff, Hessian tail of an extraordinary length; the old-fashioned flaps of his waistcoat added to the general appearance of quaintness of his figure. I had never seen anything like it before, nor could imagine who he was, nor what he came about. My doubts were, however, removed when Lord Hood introduced him to me. There was something irresistibly pleasing in his address and conversation; and an enthusiasm when speaking on professional subjects that showed that he was no common being.

Prince William had been a problem for the Crown. His father, George III, had become beset with accelerating dementia, with essentially no interest or ability in the delicate demands of raising rebellious sons or of effectively administering an empire for that matter. As a result, his eldest son, the Prince of Wales, became a free-ranging and dissolute lothario, possessive of stature and authority but without a whit of judgment or circumspection. In an effort to remove William from the influence of his older brother and to instil in him a sense of pride and accomplishment, he was sent to sea as a midshipman at the age of thirteen.

William became something of a compromise between respectability and dissolution. He was, on a personal level, obstinate, often a bully, and sometimes a comical buffoon. His eye for women was always keen and undisciplined, and his appreciation of the results of his personal misbehaviour was non-existent, probably the product of royal exemption from the standards attached to mere mortals. However, he came to understand naval matters and was a competent seaman, although the command structure was always well advised to ensure that his first officer and staff were first rate. Given his royal status, superior officers thought it advisable to bestow praise upon anything he did that, in any measure, could be praiseworthy. The regard in which I held him was also affected by a degree of reverence for royalty that, as I had been taught, should border upon the absolute. The prince would play a significant role in many and varied respects of my life.

At my interview with Admiral Digby, Admiral Hood had been present, and upon hearing my disdain for short-term financial matters and my commitment to defending the Crown's longer-term interests in the Caribbean, I believe that Admiral Hood recognised in me a young officer whose professionalism was a reflection of his own. Hood requested and received my assignment to his squadron that sailed from New York to the Caribbean, arriving at Jamaica in February 1783. Soon after my arrival I captured a French ship which was fortuitously packed with masts hued from American trees, masts that were sorely needed by Hood's squadron. It also brought some prize money that I quickly assigned to my new friend and benefactor, Alex Davidson. High commendation from Hood followed, and I was euphoric in writing to Captain Locker:

My situation in Lord Hood's fleet must be in the highest degree flattering to any young man. He treats me as if I were his

> *son, and will, I am convinced, give me any thing I can ask of*
> *him ... nor is my situation with Prince William less flattering.*
> *Lord Hood was so kind as to tell him (indeed I cannot make*
> *use of expression strong enough to describe what I felt), that if*
> *he wished to ask questions relative to naval tactics, I could give*
> *him as much information as any officer in the fleet.*

This commendation was worth far more to me than money from a score of American prizes.

Sailing with the Prince

The Caribbean operations with Admiral Hood's fleet did not last long, as in January 1783, an accord of peace was signed with France and Spain. A result of the peace treaty was that the government office in London suggested – and the king agreed – that Prince William should make a three-day visit to Cuba as a goodwill gesture. Admiral Hood ordered me to command the convoy transporting the prince and to act as his aide-de-camp.

The convoy arrived at Havana harbour in full-dress parade. Salutes were fired and answered, and I remarked, "Someday I imagine these guns will be fired upon this same spot but with a steady aim and full shot." However, for the time being, goodwill and rituals were the order of the day. At a formal ball in the governor's palace, I basked in the glory of presentation as a ranking visitor, second only to the prince himself. As for the prince, he came to show his undisciplined side in a near catastrophic manner. At the ball he was introduced to the daughter of the Spanish admiral commanding in Cuba. She was a true beauty of striking features and regal demeanour. Her invitation to Prince William and to me at a reception the following day set the stage for the prince to become romantically obsessed, and when we returned to *Albemarle* that evening, the prince announced that he planned to seek her hand in marriage.

Astonished by the prince's announcement, I responded, "That, sir, will be a tragic mistake."

"Why?" responded the Prince, "She has the status of near royalty and she has my heart. I will be blessed to spend my days at court with her beauty and my nights in bed with her bosom and loins that will give me such pleasure that I could not want for more. And, I think she fancies me."

I responded, "Sir, her smiles and pleasant conversation have meant only that she has been obliged to accord to you a proper reception. Please consider these obstacles. First, as you stand once-removed from the line to the throne, the King and Parliament would not hesitate to refuse a union with someone so closely associated with a country whose entire economic and military policy has collided with the interests of our nation and will continue to do so. When we again go to war with her country, she will be estranged from everything in our country and her bed will probably be closed to you. Finally, these things will be readily apparent to her father and his superiors. She will not be given permission to accept your offer."

"I do not think she will refuse a union with royalty," the Prince retorted.

"Your Highness, and my dear friend, I guarantee that no matter how she feels, her father will not allow it, and when she refuses you, you can only walk away with your head held low. Please know that His Majesty's son cannot walk away from anything having to do with Spain with his head held low! Besides, I can guarantee that there are scores of beautiful women of aristocracy who will become a garden from which you can pluck the most beautiful flower. Please, set this thought aside and look forward to your future."

The prince never outwardly conceded to my remonstrance, but he did not persist in a proposal that would have been both unsuccessful and foolhardy.

Home Again and France

From Cuba, *Albemarle* was parted from the fleet and sailed home to England. Shortly after arrival I was further encouraged by Lord Hood, who invited me to a "Sovereign's Levee," a reception at Windsor Castle, where I was introduced to King George in very flattering terms as an officer of promise and valued acquaintance of his son, Prince William. My sense of satisfaction was ablaze at the attention given by what I considered to be the very peak of the world to which I was completely committed.

My growing appreciation of networking with persons of influence had also become acute, and my penchant for communication, with appropriate and tactful self-aggrandizement, began with a stream that would flow for the rest of my life. I wrote to friends I had made in Jamaica, particularly those who had major interests at home, including traders, transport officials, government functionaries, and fellow officers. Much of my correspondence was with members of the Admiralty office in praise of subordinates who had served with me. This correspondence was copied to those whom I had praised, imparting a double-positive effect.

The conclusion of the American war of independence and the cessation of hostilities with France forced me into a leave from service at half pay. I had a little money from prizes taken as part of Admiral Hood's fleet, but it certainly was no fortune; however, I had enough, with the encouragement of Prince William, to finance a trip to France in order to become more familiar with the French language and *their ways*, both of which I thought would be beneficial when the ever-simmering conflict of interest between England and France would again come to a head. With a six-month leave granted by the Admiralty, I set off to discover a country for which I had previously held nothing but contempt.

As a companion for the trip, I found Captain James Macnamara, a frigate captain I had met in Jamaica whom I found to be intelligent – and a bold spirit. Indeed, Macnamara's temper would later lead him to kill a man in a duel. I must admit that our activities on the continent became more of an escapade than a serious effort at language and social study. In Calais, Macnamara sought out establishments where women were present and amenable if not eager to be entertained at dinner and in bed for the night. Macnamara came to know me as Horace, the name my family had called me as a boy, and used it as an informal appellation. He was also more fluent in French than I, who had little attraction, let alone dedication, to their language - or anything else to do with them.

On the first day in Calais, Macnamara announced, "Horace, I have information that at the dining house they call *La Maison Blanche* you can get a good dinner and a good woman at a reasonable cost. Let's give it a try, eh?"

"Why would I want to do that?" I responded.

"Well, we are both very hungry and a little yearning for company, don't you think? And besides, it would be most efficacious in learning things about the French."

I reflected and agreed to go, adding, "Mac, understand that I have no intention of buying a prostitute. They can give you a pox."

"Fair enough," Macnamara said, "but I shall not be dissuaded from taking advantage of a bargain if goods that seem to be clean are worth the price."

La Maison Blanche proved to be a very comfortable place, a warm restaurant lit with oil lamps and smelling of rich stews with ample spice. It was also part of an inn which provided rooms above the dining hall. We were asked if we would like to have companions for the evening to explain the cuisine of the house and to recommend wines. Without consulting me, Macnamara asked if there was a price for the companions and when told, "*Mais non*," Mac responded, "*Bien sûr!*" and we were seated at a corner table.

"Mac, you understand French passably well. Why do we have need of companions to do that for which we have no need?" I asked.

"Horace, my dear and naive friend, my concern is that we have no real idea of what we need, and I have no reservation against a balm for a need that is pressingly real but not realised," Macnamara responded with a condescending smile.

"I simply have no idea of what you mean," I dismissingly replied.

Two women appeared, talking among themselves and laughing as they approached. One had black hair, and she was tall and rather lean; the other was smaller with a fuller figure and blondish brown hair. Both were quite attractive.

"*Bonjour, messieurs*," the tall one greeted. "*Ce sera notre plaisir d'être utile ce soir*," the tall one said. She looked at both of us and took a seat next to Macnamara. The small one seated herself next to me.

"These are our helpful companions tonight, Horace," Macnamara advised.

"Wonderful," I replied. I looked at the small one and noticed immediately and without thought her dark brown eyes, pleasant face, and the full cleavage of her breasts modestly revealed by the low-cut neck of her peasant's frock.

"*Quelle est les meilleure nourritures à cet endroit?*" Macnamara asked of the tall one.

"We can speak English, monsieur," the tall one replied.

"Then you should," Macnamara replied. "You see, I speak a little French, but my friend does not. So that would be very well. Tell us. What are your names, and where are you from?"

The tall one said, "I am Catherine de Planvue, and my friend is Celeste de Calais."

"I am Mac," Macnamara said, "And my companion is … well, call him Captain."

They discussed the cuisine of the day, and Catherine suggested the *agneau printanier avec la sauce Bauvais*, which Macnamara translated as spring lamb with local sauce. Celeste asked if I liked lamb, and I answered that I liked almost everything well prepared.

"Do you think I am well prepared?" Celeste asked.

Taken aback at the boldness of the question, I nevertheless recovered quickly and answered, "I think you are lovely, my dear, and I am pleased that you can dine with us."

"*Mais, non*, Captain. We have eaten, and our company with you is for your pleasure and not your cost. But I will have a glass of our house Beaujolais … if you please."

Having been so long without the close company of an attractive woman, I could not avoid glances at Celeste's shoulders and breasts, and the thought of having her, as suggested by Macnamara's earlier remarks, caused a natural and pleasurable stir within me, one that I did not repress.

Separate conversations were carried out with our respective companions, and dinner was served. The lamb was well turned and served with minced potatoes under a sauce that was the best I had ever tasted. The claret Mac had ordered was Beaujolais fortified with brandy. After several glasses its effect was to dissolve inhibitions and to excite everything about the evening.

After dessert of finger cakes and figs Catherine asked, "Can we entertain you in house rooms, messieurs? It would be too soon to end the evening now."

"Is there anything we must pay?" Macnamara asked.

"Well, the room cost is six francs, but our time spent with you shall be our pleasure," Catherine answered with a full smile.

"Excellent! Horace, how can we deny such a wonderful invitation?" Macnamara responded and looked to me. Then he added, "This is a much better opportunity than to spend a cold night in a post house, don't you think?"

I was surprised and relieved that payment was for the room, and the reprehension of paying money for a woman was avoided. I looked at Celeste, whose attractiveness had grown in pace with the glow imparted by the fortified wine, and said with repressed excitement, "Celeste, I shall be delighted to spend more time with you."

"And I with you, my captain," she answered.

The women led Macnamara and me hand in hand up narrow stairs to separate rooms. I was not surprised that when I entered the room with Celeste, without speaking, she took my jacket and carefully laid it aside and then approached me and kissed me with an open mouth, flicking her tongue over my lips. The effect was ecstatic, igniting a response that had been latent for so long. I fumbled with my clothing, and she placed her hands on mine, saying, "Take your time, Captain. You must not rush." I then more slowly removed my clothing, and when I looked up, I saw her already unclothed, standing before me with a slight smile and outstretched arms.

Our coupling was unrestrained. Kissing with parted lips and touching of tongues was new to me and a perfect accompaniment to the entry and thrusts of my eager coverage. In response to the immediate fury of my motion, Celeste repeated, "Take your time, Captain. You must not rush." I slowed my assault and savoured the contact, becoming attentive to her breathing and the movement of her hands upon my back. She said, "Slowly, my captain, slowly." As our union progressed, I felt her stroking of my back change into a firm grasp and heard her breathing become mounting susurrations of pleasure. Then as she raised her legs along my sides, I could not restrain my release. We lay together afterward, and Celeste whispered, "*Parfait, le mieux, parfait.*" I did not know what it meant and did not care. In the morning Celeste was gone, and Macnamara's knock on the door awoke me from a perfect sleep. "Horace, are you fit to travel?" he asked.

As we set out, the first intention was to travel straight to St. Omer, our planned destination, but we decided to detour through Boulogne because it was considered one of the major French cities. Travel was arduous, largely because we had decided to save money by travelling in a postilion carriage which ran from one post-house inn to another, carrying mail and general commercial cargo along with passengers. Our carriage was un-sprung, and every rock or rut in the road was felt with jarring and exhausting effect. The pace was also slow, covering hardly three miles in an hour because of the weight of the carriage. By the time Macnamara and I reached their next inn, we were done for the day.

To make matters worse, as I wrote to Captain Locker, "*The inn should have been called a pig sty. We were shown into a room with two straw beds, and with great difficulty, the inn keeper mustered up two clean sheets, and gave us two pigeons for supper, upon a dirty cloth and wooden-handled knives. Oh, what a transition from happy England!*"

When we finally reached Boulogne, I was disappointed to find that it was filled with English vacationers attracted by inexpensive lodging, good food, and high-quality local wines. We pushed on to St. Omer, where lodging with a French family had been arranged. St. Omer proved to be a pleasant surprise. I wrote that "*instead of a dirty, nasty town, which I had always heard it to be, I find a large city, well paved with good streets, well lighted.*" We settled in the home of a Madame La Mourie, who had two daughters who were, as I wrote, "*very agreeable young ladies ... who honour us with their company pretty often.*" The young women, however, spoke no English, and I again wrote to Locker, "*The French goes on but slowly. Patience, of which you know I have not much, and perseverance will, I hope, make me master of it.*" I would not become master of French partly because of the discovery of other attractions in the English expatriate community. Shortly after our arrival in St. Omer, I wrote to my brother, "*Today, I dine with an English clergyman, a Mr. Andrews, who has two very beautiful young ladies, daughters. I must take care of my heart, I assure you.*"

One of the daughters, Elizabeth Andrews, lit a fire that consumed my amorous vulnerability, much as Mary Simpson had done in Quebec. Within a month I again wrote to my brother, "*My heart is quite secure against the French beauties. I wish I could say as much for an English young lady, the daughter of a clergyman, with whom I am just going to dine and spend the day. She has such accomplishments, that had I a million of money, I am sure that as of this moment, I would make her an offer of it; my income at present is by far too small to think of marriage, and she has no fortune.*" Within the next month I became so smitten that I wrote to my uncle, Maurice Suckling, whose financial accumulation from a very successful naval career might prove to be the enablement of marriage to Miss Andrews. I wrote a letter that, I must confess, resembled poetic blackmail, describing my penurious status as an officer furloughed on half pay but whose heart has been captured and whose life hung in the balance. My financial request was for Suckling to "allow me" a hundred pounds sterling per year, with the plea.

The critical moment in my life has now arrived, that I am to be happy or miserable – it depends solely on you ... life is not worth preserving without happiness, and I care not where I may linger out a miserable existence. I am prepared to hear your refusal, and have fixed my resolution if that should happen; but in every situation, I shall be a well-wisher to you and your

> *family, and pray they or you may never know the pangs which*
> *at this instant tear at my heart.*

Suckling was not as poetic in his response. He simply made a note on the back of the letter that he would consent to help. However, in the meantime the need was obviated by Miss Andrews herself. She told me that she was not a candidate for marriage. Spurned by the object of my infatuation, I wrote to my brother, "*I shall return home to many charming women, but no charming woman will return with me.*"

Back home I visited my father, taking cures at Bath. I also found that my friends were caught up in a storm of excitement preceding the forthcoming general election. My own political opinions were strongly influenced by Admiral Hood, who opposed Charles Fox, an earlier supporter of the cause of the American colonies and whose "Francophile friends," Admiral Hood said, were striving to ruin the country. I became a frequent guest at the home of the admiral, where I renewed my friendship with Alexander Davison, who was then living in comfort, having made a fortune as a government contractor and factor of war prizes. There was talk of me standing for Parliament, but nothing came of the talk. I returned to visit with my father and favourite sister, Kate, where I received news that would again point to the path of my destiny. I had been appointed to command of the twenty-eight-gun frigate HMS *Boreas*.

Chapter 4

Boreas

I remember being amused when my older brother, Maurice, asked how I managed to be appointed command of a ship when so many officers senior to me were still relegated to enforced leave at half pay. I answered that it was probably because of reports to the Admiralty of my command fitness. I suspected, however, that Admiral Hood had been instrumental in the appointment not only because of his respect for me as a commander but in part as a result of my political views and support of the admiral's positions in the recent parliamentary election. Such was part of the tapestry.

During the weeks before the election I had also, in Maurice's critical description, *"run at the ring of pleasure"* by coming to know a woman somewhat older than I was at a party given by Admiral Hood. As a result of my attraction to the woman and feeling no emotional resistance, the acquaintance developed into a brief but tumultuous bedroom romance that was confined to discrete secrecy and accommodated by the fact that she was married to a government official whose duties required frequent foreign travel. Our last activity together was a horse ride during which my horse bolted out of control and ran through the common and past the London gate, where I encountered a wagon on a narrow street. My horse could hardly pass, and I described the incident to Maurice, *"To save my legs, and perhaps my life, I was obliged to throw myself from the horse, which I did with great agility, but unluckily upon hard stones, which hurt my back and my leg, but caused no other mischief. It was a thousand to one that I had not been killed."* For several weeks afterwards I walked with a limp but, I confess, also with a self-satisfied and randy memory. I did not feel guilty. Perhaps I should have. I did not.

My orders for *Boreas* were quite simple. I was to take the ship once again across the Atlantic to the Leeward Islands of the Caribbean. However, although the orders were straightforward, they were not without complication. I would have passengers during the transit, including thirty midshipmen for disbursal to a number of Caribbean ships. In addition, I would host Lady Hughes, wife of Admiral Sir Richard Hughes, and their rather unattractive daughter, Rose, who was unabashedly in quest of a husband.

The cruise, which ended in Barbados, was uneventful except for the constant presence of Lady Hughes, who seemed to have the attitude that it was she who was in command of the *Boreas*. She would mention frequently that Sir Richard had previously commanded the ship, although I would constantly correct her by advising that although her husband had commanded a ship named the *Boreas*, it was a very different ship. She gave this incidental fact no significance and continued to refer to the ship as "our dear *Boreas*." There were times when I was driven almost to distraction by her eternal clack and vapid conversation. I would avoid her whenever possible but had to respond when she summoned me for some idle remark or request. At the same time Rosy was doing her utmost to attract the attention of officers on the ship and even some of the older midshipmen.

One afternoon in the middle of the ocean, on a whim I proposed a bet with my first lieutenant, James Wallace, a bachelor. "Wallace, I am of a mind to wager you a guinea, perhaps two if you like, that if you go to young Rosy and offer to meet with her in discreet quarters so that you might teach her the fundamental elements of physical intimacy that her future husband should like her to know, she will accept. In fact, I will allow my own stateroom for the assignation when she accepts."

Wallace responded, "Sir, may I amend the bet?"

"Of course. How so?" I responded.

"Well," said Wallace, "my major concern is that you will win the bet, in which case, I would join your side of the wager and insist upon being offered a hundred guineas."

In one of three circumstances during the transit, I allowed myself to laugh out loud and replied, "No bet, Wallace, no bet!"

Because the *Boreas* crew was new to me, I used the transit as an opportunity to exercise them in gunnery and seamanship, as I had done aboard *Albemarle*. I also showed particular interest in quizzing and drilling the midshipmen. I would call them to my side and say, "Sir, please point to the fore royal sail. Now point to the main gallant sail. Now to the mizzen skysail." Then I might say, "Go and take hold of the sheets you would use to lay on a flying jib," or I would order them to climb the rigging and put their hands upon the mizzen topsail yard. After a few days of such interrogation, the midshipmen became intent on walking the ship from bow to stern, learning everything about sails, shrouds, backstays, bowsprits, and lanyards. I believe that they despaired of embarrassing themselves in my eyes, and the process of schooling these boys honed my own knowledge of my new ship. I believe that the crew also took note not only of my demonstrated knowledge of seamanship but more importantly, my high expectations of those who served with me.

James Wallace noted to the master gunner that because Lady Hughes and Rosy would stay in their quarters during gunnery because of intolerance to the deafening sounds, and after gunnery, because of their aversion to the stench of powder smoke, gun crews should be prepared for frequent drills. And so it was. By the time *Boreas* reached Barbados and I returned wife and daughter to Admiral Hughes, they had cost me £200 for their food and entertainment. Lady Hughes did show her gratitude, however, by giving to me a silver tea caddy worth perhaps five shillings. There was some other consolation, however, because James Wallace, the *Boreas* first lieutenant, noted that "*it was no small satisfaction to Captain Nelson to find himself senior captain, and second in command of the Barbados station.*"

Admiral Hughes was the product of the genteel English aristocracy. He was the son of a baron who had accumulated a sizable fortune as commissioner for the naval base at Portsmouth. Sir Richard, therefore, was well situated financially, although his natural inclination was to be quite frugal. I observed that the quarters in which he had chosen to live were not at all equal to the station the commander of the Caribbean should have. Hughes was a pleasant and easy-going man who seemed far more intent on being a gentleman rather than a senior naval officer, and my first impression was that I could neither fully respect nor like the man. I wrote to my father, "*The Admiral and all about him are great ninnies! I do not like him. He bows and scrapes too much for me.*" Hughes also spent a great deal of time practicing the violin and was considered an excellent fiddler. I observed once to my first lieutenant that "*he spends so much time tuning his violin that his squadron was totally out of tune.*"

As I set out for a general cruise of the islands, I encountered trouble at English Harbour, Antigua. There I noticed that the ship attached to Captain John Moutray, the commissioner of the harbour, was flying the broad pennant of a commodore to which, as a captain serving in a civil appointment on half pay, Moutray was not entitled. It also indicated a formal rank that would be senior to me. I summoned the ship's captain to *Boreas* and frankly interrogated him. "*Have you any order from Sir Richard Hughes to fly a broad pennant?*"

"*No,*" the captain answered.

"*For what reason do you then fly it in the presence of a senior officer?*"

"*I hoisted it by order of Commissioner Moutray.*"

"*Have you seen by what authority Commissioner Moutray was empowered to give you such orders?*"

"*No.*"

"*Sir, you have acted wrongly to obey any man you do not know is authorized to command you.*"

He responded, "*I feel that I may have acted wrong, but being a young captain myself, I did not think it proper to interfere in this matter, even though there were you and other senior officers upon the station.*"

Shortly thereafter I wrote a letter of protest to Commissioner Moutray himself and dispatched two additional letters to Admiral Hughes. I noted that until the commissioner was properly appointed, I would not obey any order I received from him and that I recognised no senior officers besides the Lord Commissioner of the Admiralty's appointed senior officers whose names appeared on the formal post list. I then went perhaps a bit too far in dispatching letters to the secretary of the Admiralty in London. Such appealing directly to the Admiralty over the head of his superiors on station earned me a direct rebuke. The Admiralty responded, "*Captain Nelson ought to have submitted his doubts to the commanding officer on station instead of having taken upon himself to control the exercise of the functions of his appointment.*"

Although I was correct in all of my observations of command protocol and order of seniority, the Admiralty apparently preferred genteel tact and even tolerance of non-observance of a correct order.

The Navigation Acts

The great Gulf Stream of the northern Atlantic Ocean flows in the form of a great triangle that begins in the Caribbean Sea and passes northward along the coast of North America, crosses the Atlantic to the western coasts of Ireland, and then proceeds southward to Africa and back across the Atlantic to its point of origin in the Caribbean. During the great age of sailing ships in the past century, the Gulf Stream acted as the great road upon the sea, carrying rum or molasses from the islands of the Caribbean northward to the cities of the North American coast, where lumber and cotton were added and then taken across to Great Britain.

There the raw materials from the islands and America would be offloaded and replaced with finished goods. The ships would then sail south to the west coast of Africa and back to the Caribbean islands and then to North America to deliver commercial – and human – goods.

Following loss of its North American colonies, Parliament passed the famous (or infamous, depending upon one's commercial interests) Navigation Acts, which strictly forbade any trade from its remaining colonies with any country other than Britain itself. The intent of the Navigation Acts was to preserve the bounty of our colonies exclusively for the benefit of the homeland. The effect of them, if observed as Parliament clearly intended, was to break the great triangle of trade. Trouble would follow.

As a result of severe lobbying by planters, merchants, and officials at the customhouse in Antigua, Admiral Hughes had been prevailed upon to waive enforcement of the Acts. English shipping revenues were not a problem when the American colonies were part of the British Empire, but they became a severe disruption of the islands' natural commerce when the colonies became the new American nation – and foreign to the empire.

I wrote to Captain Locker that the admiral had become "*a dupe of some artful people*" and had no lawful right to waive laws which had been passed by Parliament. I contended that the Navigation Acts must be enforced, whatever the difficulties, because they were His Majesty's laws and intended to promote interests of Britain and its commerce. To clarify the application of the laws, I confronted the admiral himself. "*Sir, with respect, I must state that I am duty bound to obey the plain letter of the Navigation Acts and to prevent trade upon the seas by these islands with any nation other than our own.*"

The admiral responded, "*Captain Nelson, these are complicated matters and I am not sure what the Navigation Acts are all about.*"

I answered directly, "*I find this very odd since every captain of every warship is furnished with the statutes of the Admiralty in which the Navigation Acts appear. I will be happy to let you read my copy, if you like.*"

"*That will not be necessary, Captain,*" responded the admiral, brusquely ending the colloquy.

Thereafter, Hughes wrote a formal notice that the Navigation Acts ought to be enforced. However, after repeated complaints by men who were not only planters and merchants but also close social friends, he changed his mind and decreed that "*residents of the various islands should be allowed to decide the various trade cases for themselves.*"

Hughes had neither the mood nor the strength to go against the commercial interests of influential associates whose trade with the Americans was far more convenient and profitable than sending their goods directly to England at drastically increased cost and to a market that was much smaller and whose prices were much lower. I was both incredulous and frustrated by the manner in which Hughes had been seduced by his island friends to the point that he would not enforce the fundamental laws of the Crown. I was later dismayed upon receipt of an order that ship captains should detain all foreign ships, but "*if the governor or his representative should give leave for admitting such vessels, they should not be hindered or interfered in their subsequent proceedings.*" Incensed, I wrote to Captain Locker, "*Our commander has not the opinion of his own sense that he ought to have. He is led by the advice of the islanders to allow the Yankees' trade or, at least, to wink at it. I, for one, am determined not to suffer the Yankees to come where my ship is.*"

In an act of direct defiance I wrote to Hughes, "*No governor will, I am sure, do such an illegal act at a time when Great Britain is using every endeavour to suppress illicit trade at home, it is not wished that the ships upon the station should be only spectators of an illegal trade which I know is being carried out in these islands.*"

I added, "*General Shirley told me ... how much he, as Governor of the Leeward Islands, approved of the methods that we were carrying out for the suppression of illegal trade with America.*" I also referred to a letter from the Secretary of State, Lord Sydney, confirming that Parliament "*was determined that American ships and vessels should not have any intercourse with our West India islands.*"

I then essentially fired a direct shot across Hughes's bow by adding further, "*Whilst I have the honour to command an English man-of-war, I shall never allow myself to be subservient to the will of any governor, nor cooperate with him in doing any illegal acts.*" I made clear that I was determined to keep on punishing the Americans by invoking the letter of law and insisted that it was not for me to speculate as to what might or might not be best for England in the longer term or whether winking at the law would serve the better interests of the islands. It was clear to me that Parliament had made that decision. I had not.

In consequence of my firm resolve I found that I became a pariah to the island gentry and wrote to Captain Locker, *"You will believe I am not very popular with the people of the islands. They have never visited me and I have not set a foot in any house since I have been on station – and all for doing my duty by being true to the interests of Great Britain. The residents of these islands are American by connection and by interest. They are inimical to Great Britain. They are as great rebels as ever were in America, had they the power to show it."*

Committed to my course of action and convinced that I was correct, the ship captains under my command and I systematically challenged and boarded vessels that we believed were violating the Navigation Acts. I would impound any trading vessel found to be of American origin and carrying produce of the islands, particularly if they were sailing under fraudulent British or Spanish colours. Even though my campaign of seizures was confirmed as justified and appropriate by the Admiralty courts in Nevis and fully supported by the Admiralty's lawyers, I became a hated man, and after seizure of two American ships at Nevis, enraged island traders joined with the masters of the vessels to claim damages of £4,000 against me for wrongful assault and false imprisonment.

For several months I became a virtual prisoner within my own ship. But later in response to the flurry of correspondence with the Admiralty and the administration of Parliament, a letter was received, which I described in a letter to Captain Locker as *"signifying His Majesty's approval of my conduct and upon orders from the Crown's lawyers, authorising my defence, at the Crown's expense, from all civil prosecutions."* Throughout the whole affair I had tried to be politic and circumspect by not directly or personally criticizing Admiral Hughes, nor had Hughes cast aspersion upon my conduct in my official capacity, largely because Hughes was not a confrontational person. He also had the acumen to know not only that I was legally correct but that the administrators of Parliament in the end would support my actions, notwithstanding the economic difficulty that would result to island merchants. As matters developed, Hughes ameliorated his relationship with me by words and actions that reflected warmth and flattery. In time I also became a regular guest at the admiral's home and wrote, *"The Admiral is highly pleased with my conduct here ... I well know I am not of abilities to deserve what he has said of me, but I take it that they are meant to show his regard for me, and his politeness and attention to me are great, nor shall I forget it. I like the man although not all of his acts."*

Mary Moutray

The period in Antigua that had been marked by severe tension, and conflict became somewhat relaxed over time. It was also suspected that much of the trade was now being carried out by the secret passing of warship orders to merchants, which allowed them to arrange their harbour visits at islands where I or my squadron of ships would not be present. Whatever the case, I was able to be largely free from the confines of my ship and could venture into English Harbour and other towns without fear of shouts of defilement by incensed merchants.

Ironically my social emancipation had much to do with Commissioner John Moutray, whose flying the pennant of a commodore had precipitated my first conflict with Admiral Hughes. In Antigua, Moutray served as commissioner of English Harbour. His naval career had collapsed several years earlier when, as commander of the escort force for a valuable convoy, he had lost the convoy to a French squadron but had saved his warships and himself. The result was outrage in the Admiralty, where it was expected that the commander of a military escort should at all cost protect the convoy under its charge. By losing the convoy and maintaining his warships essentially intact, Moutray had committed an unpardonable sin for which he was court-martialled, found guilty, and dismissed from his ship. He was, however, well connected in political circles, and several years later he was appointed commissioner at English Harbour.

My objection to Moutray's flying of the commodore's pennant was not taken by him as a personal affront but was recognised as an objection that was technically appropriate and not out of line by myself as a young captain who was intent on exerting a rightful authority. As time went on, my relationship with Moutray became amiable. In fact, the relationship developed into one that would be a high point in my memory of the Caribbean. Central to that high point was Captain Moutray's wife, Mary. She was twenty years younger than he was and could have been cast in the quintessential role of a proper English wife. She was a natural hostess, whose dinners were well planned and carried out in an atmosphere of graciousness and warmth that were genuinely enjoyed by everyone within their circle of friends.

Mary was also a woman of intelligence with a keen appreciation of character. She had heard much of me and was somewhat apprehensive of the description people had generally attached to me, that of an absolutist

Hotspur of dour demeanour. However, when she first met me, her opinion would be deflected toward an understanding of me as a man with driven convictions but whose heart was open to warmth and generosity. The Moutray house stood atop a prominence that offered a grand view of English Harbour. It was called Windsor Hill, and it was there when I attended my first dinner party as a guest of John Moutray that I was introduced to Mary.

"My dear, I have the pleasure of introducing Captain Horatio Nelson, second in command of these islands and captain of HMS *Boreas*," Moutray said to his wife.

"Captain, I have heard much of you and am delighted to welcome you to Windsor Heights," Mary said.

"Madam, it is indeed my pleasure to be welcomed into the great hospitality that you and your husband have offered this evening, for it is a wonderful respite from the hard times I have thus far experienced in these islands," I answered.

"My understanding, Captain, is that you insist upon carrying out the laws of His Majesty's government, even if it impinges on local interests," Mary said.

"That is true, madam—"

"Captain, please call me Mary."

"Thank you. That is true, Mary. I find it my unavoidable duty, however inconvenient, to be true to the statement of the interests of the Crown, and I very much appreciate your recognition of my sense of ethics," I answered.

"We must all be true to our ethics, Captain," Mary said with a gentle smile and a look of warmth in her eyes.

"Mary, that is the most reassuring thing that anyone has said to me since I have been in these islands," I responded. "And I very much look forward to further discussions with you concerning duty, honour, and commitment to our king."

"As shall I," Mary answered.

I reached for her hand, kissed it, looked into her eyes, nodded and then went to join the dinner party.

During the hurricane season the port of English Harbour was considered by most mariners to be a hellhole. Ships were docked or anchored for complete refitting and replenishment. As a result, they stank of paint, gunpowder, and fresh tar in the heavy heat of late summer that was made more intolerable by the oppressive humidity of the Caribbean. To me, however, the invitation extended by the Moutrays to stay at Windsor Hill was a deliverance. Instead of my cramped cabin aboard the *Boreas*, I was given a bedroom at the top of the hill, where cool trade winds would soothe the body. Rum cocktails would refresh the spirit, and dinner parties of local game, greens, and brandied fruit would remind officers that they were still gentleman within a society of pleasurable civility. And of course, there was Mary. To me, she was a bright ray of sunlight beaming through what had previously been only dark nimbus clouds. The sound of her voice, the rustle of her petticoats, and the finely sculpted beauty of her face were intoxicating to me. She seemed an icon of what the perfect woman should be, and my thoughts constantly dwelled upon her.

For some time before I became his guest, Captain Moutray had become chronically ill. Local physicians were unable to find a true diagnosis, and the treatments administered to him had little effect. Mary, however, continued to entertain her guests in an unbroken string of dinner parties and receptions.

While a guest at Windsor Hill, I would devote my mornings to work at the *Boreas* and then would return to Windsor Hill for the afternoons and evenings. My friend and subordinate captain, Cuthbert Collingwood, was also a resident guest. Very often afternoons would be spent in conversation with Mary and in assisting with estate matters during the extended times when John Moutray was confined to his bed. It became apparent to both Collingwood and myself that we both had fallen in love with Mary. It was, however, a love that could not be requited, as her obvious devotion to her husband was clearly exclusive. As Captain Moutray's health worsened, Collingwood wrote to a friend, "*I'm afraid we shall lose them. They are very desirous to get home and if he is not recalled, I think he will resign. I shall miss them grievously. She is quite a delight and makes many of our days cheerful that without her, they would be dead weight.*"

When John Moutray's request to be recalled was approved, I wrote to my brother, Maurice, "*My dear sweet friend is going home. I am happy on her account but truly grieved were I only to consider myself. Her equal I never saw in any country, or in any situation.*"

On the evening before their departure, with boxes and chests stacked on the veranda, Mary stood alone, looking out over English Harbour. From my bedroom I saw her silhouette against the grey dusk of evening. My heart ached as I approached and stood next to her at the railing. For a long moment we did not speak. I broke the silence.

"Mary, I must tell you that I love you. I am very sorry and do not ever want to offend, but I must say it. From my heart I simply must say it."

She waited. She looked down at her hands and then at me. "I cannot say that I love you, Horatio. I cannot say it, no matter how I feel." She moved to me and kissed my cheek. "I pray that your future will be filled with fair winds, my dear one." She turned and went inside.

As I lay in his bed that evening, I waited for sleep that would not come. A sense of despair covered me like a shroud. A soft, warm breeze passed through the door to my room, and a gibbous moon cast a faint light over the porch and surrounding trees. Then a slight figure appeared at the door and slowly approached my bed.

"My dear Horatio, I am glad you are awake." She slowly pulled down my coverlet and lay gently beside me. She placed her finger upon my lips and whispered, "Although I could not stay away, you must understand that I am not here."

"Yes," I said. "Yes, yes."

"I am not here," she repeated.

For years afterwards my reverie was of the scent of her hair, the touch of her flesh, and the soft urgent sounds of her breath as we coupled in an act of perfect and exquisite love. Never will I forget being one with her and the delight that consumed me as I found that she seemed to take as much pleasure as I did in our most tender and intense movements of union. I soon approached and found the heights of our connection that I had so longed for but never thought possible.

When later she rose from my bed and quietly walked away, she paused, turned to me, and spoke, "For me, the Caribbean is now complete. Farewell, my dear man." My ambivalence was intense, a conflation of perfect satisfaction and contentment confounded by the knowledge that fate had again placed the object of my desire beyond my reach.

After the Moutrays sailed for England and Windsor Hill was closed, I wrote to Maurice, *This country again appears intolerable, my dear one being absent. It is barren indeed, and nothing can give a spark of joy to me. English Harbour I hate. The sight of Windsor I now detest. I went once up the hill to look at the spot where I spent more happy days than in any one spot in the world. Even the trees droop their heads and the tamarind tree died – all is melancholy. The road is covered now with weeds. Let them grow. I shall never pull one of them up. By this time, I hope she is safe in old England. Heaven's choicest blessings go with her.*

The island of Nevis was a major point of British trade in the Caribbean. It is dominated by a volcanic mountain called Mount Nevis, whose lava had, over the centuries, become transformed into a vibrantly fertile medium for the growing of sugarcane. Its slopes were a sea of green cane fields undulating in the caresses of gentle Caribbean breezes and dotted by large white plantation houses and sugar factories emitting a rich smell of intoxicating sweetness. Nevis was one of the first islands settled by the British and had become the richest and most fashionable in the Caribbean. One of the most charming among the great houses of the island was Montpelier, owned by John Herbert, the president of the Council of Nevis. The lady of the house was Herbert's niece, Frances Nisbet, known to her friends as Fanny. She had been brought up on the island, where her father had been a senior judge. As a young woman, she married a doctor named Josiah Nisbet and bore him a son whom they also named Josiah. Shortly after their marriage she and her husband went to England because of what was believed to be his intolerance of the Caribbean sun. However, his illness persisted in England, and after a short time there he died. Having no close family or contacts in England, Fanny returned to Nevis.

By coincidence, John Herbert, a widower, had quarrelled and fallen out with his daughter. He was then in need of someone to tend to the affairs of Montpelier and to act as a hostess for its social events, and Fanny was perfect for the role. For a young woman within the small community of Nevis, finding a husband was not an easy matter. Most of the eligible bachelors in the island would go to England to find a suitable spouse, resulting in the number of the island's eligible bachelors to be very small. However, the island did provide something of a compensating effect. The slopes of the volcano would collect tropical rains into streams and pools of pure quality, and ships were often put into harbour at the island's capital, Charlestown, to replenish their casks. When a British warship would arrive, its unmarried officers would become targets of opportunity for young women in the Nevis social circle. Such was the case in the spring of 1785, when the *Boreas* anchored off the Charlestown harbour and I came ashore.

When I arrived at any of the British islands, it was customary that I would pay respects to the island's senior official. Thus, at Nevis, I did so with its senior official, John Herbert. Prior to meeting Herbert, I had been made aware that he was one of the most successful and richest officials in the Caribbean. I wrote to my brother, *"Herbert is very rich and very proud. Although his income is immense, yet his expenses must be great as the house he operates is open to all strangers and he entertains most hospitably."* On two occasions I was invited to dinners at Montpelier. However, Fanny was visiting friends on the neighbouring island of St. Kitts. Following the second dinner, another of Herbert's nieces wrote to Fanny, *"We have at last seen the little Captain of the Boreas, of whom so much has been said. He came up just before dinner, much heated and very silent. He declined drinking any wine but after dinner, when the President offered his toasts to the King, the Queen, the royal family, and Lord Hood, this strange man regularly filled his glass ... It was impossible during this visit for any of us to make out his real character. There was such a reserve and sternness in his behaviour, with occasional sallies that indicated a superior mind. I endeavoured to rouse his attention by showing him all the civilities in my power, but I drew out little more than a yes or a no. If you, Fanny, had been there, we think you would have made something of him for you have been in the habit of attending to these sorts of people."*

Fanny

I would from time to time call upon Governor Herbert with respect to matters having to do with the Charlestown harbour and to cultivate a relationship with a man of high political stature. The relationship developed fairly well, and aside from my generally stern and dour side, I believe that Herbert also came to know the more likable aspect of my personality. He wrote to a friend, *"Good God, if I did not find this great little man, of whom everyone is so afraid, playing in the next room, under the dining table with Mrs. Nisbet's child."*

Soon thereafter Fanny would be able to make her own opinion of me at a small dinner party given by her uncle. When I arrived and came through the door, I saw Fanny and was immediately struck by her rather fine features and poise. She resembled Mary Moutray not only in her appearance but also by the manner in which she carried herself.

"Captain Nelson, I've heard much about you and am pleased finally to make your acquaintance," she greeted me.

"The pleasure is mine, Mrs. Nisbet, and I hope that the things you have heard do not reflect the general disfavour with which I am held in these islands," I answered.

"Not at all, Captain, as my uncle has advised me that you are simply carrying out the laws of the Crown."

"Splendid. I am very pleased that your uncle has said that, as he is a responsible and dedicated man, and I have simply sought only to carry out my duty to the best of my ability," I said with a smile.

"I am sure that it is the best one can demand of every officer in the Royal Navy," she responded, returning my smile.

I was immediately and profoundly attracted to Fanny. She was lovely. She lived in very comfortable circumstances, and she was closely connected to the governor, a man of authority and influence. I inquired from friends on the island whether she was the object of any suitor and was told that there was none. Delighted, I set out to court her, and when I asked Governor Herbert if I might call upon his niece, the governor answered to my great delight, "Of course you can, sir, and I will set the stage for it by inviting you frequently to dine with us."

There followed with Fanny a whirlwind courtship. As one whose heart was, I admit, vulnerable to the appeal of any attractive woman, my initial attraction soon became captivation. Within a month I wrote to my brother, *"Her sense, polite manners, and to you I may say, beauty is wonderful. I have not the least doubt but we shall be a happy pair. The fault must be mine if we are not."* Fanny responded very positively to me, whom she considered, I dare say, a man of consequence and responsibility and who also had a delightful and natural gift for entertaining her child. However, during the entirety of our courtship I spent most of my time away from Nevis, chasing after American schooners whose design for speed so often took them beyond the reach of our frigates. Otherwise I tended to administrative matters generally in other islands. I was, however, a frequent writer. In one of my many letters to Fanny, my infatuation was summed up, *"My heart yearns for you. It is with you my mind dwells, and upon none but you. Absent from you, I feel no pleasure. It is you, my dearest Fanny, who are everything to me. It must be real affection that brings us together, not interest or compulsion, which makes so many unhappy."*

My visits to Montpelier were many and frequent, a release from the visitations of memory that haunted me in recalling Mary, my momentarily perfect possession and immutable loss. I dined with the governor and spent hours of private time with Fanny in conversation on the veranda. My newly kindled amorous intentions, marked by caressing her arms and gentle kissing of her cheeks, were held in check by Fanny to little more than loving flirtations, which were frustrations I nevertheless endured with the hope and anticipation of greater intimacy to come.

Enter the Prince

Admiral Hughes returned to England in the summer of 1786, leaving me as senior officer of the station. I immediately set out to administer the harbours and dockyards of the various islands in the manner I found to be necessary and appropriate, tightening administration and accountability, which I had always thought to be too loose under Hughes. I also ordered my ships to sea with orders to enforce the Navigation Acts without exception. For five months I essentially had a free hand without direction or orders from the Admiralty.

In the summer of 1786, Prince William Henry arrived as commander of the frigate HMS *Pegasus*. I remembered meeting the prince in New York harbour on board Admiral Hood's flagship when the prince was a midshipman. After he returned home, William spent two years in the courts of Europe, ostensibly absorbing the dynamics of international politics. However, apart from what he may have learned about politics, he demonstrated a remarkable penchant for irresponsibility, lack of control, and poor judgment. I learned that at Hanover, he fell in love with the fourteen-year-old Princess Charlotte of Mecklenburg and had affairs with the daughter of a merchant, the daughter of a general, and several other women without regard to their social station or practice of hygiene.

He had written to his brother, the Prince of Wales, "*Oh for England and the pretty girls of Westminster, at least such as would not clap me or pox me every time I fucked.*" In another letter to the Prince of Wales, one written shortly after he arrived on station in the Leeward Islands, he described pursuing carnal knowledge "*with a lady of the town, against a wall.*"

The prince was a marginally capable naval officer, although the degree of his competence did not quite match the meteoric rate at which he had been advanced to command of a warship. On several occasions directing officers of the Admiralty had decided that William's pace of advancement should match that of most other officers, which was eventually overridden by the king's orders. In each of his command assignments the Admiralty was careful to ensure that his supporting officers were fully competent. This did not mean that William valued them or even that he got along well with them. His ham-fisted and autocratic manner, un-tempered by any sense of circumspection or tact, usually resulted in resentment and lack of respect among his officer corps.

William joined the forces under my command at Dominica in December 1786. He brought with him a portfolio of information and directives from the Admiralty, and as soon as I had broken the seal on the portfolio, the prince asked that he be shown the contents. Somewhat taken aback, I nevertheless gave him the portfolio, which he reviewed at length. He smiled and then read aloud from the directives, "*The Prince shall travel among the islands so that he might come to know his possessions, their trade and their inhabitants.*" He then added, "*Well that certainly gives me a free hand, doesn't it?*"

"*Does the Prince not expect to travel under orders that are coordinated with the operations of the station?*" I responded.

"*Captain Nelson, we should come to an understanding. You should know that my father is not well and that my brother, for all purposes, is acting as Crown Regent. After my brother becomes King, he will appoint me to oversight of the Admiralty. Now, I happen to have a high regard for your abilities as a naval commander and I believe that you will find great value in having me as a friend. To that purpose, I would expect from you full respect and an even greater accommodation,*" he stated.

My father had always been a strict and unswerving monarchist. Our family had always adored the royal family, whoever they might be, and held strict allegiance to them as a high calling. The sense of unquestioned devotion to the Crown had been inculcated in me from the time I was born. Thus, my unfettered allegiance to the Crown together with the stark reality of what the prince had just said framed my response.

"Your highness, you may always count on me as being both your friend and your staunch supporter."

"Then we are agreed," the prince answered and extended his hand.

There followed a general three-month tour of the islands with William, and I wrote to Fanny, "*The Prince is a very gallant man. He has some characteristics that people may criticize. He can be loud and volatile but he has great good humour.*"

In Antigua, the prince spent three straight nights in what he called "pursuing the dark rum," which consisted of eating, dancing, drinking, and fornicating in back rooms with local women of every station and colour.

In several letters I described the prince's aggressive and usually successful ways with young ladies of Dominica, Barbuda, St. Kitts, and two of the inappropriately named Virgin Islands. Frequently he would fall asleep in bed with his sex partner of the night, and I would have to rouse him, dress him, and lead him, leaning against me, back to his ship. But notwithstanding conduct that would have ended the naval career of any ordinary officer, I decided that my unconditional regard and devotion to the prince must be unwavering. It was quite clear that the concept of "the king can do no wrong" applied for me not only to the king but to his frequently profligate offspring as well. The royal family had been placed by almighty God at the head of the British nation, and it was my duty to make the best of circumstances.

Aboard *Pegasus*, the prince was considered to be something between a burden and a disgrace. This sentiment resulted from two things: the prince's lack of thorough competence in command seamanship and his conduct toward officers and sailors, which reflected few elements of wisdom or basic judgment. The discord present in *Pegasus* came to a head in a series of offences which the prince attributed to his first lieutenant, Isaac Schomberg.

Schomberg was descended from a soldier of fortune who had come to England a century earlier. His grandfather and other members of his family became prominent in English military affairs. Schomberg himself was considered to be an officer of high abilities, and it was Admiral Hood who had placed him as first lieutenant of *Pegasus*, hoping that his competence would compensate for the prince's inexperience and lack of commitment to learning the complex dynamics of ship handling. The prince had issued a series of orders that were unnecessary, petty, or both. As an example, he posted the following: *"As it is too frequent the practise on board His Majesty's ships to make use of that horrid expression 'bugger,' so disgraceful to a British seamen, if any person shall be heard using this expression they may be assured that they will be severely punished."* He also ordered harsh punishment for any sailor or marine who would hang up their wet clothing to dry between decks. Punishment would be ten lashes with a cat o' nine tails. When Lieutenant Schomberg suggested in private that this punishment may be unduly severe, the prince told him straight away not to give any sentiments that were not asked for. Another time, this time in my presence, when a civilian visitor came to visit the *Pegasus*, the crew was dressed in formal uniforms but without their blue woollen coats.

The prince fumed, *"Schomberg, it was my order that the crew be dressed in blue uniforms. This means that they must wear their blue coats."*

"*But Captain, the manner of dress for blue uniforms allows for the wearing of coats or their omission when the weather is intense, and it was my judgment that the torrid nature of temperature today would have made the woollen coats unbearable,*" Schomberg responded.

"*Schomberg, my order is my order, and I do not expect it to be disobeyed,*" Prince William retorted in a loud voice on the quarterdeck, where the rebuke could be heard by officers and men of the ship.

Schomberg responded, "*Captain, the men are dressed in the manner that is allowed by general orders, but if the captain would like the crew to don their woollen coats, I will order it.*"

I witnessed the exchange, one which contradicted fundamental principles of naval etiquette, namely that a superior officer never should criticize a subordinate officer in a public place. However, I decided to say nothing to the prince.

Later matters would come to a boiling point. Lieutenant Schomberg, while *Pegasus* was at anchor, sent a boat ashore without William's express permission. For this act, which was not against any written orders and which, under any circumstances, would be considered trivial, Prince William wrote an official rebuke of Schomberg for neglect of duty. Considering this unfounded discipline to be an act beyond the pale of tolerance, Schomberg wrote to me, requesting a court-martial to determine officially whether he had breached any standing order or whether he had neglected a duty. When I received the court-martial request, I summoned Schomberg. "Lieutenant, what is the meaning of this?" I asked.

"Sir, I am dangling at the end of my rope. I have used utmost care under our present captain to carry out my duties aboard *Pegasus*, all in conformance with the general orders of the navy as well as all posted orders of the ship. However, it seems that there is nothing that I can do – nor for that matter is there anything that any officer can do – that will not in some way find criticism from the captain. In addition, the criticism frequently has no foundation whatever. For example, any officer of the deck can give orders for boats to go ashore when it is required by the normal routine of the ship. In the instant matter, several members of the ship's crew were ashore and waiting to be returned to the ship. I ordered a boat ashore to retrieve them. This was not only appropriate but necessary in the circumstances. But for no reason that I can imagine and without any foundation in any standing order, the captain has made a formal notation of neglect of duty, and this can have a devastating effect upon my career. Quite simply, sir, I am not, nor have I ever been, guilty of any neglect of duty."

I paused, shifted in my chair, and looked out the window of my cabin. I knew of the positive reputation of the officer standing before me. I understood clearly that as a matter of equity, I should defend this lieutenant and protect the integrity of the principles he represented. It would, however, almost assuredly determine a course that would run upon the rocks of conflict with the prince. To criticize the prince and to take the side of Schomberg would enrage the prince and put me in serious disfavour of a man who might generously help or grievously injure my career in the future. I sat motionless for a long while. Suppressing what I knew was the course of rectitude and integrity, I chose a course that I came to regret for the rest of my days.

"*Lieutenant Schomberg, I am issuing an order today that all officers under my command shall make no requests for court-martial over matters that are trivial. This matter is trivial and I am placing you under arrest, to be confined to your ship until otherwise directed.*"

Schomberg stood at taught attention. It is probable that a chill passed through his body as he realized that his time-honoured request for a fair review of an unjust action was being betrayed by me, a man he had surely held in high esteem. Until that day, Schomberg had likely considered the Royal Navy to be a true meritocracy, and while some men gained advantage over others by personal contacts with superiors, in the whole the Royal Navy had been a service based upon attention to true duty and the protection of integrity.

Soon afterward I wrote what I knew to be a lame justification to Captain Locker. "*His Royal Highness keeps up strict discipline in his ship and, without paying him any compliment, she is one of the first order frigates I have seen. He has had more plague with his officers than enough: his first Lieutenant will no doubt be broke. I have put him under arrest.*" I knew in my heart, however, that Schomberg was a fine officer and pondered a way out of the predicament.

For three months I carried the prince throughout the Leeward Islands. We were received with full twenty-one-gun salutes and lavish receptions followed by elaborate dinners. Fulsome toasts were offered. Women were sought after. Some were attained. The prince feasted. The prince usually became drunk. Frequently he would miss the morning call to muster, still recovering in his bed from the excesses of the previous evening. Schomberg and his fellow officers performed the functions of the ship, maintaining it, in my own description, as a frigate of the first order.

After six weeks of laboriously touring the islands with the prince, I returned with great relief to Nevis. My intent was certain. I would ask for the hand of Fanny in marriage.

Chapter 5

Montpelier and Engagement

I remember my return to Montpelier as a mixture of relief from the prince's tour of the islands and great anticipation of being again with Fanny. When I arrived, she greeted me formally but lovingly. "My dear Horace, how wonderful to see you back at Montpelier. I have treasured your letters and look forward to spending many hours of graceful time with you."

"Fanny, my love," I responded, "the visage of you this morning is very much like a wonderful sunrise after a fierce storm." We embraced, and I felt with true loving intensity the warmth and form of her slender torso. Her touch upon my neck and the floral scent of her hair rekindled in me all that I feared might be lost after the departure of Mary. I knew, however, that I had to seek out and write a new chapter in my life with this woman, who now seemed both beautiful and inviting.

Fanny

I had ordered the squadron to stand down for repair to ships and recuperation of crews. They had been at sea for several weeks, and it was a needed time for restoration. The respite would provide a time to recover, while I pursued what had become the newly idealized object of my desires. Afternoons at Montpelier were spent in Fanny's company, followed by elegant dinners with the governor. All seemed almost sybaritic compared to the hardscrabble shipboard conditions of the past weeks that had consisted of tedious dinners during which my constant attention was focused upon attempting to keep the prince within some bounds of tolerance and correcting circumstances where he had ventured outside of those bounds. Back at Montpelier, I discussed with Governor Herbert at length the itinerary that should have afforded the prince a full appreciation of His Majesty's possessions in the Caribbean. I was also keen to detail the measures I had taken to ensure that my force was maintained in a ready state to defend against any potential French or Spanish incursions. My hope was that these commentaries would find their way into favourable accounts that the governor would send to London, and judging from the governor's reactions, I felt relatively confident they would be.

With Fanny I was more than pleased. We spent time in long walks throughout the spreading gardens of Montpelier with pleasant and sometimes endearing conversation. Although the depth of her intellectual command was not profound, she was very engaging and seemed a worthwhile match for the rising captain I intended myself to be. I was becoming confident that she had come also to regard me as a promising mate, one with obvious dimensions of achievement that were appreciated by my superiors, including a member of the royal family. I also fancied that she considered me as a promising protector and a strong stepfather to her son. One evening in Montpelier's gardenia garden she picked a flower and held it close to her face, softly inhaling its scent and regarding its perfect pale form. I quietly approached her from the back, placed my hands on her waist, and softly kissed the side of her neck. I spoke to her, "My dearest, there is a question I have been restraining for the longest time. I have told you that I love you, and it is the truest thing I have ever spoken to anyone. You have become the most important thing in my life, and I cannot spend another day or, for that matter, endure another minute without asking that you become my wife. I do now pray that you consider that prospect and tell me that you will. Your consent will fulfil my dearest dream."

She turned her head to me. "My dear Horatio, my answer is yes. I have waited upon this moment and have waited upon that question, and yes, I love you and would be proud to be your wife." I kissed her lips fully as she turned to me, and we became suspended in the fullest embrace we had ever known. But as we broke the embrace, she looked down and added, "I must append a condition to what I have just said, and that is that our becoming married must be approved by my uncle, as he needs me most dearly. He has been a father to me as well as a wonderful provider for Josiah. I know that he holds you in the highest regard and do not question that he will consent."

I had been fully aware of her role at Montpelier and her importance to Governor Herbert. In the euphoria of her acceptance I quickly conceded to the condition. "My dear, I will ask him tonight."

That evening it seemed that dinner would never end, as I waited eagerly and with no small amount of anxiety to place my proposal before the governor. When we finally finished, it was our habit to take a brandy or glass of Madeira on the veranda. After we poured our glasses, the governor methodically packed his clay pipe, and I spoke. "Sir, there is something of great moment that I would like to put before you. I have asked Fanny for her hand in marriage, and her response was positive to my greatest delight. We have both thought it advisable to obtain your blessing upon our union before making any plans, and I now ask for that blessing."

Herbert puffed his pipe, took a drink from his glass, looked out over the sea, puffed some more, and responded rather formally, "Captain, this prospect does not surprise me, as I have noted the development of closeness between you and my niece. Should she leave Montpelier, it would place a great strain upon me and my ability to carry out the affairs of the Crown here in the island. I shall give the matter my attention and will give you my response shortly."

"I leave tomorrow morning to take the prince to Barbuda and Antigua as part of his tour of the islands. How long we stay will depend upon the prince's pleasure," I advised.

"Very well then; I will write to you in a confidential note sent in the communication schooner," Herbert responded. He then rather abruptly turned and took his glass with him to his bedroom, puffing as he went.

I immediately went to Fanny and told her with some apprehension of the exchange. She smiled and said, "He will approve, my love, but I believe he is most concerned with how he can manage Montpelier. I am the only one he can depend upon to help with his important affairs here at Montpelier."

"Then we shall wait," was the only reply I could make. I kissed Fanny good night and returned to my ship to review matters for getting underway the next morning.

On the midmorning tide we set sail for Barbuda, where the prince found little that interested him, and he suggested that we go on to Antigua. As we weighed anchor, the communication schooner arrived. I went quickly through the contents and found reports and passage alerts but no letter from Governor Herbert. I wrote to Fanny,

> *To say how anxious I have been to receive a line from Mister Herbert would be far beyond the descriptive powers of my pen. Most fervently do I hope his answer will be of such a tendency as to convey real pleasure not only to myself but also to you for most seriously do I love you and I trust that my affection is not only founded upon the principles of reason but also upon the basis of mutual attachment, indeed, my charming Fanny, should I possess one million, my greatest pride and pleasure would be to share it with you and as were I to live in a cottage with you, I should esteem it superior to living in a palace with any other I have yet met with.*

On the second day after we arrived in Antigua, the schooner appeared, and in its portfolio there was a letter from the governor. His response was disappointing. While he cast no negatives on the prospect of our marriage, he stated that he and I should discuss important matters before his final decision. I was very much aware that Herbert was wealthy and suspected that he probably had reservations about his niece having to live on the pay of a captain who had not amassed any fortune.

When I returned to Nevis and spoke directly with the governor, I found that my suspicions were well founded. Herbert advised that Fanny would inherit a significant sum from him but that during his tenure at Nevis the expenses of Montpelier would be so high that he could not settle an annual income upon her of more than a very modest amount. He was also very insistent that she continue to assist him as the hostess of Montpelier until his return to England, which would not happen until perhaps two years later. He allowed that he thought highly of me and said that if Fanny and I waited for two years, his assent to our marriage would be firm.

To assuage my financial penury, I again decided to seek assistance from my uncle, Maurice Suckling, who had responded positively earlier when I contemplated marriage with Elizabeth Andrews. I wrote, "*My dear*

Uncle, I open a business which, perhaps, you will smile at in the first instance and say that Horatio is forever in love." I described Fanny in glowing terms and expressed at length my delight at her acceptance of my proposal but stated that marriage would have to wait because of Herbert's concern for my financial limitations as well as the fact that Fanny was needed to carry out her essential functions at Montpelier. Then I sought his financial assistance, *"My future happiness … is now in your power … if you will either give me assistance … either 100 per year for a few years, or 1,000. How happy you will make Fanny and me as a couple, who will pray for you forever. Do not disappoint me or my heart will break."*

Suckling responded positively but indicated in his response that my request seemed a bit presumptuous. Although greatly relieved by the prospect of an increase of financial security, my pride was seriously bruised, and I answered,

> *Had it not been for one sentence in your letter – "your application has in a great degree deprived me of my free agency" – I should have been supremely happy; but my feelings are too quick. I feel sharply what perhaps others would not. That sentence would make me suppose that you thought I conceived I had a right to ask the pecuniary assistance: if you think so, you did me a great injustice … Oh, my dear uncle, you can't tell me what I feel – indeed, I can hardly write, or know what I am writing – you would pity me if you knew what I suffer by that sentence – for, although it does not make your act less generous, yet it embitters my happiness."*

Notwithstanding the expressed tinge of resentment, I felt more comfortable with the assurance of assistance. After all, it removed one of the obstacles to our marriage. It also heightened the ardour with which I would pursue affection and intimacy with my new beloved. After dinners at Montpelier the governor and I would continue our habit of brandies on the veranda, and our exchanges continued to be most cordial. Herbert would then take his leave, allowing Fanny and me uninterrupted time together. In the progress of our affection Fanny was receptive but somewhat guarded. With each positive response from her, I would, in satisfaction of my growing and natural instinct toward becoming ever closer, interpret positive responses on her part as an invitation to proceed further. Fanny truly exhibited a love and attraction toward me but harboured a deep concern for the pain she confessed she had experienced in the sexual consummations of her first marriage. When she allowed me to lead her to my room and to my bed very late one evening, she allowed me the pleasure of disrobing her. However, the visage of her white and slender body, the beauty of her supple form, and the prospect of having her for the first time enflamed my intemperate eagerness. I can only conclude that the intensity of my immediate entry into her with what I imagine was an insufficiency of caressing to make her fully receptive caused her to cringe.

"Oh Horace, be gentle. Please be gentle, for I am not yet ready."

I immediately withdrew. "My dearest, I'm sorry. The last thing in the world that I want is to hurt you."

"Just hold me for a while," she entreated me. "Pray, just hold me."

"Of course, my love," I responded immediately. "I will hold you closely for as long as you desire."

We remained embraced. I caressed her, stroked her hair, kissed her, and whispered expressions of my love. She answered, "I love you, my dear beloved, and know that you will be gentle with me." When I felt that she was relaxed and prepared, I slowly entered her and advanced with care and attention to her every wince of response, which bespoke a willing receptivity but very clearly no excitement or true enjoyment. Slowly and gently I attained my release and lingered over her with soft professions of love. However, throughout our union I never heard the accelerated breathing or sounds of pleasure that had come from women to whom I had made love.

At breakfast I gazed at her constantly and faintly smiled. Fanny blushed, returned my look, and smiled as well. My feeling was a lingering sense of satisfaction. I believe that her sentiment was a feeling of love for someone she thought would be loving and attentive. She had exhibited no deep physical pleasure from the night before, but in the morning light she seemed pleased.

I departed Nevis again for Antigua in August 1785, and from that time until the day of our marriage in March 1787, Fanny and I would spend no time together. I would write frequently, and she would save all of my letters. Letters she wrote to me were not saved, for I believed that I would retain in my head and heart all of the important things she wrote. My writings to her contained a constant refrain of my commitment and affection, and all were honest feelings from my soul. I wrote with some sense of insecurity,

> *I declare solemnly that did I not conceive I had the full possession of your heart, no consideration should make me accept your hand ... my heart yearns for you. My mind dwells upon naught else but you. Absent from you, I feel no pleasure. It is you, my dearest Fanny, who are everything to me ... It must be real affection that brings us together, not interest or compulsion which makes so many unhappy.*

From time to time we would have disagreements arising chiefly from complaints that I had been away for so long. This was a complaint that later would become a refrain of difficulty between us. In response to one letter in which she implied that I held my duties to be foremost, I felt it necessary to respond. *"I will not begin by scolding you although you really deserve it for sending such a letter ... You will not send me such another I am certain."*

In Antigua, during the time when my duty and commitment for enforcement of the Navigation Acts resulted in ostracism by the local island society, I wrote,

> *From sunset until bed time, I have not a human creature to speak to who will feel a little regard for me ... I am not used to be left sitting alone ... I felt pleasure at receiving your kind and affectionate letter. My thoughts are too big for utterance; you must imagine everything that is tender, kind and truly affectionate has possession of my whole frame. Words are not capable of conveying an idea of my feelings.*

Because I had deep longings for a physical connection between us, I wrote, *"Every morning since my arrival I have had six pails of salt water at daylight poured over my head, and instead of finding what the seamen say to be true, I perceive the contrary effect: and if it goes on so contrary to the prescription ... and, as you begin to know something about sailors, have you not heard that salt water and absence always wash away love? Now I am such a heretic as not to believe that."*

There were many aspects of the squadron's progress through Antigua, Montserrat, Barbados, and Grenada that I did not share with Fanny. The prince was, however, very open to full descriptions of his affairs and conquests in letters to the Prince of Wales. By the end of the tour he was beset by an unfortunate result of what he had described as the pursuit of the "dames de couleurs." He had contracted a venereal disease.

In a visit to *Boreas*, which was anchored in Grenada, he burst into my stateroom and bellowed, "Nelson, I am pissing fire and have done so for the past two days."

I answered, "Your Grace, it is probably what the men call the 'the devil's love clap.'

In time it will pass. It will be difficult, but patience and endurance will bring you through."

"Damn it all to hell, man. There were two lovely opportunities that I have had in this wretched island, but I had to forego both because even springing my seed is impossible. The pain is too much. I tell you it stings beyond description."

"Have you taken quinine from the surgeon?" I asked.

"Yes, I have – in buckets – but it does not a damned thing," the prince answered as he left the stateroom, slamming the door as he went.

I considered it my duty to be ever-protective of the prince, overlooking not only the numerous discretions that would have doomed an ordinary officer but disregarding also the obvious contempt in which he was held by all of the officers under his command. I wrote to Fanny, "*I would if possible or in my power have no man be near the Prince who can have the smallest impeachment as to his character for as an individual I love him, as a Prince I honour and revere him.*" No matter what the inconvenience, I considered it my duty to serve and protect this obviously imperfect royal man.

The prince had also thoroughly involved himself in the forthcoming marriage. I wrote to Fanny, "*His Royal highness often tells me he believes I am married for he says he never saw a lover so easy or say so little of the object he has regard for. When I tell him I certainly am not, he says that he is sure I must have a great esteem for you ... He is right, for my love is founded on esteem, the only foundation that can make love last.*" Toward the end of his tour in the Caribbean, the prince forcefully interjected himself into the timing of the marriage, and I again wrote to Fanny,

I am now feeling most awkward. His Royal highness has been with me all this morning and has told me that as things have changed, if I am not married

the next time we go to Nevis, it is hardly probable that he should see me there again. I had promised him not to be married unless he was present and to show his esteem for me, he would be mortified if any impediments were thrown in the way to hinder his being present, and he told me this morning that since he has been under my command, he has been happy, and has given me to understand that there is no doubt whatever that he may be placed in a high situation that I will find him sincere in his friendship – and by keeping in his esteem, there is no doubt but I shall have my right in the service if nothing more. I hope Mister Herbert can have no objection, especially if he considers how much it is in my interest to be well with the Prince.

When the squadron finally returned to Nevis, no date had been set for the marriage. However, because of the impending return of the prince to England, our marriage was arranged by the governor, acquiescing to the prince's request that he, the prince himself, would give the bride away. Actually the prince had been very positively impressed with Fanny and copied to me a letter he wrote to Lord Hood, "*She is a pretty and sensible woman and may have a great deal of money if her uncle, Mister Herbert, thinks proper. Nelson is over head and ears in love. I frequently laugh at him about it. However, seriously my Lord, he is more in need of a nurse than a wife … I had, my Lord, the honour of giving her away. He is now in for it. I wish him well and happy and that he may not repent the step is taken.*"

Our marriage took place at Montpelier on 11 March 1787. The estate was gaily decorated, and the day was pleasant. Some sixty people arrived as guests, including the prince, who, as promised, gave the bride away. There were many personal friends and acquaintances of the governor. However, Mr. Herbert, who was in high spirits for the occasion, confided that several planter and merchant friends had given apologies and very thin excuses for not being able to attend. Apparently they still held me accountable for the commercial inconvenience of the Navigation Acts. I did not care and surely did not need them to be there. It was a great day joyously celebrated by all and quite special for all attendees who, for the only time in their lives, would be able to shake the hand of a member of the royal family. To my delight, the prince was in a very good mood and tactfully gracious. In fact, his toast at dinner was very memorable as he congratulated me on capturing "*the principal favourite of the island.*"

Afterward Fanny and I were given the main guest room at Montpelier as our quarters, an expansive room with large French doors opening to a wonderful view. On our wedding night and for the next two weeks before I sailed again, I did my best to conceive a "honeymoon child," being attentive to Fanny's sensitivities and intent upon sowing the first seed of our children. However, it would not be, as on the day before I sailed, Fanny told me that her flow had begun. She was not pregnant.

Schomberg Resolved

As soon as I returned to the squadron, I had to confront a troublesome and unresolved problem. The return of Prince William to England following his prescribed tour of the Caribbean was imminent, and the lingering matter of Lieutenant Schomburg's request for court-martial remained unsettled. As there had never been a sufficient number of ship captains to convene a court-martial at Nevis and because I had developed a personal friendship with the Prince, I decided to pass the entire matter to a more senior officer named Commodore Alan Gardiner in Jamaica. He ordered the prince's ship, *Pegasus*, to Jamaica before its return to England. The court-martial could be convened there. It was then that I felt responsible, should it result in Schomberg being broken in rank and perhaps dismissed from service.

When I laid the matter before Gardiner, he reviewed Schomberg's service record and the matters relating to his request for court-martial, namely that in dispatching a boat from *Pegasus* to retrieve men who were ashore, he had broken no order of the ship and had taken action within the purview of his authority as first lieutenant of the ship. Gardner was keenly aware of numerous and consistent commentaries regarding the prince, accounts that had been conveyed to him by officers whose judgment he respected. He called for written records of the *Pegasus* to determine whether there was any written standing order that boats could be dispatched only upon orders of the prince and found that no such written order existed. He then called members of the ship's officer staff and questioned every one as to whether the prince had given a verbal order to that effect. Each officer recounted that no such order had been given.

In a memorandum to Gardiner, I provided details of the dispute together with a personal and rather obvious observation that "*the Prince stands in a very different situation than any other captain.*" Gardiner, however, knew that the prince's official rebuke of Schomberg would be an indelible stain on his record, probably ending his career. He pored over the documents, wrestling with the conflict of what he believed to be justice counterbalanced against the prospect of offending a member of the royal family. In profound frustration regarding any workable solution of the dispute, he summoned me to vent his frustration.

"I am called upon to convene a court-martial and to command that they seek justice. But I know that true justice will be covered with thorns, and every captain who sits on the court will know that as well. We have a man who stands as captain of the ship but whose personal conduct and lack of professional capabilities would never have allowed him to attain such a position were he not royalty. We have this man who poses as a naval officer and whose constant embarrassments are overlooked because the accident of his birth has given him a license to live as a pig and to wallow despicably wherever and with whomever he likes. He has now accused a true and capable officer of wrongdoing, for which there is simply no whit of evidence. Every officer aboard *Pegasus* has related that what Schomberg says is true and that their royal captain is a liar. Finding justice in this court-martial will endanger the career of every man who sits on the court, and I cannot keep company with myself to allow that to happen."

"Perhaps, sir, there is a way out," I suggested.

"Yes, I can dismiss the court and obviate the burden that will otherwise be placed upon the fine officers who will be called upon to find grounds for real justice," Gardiner responded.

"True, you can do that, but there may be something to deflect the wrath of His Royal Highness," I replied.

"What do you think that might be?" Gardiner asked.

I paused and then suggested, "Why not order Schaumburg to apologise to the prince? It can be an apology based upon the possibility of misunderstanding, and given that we are all capable of misunderstandings, perhaps it will salve the prince's sensitivity."

Gardiner slowly walked the length of his office, turned, and replied with a smile, "Yes, perhaps that will work."

Gardiner thereafter issued a letter of dismissal of the court-martial and ordered Schomberg to apologise. Probably with mixed sentiment of relief and resentment, Schomberg wrote a formal apology.

I also felt some significant release of anxiety about the whole affair and wrote a rather patronizing letter to the prince,

If to be truly great is to be truly good ... It never was stronger verified in your Royal Highness that in the instance of Mister

> *Schomberg ... Resentment I know your Royal Highness never had, or I am sure will ever bear anyone ... it is a passion incompatible with the character of a Man of Honour. Schomberg was too hasty in writing his letter requesting court martial; but now, pardon me my Prince, when I presume to recommend that Schomberg may stand in your Royal Favour. The only want of this is to place your character in the highest point of view. None of us are without feelings: Schomberg's was being rather too hasty; but that, putting competition with his being a good officer, will not, I am bold to say, be taken in the scale against him. Princes seldom, very seldom, find a disinterested person to communicate their thoughts to. I do not pretend to be otherwise: but I am interested only that your Royal Highness should be the greatest and best man this Country ever produced.*

The prince accepted neither the suggestion to be circumspect nor the recommendation to be forgiving. He huffily responded, "*I have had two courts-martial, one on a master at arms, who was broke and received a hundred lashes, and the other one a seaman who received fifty lashes.*" The prince's disaffection with the other officers of the ship continued to the point that he sent one of them, Lieutenant William Hope, back to England without a certificate of service that he would have to produce before he was paid. For his part Schaumburg returned to England without a blemish upon his record and was appointed first lieutenant on Lord Hood's flagship, HMS *Barfleur*. The prince was outraged and wrote a strong letter of objection to Admiral Hood, which the admiral had copied and sent to me.

The prince's letter stated, "*There is nothing I feel so sensibly about as an attack on my professional conduct, under which I now labour by your Lordship's support of Schomberg and Lord Howe's disapproval of my conduct ... Much as I love and honour the Navy, yet, my Lord, I, shall beyond doubt resign if I have not a satisfactory explanation from both your noble Lordships.*" However, no such satisfaction came, and the prince did not resign from the naval service.

Home Again

I fell ill again on the transit home, so much so that the officers of the ship spoke openly of their fear once more that I might not survive the voyage. One midshipman wrote in his log that I had ordered a cask of rum to be held ready for my body should I die en route, although I do not recall giving such an order. Toward the end of the voyage, however, I recovered but suffered a relapse after I reached England. The hot weather and stress of the Caribbean had given me a slow fever. The rain and cold of England added a painful throat with its own fever and hacking coughs. I wrote to Captain Locker, "*It is not kind in one's native air to treat a poor wanderer as it has done me since my arrival.*" My maladies were not enough to keep me in bed, but they did prevent me from undertaking any meaningful work. Fanny had also been ill both during and following the voyage home aboard a comfortable Indiaman when she was accompanied by Governor Herbert. Upon her arrival she was not able to join me, as I had been ordered to a station on the Thames to oversee the pressing of men into service. After several weeks, however, I was able to join Fanny at a house Governor Herbert had taken in London.

Several significant matters preoccupied me in London. Fanny was chronically unwell, claiming that the smoky air of London disturbed her lungs. There was also the need to respond to several inquiries regarding claims against me for strict enforcement of the Navigation Acts in disregard of merchants' claims of exemptions under terms of the Acts. There was also the matter of allegations of fraud which had been raised by several junior officials in the Nevis customs house, brought initially to the attention of Prince William, who, not wanting to be bothered, had referred the problem to me. With a sense of duty for enforcing the letter of the law, I had embarked upon a series of inquiries that, when I returned to England, was still open. I spent a great deal of time at the Admiralty, recounting and explaining my actions, all of which tended to make senior members of the Admiralty staff somewhat discomforted by what was said to be my sense of "strict and non-circumspect adherence to the letter of the law." In the end my actions under the Navigation Acts were upheld, and the claims against me were dismissed. As to the issue of fraud in the customhouse, Admiralty officials simply dropped the inquiry. It appeared to me that their preference for the convenience of simply passing over matters that would cast inconvenient aspersions upon certain well-connected officials eclipsed their devotion to the strict upholding of duty.

As Fanny wanted very much to escape the congestion and smoke of London, I took her first to Bath for a treatment of the waters and then home to Burnham Thorpe, where I introduced her to my father. Father had felt some anxiety about Fanny's ability to acculturate to the slow pace of English country life after the high-minded and luxurious conditions she had experienced in Nevis. He was also exceedingly self-conscious about his deteriorating condition and wrote to my sister, "*I am in no haste to see and receive a stranger ... Every power of mine is in decay – insipid, whimsical and very unfit for society in truth, and not likely to revive my practice.*" However, after Fanny and I arrived, he found Fanny to be very gentle and accommodating, and as time passed, he came not only to tolerate her presence but very much to appreciate it as adding a lively new dimension to the family home.

On the Beach

With the *Boreas* now paid off, I was furloughed on half pay and began the longest idle and frustrating period of my life. It provided time to do whatever I wished but kept me from my dearest longing, namely to be at sea. I wrote frequently and at length to colleagues, particularly my old friend Captain Locker. I spent extended time with my brothers and sisters and came to know them as though we had been just introduced. I was also relieved to find good companionship with their husbands and wives. To pass time, I sought out endeavours that occupied my mind and had a semblance of being productive. I laid out, planted, and tended to Father's garden, and I became involved in a number of countryside events, including partridge hunts. However, I found that although they passed the time, they did not provide a true satisfaction of accomplishment. In a letter to Locker I flatly admitted the truth of my failure at hunting, "*Shoot, I cannot! I don't know why I do it.*"

During the first year a child was born to my brother William, something which put an edge on my continuing awareness that Fanny had not become pregnant. Although our intimacy had been far less frequent than I had wanted, Fanny was not unreceptive, provided that I proceeded in the slow and careful ritual that she required. I was intent upon not appearing to be intolerant or impatient with her anxiety, and I looked upon the progression of caressing and whispering of endearments as perhaps the norm for having love with a lady of proper instincts, even though Fannie's sensitivity was far greater than any of my other intimate partners, and in each of our couplings, any intense activity or pleasure continued to be mine alone. Although receptive, Fanny seemed simply resigned to her participation in my need. She never evinced an indication of true enjoyment, and when I would reach the height of my release, she remained stoically passive with no movement or utterance to indicate to me that she had reached any level of ecstasy to match my own. And each month when she would advise me of her unavailability for intimate contact, it would yet again signal to me that another month had passed without the promise of a child.

At first Fanny and I had planned to go to France, where I intended a second chance at becoming fluent in French. But when Father suggested that we stay at Burnham Thorpe, I agreed that it was best to stay in England. The first two winters were severe. All of Norfolk was, in the words of Father, *"clothed with frosted robes, all powdered with snow and trimmed in glittering icicles."* The weather was so cold that Fanny spent most of her time in bed to guard against the drafts that circled the house and to avoid having to walk on cold cobblestone floors. I busied myself with nautical charts and books, particularly the adventures of the dashing pirate William Dampier. I also wrote a seemingly endless stream of letters to the Admiralty, usually in response to inquiries relating to the issue of the customs graft at Nevis or the Navigation Acts claims of the merchant seamen. At one point while I was away, a legal process server appeared at the door and presented to Fanny an action being brought against me with an outrageous damage claim for £20,000. I was enraged when I returned home, writing to the Admiralty that a profound insult had been foisted upon *"the wife of a Sea Officer in his Majesty's Service."* I shot off another stinging letter to the Admiralty in which I stated that I would leave England altogether and would enter service for the Russian Navy or that I would even go to live in France, *"even though it was that I hated their country and their manners."* Upon reflection it was a petulant outburst, and as time passed, I became calmer, though never happy. I began to busy myself again with the grounds of father's home, the digging of a small lake, and the planting of a rose garden. The weeks and months at Burnham Thorpe passed into years, and I languished, bored and profoundly unhappy.

Meanwhile, on the continent events were unfolding that would end my suffering. After years upon years of royal decadence amidst economic failure and political repression, passions flared in France. On 14 July 1789, the Bastille was stormed, and in June 1791, King Louis XVI was jailed and subsequently beheaded. The monarchies of the continent were aroused by fear that the republican movements of America and France could spread and threaten to alter the very nature of their governing lives by sparking a recrudescence of populist uprisings as had temporarily flared during the English Civil War and the Pugachev uprising in Russia. Their fears were well taken. In France, it seemed that a great fire of republican enthusiasm was furiously burning and consuming everything having to do with monarchy. Within the revolutionaries there came to be a firm commitment to end permanently any form of monarchy rule. Throughout France, royalists and every form of disloyalty to the revolution were stamped out, and outright assertions were made by the National Council that France was to be the protector of all other revolutions – anywhere. Young men poured into the *Armie de la Republique*, and a new song, the "Marseillaise," spread through the land, intoxicating the blood of France like rich wine. In the streets of Paris, Le Havre, Boulogne, and in small towns throughout the countryside, it seemed that the population of France had awakened to the spirit and words of deliverance of the common masses, singing,

> *Drive on sacred patriotism,*
> *Support our avenging arms for liberty, cherished liberty.*
> *Join the struggle with your defenders under our flags,*
> *Let victory hurry to your manly tone so that in death,*
> *Your enemies see our triumph and our glory.*

In September 1792, an invading Prussian Army was defeated and turned back by a republican army that was inordinate and ragtag by general military standards but driven to victory by verve and commitment that appeared to be nothing less than a storm of fierce determination.

Goethe was quoted in the *London Sun* as writing, "*On this day, at this place, a new era opens in the history of the world.*"

The republican army not only repelled attacks but pushed beyond their borders into Belgium, the Piedmont, and Holland. The National Council of France then took a profound step. Enraged by our expulsion of its representative following the execution of Louis, it declared war against England.

England would mobilize. I would be saved, and the epoch that would define my life would begin to unfold.

Chapter 6

Recall to Duty

I remember vividly how 1793 brought a new and aroused return to strength for the Royal Navy. Orders went out to all suitable captains of warships, so many who had been living, like myself, in a state of uncertain expectancy. With relief and renewal, we were called back to service, and to all of the Royal Navy it seemed a return to our natural condition – at full force and at war with the French. I received notice that I had been appointed to command the sixty-four-gun frigate HMS *Agamemnon*, which was docked at Chatham and being fitted out again for service. When I first walked on her decks, I must confess that I was ecstatic, filled with anticipation of again engaging in the life that I unabashedly treasured – the life at sea, standing on a quarterdeck, commanding a warship in a time of war. From my new stateroom and with a sense of euphoria, I wrote to Fanny, "*Post nubila phoebus – after clouds comes sunshine. The Admiralty so smile upon me that really I am as much surprised as when they frowned.*"

Upon my return to Norfolk, I enthusiastically began the recruitment of a crew and immediately sent a lieutenant and several midshipmen to recall experienced sailors from every village and seaport in the county of Norfolk. I ultimately chose a core of officers and sailors I knew and who had earlier served with me, including Martin Hinton as my first lieutenant, a very capable man who had served with me in HMS *Albemarle*. The man who would be in charge of sails and rigging would be Joseph King, earlier a boatswain's mate aboard *Boreas*. It was also decided that I would take Fanny's son, Josiah, as a midshipman. This was fortuitous, as Governor Herbert had recently died, leaving only a very modest amount of his wealth as Fanny's inheritance. Surprisingly he had also left an amount to me, which, at prevailing investment rates, would return an amount equal to half my pay. However, Herbert's contribution toward Josiah's education was discontinued, and that expense would now be obviated by appointing Josiah to serve as an *Agamemnon* midshipman. I did not know that the decision would perhaps later save my life.

I believe that my entire countenance became enlivened with the new command. My step became quicker, my voice stronger, my outlook bursting with expectation, and my general ardour for life rekindled in a new fire of energy and purpose. With Fanny, my understanding and affections exceeded anything that we had experienced, and on the evening before my departure the patient and measured progression of my lovemaking actually brought more pleasure to her than she had ever exhibited. When we retired to our bed, we twice coupled. To me, the consummation of my needs seemed almost matched by a feeling that I had brought pleasure to her, and although her response did not indicate the great passion I would have wanted, she was quite willing to receive my gentle but intense assault, even though the quickened sounds of my breathing at the peak of my pleasure were, as always, never matched by her own. The next morning as first light shone through their window, I again stroked her to a point of receptivity and took my pleasure with her once more. Later that day after I received formal deployment orders from the Admiralty, I penned, "*My dear Fanny, never a finer night was seen than last night and I am not the least tired*—" The note would signal the highest point of our love and affection as husband and wife, never again to be equalled.

My orders were to take *Agamemnon* to Gibraltar and to join the Mediterranean Fleet under command of Admiral Samuel Hood. At the time Spain was still allied with England. It remained a monarchy fearful of the populist tide sweeping the continent and staunchly opposed to the brutal uprising that had consumed France. French royalists had captured the naval base at Toulon, and orders to Admiral Hood were to proceed to Toulon to support royalists, who still held the greater part of the city. In response to pleas from the royalists, Hood landed 1,500 troops and two hundred seamen and marines to assist in their defence. This, however, was a very marginal assistance, as the revolutionary forces numbered some thirty thousand. Needing further support from any source available, Hood sent me to seek additional reinforcements from King Ferdinand IV of the kingdom of Naples and the Two Sicilies.

Our extended time at sea with only a brief replenishment stop at Cadiz had taken its toll on the *Agamemnon* and her crew. I wrote, "*My poor fellows have not had a morsel of fresh meat or vegetables for nineteen weeks, and during that time I have only had my foot twice on shore. We are absolutely sick with fatigue.*" Thus, the trip to Naples to lay before King Ferdinand the immediate and urgent need for assistance served not only that purpose but also an opportunity to repair *Agamemnon* and to recuperate its crew.

Naples

Agamemnon arrived in Naples on the evening of 10 September 1793. A midshipman wrote in his log that looming behind the city, Mount Vesuvius was erupting in a spectacular display with *"lava spreading from the top and rolling down the mountain in great streaks of fire."*

A meeting with King Ferdinand was arranged by the British ambassador, Sir William Hamilton. At the meeting the king and his wife, Queen Maria Carolina, not only expressed a willingness to provide assistance but also made clear that they expected a permanent bond between the kingdom and the British fleet. Fearful that the republican forces were pressing into northern Italy with considerable support from Italian populists, the queen, a sister of Marie Antoinette, had convinced the king that support of the Royal Navy would be essential for the survival of their throne in the event of an attack by the French republicans.

Before I left Naples, Sir William Hamilton suggested that I host a formal dinner in honour of the king and queen. Because he was aware that the galley of the *Agamemnon* was ill-suited for such an event, Sir William arranged that it would be fully catered by the staff and kitchen of his embassy. The event turned out to be a most sumptuous and successful affair. Offering a toast, the king announced that he would send four thousand troops to bolster the defence of Toulon. Later it would become known that at first the king was hesitant to make a substantial commitment of assistance but that his mind had been changed by the reasoning and insistence of the queen, who knew that the existence of the kingdom may ultimately be dependent upon English support. It also became known later that the queen's decision had in significant measure been influenced by Sir William's wife, Lady Emma Hamilton.

At dinner aboard *Agamemnon*, Sir William and Lady Hamilton basked in the glow of their success. Sir William offered several toasts that were patronising to the royal couple, emphasizing the strength of the new bond between England and the kingdom. For her part Emma Hamilton sat next to the queen, and by her constant attention, she demonstrated that there was a very strong connection between the two women. I found myself looking frequently in the direction of Emma Hamilton. She was a beautiful woman of fine features with light brown hair tied back in a manner that emphasised the beauty of her face. At times I also felt some excitement when her glances toward me were longer than I would have expected and were accompanied by a lingering and demure smile. When Sir William and Emma departed the ship, Sir William was buoyant.

"Captain Nelson, I find words hard to come by which will express my satisfaction and happiness with your visit to Naples. There has been a great success, and I am most impressed by both you and your ship."

Sensing an opportunity, I replied, "Thank you, sir, and I would be most pleased if you would reflect that sentiment in your dispatches to London."

"Indeed I shall, my good man. Indeed I shall!" Sir William responded.

Lady Hamilton offered her hand and said, "Captain Nelson, this has been a most wonderful evening, and you have a great ship. It also appears that you are a fine captain, and I trust that we shall meet again." To my surprise, she touched my cheek and smiled and then repeated, "I do hope that we shall meet again."

"Thank you, madam," I responded, "and please know that it shall equally be my great pleasure to see you."

In the meantime Fanny's correspondence indicated very clearly that she was taking my extended absence very badly. She constantly expressed fear for my safety as well as the safety of her son, Josiah, a fear constantly repeated in letters that were morose and complaining. To me, the effect could not have been worse. My naval career was the polestar of my life, and her constant interrogations of when I would return to England were contrary to my very nature and alienating at a time when I expected not only support but encouragement from my wife. I wrote to her,

> *My dear, I cannot convey in greater terms the sense of disparagement that I felt in your last letter. I cannot guarantee you a time when I will be home. My place is here, as happily I seek to do my duty to its utmost, and I ask that you not express any sentiments other than that of support. Please do not ask again when I shall return to England and it will do no good whatever to despair for my safety. I must do my duty.*

However, my protestations to Fanny had little effect, as her letters continued with sentiments of a distraught and unhappy wife. She remained at Burnham Thorpe, doing little more than sitting bundled next to the fire, reading and knitting shawls. She seldom went out and did nothing to encourage contact with other members of the family. Her isolation was also not affected by father. He was a man of very timid social skills, and the effects of his aging made him become all the more sedentary. Her isolated life, made so by her largely self-imposed inactive existence, was reflected in repeatedly morose correspondence at a time when I was exulting in a triumphal mission to the kingdom of Naples.

On the day before my departure King Ferdinand made a grand and ostentatious display at the embarkation of his troops into my squadron of ships. The king rode at the head of his four brigades and paraded them before our squadron, all in full-dress uniforms of red and green with polished brass sparkling in the morning sun and high-top hats mounted with curled cock's feathers waving in the breeze. As *Agamemnon* weighed anchor and sailed from the bay, we fired a salute of twenty-one guns, answered by the king at the dock raising his hand in salute amidst a spectacular entourage of Neapolitan nobles and staff of the English embassy. I admit that I relished the sight.

My mission to Naples had been completed with the success that magnified my sense of confidence and self-assurance. I also left with a very positive impression of the Hamiltons, not only of Sir William, whom I had come to admire, but also of his wife, the young and beautiful Emma. The embassy adjutant had in confidence recounted to me that Emma had been married to Sir William after she was his mistress for five years previous. In fact, she came to him following several episodes of intimate relations with members of the English gentry. By one of them when she was still in her teens, she had given birth to a child. Sir William was a true English gentleman, a man of intellectual capacity with a well-developed appreciation of history and antiquarian art. He had been well educated and was immensely effective in both the spoken and written word. Emma Hamilton had, notwithstanding her low born and socially chequered past, developed an ability to be very effective in interpersonal relationships, particularly with Queen Maria Carolina. She was also genuinely warm and personable. During my stay in Naples, she had paid particular attention to my stepson, Josiah. The noted English artist, George Romney, had painted several portraits which reflected both a beautiful and warm countenance. I wrote to Fanny, "*Lady Hamilton is a young woman of amiable manners and who does honour to the station to which she is raised. She has been wonderfully kind and good to Josiah.*"

As the *Agamemnon* departed Naples, my last long entry in the captain's log was, *"God sent us good success. I believe we carry with us the good wishes of Naples and of Sir William Hamilton and Lady Hamilton in particular, which I esteem more than all the rest. Farewell Naples. May those who were kind to me be repaid ten-fold."*

Return to Toulon

The return passage to Toulon was a time of exultation. I basked in the confidence of having triumphed in my mission and anticipated a rich adventure of action that would lie ahead. Each morning I enjoyed the act of walking to my first lieutenant without forewarning and saying, "Mister Hinton, beat to quarters and prepare for battle action port and starboard." Hinton eagerly complied. The ship's bell rang out, and the stirring beat of marine drummers called the crew to general quarters. All work was stopped. The men cast aside their tools and swabs where they were and dashed to battle stations. Gun ports were flung open. Cannons were untied from their secured states and made ready for loading. As a readiness for action proceeded, I would stand on the quarter deck, beating my palm against the railings, noting how long it would take for the ship's batteries to be ready to unleash their hail of destruction. With sandbags in place of shot, guns were loaded and run out the gun ports, ready to fire. When this was done, each gun master would raise his hand to the quarterdeck, signalling that the gun was ready to fire. I continued my tapping count until every gun was ready to fire and would then give the order, "Horizon fire." This order meant that each gun master would have to take the time to aim at the horizon as he would aim at a target during battle. I then barked out, "Fire at will!" and the continuous roar of cannon fire would deafen all sound upon the decks. Powder smoke would fill the ship in a great yellow-grey cloud.

I allowed the battle station gun drills to continue for some minutes and then ordered a cease-fire. I would ask each gun master to count the sandbags fired. On each succeeding day and following each drill, the progress achieved in rapidity of fire was noted. It also became my habit after each drill to walk the length of the gun deck on both port and starboard, looking into the face of every gunner. It was a simple act, but it conveyed to every man that there was a bond between each man, however senior or junior, and his captain. The guns of our ship became as a single unit, and the commitment of every man, strengthened by a sense of his importance to his gun and his ship, became real and very personal. I intended to hone the sharp edge to the fervour of their morale when I would order in a loud voice at the end of every exercise, "Mr. Hinton, splice the main brace. A half ration of grog to the crew and a quarter ration to the midshipmen."

At Toulon, I found the siege of the city to be in a furious deadlock. The great majority of the population had joined forces with the republicans, and the combination of royalist forces with British support was still seriously outnumbered. Although we controlled the waters around the city, very little success had been made in gaining a foothold on land, and every new day brought additional support flowing in to the republicans from the mainland. Although I preferred to stay at Toulon and made several suggestions to Admiral Hood directed chiefly at capture of the republican-held forts that commanded the harbour, Hood remained unconvinced that his force would be successful. It simply wasn't large enough. Believing that capture of Corsica would be most important to long-range strategy in the Mediterranean, Hood gave me orders to join Commodore Linzee, who had been sent to attack Corsica.

Following my departure from Toulon, the fortunes of the combined royalists and British forces did not improve. Although they continued to hold the bay that was essential for resupplying the city itself, they were essentially confined and surrounded in those positions. Resolution of the conflict would come about through the actions of a young republican captain of artillery who spoke French with an Italian accent. I was advised that his name was Napoleon Bonaparte, and he had requisitioned artillery from all of the surrounding countryside and amassed a combined battery of more than a hundred artillery pieces of various sizes. He placed his new batteries on a prominence above the royalist forts and began a constant barrage. Fearful that they could not last, the royalist and British forces made an attack upon the French positions but were pushed back in a counterattack led by Bonaparte himself. During the counterattack British General O'Hara, commanding the combined royalist forces, was captured with most of his troops. He sued for peace. The city was ultimately surrendered, and the victory of the French at Toulon signalled a rising star in the French Army by the name of Bonaparte. For the next twelve years that name would be spoken on the lips of the British people as an icon of hate tinged with begrudging respect.

First Engagement at Sea

On 9 October 1793, I set sail in *Agamemnon* for Corsica. I worked my men tirelessly at gunnery and ship-handling drills in every sea and wind that came our way. On 18 October, the drills would become reality, and the sandbag shot would be replaced with iron shot. What would ensue would be my first battle engagement as the commander of a warship.

During the night lookouts in the crow's nest high above on the foremast had spotted rocket signals over the horizon. The officer of the watch apprised First Lieutenant Hinton, who immediately raced to my stateroom and awoke me with the announcement, "Captain, there are rocket signals that are reported in the distance. We believe them to be from French ships."

I sprang from my bed and ordered, "Set full sail, Hinton, and make a course to intercept the signals." I donned my uniform, splashed water on my face, and raced to the quarterdeck. At first light the silhouettes of five ships could be seen in the distance. From time to time signal rockets were again fired in the air. At dawn the closest of the ships, at the rear of the group, was in hailing distance, and not knowing whether the ships were French or perhaps a merchant convoy from a neutral country, I hailed the ship to identify itself. It did not respond, and I ordered, "Mister Hinton, beat to quarters and fire a shot across her bow."

The sound of the ship's bell and the beat of the quarterdeck drums sent every man again scurrying to his battle station. Hinton came close and said, "Captain, if they are French warships, there are five of them."

"I can count, Mister Hinton. I can count," I responded sharply. "I intend to do business with the ship in the rear and, if necessary, with the rest of them. To start with, Hinton, have the even guns loaded with round shot and the odds loaded with chains shot or angles." Chains shot and angles were to round shot connected by either four links of chain or a straight piece of iron. They were used to tear away rigging and sails of the opponent. I walked to the forward railing of the quarterdeck and shouted, "Master gunner, tell your men that this shall be yet another drill but a drill of reality, and we shall expect a quick but sure aim. Make sure that our rapid fire will win the day." The decks were sanded. Cannons were loaded and run out of their ports.

As I spoke, the unidentified ship hoisted the French tricolour and fired at *Agamemnon*. It was the French frigate *Melpomene*. Her first shots fell short, sending high plumes of water into the air. As the *Melpomene* closed, I ordered, "Helmsman, port your helm. I want to be downwind of the Frenchman." The advantage of having *Agamemnon* downwind would mean that we would be heeled up and all of our gun ports would have clear view of the enemy. Meanwhile, the *Melpomene* would be heeled down, and her gun ports would have an occluded view of the *Agamemnon*. The Frenchman continued to fire, most of the shot landing short. However, some struck home, tearing through our sails or sharply banging against the hull. Some of the shot passed overhead with an ominous whooshing sound. Because manoeuvring was not of significance, I ordered the main and main foresail reefed, and soon thereafter the Frenchman did likewise. We approached the enemy.

"Master gunner, cock your locks and fire as the target appears."

The roar of the ensuing broadside from *Agamemnon* came at the same time as the *Melpomene* fired her broadside. Great clouds of smoke enveloped each ship, and as successive volleys were fired, the portrait of the engagement was one of continuous flashes of muzzle fire and great clouds of yellow-grey smoke. Shots that struck the *Agamemnon* tore at our sails and broke some of our rigging with sharp, loud snapping sounds. The gun crews worked their feverish pace of firing, swabbing hot barrels with a wet plunger to extinguish any burning power, ramming powder sacks and shot, and then heaving again at the gun tackle as the gun crew master shouted orders to aim his gun. The firing was continuous, and I took great delight in seeing that our guns were being fired with greater rapidity than those of the French. I could see that *Melpomene's* mainsail and foresail had been shot away and that she was manoeuvring with only her jib and spanker. Considerable damage had been suffered to her hull with almost half of her gun ports out of commission.

"Captain, we are faring well," Hinton shouted to me, "and I believe we can take her measure." But as he spoke, one of the *Melpomene's* shot struck squarely upon the *Agamemnon's* mainmast, snapping it in half. It fell to the deck in a thunder with all of its massive rigging and the top mainsail covering the deck like a great white shroud. As all hands frantically worked to clear the deck, Hinton spoke, "Captain, the others are closing, and we shall soon be in for warm work." The other ships were the frigates *Minerve*, *Fortune*, and *Mignonne*, each of forty guns, and the brig *Hasard* of twenty-eight guns. To me, the battle plan had been changed considerably. *Agamemnon* would no longer be in a fight with another ship but would be engaged in a battle of outnumbered odds. An aggregate of more than 180 French guns would be brought to bear against the sixty-four of the *Agamemnon*. I nevertheless answered, "Let them come, Hinton. We have an armoury of shot and the best seamen in the world. We will do what we must do."

My inner thoughts were quite different from the bravado of my words. I was keenly aware of their advantage in gunnery numbers and knew that if they decided to board the *Agamemnon*, their numbers would be overwhelming. Could I possibly strike our colours and surrender? And could I endure the surrender of my sword to a French captain? The alternative was to continue the fight and, in all likelihood, have the *Agamemnon* shot to pieces by an overwhelming enemy. I was fully willing to lay down my life for king and country, but could I sacrifice the lives of my crew for the sake of personal defiance?

At that moment, however, fate provided deliverance. The wind died to a total calm, and *Agamemnon* drifted away from the *Melpomene*. The crew cleared the deck and rigged the remains of the main topmast between the foremast and mizzen. Our loss of men had been light with one man killed and six wounded. The gun crews cleared their stations, again sanded the decks, and reloaded the guns. *Agamemnon* would continue the fight. However, our readiness became unnecessary. When the calm was broken by a light wind in the late afternoon, the French ships tacked to the north and inexplicably withdrew. As they had such an advantage in number, I could not understand.

Night fell on a calm sea with light winds. I ordered the loaded guns discharged into the night air in what seemed to be a volley of salvation. We had been saved. Sensing a moment of great relief and with a deep and abiding gratitude and respect for the men of my ship, I said to Hinton, "First Lieutenant, please call the officers to conference, but not in my cabin. We will have it on the main deck." I ordered the issue of a full ration of grog and called the men close around the officers, tankards in hand. I gazed about the faces of my officers and men and spoke, "Today, my dear brothers, we have done battle. I have seen in each of you that which every captain prays for in a crew. You have shown a skill that was far greater than that of the enemy. You have been dedicated and fearless. You have shown the courage of lions, and tonight you will be able to sleep as lions. I bid you good night."

I returned to my stateroom and wrote in the captain's log,

How thankful I ought to be and I hope am for the mercies of Almighty God manifested to me this day. We lost only one man killed and six wounded, although my ship was cut to pieces ... I commend myself to the care of my Almighty God ... I give myself up to His direction, amidst all the evils that threaten me, I will look to Him for help, and question not but He will either avert them, or turn them to my advantage, though I know neither the time nor manner of my death, I'm not at all solicitous about it, because I am sure He knows them both, and that He will not fail to support and comfort me under them.

I felt within the beating heart of my chest that I, who had grown from a motherless boy to become a man, must forever seek love and protection from God himself. With a renewed spirituality and a strong faith that bound me to the Almighty, I would go forward with a surge of confidence, inspiration, and courage that I prayed would also become a source of strength to those who served with me.

In the dark night I walked to the quarter deck and looked to the stars above. I spoke aloud, "Thank you, Lord God. I bow to you with total resolve to do my utmost in service to you, my country, and my king, who reigns by your divine right."

Tunis

With jury-rigged sails *Agamemnon* limped back to Corsica and joined with the fleet at Cagliari under command of Commodore Linzee. From the beginning there was a lack of understanding and respect between Linzee and me. I explained my delay and the reason for my ship's condition by recounting the entire engagement with four French warships, but Linzee was neither understanding nor sympathetic. I wrote,

The Commodore did not think it right to give us the least assistance, but sent for me to give my reasons if I could not go to sea with him the next morning, totally unfit as my ship was, which he knew. I would not say Agamemnon was ever unable to go in search of an enemy. We worked all night fixing our masts and stopping holes, mending our sails and splicing our rigging.

With my crew still working to mend the ship, we sailed with Linzee's squadron for Tunis with orders to capture a French convoy that included the eighty-gun *Duquesne*. Linzee's orders were to *"expostulate with the Bey (the King of Tunis – and obviously a monarchist) on the policy of giving support to so threatening a government as the present one in France, composed of murderers and assassins who had recently beheaded their queen in a manner that would disgrace the most barbarous savages."* The Bey allowed that the murder of a member of a royal family was a heinous crime, but *"if historians told the truth, the English had once done the same,"* an obvious reference to the death of Charles I. My reaction to this observation was to encourage Linzee to seize the French ships straight away. In the alternative I suggested that Linzee offer the Bey a bribe of £50,000 to surrender the convoy (valued at £300,000). The commodore, however, refused the suggestion and continued with negotiations that ultimately proved to gain us nothing. I also suggested that we simply take the French ships. After all, when the Barbary pirates captured American ships and took refuge in Tripoli, the Americans went in under cover of night, boarded, and seized their ships, then defiantly sailed them out. That was gallant action, and could we not do the same? But Linzee continued to be a timid man. When Admiral Hood was apprised of the stalled negotiations, he ordered Linzee's squadron to withdraw out of fear that the Bey might be driven to end the neutrality of Tunis and join the war on the side of France.

Squadron Command

My disgust at the way things turned out in Tunis was, however, turned around by a passage in Hood's orders that commented favourably on my near capture of the *Melpomene*, and, more importantly, he gave to me command of a newly appointed squadron of ships ordered into a new action. I wrote delightedly to Captain Locker,

Thank God! Lord Hood has ordered me to command a squadron of frigates for Corsica and the coast of Italy, to protect our trade, and that of our new ally, the grand Duke of Tuscany, and to prevent any ship or vessel of whatever nation, from going into the port of Genoa. I consider the command as a very high compliment, there being five older captains in the fleet.

To my great relief, I would be acting independently, able to use my judgment and initiative, no longer having to act under what I considered to be the weak leadership of Commodore Linzee. My orders were very general, and I set out with my new squadron for Corsica.

At the same time Fanny's condition at Burnham Thorpe continued to deteriorate. It was reflected in her letters, which were listless and mundane, still complaining of my absence and asking repeatedly when I would return home. In one of her letters she fussed about her indecision whether or not to go to Bath after Christmas. In my reply I commented with some impatience, *"As you desire my opinion about Bath, I have only to order that you do what is best for you. You have my consent to your own wishes. That is settled."* It had become clear to me that the excitement of my new station meant little to Fanny and that any encouragement or support from her would not be forthcoming.

Corsica

The fall of Toulon, securely in the hands of Bonaparte, meant that the most favourable base for British operations in the Mediterranean would be Corsica. San Fiorenzo, with a wide bay and sheltered port, would be an ideal post from which to operate, as it lay only about a hundred miles from Toulon and the coast of France. There was one major problem with Corsica. It was currently in the hands of the French, having been ceded to them by the Genoese some twenty years earlier. The political situation in Corsica was, however, troublesome, with sentiments of most official governors lying with the republicans following the fall of Louis XVI. However, Corsican nationalists' hopes of independence were dashed following the French Revolution, when the National Assembly issued an order formally annexing the island to the French republic. The leader of the Corsican nationalists, Pasquale Paoli, had spent twenty years in exile in Britain and was considered an ally. In January 1794, we concluded an agreement with General Paoli under which the British would provide assistance to the Corsicans and they would attempt to take control of the island for British operations against Napoleon. Commodore Linzee tried to take the fort at San Fiorenzo through a frontal attack but was beaten back, with fifty-six men killed or wounded. I wrote again to Captain Locker, *"Linzee failed and did no good whatever. I am glad Lord Hood did not leave me under his command."* Hood decided to make another attempt at capturing

San Fiorenzo and gave me orders to blockade the town of Malcinaggio, directly across from the bay and port of San Fiorenzo.

I decided to be direct and aggressive. I sent an officer under a flag of truce into the city, offering to be a friend of an independent Corsica, and stated that if a musket were fired, I would burn the town. The Malcinaggio commander replied haughtily and immediately,

> *Nous sommes Francais Republicans! That phrase alone ought to satisfy you. It is not too much for Malcinaggio, a place without defence that you want to address yourself. Go to San Fiorenzo, to Bastia, or to Calvi, and they will answer you according to your wishes. As to the troops to my command, they are ready to show you that they are composed of French soldiers.*

I read the response and then ordered, "Hinton, muster the marines and assemble an additional company of forty able-bodied seaman. We will show them what a company composed of British men can do." I decided that I again would lead the assault.

Later, I wrote in my journal, "*I landed and struck the French colours with my own hand on the top of the old castle and ordered the tree of liberty in the centre of the town to be cut down, not without great displeasure from the inhabitants. The military commandant retired to a hill some two miles away, where he paraded his troops, with the national flag flying all day. We destroyed about 500 tons of wine ready to be shipped and 10 sailing vessels.*"

Not having sufficient troops to hold the town, I withdrew and sailed around the northern coast of Corsica to Bastia some fifty miles away. I had orders from Admiral Hood to search for French privateers. Fearful of the potential of offending neutral countries, I was ordered not to fire upon ships coming out of the city of Caprera, but one circumstance negated that order when a departing ship fired upon *Agamemnon*. I immediately returned fire, raking the ship and causing it to strike its colours. But that did not satisfy me, as I considered this act to be a licence to act against the city itself. I later wrote, "*This was too much for me to suffer. I took boats of troops and the Fox cutter and went to the cove, where a number of people were posted behind rocks, where we could not land, who fired on us. It was a point of honour to take her; and after attempting in vain to dislodge the people, I boarded the boat, and brought her out, I am sorry to say with a loss of six men wounded. The ship that had fired upon Agamemnon was a French courier from Bastia to Antibes; an officer with a national cockade in his hat was killed, with several other people."*

Having been given orders to assist generally in the conquest of Corsica, I landed sixty troops at Lavisena and marched to within gunshot of Bastia, accompanied by two hundred Corsican nationals dispatched by Paoli. By this time I had come to be known to Corsican nationalists as "Piccolo Capitano," meaning *the little captain*, admired as an aggressive ally to the nationalist cause. When I met with the mayor of Erbalunga, a committed nationalist, I was told that the local people in the countryside surrounding Bastia had declared for Piccolo Capitano and the English. I immediately dispatched this information to Hood and wrote in my journal, *"I am well, never better, and in active service which I love."*

The Corsican campaign would begin a new and very positive chapter in my life. I would work with and for a superior officer, Admiral Hood, for whom I had consummate respect. I wrote to my brother, *"The Admiral is as active as a man of 40²who writes his own orders and correspondences with all the Italian states. His business is enough for three common heads, but to him it is easy."*

The relationship between Hood and myself became increasingly strong. We both had a natural tendency to be direct and aggressive, and each fed upon the other with a very positive effect. With mutual respect I would come to serve Hood with total allegiance, and Hood came to respect and rely upon me as a most valued assistant and subordinate.

Bastia

There were two major republican strongholds remaining in Corsica – Bastia on the north-eastern coast and Calvi on the north-western. The first order of business was to capture of Bastia. British soldiers under command of General Sir David Dundas had taken positions surrounding Bastia's fort. I was laying in *Agamemnon* opposite the harbour, and when the HMS *Victory*, under command of Admiral Hood, arrived with five other warships, it seemed that the effect of the combined forces would mean a quick and certain victory in taking the city. However, inexplicably General Dundas ordered his troops back to San Fiorenzo. Appalled by the abdication of a perfect opportunity, I wrote, *"What the general could*

---

² Hood was actually 70 years old at the time.

have seen to have made a retreat necessary, I cannot conceive, the enemy's force is 1,000 regulars and 1,000 or 1,500 irregulars … Agamemnon with only the frigates now here laying against the town for a few hours, with 500 troops ready to land … would to a certainty carry the place."*

After Dundas's retreats to San Fiorenzo, I met with Admiral Hood and thereafter wrote in my journal, *"I presumed to propose to Lord Hood, and his Lordship agreed with me, that he should go to Fiorenzo and hear what the general had to say."* Impressed with the series of aggressive and effective actions taken by myself, Admiral Hood offered me the command of the larger seventy-four-gun HMS *Courageux*. However, I turned down his offer and wrote, *"I declined – if Agamemnon sticks by me I will do the same by her. My seamen are now what British seamen ought to be … almost invincible. They really mind shot no more than peas."*

The retreat by Dundas from Bastia would also mean that taking the city would become ever more difficult with time. I could observe new batteries being constructed above the town, with the field of shot clearly covering landing places that would be used by any attacking forces. At San Fiorenzo there raged major differences between Dundas and Hood. First General Dundas did not accept Hood as commander of all military and naval forces in the area and denied the importance of an immediate attack upon Bastia. In response Hood insisted that an immediate attack upon Bastia was essential, and he further said that if necessary, he was ready and willing to undertake the capture of the city at his own risk with the force of hand. He later remarked to me, *"The general's faculties seem to be palsied – we must therefore do the best we can."* Because of ill health, General Dundas was soon forced to retire from the theatre and was replaced by General Abraham D'Aubant. The new general was not willing to remove his entire force for an attack upon Bastia but did agree to send artillery officers to examine the possibility of directing artillery batteries for bombarding the Bastia fort, and most importantly he agreed to allow Admiral Hood to command the assault.

Arriving at Bastia, Hood sent a single officer under a flag of truce to request the surrender of the Bastian fort. The officer returned with notes of the fort commander's response, *"I have hot shot for your ships, and bayonets for your troops. When two thirds of our troops are killed, I will then trust to the generosity of the English."*

With four hundred troops given by D'Aubant and an equal number of seamen and marines, the admiral ordered that positions be taken to prevent any retreat from the fort, and I was assigned to command the naval contingent. When the land batteries were in place, a red flag was hoisted aboard the *Victory* as a general order to commence fire upon the fort. What began was a very long and largely ineffectual bombardment. The French guns answered, but because of the distance from the targets on both sides, very few shots landed with any effective result. For five weeks and after the expenditure of vast amounts of powder and shot, the standoff remained. I remained confident and committed to the action, constantly repositioning our guns and exhorting my men. I wrote, "*The expedition is almost a child of my own, and I have no fears about the final issue, it will be victory, Bastia will be ours. If so, it will be an event which the history of England can hardly boast its equal.*"

Five weeks after commencement of the bombardment the Bastian fort raised the white flag of capitulation, and I wrote proudly, "*At daylight this morning the most glorious sight which an Englishman and I believe none but an Englishman could experience was to be seen – 4,500 men laying down their arms to less than 1,000 English soldiers. Our loss of men in taking this town, containing upwards of 14,000 inhabitants, and fully inhabited would contain 25,000, was the smallest possible to be conceived.*"

In fact, Bastia had been starved into submission, and the surrendering officers stated that during the five weeks of counter-bombardment, they had essentially expended all of their munitions. Nevertheless, it was a victory, and Admiral Hood was generous in his praise. He wrote to me,

> *The Commander in Chief returns his best thanks to Captain Nelson and desires he will present them to his officers, as well as to every soldier and seaman employed in the reduction of Bastia. Notwithstanding the various difficulties and disadvantages they have had to struggle with, which could not have been surmounted but by the uncommon spirit and cordial unanimity that has been so conspicuously displayed. It must give a stamp of reputation to their character not to be effaced, and it will be remembered with gratitude by the Commander in Chief to the end of his life.*

Clearly the image that Hood had of me and my men had been reinforced. I had proved to be a captain who, through constant energy and directed force, could obtain significant results. It was also clear that my allegiance to the admiral was beyond question. I also revelled in some satisfaction and wrote to my brother Maurice, "*Lord Hood has gained the greatest credit for his perseverance and I daresay he will not forget that it was due to myself in great measure that this glorious expedition was undertaken. Lord Hood's thanks to me, both public and private, are the handsomest that man can pen. Having ever since our leaving England been in the habit of getting thanks and applause, I look for them as a matter of course.*"

Calvi

I was then ordered to convoy troops from Bastia to San Fiorenzo and to off-load them at Calvi, thirty miles to the south. Royalist forces at Calvi represented the last remaining obstacle to British control of Corsica. Having received a report that six French warships had departed from Toulon and evaded the British blockade, the admiral removed all of his fleet, except for my squadron, in pursuit of the French. In *Agamemnon*, I took a group of four English warships and six merchant vessels to a small inlet named Porto Agro to the immediate west of the city and fort of Calvi.

From the beginning it was apparent that Calvi would be a difficult assignment. On three sides of the fort great granite walls rose from the rocks on the shore, and towering bastions guarded the fort. Commanding our army contingent of 1,450 troops was a new commander named Lieutenant General Charles Stewart, who had recently been dispatched from England. He was a far more aggressive and collaborative man than his predecessors had been. Stewart and I arranged a conference to outline the battle plan for taking Calvi.

Stewart began, "This is what I see, Captain Nelson. The fort is situated in the centre of a peninsula that juts out northward into the sea. If we arrange batteries on the land promontories to the west of the fort, it will be within a convenient range of artillery. However, we have brought only light artillery with our troops, and I wonder if I might impose upon you for the use of guns from your ships."

"General, I am very willing to commit whatever guns may be appropriate," I responded. "For purposes of bombardment by sea I will be able to use only my deck guns since those on the lower decks cannot be trained high enough to reach appropriate targets on the high ramparts of the fort. Also, my ships in open sea will be perfect targets for the

French guns high on the ramparts firing down upon them, and in order to be effective from our lower perspective, we will have to get close to the fort, exaggerating our disadvantage. The exchange of fire would not be advantageous from the sea. Therefore, all of my lower deck guns can be committed to the ground action."

"Excellent!" replied Stewart.

"I can also commit to the land campaign two hundred or perhaps three hundred seamen and marines," I added.

"That will be very helpful," Stewart replied, and then he added, "It would please me, Captain, if you would oversee the batteries that are created using the guns from your ships."

"I am absolutely willing to do that," I replied with delight.

On 18 June, 1794, the landing of weapons and stores began. Throughout the next two weeks, cannons, munitions, and stores were carried to the island. Each gun weighed more than two tons and was approximately nine feet in length. The French had not anticipated that they would have to exchange fire with batteries being placed on the promontories to the west of the city because they believed that carrying ship cannons to such heights up severe and rocky slopes simply would not be possible. They underestimated, however, the nerve and commitment of both myself and Stewart. The next fortnight was hard labour, manhandling and dragging guns, shot, barrels of powder, and rations up the steep slope from the beach and over the broken, boulder-blocked ground. However, under the constant attention and exhortation of Stewart and myself, cannon and equipment for four batteries had reached the promontory, and on 4 July, our bombardment began.

I recorded in my journal, *"Both sides kept up a heavy fire. They totally destroyed two of our 24 pounders, greatly damaged a 26 pounder, and shook our works very much. One of the shells burst in the centre of our battery, but, wonderful to say, not a man was hurt. We, on our part, did considerable damage to several of the batteries in the fort."*

"I Got a Little Hurt This Morning"

Four hours after the bombardment began, the captain of one of my accompanying ships had his head taken off by grapeshot fired from the fort. Two soldiers and a seaman from *Agamemnon* were also killed. That evening I dashed off a short letter to Fanny, *"It is possible you may have heard that a captain of the Navy has fallen. To assure you it is not me, I write a few lines, for if such a report should get about, I will know your anxiety of mind. I am very busy yet I am all in my glory. I would not be anywhere but where I am, for all the world."*

I also wrote admiringly of General Stewart, *He was constantly active among his troops, leading by example. He every night sleeps in the advanced battery."* On 12 July, I was watching the bombardment and exchange of fire from an exposed vantage point next to our northern battery when a shell burst on the rampart with a furious shower of sand and stones. I was thrown to the ground, and when I slowly tried to stand, blood flowed from my face. A stone had cut into my forehead and eyebrow, and the concussion from the explosion had caused a rupture to a blood vessel in my right eye, which forever thereafter would eliminate any effective use of the eye. For the remainder of the day and disregarding the pain to my face and eye, I continued the active command of my batteries.

I wrote to Fanny of *"a very slight scratch toward my right eye which has not been the slightest inconvenience."* I intended to be equally dismissive of the injury in an operational note to Admiral Hood,

> *I got a little hurt this morning, not much as you may judge by my writing ... and, later, when I was on the beach, seeing how necessary it was to give encouragement to the people to exert themselves in getting stores on shore, I gave them some provisions rather than any delay should be made, but I did not feel myself justified in always continuing it. However the people behaved well and have worked all day and were ordered to work all night. If your Lordship will allow me, I will order them a little more wine as encouragement.*

Hood replied to me, *"I am truly sorry to hear you have received a hurt, and hope you tell the truth in saying it is not much. I shall be glad if you order the crews wine, upon any occasion you may judge necessary."*

Nothing of major consequence occurred thereafter as a result of the loss of my eye. At first the condition denied me the ability to use the eye to perceive and focus upon any object, allowing me only to distinguish between light and dark. Later the sight of the eye would deteriorate, and ultimately it became totally blind. There would be recurring painful periods, and from time to time I would seek treatment from ships' surgeons; however, there would be no disabling disease, and no pain would ever prevent me from doing whatever I considered had to be done.

Calvi Drags On

The battle for Calvi dragged on with little effect except for the great expenditure of ammunition on both sides. Although the capture of Corsica was important to Admiral Hood, he was chiefly occupied with the blockade of the French fleet at Toulon. Constant requests from General Stewart for more troops, more seamen, and more ammunition went unsatisfied. However, Hood's primary focus upon Toulon became well placed when the French attempted a major sortie. Hood intercepted them near Gulf Juan, opposite the coast of the Riviera, and seriously battered their fleet, capturing several ships and forcing a retreat of the remaining fleet back to Toulon.

At Calvi, the stalemate continued. General Stewart's chief of artillery, Colonel Moore, had begun to voice criticism of Hood's commitment to the siege. Having worked my men to the point of exhaustion, I wrote to the admiral,

> *I hope to God that the general, who seems a good officer and an amiable man, is not led away, but Colonel Moore is his great friend. The general took me aside today. There seems to be a little jealousy of my communicating with you daily. Your Lordship will be so good as not to notice any part of this letter to the general, but indeed I don't say yet that he is to blame. I wish Moore was a hundred leagues off. He will injure the general with the Army.*

I then added, "*I beg your Lordship to burn this letter.*"

Stewart gathered his forces together for another push against the fort. I landed additional ships' cannon, and attacks were made on two outlying gun positions beneath the fort. Both were taken. However, the assault came with its price, and the fire was so intense from the fort that eighteen of Stewart's men were either killed or wounded. Again Stewart sent an officer under a flag of truce to request capitulation of the fort. The answer came defiantly, "*Civitas Calvi, semper fidelis.*"

After the assault, which had only marginal tactical effect and was accomplished with significant losses, Colonel Moore approached and said to me, "Why, in God's name, does Hood not land another five hundred troops? Our soldiers are tired, and if he were to give us greater support, I am sure that the fort could be taken."

I answered, "Admiral Hood is more than fully occupied elsewhere, and the new report of his victory off Gulf Juan indicates that he has prevented the landing of a thousand French troops who would have meant the end of us in Corsica. He has his job to do, and we have ours. Our mission is to carry it out the best we can and with the forces we have."

Suffering from considerable stress, fatigue, and fever, I wrote to the admiral, "*I am far from well, but not so ill as to be confined. My eye is troublesome, and I don't think I shall ever have the perfect sight of it again. The general may have his causes to be displeased, but I am confident they cannot be concerned because by any part of the Navy.*"

Hood answered, "*I can only repeat to you my earnest desire that you comply with the general's wishes as far as you can and should they be beyond your powers, let me know them. I am quite unhinged.*"

Admiral Hood

Toward the end of July 1794, General Stewart concluded that his beleaguered troops were unlikely to withstand another month's ordeal and told Admiral Hood that after another ten days he would either have to attempt a final assault or give up the siege. However, conditions inside the fort became grave, and on 28 July, a lone French officer appeared with a flag of truce and announced that the fort would surrender. With more than half of their men critically ill, the defenders had simply run out of necessary ammunition to continue the fight. Thus, Corsica became a British possession.

General Stewart wrote a rather brief report to the war office, announcing the capture of the fort and the end of hostilities in Corsica. It was a strange and lacklustre description of what could have been described as a glorious and determined effort. However, Stewart simply seemed too exhausted to seek praise or give laudable accounts to any of his subordinates, including myself. Again I felt acutely aggrieved that my extraordinary efforts and those of my men were not publicly recognized. Writing to my uncle, I remarked bitterly, "*I am without reward. Nothing but my anxious endeavours to serve my country makes me bear up against it, but I sometimes am ready to give all up. Never mind, however, someday I shall have a Gazette of my own.*"

I was, however, lifted considerably when I received copies of Admiral Hood's dispatches, which reported the conquest of Corsica and added that it was achieved in part by the "*efforts of Captain Nelson, who had the command of seamen, and whose unremitting zeal and exertion I cannot sufficiently express.*"

In the meantime political developments in London were significant to the future direction of the Royal Navy in general and for me in particular. The Whigs had formed a coalition with Prime Minister Pitt, and Lord George Spencer, an active Whig upstart, had been appointed First Lord of the Admiralty at the age of thirty-six. Spencer set about his office with zeal, poring over fleet deployment and status reports with a full appreciation of the crucial role that British sea power would play as the critical instrument of protection against a French invasion of the home islands. He read Hood's report of the capture of Corsica with intense interest, noting particularly his comment regarding me. I was told that he reviewed the personal portfolios of more than sixty ship captains in active duty and stacked them in order of the merit he attached to each. I was also told that my portfolio sat atop the stack.

Chapter 7

Intermezzo

I remember how the Admiralty's focus of defence shifted to the Mediterranean in 1794. French armies had occupied Belgium, and their conquest of areas neighbouring the French borders was considered secure. The National Assembly, still involved in cleansing French society of remaining vestiges of royalist sentiment, began a renewed effort to build its naval forces. Rear Admiral Pierre Martin, in command of the fleet at Toulon, was painfully aware that his fleet was inexperienced and unreliable chiefly because many officers had largely come from the French aristocracy and had been dismissed and frequently imprisoned. Some had been executed.

Admiral Hood, ill and aging, had been allowed to return to England and was replaced by Admiral Sir William Hotham, who, very much unlike Hood, proved to be a commander devoid of aggressive inclination and who considered small victories to be triumphs. Following another fierce storm that stripped the *Agamemnon* of most of its sails and much of its rigging, I was allowed to put into Leghorn for long-needed repairs to my ship and recuperation of its crew. As *Agamemnon* lay idle in refurbishment, I wrote mournfully to my brother,

> *What can be expected from a worn-out ship and ship's company? Notwithstanding I'm in the best possible health, yet I don't like any longer being kicked about. I am tired. Now that services are over I believe for the present, I have more time to think and no person has been treated so ill as myself ... I now think, knowing it to be true, that I was the humble instrument of Corsica's being taken, the active instrument for Bastia's being attacked by the English and without vanity, that I was the cause of 4,500 French troops laying down their arms to 1,000 English marines and seamen.*

As further discouragement, I became aware of reports that the French fleet was at sea while *Agamemnon* lay in port, dismasted and immobile in an extended period of inaction. I wrote, *"It would go nigh* to break my heart, but I will hope the best." I added, *"Lying in port is misery to me."* My misery, however, would not last for long. I was received and treated with formal honours at a dinner in the doge's palace. His reception, with formal dignity and effusive expressions of appreciation by the doge himself, salved my pride and lightened my spirit. I also met and was treated with adulation by the British consul, who introduced me to an attractive, dark-haired opera singer named Adelaide Correglia. Her beauty attracted me, and her remarks of respect and praise were most thankfully received.

"Captain, please know that everyone here of refined sentiment believes that you can save us from the threat of invasion by the military power of the unwashed and cruel masses of France."

I responded, "Please know, Madame, that I shall do my utmost. My king and his government are committed more than anything to preservation of the countries and states under the rule of those with judgment and stature that befit a responsible ruling class."

Throughout the evening she stayed near to me, and whenever in conversation she wanted to make a point, it was emphasized by her touching of my arm followed by a smile. The doge must have noted her attraction and instructed that the seating arrangement be amended to have Signora Correglia sit next to me. As the evening progressed, her conversation and questions indicated an intelligence that was equal to her attractiveness. She was both knowledgeable and articulate with regard to the nature and development of politics among the Italian states, and she was keen to know about the disposition of the Royal Navy and its potential for checking a French invasion of northern Italy. This impressed me, and I was eager to describe in detail my assessment of the strength of the Royal Navy as well as its ability to overcome anything that France could put on the water. At the end of the evening I had become besotted by the Italian woman and invited her to tea at the small villa I had taken while the ship was being repaired. Her immediate acceptance was a particular excitement to what had been a totally fallow field of feminine contact during my continuous duty at sea for more than two years.

Toward the end of the banquet the doge sent a note to Signora Correglia, one asking her to meet with him the next morning. She told me that at the meeting he made a request that was essentially an instruction. She recounted him saying, "Signora, I would like you to develop as close a friendship as you can with Captain Nelson and to determine with as much precision as is possible the ability of the Royal Navy to support us. Let him know that we stand with England against the French and shall rely upon their support against the threat of French encroachment."

Signora Correglia said that she received the instruction with enthusiasm and responded, "I find Captain Nelson to be a very interesting and attractive man. He seems committed to us and is totally against the French both militarily and politically." The doge replied, "Well then, I shall await with great anticipation any information you may obtain."

Correglia prepared herself for our afternoon tea by dressing up her dark tresses in a net interspersed with small pearls. She chose a dress of dark red silk that was cut low in front, similar to the one she had worn at the banquet, revealing the distinct cleavage of her breasts, which she likely remembered that I had glanced at with some frequency during our first meeting. At the time for afternoon tea she arrived promptly and was greeted with some excitement on my part.

"Madame, I am delighted that you were able to come this afternoon. I had ordered tea cakes and sandwiches, but my Italian valet had no idea how to prepare them, so he bought this assortment of pastries that I do not recognise," I said in my welcome to her.

She inspected the pastries and replied, "Oh my, your valet has done very well. These are ciarduna and bocarroto, which are delicious pastries from different parts of Italy. I like them all very much and believe that you shall as well."

We sat and talked at length, initially about the threat of French invasion and British command of the Mediterranean. Correglia described the political interplay among the Italian city states and recounted a theme of consistent fear. She noted that some of the states, particularly those in the Piedmont, seemed on the verge of making an alliance with France rather than enduring military conquest. She opined that to save themselves, the rulers thought it best to sacrifice their political principles for the sake of survival of their families as well as their rule, even though it would be under French domination. All of the information she imparted was eagerly taken in by me as significant intelligence that I would relate to the Admiralty and the British Foreign Office. In return, I assured her that the British exerted present dominance over the Mediterranean and would continue to do so. I opined confidently that it was not simply a matter of strength in number of British ships but a matter of professional competence that would enable the Royal Navy to overcome any French fleet.

Having exhausted political and military discussion, the conversation turned to Correglia's operatic performances in Leghorn, Padua, and Florence. I knew nothing about Italian opera, but I was entranced by the woman's beauty and enthusiasm. I asked if she would sing her favourite aria, and after pausing to think, she agreed to sing a short piece by Marco Marazzole from his opera *Dal Male Il Bene*. I had never heard of the man or the opera, but as she stood and sang in a quavering, thin soprano, she acted out the piece, which ended with her approaching me and touching my face as she finished with an emotional stanza that was apparently about something having to do with *amore dolce*. The moment was electric, and I found an excitement well within me that had been totally latent for so long. She finished her piece with a gentle smile as she looked into my eyes, her hand still touching my cheek. The touch was exciting and wonderful.

"I must go, for I believe that I have stayed longer than is customary for an afternoon English tea," she announced.

"My dear lady, I have enjoyed this afternoon immensely and would like to see you again," I replied.

"Then please come to my villa for dinner tomorrow evening. It has been some time since I have prepared a dinner for a man, and I would very much like to prepare one for you," she said.

"I shall be delighted, Madame."

"Please call me Adelaide, Captain, or better, "Delie." It is what my friends call me."

"Very well. "Dolly" it shall be." Later I would learn that I had misheard her accent.

Correglia went to the doge's palace and reported the content of our conversation. The doge was concerned that she had advised me of weaknesses in some of the Piedmont states and said that his fear was that a sense of lack of resolve in those states might diminish British commitment to the other states. Correglia told him that he should not be concerned because for all of the states that remained allies with the British, the Royal Navy would do its utmost in their defence. The doge recommended that she continue her relationship with me and report any new information she gleaned. She would thereafter report nothing new, as everything that I knew at the time had already been told to her in detail. She was, however, very keen on continuing the relationship, and she set about the preparation of dinner for that evening.

As I mused about the forthcoming dinner with Dolly, I reflected on the circumstances where several of my fellow naval officers had entered into intimate liaisons with women in distant ports, especially when they had been at sea for extended periods of time. Without deciding a specific intent in the development of my relationship with Dolly, I went to her villa with a vulnerability resultant from years at sea and an innate yearning for a woman's company, which I would not deny. I was a mortal man after all.

"Welcome, Captain," she said upon my arrival. "You are so prompt that I am sure the time of day can be set by your actions."

"You flatter me, Dolly, but I have so anticipated this dinner with you that I almost came early. Also, I would be pleased if you would call me Horatio."

"Thank you, Horatio."

The dinner was marvellous, consisting of thin pasta with red tomato sauce and pieces of lamb. I particularly relished the warm and delicious bread rolls and salad of mixed greens covered with a light dressing of cream and pesto. It was followed by baked pears in a sauce of reduced wine and honey. Nothing that I had been served in *Agamemnon* could compare, and to my taste, the dinner eclipsed even that which had been served at the doge's banquet. After Correglia brought an ornate snifter with Italian brandy, I sipped it deeply, feeling totally sated and at peace with the world. She asked if I knew what my mission would be after my ship and been repaired, and I replied that I knew only that I would again join the fleet of Admiral Hotham in the blockade of Toulon. Our conversation then turned to personal matters with my asking where she was born and grew up. Correglia answered that she was born in Florence and grew up chiefly in Parma. Much of her schooling had been attained in Switzerland, where she learned French and English. She then put her hand on mine, stroking it lightly, and asked about my childhood. I described growing up in Burnham Thorpe, the death of my mother, and my experiences as a midshipman in the Royal Navy. I described in some detail the illnesses I had suffered in the East Indies. I described my tour of duty in the Caribbean and my relationship with Prince William Henry, and I spoke proudly of my recent role in the capture of Corsica.

At the end of my story I added, "Through all of the misfortunes I have had to endure, I believe it is for a reason, and I feel with all my heart that I shall have a great destiny."

"I am certain that it will be so, Horatio," she responded. She then took both of my hands and stood up. I rose and looked into her face. She paused for a long moment and said, "Horatio, I am deeply pleased to be with you in these momentous and troubling times. I have the strongest of attraction to you because you are a strong man at a time in our history when there is a desperate need for good and strong men." She then kissed me on the cheek and looked admiringly into my eyes. The moment for me was precipitous, breaking into a growing flood of emotion as she added, "Horatio, I would very much now desire to take you to my bed and to have love with you there." Without thinking, I placed my hands upon her face and kissed her, rekindling a passion that had for two years been unknown. She led me into her bedroom and slowly undressed, revealing the ample figure of a mature and beautiful woman. When I began to unbutton my uniform, she stopped me and methodically undressed me. Our first lovemaking was brief but tumultuous, as I could not – nor did I feel the need to – restrain the passion that took me to an explosive consummation. Unlike my years spent with Fanny when her response had been restrained and sometimes cold, Dolly was not simply responsive but active, encouraging, and resonant with sounds of excited breathing that were reactive to my every movement. When I had reached my apex, it had been magnified by her gasps and the tightening of her hold upon me. As we lay together in the afterglow, Dolly slowly stroked my chest and whispered Italian phrases in my ear that I could not understand except that they were evidence of shared satisfaction and contentment. We slept embraced, and before we rose in the morning, I remembered the instructions that had been given by Elsinore so many years earlier in Jamaica. I kissed Dolly softly to awaken her and began the methodical and gentle exploration of her as I had done with Elsinore so many years before.

For the next four months I was a contented man and simply dismissed any thought of guilt over breaking my marriage vows, accepting the relationship as a marvellously satisfying interlude within the drama of conflict that otherwise would define a life at sea. I would frequently and openly entertain fellow officers at my villa over dinners prepared by Dolly, and frequently they would correspond about the affair and the doting way in which I treated my new mistress. She was a hot, rich cup served up by the fortunate hand of fate, from which I was happy to drink deeply.

Meanwhile, my infrequent letters to Fanny continued to be a general reportage of circumstances within the fleet with some expressions of endearment from time to time. Just prior to my departure from Leghorn in March 1795, I wrote to Captain Locker, *"My health is extraordinarily good and I feel myself seven years younger than when I left England."* It was perhaps in part the effect Adelaide Correglia had upon me, but when I left Leghorn, I knew that the sweet affair was over.

Action with the Ca Ira

My return to the fleet brought immediate action. Four days after our sortie from Leghorn, I joined with Admiral Hotham's fleet at a time when orders from the *Directoire Nationale* in Paris commanded that Admiral Martin, then commander of the French fleet, sail out of Toulon in order to protect a convoy of troops bound for an attempt to retake Corsica. Martin's reservations about the preparedness and competence of his fleet would prove to be well placed, as two of his ships, the *Ca Ira* and *La Victoire*, collided shortly after they left Toulon. The *Agamemnon* was part of a squadron shadowing the French movement. From the quarterdeck of *Agamemnon*, I saw the collision. The *Ca Ira*, a frigate of eighty-four guns, lost her foremast and main topmast. To make matters worse, the masts with all of their sails and rigging crashed down upon her deck and covered not only the deck itself but all of the shrouds and sheet lines that were attached to the other manoeuvring sails as well. She became a crippled ship, and feeling very much like a lion noticing a crippled zebra, I went on the attack. The fact that *Ca Ira* carried twenty more guns than my *Agamemnon* meant nothing.

After I evaluated *Ca Ira*'s condition I shouted, "Mr. Hinton, clear the decks and beat to quarters. Have the gunners double load the cannon with round shot," I added. "Wear to port and make for her stern. Then backhaul the sails. We shall sit there and have our business with her."

As *Agamemnon* approached, the broadside guns of *Ca Ira*'s starboard quarter were able to train upon us and began firing with some effect. I had ordered full sail to minimize the time when our ship would pass through the rain of fire. I intended the action to be very close and instructed Hinton to manoeuvre *Agamemnon* athwart the stern of *Ca Ira* and then to reef and backhaul sails, and deploy sea anchors, bringing *Agamemnon* essentially to a dead stop. The first broadside we fired at the stern of the crippled ship destroyed her stern guns, and each successive cannonade tore gaping holes in her thin oak siding until the entire stern was effectively blown away.

Each successive broadside of double shot destroyed bulkhead walls down the entirety of the ship. As each twelve- and eighteen-pound shot shattered the athwart-ship bulkheads, wooden pieces would fly out through the air as deadly shrapnel, maiming and killing with a furious effectiveness. After major structures were blown away, *Agamemnon's* guns were loaded with rounds of grape shot and fired repeatedly down the length of *Ca Ira's* decks in a veritable hailstorm of destruction. Main deck guns were loaded with bar shot and chain shot that effectively shredded sails and tore away her yard arms and rigging.

Agamemnon and Ca Ira

I wrote in the captain's log, "*Scarcely a shot appeared to miss, and by one o'clock in the afternoon the Ca Ira was a perfect wreck, her sails hanging in tatters, topmast, mizzen topsail and crosscheck yards shot away.*" For whatever reason, I neglected to mention that almost two hundred French sailors lost their lives in what was a veritable shooting gallery exercise for *Agamemnon's* gun crews.

Meanwhile, the main body of the French squadron had turned to provide defence of the *Ca Ira*, and Hotham, characteristically reluctant to engage in a full encounter, ordered me to break off contact. The next morning the British fleet sighted the French frigate *Censeur* attempting to tow the shattered *Ca Ira* back to Toulon. After a brief action both ships struck their colours and were taken. In order to encourage a full fleet action against the French, I requested and was granted a conference with Hotham.

"Sir, we have a wonderful opportunity to deal a decisive blow to the French which will end any significant part they may play in the entire Mediterranean Sea. They have many ships, but they obviously have inexperienced officers and crew. They are ours for the taking, and we must act now," I strenuously suggested.

"Captain Nelson, we have achieved our mission for the time being. We have frustrated their attack upon Corsica, and we have captured two of their ships of the line. I am not willing to risk my fleet having any negative effect cast upon it so long as we can stand strong and continue our blockade of Toulon," Hotham responded. Then he added, "It shall be well for us to repair to Spezia for a period of repairs and recuperation, and that shall be my order."

Tame and Slow Measures

I returned to *Agamemnon* with disappointment and frustration. As the *Agamemnon* lay in Spezia, making repairs of the damage it had received in the approach to *Ca Ira*, I vented my frustration in a letter to Captain Locker,

> *We make but a bad hand of managing our fleet. I am absolutely at this moment in the horrors, fearing from our idling here, that the enemy may send out two or three sail of the line and some frigates to intercept our convoy which is momentarily expected and which, if taken, would ruin all of our affairs in this country, but we are idle and lay in port when we ought to be at sea. In short, I wish to be an Admiral and in the command of the English fleet. I should very soon either do much or be ruined. My disposition can't bear tame and slow measures. Sure I am that had I commanded our fleet, the whole French fleet would have graced my triumph, or I should have been in a confounded scrape.*

Back in England, Admiral Hood was making a formal reassessment of British resources in the Mediterranean, and in a report to the Admiralty he recommended that a minimum of twenty ships be added to the Mediterranean fleet. However, the Admiralty was generally of the opinion that the Channel Fleet had first priority, and First Lord Spencer precipitously, and very unfortunate to the effectiveness of the Royal Navy, sacked Hood. When I discovered that Hood would not be returning, I wrote to my brother,

We have been cruising here for a long month, every moment in expectation of reinforcements from England. Our hopes are now entirely dwindled away, and I give up all expectation. Oh miserable Board of Admiralty! They have forced the first officer in our service away from his command. We are tired and fatigued with our laying off here doing nothing; ... now even expectation is worn out. I hope I shall be ordered home but at present, I see no prospect of it. I am tired of this business, however, I hope peace will come very soon and send us all to our cottages again.

Peace, however, would not be at hand. On the continent the Austrians began an offensive campaign by crossing the Apennines and capturing Savona on the Italian coast near Genoa. Any further advance depended upon the British Navy's ability to prevent communication among French forces in Toulon and along the Riviera. This task had been given to me with a squadron of five frigates in addition to *Agamemnon*. However, it became apparent that far more ships would be required for interrupting commerce and communication along such an expanse. There were simply too many fortified harbours in which French coastal craft could seek refuge. Admiral Hotham retained the heavy ships under his own command for the continued blockade of Toulon and protection of Corsica. I sent numerous and urgent requests for additional ships, but all of my entreaties were ignored. The result was that French communication along the Riviera remained intact.

In November, Bonaparte launched a counterattack that pushed the Austrians back across the Apennines. Shortly thereafter the Admiralty made a momentous appointment, as Vice Admiral John Jervis hoisted his flag in HMS *Victory* and sailed for the Mediterranean to relieve Hotham. The appointment of Jervis became a master stroke at a time when a strong commander was needed. Britain's previously staunch ally, Prussia, had terminated an unsuccessful campaign on the Rhine, and in May, they made peace with France. Holland, which previously had been occupied by French troops, formally joined France as an ally, and in July, Spain announced its neutrality. This required a thinning of the Channel Fleet, as the Admiralty was required to dispatch a squadron to stand off Dutch harbours to prevent the passage of timber and hemp from Holland to French ports.

Toward the end of 1795, the French resolved to make dual thrusts simultaneously at its remaining enemies, Britain and Austria. Its two most successful generals, the twenty-six-year-old Napoleon Bonaparte and Lazare Hoche, were given momentous tasks. Bonaparte was ordered to drive across Lombardy and to take Vienna. Hoche was to assemble and prepare an army to launch an amphibious assault against the British Isles. Vice Admiral Laurent Truguet was appointed fleet admiral to provide naval support for both campaigns.

Truguet was given a free hand in reconstituting the navy and set about to restore the authority of line officers in all branches of administration and to remove the influence of political agents who had controlled naval administration during the rampant republican regime. Bonaparte assumed command of the Army of Italy and launched what I could only reluctantly describe as a brilliant six-week campaign that cleared the Austrians from Lombardy. He then captured Livorno, depriving the Royal Navy of one of its most valued ports. Palermo and Naples were also lost as allies. King Ferdinand was forced to close his ports to our ships. Corsica also became vulnerable, as military successes of the French attracted support from the majority of French nationals. An invasion by Hoche – or Bonaparte – was anticipated.

In Spain, to obviate a French invasion, the Assembly of Spain declared war against Great Britain. This was a serious blow to British fortunes, as Spanish ships were generally regarded as having excellent design and sailing qualities, even though their officers and crew were considered to be far less professional as compared with their British counterparts.

Jervis Arrives

Admiral Jervis arrived on the scene in November 1795, and I immediately sent him a full report of operations along the Riviera. In the report I was candidly critical of Hotham's non-responsiveness to my request for a sufficient number of ships necessary to carry out the communication blockade successfully. When I met with Jervis in January, my spirits were significantly raised, as he paid me high and sincere compliments for the aggressiveness of my actions and my perseverance in carrying out my duties with only a few ships under my command. To my great delight, Jervis offered me command of the ninety-gun *St. George*. I, however, requested that I remain in command of *Agamemnon* because of what I described as an ironbound commitment to my valiant officers and crew. Jervis said that he understood and admired my decision. He further remarked that when my flag arrived on my promotion to rear admiral, he would like me to stay under his command. I agreed wholeheartedly.

Admiral Jervis

The first meeting with Jervis was rather long, and we shared extensive opinions and thoughts over strategies that should be employed in the Mediterranean. I was entirely won over by all that Jervis had to say and wrote to Fanny, *"Although I wish to get home, yet my fair character makes me stand forward to remain abroad."* Concerning Jervis, I added, *"Reports say the French will have their fleet at sea again. If they do I think they will now lose the whole of them, for we now have a man of business at our head."*

My bond with Jervis was further cemented when the admiral authorised me to fly the broad pennant of a commodore, although I would not in fact be appointed formally until August of the next year. Still my sense of pride was magnified, and my commitment to the new commander was intensified.

In June 1795, Jervis recommended that I should shift command to the seventy-four-gun HMS *Captain*. The request was made because of the deterioration of *Agamemnon* after years at sea and significant damage that could not fully be repaired following the encounter with *Ca Ira*. I acquiesced to the request but took with me most of the officers and many of the valued crew from *Agamemnon*. Hinton, to my distress, remained in charge of *Agamemnon* until its new captain arrived.

Mediterranean Withdrawal

Throughout 1796, the French had steadily accumulated a sizable army in Brest under the command of General Hoche. In December, the Brest fleet consisted of more than fifty vessels, and General Hoche's army of fourteen thousand was fully embarked. On 16 December, the French fleet with Hoche's army aboard departed Brest and headed for Bantry Bay in Ireland, where support from Irish separatists was anticipated. The operation, however, was stillborn from the first day when an early winter storm with high seas and gale force winds scattered the fleet. Two other gales followed in quick succession, forcing the ships to straggle independently back into French ports. News of the ill-fated operation was received by the Admiralty in London with a jolt of alarm, and it was concluded that defence of the home islands would become the Royal Navy's singular priority. Admiral Jervis was given orders to withdraw his fleet from the Mediterranean and to evacuate Corsica. Jervis sent a dispatch to me. *"All our operations are at an end by the arrival of orders to evacuate Corsica and retreat down the Mediterranean. You must go over to Bastia immediately and cooperate with the Viceroy in retiring the troops from their outposts, keeping Leghorn under blockade to prevent a descent pending this difficult operation."*

To me, retreat from the Mediterranean was a humiliation and a negation of the years I had spent assuring control of that vital sea. I wrote to Sir William Hamilton, *"I lament in sackcloth and ashes our present orders, so dishonourable to the dignity of England whose fleets are equal to meet the world in arms, and of all fleets I ever saw, I never saw one equal in point of officers and men to our present one, and with a commander-in-chief fit to lead them to glory."*

For the moment, however, my orders were to evacuate Corsica as quickly and as orderly as possible. Of great concern was the general sense among Corsican municipalities that a renewed French control was inevitable. In fact, Corsicans at Bastia seized all English property and had stationed a ship across the entrance to its harbour. The English viceroy, Sir

Hugh Elliot, was sequestered in his quarters. When I arrived at Bastia, my action was immediate and compelling. I wrote,

> *In one quarter of an hour I settled the whole matter for I sent for the Council ... who acted for the Corsicans or French, and told them that if the sequester was not taken off and the armed Corsicans retired, and that should I be molested in taking off what I thought proper, I would blow the town down. From this moment all was quiet and I saved £200,000 worth of stores and property. In short, it is impossible to say what I did not do ... Not a sixpence worth of property belonging to the merchants was left behind. The pleasure of my own mind will be my reward, except having the honour to maintain Viceroy, Sir Hugh Elliot and about forty other persons at an enormous expense.*

When I arrived at Gibraltar, I was invited to confer with Admiral Jervis, who complimented me on reports that had been received concerning what Jervis described as my *"assiduous actions"* in the evacuation of Corsica. Jervis then ordered that I shift my flag to the frigate HMS *La Minerve* and to take another frigate named the *Blanche* to assist in the evacuation of Elba. Having utmost confidence in my judgment, his orders included the comment, *"Having experienced the most important effects from your enterprise and ability, upon various missions ... I leave entirely to your judgment the time and manner of carrying this critical and arduous service and of its execution."*

As I proceeded to Elba, two enemy frigates were sighted, and I immediately set upon them. I later described in a letter to my brother, *"When I hailed the Don, and told him, 'This is an English frigate' and demanded his surrender or I would fire into him, his answer was a noble one."*

The Spanish captain replied, *"This is a Spanish frigate, and you may begin as soon as you please."* A short and furious battle ensued with the Spanish ship, the *Santa Sabina*. I wrote:

> *I have no idea of a closer or sharper battle: the force of gun nearly the same, and nearly the same number of men. After half an hour, the Santa Sabina's mizzenmast was shattered and fell. I asked him several times to surrender during the action, but his answer was − "no sir, not while I have the means of*

fighting left." When only himself and his officers were left alive, he hailed and said he could fight no more and begged that I would stop firing.

The Spanish captain, Don Jacobo Stuart, was rowed to *La Minerve* and surrendered his sword to me, which was promptly returned with my compliments and congratulations for having put up such a noble fight. For the balance of the day action was directed toward repair of battle damage on both *La Minerve* and *Santa Sabina*. The *Blanche* had also engaged the Spanish frigate the *Ceres* after a short battle had taken her. That action had been taken out of sight of *La Minerve*, and when I saw another frigate approaching, I assumed it to be the *Blanche*; however, it was a Spanish frigate, and soon afterward several other Spanish ships were sighted under full sail, approaching and cleared for battle. In order to lead the approaching ships away, the *Santa Sabina* hoisted British colours and tacked to a different direction away from *La Minerve*. The *Santa Sabina* was soon overtaken and struck its colours rather than be destroyed by the overwhelming Spanish numbers. In that action I lost the sailing crew that had been put aboard the Spanish prize and had all of its officers captured by the Spanish, including a lieutenant whose career would be significant in the highest points of my life, Thomas Hardy. After they subdued *La Sabina*, the Spanish ships made after me. I had ordered every inch of sail to be put aloft to make as much distance as possible between *La Minerve* and the three ships in pursuit. Fortunately night soon fell, and the Spanish broke off the chase.

I proceeded to Elba and penned a letter to the General of Spanish forces at Cartagena,

The fortune of war put La Sabina into my possession after she had been most gallantly defended. The fickle dame, fate, returned her to you with some of my officers and men in her. I consent, Sir, that Captain Don Jacobo may be exchanged, and at full liberty to serve his King, when Lieutenants Culverhouse and Hardy are delivered into the garrison at Gibraltar ... I also trust that those men now prisoners of war with you will be sent to Gibraltar. It becomes great nations to act with generosity to each other, and to soften the horrors of war.

In response, Lieutenant Culverhouse and Hardy were allowed to return to Gibraltar, and Captain Don Jocobo Stuart was in turn sent to Cartagena with my good wishes.

When I reached port at Elba, I was surprised and delighted that accounts of my actions had preceded me and that Commanding General De Burgh had arranged a dinner in honour of me and my officers. When we arrived for the dinner, the general stepped forward to greet me with a firm handshake while the band played "See the Conquering Hero Comes" and "Rule Britannia". However, there was a complication. General De Burgh had received no orders to evacuate Elba. I, however, knew that my mission was very clear and direct. In confirmation I wrote to Jervis, "*I shall withdraw nearly all the supplies from this place whether the troops quit it or not, and will reduce the naval force here as much as possible. The object of our fleet in future is the defence of Portugal, and keeping in the Mediterranean the combined fleets. To these points my orders go and I have no power of deviating from them.*"

I also wrote to First Lord Spencer, "*The General is without orders, and the Army are not so often called upon to exercise their judgment and political measures as we are; therefore the General feels a certain diffidence. But let me be clearly understood in not intending to convey the slightest criticism of the General's conduct.*"

Having taken on board all of the stores my ship could carry, I divided my squadron into two convoys in order to reduce the possibility of total loss from capture by the enemy fleet, now so numerous in the Mediterranean. I set sail from Elba on 29 January 1797, with a convoy of ships packed with everything I could muster from the island. As I made the transit to Gibraltar, I decided to look into Toulon and Cartagena for signs of the combined French and Spanish fleets. At Toulon, I observed a small number of French ships, none of which were first-rate men of war, and at Cartagena, there were no ships. When I arrived at Gibraltar in February, I learned that the French fleet under Rear Admiral Villeneuve had passed through the straits weeks earlier, and just one week earlier the Spaniards had slipped into Algeciras.

Much to my delight, I found Culverhouse and Hardy at Gibraltar, where both were returned to my command. When we departed Gibraltar to join with Jervis in the Atlantic, my squadron came under chase by a large force of Spanish ships that had been watching us closely from Algeciras. Racing at full sail to outdistance the Spaniards, an unfortunate accident occurred that would be a personal test to me and – as I like to believe – a proof of my commitment and courage. One of my crewmen fell overboard, and I ordered that a jolly boat be lowered with Hardy to retrieve the seaman. Rather soon, because of current flowing through the straits, the jolly boat had been carried far astern of *La Minerve*. Hardy signalled that the seamen could not be found, and his boat crew began rowing frantically to re-join the ship. The crew was in mortal danger of being captured by the lead Spanish ship when I ordered, *"By God, I will not lose Hardy. Back the mizzen topsail."* This slowed the ship almost to a stop until Hardy and his crew could be thrown a line to bring them aboard. The captain of the lead Spanish ship was apparently disconcerted by my manoeuvre and responded by shortening his own sails so that his following ships could catch up for a combined engagement. Soon Hardy's jolly boat was retrieved and brought aboard while he and his men climbed the lifelines to safety. I then ordered every sail hoisted. *La Minerve* regained its speed and was soon out of shot range from the pursuing Spanish. The incidental action I had taken by not abandoning my crew while still managing the safety of my ship became short-term legend among the ships of my command and later became repeated over and over again by governmental officials who had been evacuated and were on board to witness the event with the same anxiety and relief as had been experienced by my officers, my crew, and me.

At nightfall I was entertaining more governmental officials who had been brought aboard at Gibraltar when the officer of the watch sent a messenger to advise me that ships had been sighted on the horizon. I immediately went to the quarterdeck to determine if it was Jervis's fleet, but as the *Minerve* drew nearer, I could see that it was not Jervis but the Spanish fleet that had chased us through the straits the day before. Apparently the ships had been dispersed and were regrouping, as they were sailing slowly with mizzen and mainsails half-reefed. Wanting to gain as much information as possible concerning the size of the fleet, I ordered the *Minerve's* sails reefed likewise and ordered the large war flag to be taken down and replaced by a smaller standard flag in order to avoid announcing the fact that a British ship was monitoring the enemy number and course. Fourteen ships were counted, but it seemed that more were over the horizon, and it became apparent that they were on a north-east course bound probably for Cadiz. As night fell and no more information could be gleaned, I ordered that full sail be set for best speed to join with Admiral Jervis.

When the British fleet was sighted the next morning and rendezvous was made with Jervis, I ordered a jolly boat to be launched and went immediately to HMS *Victory* to make a full report of the Spanish force, their location, and their course. I took with me lieutenants Culverhouse and Hardy, who had been prisoners of the Spanish and who could provide information about the condition of the Spanish ships and their crews. I was complimented in my actions by Admiral Jervis, who ordered that I immediately return to command of HMS *Captain*. He then ordered a signal that all division commanders form in a single battle line and that they clear for action.

As I returned to command the *Captain*, what was to become the Battle of Cape St. Vincent was about to begin.

Chapter 8

The Battle of Cape St. Vincent

I remember vividly and despondently how the arrival of Admiral Jervis on the Atlantic station meant that the Mediterranean had been conceded to become a French and Spanish lake. Good fortune had been embraced by the French, whose armies under Napoleon had quickly cleared northern Italy, suppressed opposition from the Italian states, and were pushing vigorously toward Vienna. Napoleon seemed invincible, and General Hoche was assembling a grand army in Brest for a renewed invasion of Britain. However, they needed a fleet to carry the army to the shores of England.

The Spanish fleet, newly allied to France and under command of Admiral Don Jose de Córdoba had departed Cartagena in early February 1797 with orders from the French Admiralty to take his fleet of twenty-five warships and a convoy of supply vessels to join with Admiral Villeneuve's force already there. It was intended that the combined fleets, augmented possibly by another squadron to be sent from Holland, would be able to outnumber and overpower our Channel Fleet and to land General Hoche's invasion army. The immediate question would be whether Jervis could take the Spanish fleet out of the equation.

Admiral Córdoba had been told by a transiting vessel that the British force consisted of nine warships, which he believed would not engage his far larger fleet or which he could overpower with little difficulty. It also meant that drawing his force into a single battle formation was not essential. Many of his ships had become scattered in the pursuit of British merchant targets of opportunity that were sailing southward along the trade route to Africa. In the early morning, hearing reports of suspicious sails, he sent Admiral Moreno's squadron of five heavy ships to investigate. As the morning mist lifted, Córdoba was surprised to see the British battle force of fifteen ships advancing from the north and cleared for action. His own fleet was caught divided, with Morino's squadron to the East.

Throughout the night watch officers aboard HMS *Victory* could hear signal guns being fired by the dispersed Spanish ships. Therefore, Jervis was aware that the enemy fleet was nearby and attempting to assemble. A signal was hoisted in *Victory* for all British ships to prepare for battle. He also sent another signal, *"A victory to England is very essential at this moment."*

As soon as the Spanish fleet came into sight, Captain Robert Calder, on the quarterdeck of *Victory* and with his telescope against his eye, counted the Spanish ships. It was at this moment that Jervis discovered how severely he would be outnumbered. The count of the enemy was relayed by Calder:

"There are 8 sail of the line, Sir John."
"Very well, Sir," Jervis responded.
"There are 20 sail of the line, Sir John."
"Very well, Sir."
"They are 25 sail of the line, Sir John."
"Very well, Sir."
"There are 27 sail of the line, Sir John."
"Enough, Sir, no more of that; the die is cast, and if there are 50 sail, I will go through them," Jervis tartly replied.

Jervis noted that in the distance, the Spanish were loosely formed into groups. He signalled to his fleet of fifteen ships, "Form a line of battle ahead and astern of *Victory* as convenient."

When his order was carried out, the British fleet had formed a single tight line of battle, sailing on a southerly course to pass between the two Spanish groups. They were, in order – HMS *Culloden*, seventy-four guns; HMS *Blenheim*, ninety guns; HMS *Prince George*, ninety guns; HMS *Orion*, seventy-four guns; HMS *Colossus*, seventy-four guns; HMS *Irresistible*, seventy-four guns; HMS *Victory*, a hundred guns; HMS *Egmont*, seventy-four guns; HMS *Goliath*, seventy-four guns; HMS *Barfleur*, ninety-eight guns; HMS *Britannia*, a hundred guns; HMS *Namur*, ninety guns; HMS *Captain*, seventy-four guns; HMS *Diadem*, sixty-four guns; and HMS *Excellent*, seventy-four guns. At a distance, the former viceroy, Sir Hugh Elliot, who had transited from Elba with me, keenly watched the unfolding scene aboard the fast sloop HMS *Lively*. The accounts of his observations would become a formal report to be repeated and embellished by newspapers throughout England.

At midmorning on 14 February 1797, St. Valentine's Day, the single battle line of British ships under full sail with decks cleared, crews at battle stations, and all cannons loaded, bore down from the north upon the divided groups of Spanish ships consisting of twenty-one ships, fifteen of which were clustered around Admiral Córdoba's *Santissima Trinidad* to the west and five ships to the East under command of Admiral Morino. As the British force approached, Jervis hoisted a signal, "Engage the enemy."

Eighteen minutes later he hoisted, "The admiral means to pass through the enemy's line."

Aboard *Captain*, after I had taken our station in the line of battle, I called all of my officers to the quarterdeck and spoke to them. "Gentlemen, this is a day that we have lived for. Each of you has committed his spirit and his soul to our great country and to its king. We are now faced with one of the greatest threats that our nation has ever seen. The French are amassing armies on the continent. They intend to invade and enslave us. The only thing that can prevent this is the Royal Navy. Today we shall indeed be the Royal Navy, each one of us. You are the finest officers on any ship and upon any sea. I know that you will fight this ship with the greatest determination and courage that will reflect the substance of your valour and the love of your country. Today we will save our country. God bless you, and now let us attend to our business."

I then walked from gun crew to gun crew throughout the ship and shook the hand of each chief gunner's mate, repeating to each gun crew, "Today we shall write a glorious page in English history. I know you will fire rapidly and true. You are the best gunners on earth. God bless you and know this in your heart – today you will save England."

I then turned to each sail-handling crew of boatswain's mates and told them, "My fellows, the manner in which you smartly fix the sails of the ship as we come through the battle will be essential to the victory we shall have. You are the best seamen I can ask for, and today we shall have a great victory." When I returned to the quarterdeck, I ordered that every cannon be loaded with double shot, which meant that an additional round was added to each of the *Captain's* twenty-eight thirty-two-pound cannon, twenty-eight eighteen-pounders, and eighteen nine-pounders.

As the lead ship, *Culloden*, passed between the Spanish groups, Jervis had a signal order hoisted, "Tack in succession to starboard and engage the enemy."

The signal essentially meant that each ship following *Culloden* would tack to the right and follow in *Culloden's* wake. Jervis decided to keep his forces together and chose to attack the larger body of Spanish ships to his right, essentially ignoring the smaller group to the left. *Culloden*, under command of my friend and colleague Captain Thomas Troubridge, tacked with such speed and verve that Jervis was reported to shout, "*Look* at *Troubridge. He tacks his ship to battle as if the eyes of England were upon him; and would to God they were, for then they would see him to be as I know him, and, by heavens, Sir, as the Dons will soon feel him.*"

At that moment I felt a frustration that rattled my soul. Oh, how I would love to be Troubridge at the head of our ships. What a glorious show of warship command! What a time to do what every naval officer dreams and lives for! Gallant Tom Troubridge, fearless friend, was taking his ship and all of England with him first into the enemy's breach and would deal the blows against an enemy who wanted to savage our homeland. I could not wait to get at the Dons. I could not wait to shred their sails and batter their freeboards. This day was a day for which almighty God had given me life.

As the middle of our line tacked to starboard, Admiral Moreno and his southerly force found their range close enough to engage our turning ships. For more than half of an hour the Spanish southerly force exchanged fire with *Irresistible, Victory, Egmont,* and *Goliath,* but soon Moreno broke off, probably fearing that severe damage or destruction of his squadron would leave his convoy of supply ships entirely vulnerable. Likely he also believed that judging from the furious and destructive effect of the short exchange, his squadron could not match the fury of our guns.

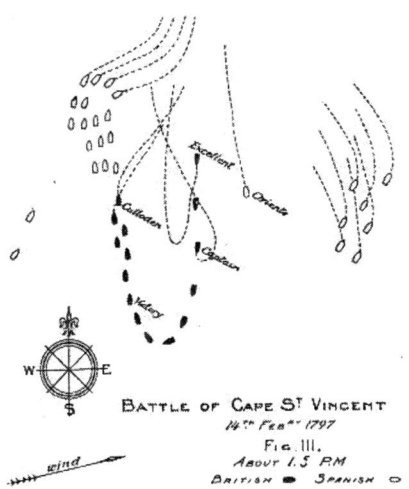

BATTLE OF CAPE ST VINCENT
14TH FEBRY 1797
FIG. III.
ABOUT 1.5 P.M
BRITISH ■ SPANISH ○

When HMS *Victory* came to her tacking point and turned toward the main body of the Spanish fleet, Jervis could not have been more pleased. He had split the Spanish forces and held off an attack by the forward van. However, he could not have been certain that his force would be able to isolate the rear. To see more clearly the disposition of all ships, he climbed a ladder to the highest point on *Victory's* rear deck. As he stood there and looked above the smoke that had enveloped *Victory,* cannon shot decapitated a seamen standing nearby, covering the admiral in blood and brains. One of the officers of *Victory* rushed to the admiral, fearing that he had been hurt. However, Jervis immediately replied, *"I am not at all hurt, but do, George, try if you can to get me an orange."* There is conflict in the account of this exchange as to whether Jervis was addressing a naval officer or a marine officer, but the solecism of addressing the officer by his first name, "George," was repeated over the years as an example of Jervis's equanimity under stress. The man who rushed to Jervis's side was probably the *Victory's* commanding officer, Captain George Grey. A midshipman was sent below and returned quickly with the orange. Jervis bit into it, rinsing his mouth, and declared, *"Much better!"* Because conclusive engagement had not been attained, he was still fearful that the Spanish might veer to the west and then southward to join up with the remainder of the Spanish fleet, gaining a much greater numerical superiority. He clearly wanted British ships to prevent a Spanish escape and to fight them on as near an equal footing as possible. He hoisted an order to HMS *Britannia* and Admiral Charles Thompson, commanding the rear division, including me in the *Captain,* "The leading ship shall tack northward and others in succession."

He then hoisted a signal to all ships, "Take up suitable stations for mutual support and engage the enemy as arriving in succession."

Jervis wanted his rear division, consisting of *Britannia* and the five ships astern, to turn for reinforcement of the lead ships beginning at that moment to engage the rear of the Spanish group. However, for whatever reason, as none was recorded, the *Britannia* did not acknowledge the signal. Nor did it turn as ordered. *Britannia's* failure to tack meant that with every passing minute, the British van became isolated and seriously outnumbered. It is also somewhat inexplicable why, if Jervis wanted the rear ships to close the enemy and to engage them more directly, he did not order a simultaneous tack, which would have brought all of the rear ships toward the enemy as a line-abreast phalanx instead of having each turn slowly in succession after *Britannia.*

Breaking Formation

I saw both signals hoisted from *Victory* and realized that *Britannia* had either failed to see the signal to tack or was not capable of tacking because of the loss of her main jib. More importantly I saw that the lead ships of the Spanish van were turning to the West, either intending to escape toward the main Spanish fleet or to envelop the isolated front line of British ships. Each circumstance was foreboding, and I then decided to take what I knew would be considered an extraordinary measure but one that the developing Spanish actions absolutely required. I ignored the signal to tack in succession and shouted an order the *Captain* to be turned away from the wind, wearing out southward in an arc that would take us to the east and north between *Diadem* and *Excellent* and toward the main Spanish force. When I gave the order to wear out of formation, Captain Miller approached and said, "Sir, we are under orders to tack in succession after *Britannia*."

In response I answered, "We are also under orders to engage the enemy, and at this point I do not see *Britannia* in a tack. It is also clear that the Dons are either trying to escape or they are turning back upon our outnumbered ships in the van. I cannot allow that. We are going to engage the enemy!"

"Very well, sir. By God, very good, and well done, sir!" was Miller's enthusiastic answer.

In the moments that passed, *Culloden* was engaged with the rear of the Spanish group. *Victory* and three others were closing, and to the east our single ship, the *Captain*, was under full sail, heading for the main body of the Spanish ships to prevent any escape or execution of any advantage they might inflict upon our outnumbered van. I would confront the first enemy that came within my reach. A freshened wind pulled at our sails, and I could hear the shrouds creak and sail ends flutter frenetically in what was otherwise a quiet deck. I ran to the forward railing of the quarterdeck and shouted as loudly as I could, "This is the time, men. This is our time." Gunners standing by their cannon, marines with rifles at ready arms, and boatswains standing by their rigging all raised their hands in response, and what had been stern and apprehensive scowls became wide eyes and smiles that told me wonderful things. They were ready. We were thrusting ourselves at the enemy, a warship ready to fight – to fight together. My fierce and gallant friend Tom Trowbridge was not alone, as we were now with him – in the lead.

My manoeuvre could have been suicidal, as our approach to the closest ship, the 112-gun *San Nicolás*, exposed *Captain* to broadside fire not only from the *San Nicolás* but from three other of the Spanish main group, all significantly larger and possessing exceedingly more firepower than *Captain*. Had their gun crews been trained in accuracy and rapidity of fire to match that of the British, my approach may have been devastating. As it was, the enemy fire was fearsome in thunderous sound, emitting enormous clouds of yellow-grey smoke, tall geysers of water rising from the sea as thirty-two-pound shot fell short or whizzed overhead. However, some of the Spanish shot did find its mark, stripping away rigging, shredding sails, and destroying the *Captain's* wheelhouse. I shifted rudder control to the manual after steerage station and continued to keep headway with the sails remaining. I was struck in the abdomen and shoulder with impact splinters. These were not serious wounds, but they broke my skin and caused stains of blood to mark my tunic and leggings. The rigorous training of gun crews of the *Culloden* and *Captain* gave our fire a deadly effect, so much that Córdoba abandoned his eastern tack and resumed a north-eastern course. On *Victory*, Captain Calder approached Jervis and said, "*Sir, the Culloden and Captain are separated from the fleet. Shall I recall them?*"

"*I will not have them recalled,*" Jervis shouted. "*I put my faith in those ships. It is a disgrace that they are not supported and are separated.*"

Following the order of Jervis to engage the enemy more closely, HMS *Prince George* sailed ahead and was also pouring effective fire into *San Nicolás*. When the *Excellent* came up (under Captain Cuthbert Collingwood), she also gave rapid and accurate broadsides into the *San Nicolás*, causing her to luff up. I exclaimed, "*Look there, Miller, my old friend and messmate, Collingwood, has passed up two prizes that he subdued and is helping us like the true Captain that he is. God save him and England love him.*" After he fired several broadsides into the *San Nicolás*, Collingwood moved ahead and joined the *Blenheim* and *Orion* in battering the *Santissima Trinidad*.

By this time the *Captain* was largely in tatters, as she had been exchanging fire not only with the *San Nicolás* but from as many as five other Spanish ships that were within an effective range. I then made a fateful decision. Even given the quality of *Captain's* crew, it would have been futile to continue to attempt to overcome the *San Nicolás* simply with exchange broadside fire. Only one option remained. We must board her. I gave the order, "Miller, have Lieutenant Pearson assemble all of his deck marines here together with all of the starboard gunners and as many seamen as can be spared. We are going to board her. Trim the sails to get every breath of wind you can and take the head of the ship into her."

Miller ordered the rudder put over, and the *Captain* lurched toward the *San Nicolás*, which, in the meantime, had lost its top mainmast and became entangled on its port side with rigging of the *San Josef*, another 112-gun battleship. I spoke to the assembled boarding party, "Men, we are going to take that ship by boarding her. You are to get into her as fast as you can and clear the quarterdeck of all their officers and crew. You are then to take as much of the main deck as shall be necessary. This is how we shall conclude our victory today."

I noticed that Captain Miller had drawn his sword and was standing at the head of the boarding party, but I then ordered, *"No, Miller, I shall have that honour. You shall remain in command of the Captain."*

The *Captain's* bow crashed into the port side of the *San Nicolás* with a thudding crunch, and our bowsprit became entangled in the enemy's rigging. To the assembled boarding party, all carrying swords, pistols, knives, and clubs, I raised my sword and shouted, "Let us go, my gallants. Glorious victory or death!"

Lieutenant Pearson, in command of our red-coated marine soldiers, was the first man into the enemy ship. He jumped onto her mizzen chains with Edward Berry, my first lieutenant, and they led the attack party of marines and seamen across the main deck.

Captain, San Josef and San Nicolas

In the rear a marine broke a gallery window on the *San Nicolás's* starboard quarter, and I jumped through the window, followed by others as fast as possible. I found the inside cabin door fastened, and I had marines batter down the door with the butts of their rifles. Some Spanish officers fired their pistols through the door, but to no effect. Having broken open the door, my marines fired through the door, and the Spanish brigadier fell while retreating to the quarterdeck. I pushed immediately onwards for the quarterdeck, where I found Commander Berry in control and the Spanish flag being hauled down. I passed with my people, and Lieutenant Pearson over the port side to the forecastle, where I met two or three Spanish officers, prisoners of my seamen. They each raised one arm and delivered me their swords with the other.

Pistols and muskets were fired onto our boarding party from the stern gallery of the *San Josef*, the other 112-gun Spaniard still entangled with the *San Nicolás*. I directed the marines to fire into her stern to suppress the fire and called out to Captain Miller, ordering him to send more men. Miller sent them straight away, and as soon as they arrived, I raised my sword and ordered the boarding of the *San Josef*. With Commander Berry and Lieutenant Pearson at my side, we led our party across the railings and onto the main deck of the *San Josef*. As we spread across the deck, the Spaniards at the guns raised their hands, as we were immediately ready to shoot them down. At that moment a Spanish officer looked over the quarterdeck rail and shouted, *"No mas. Nos rendimos!"* Lieutenant Pierson quickly translated, "Captain, they surrender!" With this most welcomed information, it was not long before I was on the quarterdeck, where the captain presented his sword to me with a bow and said that their admiral, Don Francisco Winthuysen, was below, dying of his wounds. I asked him on his honour if the ship was surrendered. He declared she was, upon which I gave him my hand and instructed him to call on his officers and ship's company and tell them accordingly. He did so. Thus, on the quarterdeck of the Spanish first-rate battleship, extravagant as the story may seem, did I receive the swords of the vanquished Spaniards, which I accepted and gave to one of my boarding party, who put them under his arm, rather like a bundle of sticks.

I remained on board the captured Spanish ships while they were made secure. Because the date was February, Admiral Jervis was concerned that night would fall quickly, and he ordered our fleet to secure the prizes that had been captured but otherwise to break off contact. As the *Victory* with other ships in company came past our *Captain* alongside its prizes, they doffed their hats and cheered.

Admiral Jervis hoisted the signal calling all ship captains to the *Victory*. As they arrived, Jervis embraced each and gave hearty congratulations for the great victory that had been won. I was the last to arrive and slowly climbed, tired and spent, onto the quarterdeck of *Victory*. I had not taken the time to wash my face or to change my uniform. Admiral Jervis had washed off the blood of the seaman who had been killed next to him, and all of the other captains stood in uniforms that were essentially unblemished. As I stepped onto the quarterdeck, I saluted the admiral and said, "Reporting as ordered, sir. I apologise that I have lost my hat." And looking at my fellow captains, I said, "Good evening, gentlemen." There was brief time of silence. I stood there before the admiral and our fellow officers. My face was still black from cannon smoke. My uniform was soiled and torn. There were bloodstains on my abdomen and trailing down my leggings.

Jervis looked me over for an extended time. He did not speak, and I believed that I saw tears well in his eyes. He walked to me and enveloped me in his arms. When he broke the embrace, he said, "There are no words to say how happy you make me feel. You have done more than I ever could have expected, and I give thanks to God that you are alive."

A very significant account of all that had taken place during the battle was made by Sir Gilbert Elliot from the decks of the frigate *Lively*, who wrote to me, "*Nothing in the world was ever more noble than the transaction of the Captain from the beginning to the end and the glorious group of your ship and her two prizes, fast in your grip, was never surpassed, and I daresay never will be.*"

Aftermath

It was now five o'clock on a glorious St. Valentine's Day, and the light of day was beginning to fade. The *Santissima Trinidad*, although she had at one point struck her colours, was never boarded and was taken by Córdoba clear of the British fleet, escorted by two Spanish frigates that had just arrived on the scene. She would later join up with the ships of Moreno's group and would be towed along with three other disabled ships back to Cadiz. Jervis ordered his fleet to a starboard tack, taking them to the north along with our four captured prizes. In retribution for his defeat,

Admiral Córdoba would later be dismissed from the Spanish Navy and forbidden ever to appear at court.

In the battle British casualties amounted to seventy-three killed and 327 wounded. Spanish casualties amounted to more than a thousand men killed or wounded. Almost one-third of the British casualties were suffered aboard the *Captain*. After the battle Captain Calder of the *Victory* had mentioned to Jervis that I had taken my ship out of the line of battle while under orders to tack in succession. Jervis tartly responded, "*It is so, but if you ever shall do likewise, I will also forgive you.*"

Full of exhilaration and pride, I wrote that I had received the praise of "*everyman from the highest to lowest in the fleet.*" And it was true that throughout officers' wardrooms and seamen's mess decks of every ship, accounts flourished about the manner in which I had taken my single seventy-four-gun frigate out of line and had dashed headlong to attack a Spanish warship of far greater firepower. The fact was repeated with praise that after I had subdued the *San Nicolás*, I myself had led my crew in racing across her deck to conquer the even larger *San Josef*. However, Jervis's formal report to the Admiralty was exceedingly brief, giving full account of the results of the action while mentioning no captain by name. Jervis had written earlier that he had come to disdain self-publicity. "*I perceive is the fashion of people to puff themselves and no doubt you have seen, or will see, some of these accounts ... I write not a syllable about myself except touching my health, nor shall I, but to state the intrepidity of the officers and people under my command.*" He did, however, send a follow-up letter to First Lord Spencer in which he did mention officers by name. The most effusive praise was given to Captain Trowbridge, who "*led his squadron through the enemy in masterly style and tact the instant the signal flew.*" He wrote that "*Commodore Nelson contributed very much to the fortune of the day as did Captain Collingwood, accounts as to both men which were payable compared to their true contributions.*"

It is important to note that formal dispatches are only part of the publicity given to battles. Of great significance were reports by Sir Gilbert Elliot and his secretary, Colonel Drinkwater, who, as I noted, had witnessed the entire battle from the decks of HMS *Lively* and were eager to make reports of what they had witnessed. I was quite aware of this and wanted to make sure that they were apprised of my own recollections. On the morning of 15 February, I was rowed to the *Lively* to see both gentlemen, but I was disappointed that Elliott had gone for a meeting with Admiral Jervis. However, Colonel Drinkwater told me that as the *Lively* would bear the glorious news to England, I should provide him with as many particulars of my ship's conduct and my own conduct in the capture of the two ships we had boarded. This provided the perfect opportunity to lay out in full detail all of the undertakings of my leadership and the role of the *Captain* in bringing the battle to a marvellous triumph. Drinkwater took copious notes of everything that I described, which included all of my actions and thought processes in taking my ship out of line, having the audacity to attack much larger ships, boarding the first and then the second, as well as describing the supportive roles of other ships, including particularly Trowbridge in the *Culloden* and Collingwood in the *Excellent*. Drinkwater's account, however, failed to mention the actions of the *Prince George*, commanded by Admiral William Parker, and this negligence would always be carried with some resentment by Parker.

Drinkwater also mentioned the subject of honours and titles to be bestowed in consequence of the action and ventured that I would probably be made a baronet. Drinkwater later wrote that his "words were scarcely uttered when I placed my hand on his arm and, looking most expressively in his face, I said, '*No, no; if they want to mark my service, it must not be in that manner … If my services have been of any value, let them be noticed in a way that the public may know me and them.*'" I had already pondered the possibility of a baronetcy and had grave misgivings about such an honour because it would require at least a small fortune to support the title. It became clear that my preference was to be named as a Knight of Bath, a designation that not only allowed me to follow my name with the honourable initials "K. B." but would also allow me to wear a very prominent star upon the left breast of my uniform.

When the *Lively* reached Plymouth with Elliott and Drinkwater aboard, they found this prominent naval city to be acutely concerned about impending attacks from French and Spanish fleets. The Bank of England had suspended transactions, and the whole of the country was in a state of alarm. News was delivered by the *Lively*, including not only the report by Jervis but more importantly, the descriptions of Elliott and Drinkwater. The immediate effect of the accounts of the battle seemed like parting clouds to bring glorious sunshine in breaking a storm of anxiety. Jervis's report was immediately published as a special edition of the *London Gazette*, and when it became known that Elliott and Drinkwater had been present at the battle, their lengthy and colourful accounts of the battle became the most important news of the year.

Drinkwater had prepared a full description, which he called the *Narrative*, including sketched diagrams of ships' positions in various stages of the battle. The *Narrative*, published in the *London Times*, the *Sun*, and local news journals throughout England, became the chronicle of a great triumph as a product not only of what Drinkwater and Elliott had witnessed but an account of the battle related to Drinkwater by myself.

As the *Narrative* was being published, eager newspapers were printing full details of another detailed account – my own. Immediately after the battle I had written letters which I called, "*A few remarks relative to myself in the Captain, in which my pendant was flying on the most glorious Valentine's Day, 1797,*" to my old friend, Prince William Henry (now the Duke of Clarence), Admiral William Waldegrave, and my mentor, Captain Locker. To Locker I had written, "*If you approve of it, you are at perfect liberty to insert it in the newspapers, inserting the name of Commodore instead of the first person pronoun, 'I'.*" My letter said, "*As I do not write for the press, there may be some parts of it which require the pruning knife, which I desire you to do without fear.*" However, Locker straightaway gave the lengthy report to newspapers without applying any cut of an editorial pruning knife. It was published up and down the length of Britain, read by all who were able to read, and discussed at parties of nobleman, church parlours, garden clubs and throughout pubs with the full pride and adoration of a relieved people. As news of the battle was fully digested in cities, towns, and villages, celebrations were held with the ringing of church bells and bonfires where officials and populace gathered for speeches and cheering.

From Bath, Father wrote to me, "*The name and services of Nelson have sounded throughout the city of Bath, from the common ballad singer to the public theatre. Joy sparkles in every eye, and desponding Britain draws back the sable veil and smiles.*"

Controversy

The combination of selective memory and personally oriented myopia among men with assertive personalities has a way of elevating oneself and one's accomplishments above those that greater circumspection would record fair praise. Thus, it was to some extent concerning the publication of my remarks. I had written that when the *Captain* crossed over, joining the van, she took her place at the head of the British line in front of *Culloden*. Because the cloud of our own smoke blowing astern may have occluded my vision, I may not have seen that the *Blenheim*, *Prince George*, and others in the van were close behind *Culloden* and joined fervently in the action. I had given no account of this action that appears to have been a true fact of the battle. The omission was particularly resented by Admiral William Parker, who had commanded the van. He took issue with my statement in a lengthy letter to me, which he arranged to have published in several journals. He stated in his letter, "*So different from your statement, very soon after you commenced your fire, you had four ships pressing on board of each other, close to your rear.*" I later altered my remarks and allowed that my description, in which he claimed to have battled for an hour without support, may not have been correct as to time.

There were some reports from other sources that I had also taken the Spanish battleship *Salvador del Mundo*, which, in fact, had been subdued by Captain James Saumarez, commanding the *Orion*. I, however, readily admitted to this correction, an act which palliated resentment by Saumarez, an active and ardent naval officer.

The honour of Knighthood of the Bath was awarded to me on 17 March, and I was given the honour, in the words of the first lord of the Admiralty, "*to mark the Royal approbation of your successful and gallant exertions on several occasions during the course of the present war in the Mediterranean, and more particularly, your very distinguished conduct in the glorious and brilliant victory obtained over the fleet of Spain by his Majesty's fleet on 14 February last.*"

Chapter 9

Frustration at Cadiz

In May 1797, I remember how splendid it was to re-join the force of Admiral Jervis, who was standing off Cadiz, blockading what remained of the Spanish fleet that was comprised of ships that had escaped the Battle at Cape St. Vincent. While most were battered and crippled, many others were fresh, as they had not taken any part in the engagement. More importantly, all of the convoy that had been escorted by Admiral Moreno was now safely sequestered there, containing the valuable equipment and stores that had been intended to be delivered to the combined fleet at Brest. I was still sailing in HMS *Captain* but was fearful that she was not fully capable of carrying on as a warship. Her masts were badly battered, and the integrity of planking along her freeboard and surrounding the gun ports would not hold up to another serious broadside. She had been a true and valiant warship, but her glorious deeds had taken a toll that would mean the end of her service.

When I joined the admiral's fleet, I was rowed to his flagship and there reported for instructions. As I entered his stateroom, the admiral rose from his desk, smiling, and offered me his hand. He then addressed me by my familiar name, which suggested that our relationship was not simply that of senior to subordinate but also as friend to friend. It pleased me greatly.

"My good man, Horatio, it is so good to see you. I hope that all the publicity and diversion following the battle has now settled down and we can tend to our work again."

"Sir, I present myself with a completely refreshed body and state of mind, ready to do anything and everything that is necessary to carry out our business here," I replied.

"As you know, I would very much like to draw out the Dons from Cadiz so that we can finish them off. There are twenty ships of war in Cadiz and probably more merchantmen full of materials that the French would very much like to get to Brest, and should they be able to do that, the combined forces then amassed there would be of major concern to the homeland. I doubt, however, that they will come out, and here we are, trailing our wakes up and down the coast waiting for something that simply may not happen."

I suggested, "Sir, I'm sure you have considered sailing into the harbour and engaging them there."

"Indeed I have, but the combination of guns not only from their warships but also from the many batteries that surround the port are simply too many. We would perhaps be able to inflict major damage upon them, but I fear that the price we would have to pay in damage to our own ships would be too dear," he responded with a grimace.

"That seems quite probable, sir. I stand ready to carry out any orders you may give me, but I have to recommend that my dear ship, *Captain*, be sent home for refurbishment. She is very wounded and presently in a very deplorable condition."

The admiral replied, "I have taken that into account and would have you transfer your pennant to the *Theseus*. She is very fresh and seaworthy. It is my desire also that you assume command of the interior squadron closest to the port. I'm quite mindful that you are the junior flag officer on the station, but it is my belief that I can count on you to carry out my instructions to the fullest, even though dangers to the interior squadron will likely be the greatest."

"Sir, I will be proud to assume that command and will eagerly carry out any operation you may deem appropriate," I immediately answered, delighted at the prospect of having command of the most important squadron within the admiral's forces. His faith in me was reaffirmed and was something that I would not disappoint.

I returned to the *Captain* and toured the ship, shaking hands with all of the officers, the master gunners, and the chief boatswains, telling each of the deep affection and admiration I had for them and would carry until my final day. I then transferred my pennant to HMS *Theseus*, a fit and ready frigate of seventy-four guns, outfitted quite similar to *Captain*.

This was also the time of the great and unfortunate mutinies within the British Navy. Seamen of the Channel Fleet, the North Sea Fleet, and at Nore had taken over many of their ships and rejected the leadership of their officers. Admiral Jervis, however, had experienced no such uprisings. The management of his ships had been distinguished by keen judgment and solicitous foresight coupled with iron-handed severity. I was quite sympathetic to the plight of ordinary seamen, observing that their lives were indeed hard. They were paid only a fraction of what the merchant crews received and worked under conditions that were, for years at sea, difficult to bear for any man. In fact, I had written to Captain Locker,

> *I am entirely with the seamen in their first complaint. We are a neglected lot, and, when peace comes, they are shamefully treated. But for the Nore scoundrels … I would be happy to command a ship against them. The Admiralty has evinced a lack of resolve to improve the lot of seamen while, at the same time, has failed to support disciplinary actions taken by commanders at sea, and went so far as to criticise a captain for hanging a convicted mutineer on a Sunday. Had it been Christmas day instead of Sunday, I would have executed him. We know not what might have been hatched by a Sunday's grog.*

I had been advised that there had been discontent and trouble aboard the *Theseus* and was keen to ensure not only that my crew was treated as well as could be accommodated but that they also understood that discipline would be severe in the event of unruly conduct. To my great satisfaction and even delight, within a month of my assuming command a paper was left on the quarterdeck, a document expressing the devotion of the ship's company to me and pledging *"that the name of Theseus should become as renowned within the fleet as the name of Captain."*

The stringent blockade we had imposed upon Cadiz presented the Spaniards with a severe dilemma. They had been requested but not ordered by the National Council in Paris to leave port and engage us, obviously because their ships and stores were very much needed to augment the force at Brest. However, they remained in port largely, I believed, as a result of the thrashing we had administered to them at Cape St. Vincent. Nevertheless, rumours of a Spanish sortie persisted, and my squadron was in a constant state of tension and excitement. I relished the prospect of action with the Dons and wrote to my brother, *"We are in the advance day and night, prepared for battle; bulkheads down, ready to weigh anchor. I have given out a line of battle – I to lead; and you may rest assured that I will make a vigorous attack upon them at the moment their noses are outside the port. I do not need another ship. If they come out, there will be no fighting beyond my squadron."*

To increase further the pressure upon the Spaniards, Admiral Jervis planned a bombardment against the town and the ships in port, the coordination of which he entrusted to me. A former Dutch frigate had been refitted in Gibraltar with a mortar and a howitzer, and it was sent to us with a new and appropriate name, HMS *Thunder*. On a clear moonlit night, the *Thunder*, under command of Captain Ralph Miller, the captain who had served so ably under my command at the Battle of Cape St. Vincent, took a distant position from the town beyond the range of the Spanish batteries and began the bombardment. As we had expected, a Spanish flotilla of gunboats was sent out to attack the *Thunder*. Because we had anticipated such a move, we had gathered all available boats from the squadron to resist such an attack. I ordered Miller to take an attachment of boats and head off the Spanish. However, given the number of Spanish boats, which far outnumbered those of Miller, I ordered that all remaining boats be filled with available seamen and marines. I also decided to lead those boats myself. Seamen aboard the *Thunder* seemed reluctant to leave it, but when the chief boatswains mate shouted, *"Who will follow the Admiral?"* I found that my contingent of boats was quickly filled with able men armed with cutlasses, rifles, and pistols.

The Battle in the Boats

As the enemy boats drew closer, I noticed that they were not only more numerous but also larger than ours, and I felt some anxiety as we approached. However, the stage had been set, and we had to overcome them. I lifted my sword and cried out, "Let them feel our fury, my lads. Fire your pistols and then board them. Get at them, and we shall win this thing!" To my pride and delight, my men raised their guns and swords, and I heard shouts of "Let us get them!" and "We are ready!" As we came close and could see the faces of the Spaniards, volleys were exchanged, and I saw that our fire had been most effective. The bow of our boat slammed against the lead boat. I shouted, "Attack!" and leapt across to the enemy boat followed by a stream of our men slashing with their swords and shouting furiously at the Dons. The action was intense, and even though we were outnumbered, the spirit of our fight was far greater than theirs. As providence would have it, I was most fortunate to have near by my side a coxswain named John Sykes, who on two occasions quite probably saved my life. As I was engaged with several of the enemy's men, another slashed at me with his cutlass, but Sykes raised his arm and suffered the blow that was intended to sever my head. Soon Miller's boat arrived to assist us, and when his men began leaping across, the enemy commander dropped his sword, raised his arms in surrender, and cried out, *"No mas! No mas!"*

The other Spanish boats that had not been engaged then turned and headed back for Cadiz. Miller took his men back to his boat and chased them toward the harbour while I sat on the captured boat with the wounded and bleeding Sykes cradled in my arms. I looked upon this gallant man and said, "Sykes, I cannot forget this." Later, good to my word, I made special mention of Sykes in my dispatch and recommended that he be made a

lieutenant. However, Sykes had not served sufficient time as a petty officer to qualify for promotion, but he was awarded a gunner's Warrant of Merit.

I believe it true that my leadership in the engagement of the boats was crucial to its success, for as I have found so many times, no order can ever be as effective as the force of leadership in doing what has to be done. I wrote to my brother, *"It was during this period that perhaps my personal courage was more conspicuous than at any other in my life."*

I also became aware that the description of my actions was passed throughout our ships from seaman to seaman and from officer to officer as an act of courage and leadership. I was also humbled that in the admiral's official report he described me as *"always present in the most arduous enterprise."* He also wrote personally to me, *"Every service you are engaged in adds fresh lustre to British arms and to your character."* The regard that my fellow officer felt for me was very much like a badge that I wore upon my soul as proudly as I wore the insignia of the Order of Bath upon my coat.

By the end of spring Admiral Jervis realised that the Spanish were unlikely to leave the port of Cadiz voluntarily. He decided to enforce a total blockade, allowing no ships of commerce in or out of the port, not even those from neutral countries. He knew that Cadiz was a principal port for Spain's colonial trade and that the local economy depended upon the commerce it received for merchant ships. It was his intent to ruin the economy of Cadiz in hopes that the commercial community would insist that the Spanish fleet come out to end our blockade. He also ordered my squadron to anchor at the mouth of the harbour, within sight of the entire Cadiz community. Captain Collingwood described to his father-in-law that we were *"parading under the walls of Cadiz,"* and I wrote to my friend Dixon Hoste, *"We are looking at the ladies walking the walls and the mall of Cadiz."* We learned later that the blockade had been extremely detrimental to the spirit of the city. Bankruptcies in the commercial community increased, and the economy of the city had been effectively shut down. By July it appeared to Admiral Jervis that the standoff of inaction would continue indefinitely, and he concluded that more serious action was necessary. On the nights of 3 and 4 July, the *Thunder* began another distant bombardment of the city itself, causing serious damage to its buildings and considerable death among its inhabitants. Still, even with the continuing bombardment, Jervis concluded that the Spanish would simply not come out. On 14 July, Jervis ordered me to withdraw my inshore squadron and rejoin the main fleet. The admiral ordered a continued but more distant blockade and requested my conference with him to plan our next move.

Several other ship commanders and I dined with the admiral on roast pork with fresh greens and fruits that had been bought from merchants who were allowed to come out of the city to sell their fresh and dearly needed products. The admiral appeared in very good spirits, which was somewhat surprising to me in light of our lack of success in drawing out the enemy fleet over so many arduous months. Soon, however, the reason for his buoyant spirit was revealed.

"Gentlemen, I offer a toast to you for your very effective actions in making this blockade as tight as a good purser's money strings. The Dons sit in port and refuse to come out to fight us. Meanwhile, all of the goods and stores which are needed in Brest are here and not there. We shall continue this blockade in hopes that perhaps someday they will come out, and when they do, we shall have at them. However, something else has been made known to me that you will find interesting. Our intelligence reports indicate that there are two, perhaps three ships carrying the viceroy of Mexico that have recently departed Havana carrying a cargo of gold reputed to be worth six or seven million pounds sterling. It would be a nice trick to intercept and capture their ships and to put the gold we find in circulation at London. I believe it would probably cover the cost of our war expenses for more than a year. It is also something badly needed, as I have been apprised that there have been several runs upon the English banks. Captain Nelson, I would like you to take a small squadron of frigates to intercept the viceroy and take his bullion."

I smiled broadly and responded, "Admiral, there is nothing else that I can think of which would please me more." I had always dreamed of perhaps making my fortune by finding some Spanish ship full of gold that I could capture as a prize to be factored by Alex Davison ... and bring me a fortune. It would also mean that I had contributed not only my loyal service but also chests of gold to my king.

With *Theseus*, three other frigates, and a fast cutter, I set out for a patrol of the Atlantic sea lanes from North Africa to the southern tip of Portugal. In order to broaden the scope of our search, I ordered my ships to spread out in a broad fan of reconnaissance and drew them in every three days to assess what they may have found. Weeks passed, and there was no sign of the gold ships. Our orders were to search for three weeks, which everyone considered to be more than enough time for the viceroy's ships to have made the passage. Searching assiduously and finding nothing, we returned to the blockading force that reported to the admiral that the search had been devoid of golden targets.

"This does not surprise me," the admiral said, "for rumour now has it that the viceroy and his ships may be sheltered in the Spanish Canary Islands at the port of Santa Cruz in Tenerife."

"If that report is true," I replied, "then we can take them there."

"Yes, that is possible, but Santa Cruz is reported to be heavily fortified, and we will need a sizable contingent from the army. They can probably only come from the forces still remaining at Portoferraio in Elba. I will request evacuation orders from Governor O'Hara at Gibraltar, and you will take ships to assist in the evacuation."

"Sir," I immediately replied, "I shall be delighted to do so, and in the meantime I will draw up an outline for an attack upon Santa Cruz."

Following our meeting I researched our charts of the port of Santa Cruz and filled in an array of possible defences, which I imagined would be stationed at the port's entrance. My proposal for action was drawn up on lines very similar to my successful capture of Capraia in Corsica the year before. I projected that by landing approximately four thousand troops, we could seize command of the heights dominating the town. In addition, the squadron of frigates with perhaps a gunship could be positioned so that we could bombard the town. Once the heights were taken, a demand could be sent for surrender of the treasure ships as a price to avoid bombardment and further destruction of the town. When my plan was finished, I met again with the admiral.

"Admiral, I believe my plan cannot fail of success. It would result in a near mortal blow to the Spanish treasury and would greatly enrich our own." Desiring that he would not think that my primary motivation was the prize money to be garnered from the capture of Spanish gold ships, I added, "And I know with you, sir – and I can lay my hand on my heart and say the same – it is the honour and prosperity of our country that we wish to extend."

"This is a well-drawn plan, Horatio, and you will be pleased to know that Governor O'Hara has already ordered the evacuation of Elba. But the evacuation force is in need of armed escort. I trust that you can provide that, and I will order two other frigates to accompany you."

"I am ready, sir," I immediately responded, delighted with the admiral's positive response to my plan and eager to make it possible.

I departed that evening with three ships to accompany the evacuating forces from Elba. The passage to and through the Strait of Gibraltar was uneventful, and good winds gave us an excellent speed. Surprisingly, as we approached Elba, we found the evacuating convoy already underway and provided them escort to Gibraltar. When I rejoined Admiral Jervis off Cadiz, I found him in a rather sour mood. He had requested an assault force against Santa Cruz from General De Burgh but had been turned down, and a subsequent request had also been denied by Governor O'Hara, who stated that he believed the evacuated force from Elba was necessary to ensure the defences of Gibraltar. Undeterred, I decided to lay out an alternate plan.

"Admiral, I believe that we can still accomplish this objective with an extra force of Royal Marines from other ships. They should probably like the idea of action after the endless boredom here. I suggest that they be assigned under the command of Captain Trowbridge. I would be honoured to be charged with the entire operation. I am confident of success."

"Very well, Horatio, but this will be an operation on the edge since we will not have a number even close to the four thousand you indicated in your first plan," the admiral replied.

"I believe we can do it, sir. I am confident of success with the quality of ships and men that are available," I assured him.

On 14 July 1797, Admiral Jervis issued my orders to *"take possession of the town of Santa Cruz by a sudden and vigorous assault. In case of success, you are authorised to lay a heavy contribution on the inhabitants of the town and adjacent district if they do not put you in possession of the whole cargo of the ships present."*

The admiral assigned to me a strong force consisting of three seventy-four-gun frigates: the *Theseus*, *Culloden*, and *Zealous*; three sixty-gun frigates, including the *Seahorse*, *Emerald*, and *Terpsichore*; the fast cutter *Fox;* and a mortar gunboat named the *Terror*. I was also very pleased with the officers under my command, each considered to be shining stars of the fleet – Ralph Miller, Thomas Trowbridge, and Thomas Fremantle. In his parting dispatch the admiral also added an interesting passage that quoted from Joseph Addison's play, *Cato*, "*God bless and prosper you. I am sure you will deserve success. To mortals is not given the power of commanding it.*"

On 15 June, my attack squadron departed from Admiral Jervis's fleet and sailed with ample northerly winds toward Tenerife. I had spent days reviewing charts and imagining how the Spanish would defend the port of Santa Cruz. I knew from dispatches that had been taken from Spanish ships captured earlier in the year that the commandant general of the Canary Islands was an elderly gentleman by the name of Don Antonio Gutierrez. What I did not fully appreciate at the time was that Don Antonio was a distinguished officer who was a veteran of many engagements as well as a talented man in both organizational and leadership respects.

As we made our passage, I called the captains of the accompanying ships together with the commanders of the marine detachments for an explanation and discussion of our battle plan. At the first gathering of my supporting officers, I explained, "Our charts indicate that the port is defended by four large forts and three batteries that run along a six-mile stretch from north to east. Because the town itself is very strongly defended, it appears that a frontal attack is not practical. It is my thought that we pay particular attention to the major outlying fort, the Castillo de Paso Alta, which is about a mile to the north of the town. It has an elevation that gives it a particular strategic importance because of the destructive range of its cannons, estimated in number to be approximately ten or twelve guns. They can fire shot over the entire battle scene. If we can gain possession of the Castillo de Paso, we will control the town. Our landing will be made here on the northerly stretch of beach from which we will make a concentrated attack on the Castillo. Once that fort is captured, I shall send an ultimatum to General Gutierrez that the town will be spared further destruction upon surrender of the gold ships and all of their cargo."

Captain Fremantle asked how the landing force would be organised. I answered, "The whole body of seven hundred seamen and marines will be divided into three companies, each having a master at arms, a boatswain's mate, a quartermaster or gunner's mate, a carpenter with a short broad axe, and a midshipman or mate, all with a lieutenant to command it. Make sure that these men are exercised twice a day and drilled at target practice so that their fire will be true and effective." I looked at Captain Trowbridge and asked, "Trowbridge, will you consent to command of the landing force?"

"I shall consider it an honour, sir," was his immediate response.

"Then it is decided. Our frigates will go ahead with the landing force. We shall land before dawn under cover of darkness and beach the boats at the appointed spot. It is our intention that by this means the Castillo will be surprised and captured before the Spanish shall have time to reinforce it."

There followed a full discussion of the defensive posture of the port as well as the terrain over which the assault would take place. I then issued a set of regulations I had drawn up, ordering that the boats were to be kept together by a towline, one from the next, thus ensuring that they would arrive at the same time. A marine lieutenant was to be posted on the beach to make sure that the boats returned quickly to the ships to collect additional men and supplies. Special ladders fitted with iron reinforcements were to be used instead of the wooden ones which so often broke in the heat of action. In order to make an impression upon the enemy, the seamen should also be dressed as much as possible in spare marine uniforms so that the Spanish would think that they were being assaulted by a full body of regular troops.

Disaster at Tenerife

On the morning of 21 July, the squadron lay to, deploying sea anchors so that boats could easily pass from one ship to another. The landing parties were assembled. Two hundred men from *Theseus* went to the *Seahorse*, two hundred from the *Zealous* to the *Emerald*, and 150 from *Culloden* to the *Terpsichore*. Our total force would be comprised of approximately nine hundred men, a number I thought entirely sufficient for the operation. The transfer took most of the day, and in mid-afternoon we were able to get underway, trailing landing boats behind each ship. We made our way to Tenerife, having it in sight by late afternoon of 22 July. It was our hope that laying offshore, we could avoid being sighted by the Spaniards and could take them by surprise the next morning.

In the dark before first light of dawn the first landing parties disembarked from the *Seahorse*, *Terpsichore*, and *Emerald*. They headed straight away for their landing point, but we soon experienced conditions that had not been anticipated, conditions that would prove to be very detrimental. There was a strong offshore wind blowing, and a strong current was running from west to east. As dawn began to break, the landing party was still a mile from shore, and the Spaniards in the port came alive with alarms sounded and the running of defence forces to their positions. Trowbridge immediately realized that his boats would be naked targets for the Spanish defenders and decided to recall the entire landing force. He then immediately came to me to consult about what should be done next. We decided to adopt what had been discussed as a second option – to attack the heights above the fort to its north and storm it from there. In the meantime I would begin a general bombardment of the town and its defences. As my guns began to fire, Trowbridge landed his men on the beach north of the port and began a steep ascension of the rocky heights. However, they found that the terrain was not as it had been shown on the charts because a deep chasm lay between their appointed position and the Castillo. An attack up the near-vertical chasm on the fort side would expose his men to a constant hail of murderous fire. Trowbridge decided to retreat with his entire landing party back to our ships.

The painfully unsuccessful first landing presented me with a harsh predicament. The Spanish forces were now assembled and ready. The entire operation was at risk, and my reputation was at stake. Admiral Jervis had ordered me to take Tenerife with "*a sudden and vigorous assault.*" Everything was up to me, as I had passionately sought the operation and had all but guaranteed its success. I could not let the admiral down, and I could not have my men leave the Canary Islands with the taste of defeat in their mouths. I called a conference of my officers.

"Gentlemen, we shall not leave the Canary Islands without victory. As each of us has experienced and as we all know, the outcome of battle between two forces will always be determined in victory on the part of the side that displays the greatest will and fighting spirit. Tactically I have decided that we must do something that is not expected – something that will be a surprise and will lead to victory here. I've decided that we shall make a night assault upon the port, and I shall lead it."

The faces of each of my captains seemed stern and resolved. Nothing was spoken for a long while. Then Captain Fremantle said, "Sir, I am with you." Captains Trowbridge, Hood, and Bowen quickly voiced their assent to Fremantle's remark, something that was very dear and reassuring to me.

On the night of the attack I sent a message to Admiral Jervis that said, "We are not in possession of Santa Cruz. All has hitherto been done which was possible, but without effect. This night I, humble as I am, will command the whole force destined to land under the batteries of the town, and tomorrow I will lead an attack to grasp at victory." As our landing parties prepared, my stepson, Josiah, appeared beside me, armed and equipped to join the landing party. I commented to him that it would be a dire blow to his mother if both of us were lost in the action. He responded that he was resolved to go and serve at my side. I decided not to order him to remain on board the *Theseus*, believing that the Almighty would determine our fates. Hours before dawn on 24 July, a thousand men were assembled in the ships' boats. Pieces of canvas were tied around the oars to muffle their sounds in the water, and we began a slow and steady progress toward the shore, aided in our journey by large swells that sometimes carried us toward the beach. All went well, but as we made close approach only about a hundred yards away, sudden alarms were sounded among the Spaniards' defensive positions, and any effect of surprise was lost.

"All boats must row as quickly as you can. Get to the beach and cross to take the enemy positions!" I cried out as loudly as I could, and every boat made its best speed to the surf line. Captain Bowen was the first to reach the shore. After he landed, he made a mad dash to the closest battery, where he and his men overran it. Fremantle also landed but was wounded on the beach. Thompson followed and was also wounded. The surf was wild and heavy, and several boats smashed against rocks. By then the Spanish forces were assembled and began firing constant volleys of musket shot through the dark and into our ranks. Bowen and his first lieutenant were cut down and died. The scaling ladders that had been intended for the walls of the Castillo were lost in the surf as were many rifles along with their ammunition and powder.

165

Amidst the clamour of crashing surf and the sound of gunfire all around, my boat approached the shore, and as I drew my sword before jumping over into the shallow water, I felt a strong thud in my right arm and looked down to see that it was shot through and bleeding profusely. The effect of the shot was to spin me around, and I fell upon the planking of the boat. Josiah, who had been behind me, grabbed me and said, "Admiral, you are badly hurt." He then quickly stripped off his shoe, removed his stocking, and then tied it around my arm to stanch the bleeding.

"I am shot through the arm. I am a dead man," I cried out. Josiah comforted me by pointing out that his tourniquet had stopped the bleeding and that I would not die. His statement gave me great reassurance, and in truth, I believe that the immediate action of Josiah did save my life and prevented me from bleeding to death then and there. As the men of the barge began rowing me back, I asked that I be lifted up so that I could look about the battle scene. The thunder and flashes of cannon and musket fire continued on the island, and I could see alarmingly that the cutter *Fox* was sinking at a very rapid rate, with all of its men jumping into the water and flailing about. I ordered that two boats to be dispatched to pick up as many as they could recover. I later learned that the *Fox* had taken a hit below the waterline which caused it to go down like a stone. As we rowed away from the island, the nearest ship was the *Seahorse*, and Josiah stated that I should go board in order to be attended to by its surgeon. However, I knew that its captain's wife, Betsy Fremantle, was aboard, and I did not want her to be shocked by seeing me in my shattered state. Josiah protested that I must get to a surgeon as soon as possible, but I replied, "*Then I will die. I would rather suffer death than alarm Mrs. Fremantle since I can give her no tidings whatever of her husband.*" We rowed on. When we reached the *Theseus*, Josiah and several seamen put their hands upon me to help in getting aboard, but I refused, "*Let me alone. I have got my legs and one arm.*" I was able to ascend the ladder to the quarterdeck with my right arm dangling at my side. On the quarterdeck the officers as usual saluted me by taking off their hats, and I returned their salutes with my left hand, wanting to appear as capable and normal as possible.

The surgeon of the *Theseus*, a very competent man named Thomas Eshelby, brought me immediately to his surgery and recorded in his log, "*Admiral Nelson suffered a compound fracture of his right arm by a musket ball passing through a little above the elbow. An artery was divided. The lower part of the arm was immediately amputated and opium was given.*" I wonder now why, in the name of God, opium was not administered before the amputation, as the pain was excruciating because of the cutting of the flesh and the stark coldness of the surgeon's blade and saw. I made note and thereafter instructed all surgeons in the fleet to warm their instruments before surgery. When the amputation was over, I was asked what should be done with the arm that was taken off. Should it be embalmed and sent to England for burial? I said no and instructed that it be thrown into a burial hammock of one of the brave fellows who had been killed.

On the island I was advised later that Captain Trowbridge had joined his force with those of Miller and Hood and occupied a position near the centre of the town. Their situation was precarious, having only a bit more than three hundred men and being subject to surrounded cross fire from the Spanish forces as well as cannon shot from the Castillo and its nearby batteries. Trowbridge, stout fellow that he was, made a gallant gesture. He sent a sergeant of marines and two captured Spanish officers under a flag of truce with the demand that Don Antonio Gutierrez surrender the town. Don Antonio's reply was immediate. "*I shall not*," he said. Trowbridge then tried another bluff. He sent Captain Oldfield under a flag of truce with the threat to burn the town if it did not surrender and if the ships in port were not handed over. The general felt very confident that he commanded the entire situation and sent a reply to Trowbridge that there would be no negotiation. The matter had come to a bitter stalemate, with the British force essentially surrounded, fatigued, and dying of thirst in the heat of the day. By the end of the afternoon Trowbridge sent a message to Gutierrez that if he should be allowed freely and without molestation to remove his people, taking all of their boats and equipment, the attack upon the town would be ended. In response, Gutierrez sent a soldier under a white flag to state that a truce would be observed and the British could openly come into town, retrieve their materials, and withdraw.

When Trowbridge's men came into the square, they were reviewed by all of the forces that Gutierrez could assemble, intended to exhibit as strong a force as he could in order to discourage any further assault. Trowbridge also found that he could not really disembark his force because most of their boats had been lost. In victory, Gutierrez exhibited magnanimity. The wounded were taken to a Spanish hospital. All of the surrendering attackers were given bread and wine. Trowbridge, Hood, and Miller were invited to dine with the general. They declined the invitation and were given butter cake and lemonade. When Trowbridge's force returned to the squadron, I was apprised of Gutierrez's action and was quick to respond with what I intended to be a gentleman's touch. I sent a present to Gutierrez of a cask of English beer and several wheels of cheese with a note that offered "*my sincere thanks for your attention and your humanity to those of our wounded who were in your possession or under your care as well as your generosity to all that were landed.*" The note was written out for me and contained an awkward and hardly readable signature. It was written, as best as I could, with my left hand. The general replied to my letter with appreciative thanks and sent a present of some Malmsey wine. On the afternoon of 27 July, our squadron received our survivors along with the dead and wounded and then departed the Bay of Santa Cruz and headed north for Cadiz.

The body of Captain Bowen was buried at sea to the muffled sound of the marines' drums and gun salutes. As I looked upon his body entering into the water with hardly a splash, I could only think, *how noble, how honourable, and how glorious it is to die in the dedicated service of that which you hold dear. Good-bye, dear Bowen. Take your place among angels.*

I was feeling remarkably better and very thankful that no apparent infection had set into what was left of my arm. I would have given my whole body for a victory at Santa Cruz, but I could not dictate the terms of life and death or those of victory or defeat, except that in the future I would dictate the terms of preparation and engagement. To that task would be the dedication of whatever remained of my life. It was a grey slate sky and a low murmuring wind that accompanied the silence of our ships as we sailed away from Tenerife, slowly disappearing in the distance. With a dark cloud about my soul, I scribbled to Jervis,

You will excuse my scrawl, considering it is my first attempt ... I am become a burden to my friends and useless to my country ... When I leave your command, I become dead to the world. I go hence and am no more seen ... A left-handed Admiral will never again be considered as useful; therefore, the sooner I get to a humble cottage the better, and make room for a better man to serve the state.

After a slow and tedious voyage during which grey skies and a persistent headwind almost seemed admonishments of our failure, we rejoined the fleet off Cadiz on 16 August. Troubled in spirit and broken in body, I met with the admiral and reviewed my dispatches of our Tenerife action. Throughout the audience Admiral Jervis was warm and solicitous but somewhat taciturn. As I left, he handed me a small envelope, which

I placed in my breast pocket. I was rowed back to my ship and returned to my stateroom, desperately hoping to have some restful sleep that had eluded me for days. As I removed my coat, I noticed the admiral's envelope. I opened it and read his note. *"My dear Horatio, mortals cannot command success; you and your companions have certainly deserved it, by the greatest degree of heroism and perseverance that ever was exhibited."*

When I finished reading, a knot came to my throat, and tears of gratitude filled my eyes. With a sentence he had reached into the pit of my despair, lifted me out, and patched my broken spirit.

Recovery

On 20 August, I was taken to HMS *Seahorse* for the voyage home, and I was very pleased to be welcomed by Betsy Fremantle, whose husband still suffered severely from the wound in his arm. In this particular condition, we again shared a bond. Sailing home was a horribly depressing experience, with headwinds and heavy seas. As the ship was littered with the wounded, the constant banging of the ship's bow into the waves amplified our misery. Throughout the ship there were moans of pain and despair. Captain Fremantle had lost much colour and grieved that his wound was not healing. My own stump of arm, which previously had not given me great trouble, began to pain me very much, requiring from time to time more ministrations of opium. After twelve days we finally reached Portsmouth. As I was helped off the ship and walked awkwardly down the gangway, I was surprised and greatly delighted to be greeted by a cheering crowd. Apparently praise contained in Admiral Jervis's dispatch of the Tenerife action had preceded us and was made known to the populace, most particularly to the people of Portsmouth, who were constantly attuned to everything of importance in the Royal Navy. Waves and cheers of these good people were a salve to my spirit, better than any doses of opium ever could have been.

Fanny was there to greet me, and gingerly embraced my body with a warm kiss upon my cheek. She took me to Admiralty House, the residence of Sir Peter and Margaret Parker, who would always have a great affection for me and whom I had not seen since my convalescence in Jamaica. They were the perfect people to host my return, as I felt that they had always considered me to be something akin to a son. I sent a letter of request to the Admiralty in London, asking that I be permitted to spend a leave time on shore for the recovery of my wounds. While I was at the Parker residence, a number of heart-warming letters of congratulation arrived from Lord Hood, the new comptroller of the navy, members of the Admiralty Board, and Prince William Henry, now the Duke of Clarence, who wrote, "*I congratulate you with all my heart on your safe arrival at last, covered with honour and glory.*" Shortly thereafter, hoping very much that my battered self might still be of some value, I wrote to Admiral Jervis, "*The moment I am cured I shall offer myself for service; and if you continue to hold your opinion of me, I shall press to return with all the zeal, although not with all the personal ability I had formerly.*"

My optimism and spirit had recovered. My arm had not.

From Portsmouth, Fanny and I travelled to Greenwich to visit with my old friend Captain William Locker, who had been appointed lieutenant governor of the Royal Hospital in Greenwich. It was fortuitous that I should go to hospital because my stump had become a fitful problem. There was constant inflammation and pain such that sleep was not possible without the taking of opium or laudanum. The ligatures and dressings that had been applied on board *Theseus* had adhered to the base of the stump and were apparently the cause of a troublesome infection. Changing of the dressings had often been relegated to Fanny, whose sensitive nature did not allow her to tend the wound as it should have been treated, as she did not even like to look upon the ugly, festering area of the stump. I was also experiencing some stinging in my blinded eye that was inspected at length by a team of physicians, including the surgeon general of the army. After much collaboration they decided to do nothing about it, for there was little they could do, concluding that the problem was secondary to the infection of the arm. By a stroke of fortune a doctor named Michael Jefferson, who had been an old service colleague from my midshipman days, came to my treatment. He administered a series of baths and soaks to the stump and tenderly removed all of the dead tissue. The result was that, within a matter of just a few days when he removed the bandages, all of the ligatures came away from the flesh. The pain ceased, and full healing of the stump began, which brought to me a great relief and sense of thanksgiving.

My true recuperation could then begin in earnest. I even began to look upon my partial arm with a sense of humour and gave it a nautical nickname, "my fin." I was able to get about very well and visited a naval hospital at Yarmouth where I saw a young sailor who also had lost an arm. I commented to him, *"Well lad, you and I are both spoiled as fishermen."*

As I went to depart, he said something that touched me deeply. He had tears in his eyes, and choking back sobs, he said, *"Thank you, Admiral. Thank you so much for caring about a broken seaman of so little worth."*

I became suddenly frozen and transfixed in the moment, looking down upon this valiant young man who was still likely in his teen years and whose body had been broken in service to his country. I went over, stood at the foot of his bed, and said in as strong a voice as I could muster, *"My boy let it be known that this Admiral holds you as a treasure to the Royal Navy for the service you have given and the price you have paid. Mend your body and may God bless you to a full life ahead. You will go with my fullest admiration."*

As I left the wounded ward, I hoped that tears that had welled in my own eyes would not streak down my face. I also found out later that the Almighty has measures for just reward. The surgeon general of the hospital, who had accompanied me in my rounds, wrote a letter to the first admiral, Lord Spencer, describing the exchange with the seaman. The first admiral placed the letter in my service jacket and wrote upon it, *"As Admiral Nelson spoke to the boy, so should the country speak to Nelson."* I also learned that the exchange would become lore among physicians in the hospital, the scores of wounded sailors in the hospital, and their families.

During this time I had also appreciated very much the general affections of my wife, Fanny, whose solicitous nature had made her attendant and sympathetic to my needs, although for many reasons we did not share intimate embraces. She was also good enough to have fashioned for me an eating fork with a honed edge that could also be used as a knife, something that would serve me well for all of my remaining days.

As the timing of providence would have it, on 25 September, I attended a formal royal levee before King George, where he formally draped upon me the red sash of the Order of Bath. It was an impressive occasion where I was privileged to kiss the hand of the king and to speak personally with him in a private session. He was cordial and solicitous, expressing his gratitude for my service to the Crown. As I left St. James Palace, my commitment to king and country had been renewed, and within my breast, a sense of unswerving loyalty arose that could never be broken.

As I was recovering in September 1797, a *coup d'état* had taken place in Paris, giving rise to a more hard-line government that came to be dominated by the French military. Peace negotiations that had been underway in Lille were broken off. Earlier French victories had taken Austria out of the war, and it appeared clearly that France was determined to continue her hostilities against Britain, having been essentially subjugated by the entire continent. With the Spanish fleet still firmly blockaded at Cadiz, a new anxiety arose with respect to a Dutch fleet that could possibly join with the French at Brest to pose an immediate threat of invasion against England. In response, Admiral Duncan had been sent to engage the Dutch. When I heard of this proposed action, I wrote to Admiral Jervis, "*I would give my other arm to be with Duncan at this time.*"

I later learned that Duncan had sighted the Dutch fleet off the coastal town of Camperdown and had engaged them in a very unorthodox fashion. Eschewing formalistic lines of battle, Admiral Duncan had quite simply ordered each ship to attack its opposite number ship upon ship. When I heard of this, I knew immediately that it was a stroke of genius because in any engagement where a British ship is pitted against a ship of the enemy, we will prevail. A commander can do no more than to ensure that the rules of engagement should have as the objective the placement of our ships alongside those of the enemy. In that manner we are best assured of the best result. Victory over the Dutch at Camperdown eliminated the possibility of a combined Dutch and French invasion force. With the French fleet remaining holed up at Brest and checked by our Channel Fleet and with Admiral Jervis blockading the Spanish at Cadiz, circumstances allowed that we could refocus our attention upon opposing the free movement of the French out of Toulon and throughout the Mediterranean.

On 19 December, I received orders to hoist my flag in HMS *Vanguard*. At this time our intelligence indicated that Bonaparte intended an expedition not against Britain but against unknown objectives in the Eastern Mediterranean. I was advised that Admiral Jervis had recommended that a new fleet destined for the Mediterranean should be put under my command. It is not possible to describe the excitement I felt at that moment.

As an admiral in command of a fleet, I would now deal with General Bonaparte directly.

Chapter 10

At Portsmouth

I arrived at Portsmouth in March 1798. I remember so clearly boarding my new flagship, HMS *Vanguard*, whose captain, Edward Berry, was a man of experience and bearing that gave me high regard.

"Welcome, Admiral," he greeted me. "It is good to see you so well recovered from your wounds. We are honoured to have you as our squadron commander."

"Thank you, Captain. I am so very glad to be recuperated and am most ready to be at sea again."

"Admiral, I have read the accounts of your management of ships and have been most impressed. It has been my intent to manage *Vanguard* as closely as possible to your manner of command."

"Very well. I am honoured, sir," I replied, "Please have my chests delivered to my stateroom and, if you please, conduct me through a tour of the ship."

"I am delighted to do that, Admiral," he replied, and we began a full walking of the decks of the ship. He first introduced his officers and then the chief mates of the crew. We toured the main deck, and he introduced me to the boatswains and gunners, most of whose names he knew, which impressed me greatly. The gun decks, rigging, galley, and storage decks were in excellent order. It was obvious that the ship was ready to sail.

As we returned to the quarterdeck, he commented, "Sir, we have not received orders for transit or action, and I am advised that you should speak with the fleet office to be apprised of our instructions."

"I will do that this afternoon after I have settled in," I replied.

Unpacking my chests, I became very irritated because so many of the things I had asked Fanny to pack simply were not there. She had not only packed the wrong clothes but had forgotten to include a number of items that I had specifically mentioned. My watch was not there. Nor was the piece of Portuguese gold that father had given me and that I valued as a token of good fortune. I found but one pair of white silk stockings and no black socks. Missing also were my buckler and the keys to my dressing stand. I wrote to Fanny of my disquietude concerning the missing items and the wrong clothing, but she replied with a rather superficial air. In her response she stated that she rejoiced that I was "so exact," but she did not send the missing items or the appropriate clothing. It was necessary to dispatch a midshipman to various merchants in the harbour to obtain very basic things I needed.

In the afternoon I went to the fleet office with Captain Berry and conferred with various Admiralty officials and intelligence men. They advised that the revolutionary zeal of France had been recently magnified by Bonaparte's victories over the Austrians, something that had served to cow virtually all of the governments on the continent. Holland, Switzerland, and the northern Italian states had essentially become French outposts occupied by divisions of Bonaparte's troops. Although the Austrians had not capitulated formally, that development was expected soon to occur, and in any event the Austrians were effectively out of the war. So was Prussia, which seemed to be satisfied in sitting by in defensive isolation. In addition, the possibility of assistance from Russia seemed to die with Empress Catherine, as the government of her successor, young Czar Paul, showed no intention of doing anything to anger the French. The senior intelligence man advised, "Our secret sources in Paris cannot be certain of what specific plans the French have. They only know that with French control of the Mediterranean, it is quite likely that their view is toward the east, either to take control of all islands in the Mediterranean, possibly to take the Levant or Egypt, or possibly both. It has even been rumoured that Bonaparte has spoken of his plans to act toward the east as a new Alexander the Great, now that he, like Caesar, had taken control of the continent of Europe. Whatever the true intent of the French may be, it is most likely that it will take place not directly against the British homeland but in the Mediterranean. Bonaparte has also been rumoured to say that he would love nothing better than to liberate India from our control."

The chief officer from the Admiralty then added, "Admiral, you are to go to Lisbon and then to the Mediterranean to counter any seaborne French force, wherever it may go or whatever its intent may be."

At that moment I was overcome with a great exhilaration. For the first time I truly realized the enormity of the mission I was about to undertake. After a moment of silence I responded, "It shall be my task to find the French forces at sea. It is my hope that Bonaparte will be aboard, and in that case I shall capture or kill the little Corsican bastard."

174

The officers of the foreign office chuckled at my statement, but I looked at them intently until they were quiet for a moment. Then I added, "Gentlemen, I meant exactly and fully what I have said."

I returned to the *Vanguard* with an exhilaration that I had never felt before, except in the midst of battle. I read my orders and was further pleased beyond measure to read the copy of a dispatch sent from first Lord Spencer to Admiral Jervis, commander-in-chief of the Atlantic fleet. Lord Spencer's letter read,

> *I am very happy to send you Sir Horatio Nelson again. Not only because I believe I cannot send you a more zealous, active, or approved officer, but I have reason to believe that his being on your command will be agreeable to your wishes. The circumstances in which we now find ourselves oblige us to take a measure of a more decided and hazardous complexion that we should otherwise have thought ourselves justified in taking; but when you are apprised that the appearance of a British squadron in the Mediterranean is a condition on which the fate of Europe may at this moment be stated to depend, you will not be surprised that we are disposed to strain every nerve and incur considerable hazard in affecting it.*

The letter pleased me greatly. It also further weighed upon the gravity of my responsibility.

Our small squadron of four ships sailed immediately to Lisbon and took on provisions and then joined with Admiral Lord Jervis off Cadiz. I went immediately to the admiral's flagship, where he greeted me with an embrace and said, "Horatio, seeing you here and recovered is the best sight that these old tired eyes have seen in quite some time. As you know, we are going against the French in the Mediterranean, and I have written to Lord Spencer that I am an old man and that I would like to send the best young man I can to command our forces there. You are that man."

"I am at your service, sir, and shall do my absolute utmost to fulfil any expectation you may have of me," I responded. "I have met with the Admiralty's intelligence men in Portsmouth, and although they have concluded that the French objective is not against the British Isles, they seem bereft of any solid information concerning French objectives in the Mediterranean."

"Quite true," Lord Jervis responded, "and all that we really know is that a major French force is being assembled chiefly in Toulon but in other places as well, including Marseille. We believe they have more than twenty warships in preparation and countless numbers of convoy ships to carry troops and equipment, wherever they may intend to go. We are not apprised of the size of the army they have assembled, but I am sure that it is thousands upon thousands."

"Wherever they go and whatever they may set out to do, it may be that our best play shall be to keep a close eye at Toulon. That has always been their primary port in the Mediterranean, and whatever their intention, what comes out of Toulon shall probably show their hand," I suggested.

"I agree entirely," Lord Jervis responded, "and your first task shall be to do just that. Lay off Toulon and watch them. I will send, as soon as I can, as many ships as can be spared from the Atlantic to provide you not simply with a scouting squadron but hopefully in time a full fighting fleet."

"I know that what your lordship shall provide will be the utmost you can to give me the force that I shall need, and that force is what I shall use to defeat the Corsican scoundrel," I replied with a firm belief that I could do just that.

When I left Lord Jervis's stateroom, he shook my left hand firmly and placed his other hand upon my shoulder, looking directly into my eyes with the visage that was not only warm and encouraging, as was his manner, but that showed also the great strain of crisis that surrounded us. I returned to *Vanguard* straightaway, and on the next morning I set out for Gibraltar, where our reconnaissance squadron would be organized before proceeding to Toulon.

I later came to understand that my Mediterranean command had caused some anguish within the fleet, particularly with Admiral Sir William Parker, who was considerably senior to me in time of command and was an officer well thought of, having been made a baronet after the battle of Cape St. Vincent. He stated in several formal letters to various persons in the Admiralty that he believed the Mediterranean command should rightfully have been given to him. One of the letters went to Admiral Jervis, who responded that he had been ordered to place me in that command, a response that was not fully accurate since my appointment had in very large measure been decided between himself and Lord Spencer.

However, I believe that a distinct sense of resentment remained with Admiral Parker.

When I arrived at Gibraltar, I was advised that my squadron would consist of my flagship, *Vanguard*, and would have under my command two other seventy-four-gun frigates, the *Orion* and the *Alexander*, together with three thirty-six-gun ships, the *Caroline*, *Emerald*, and *Flora*. We would also be accompanied by two fast cutters, the thirty-two-gun *Terpsichore* and the twenty-gun *Bonne Citoyene*. I called the captains of my squadron ships to conference in my stateroom the evening before we departed.

"Gentlemen, we shall sail into the Mediterranean with very specific orders to reconnoitre French activity out of Toulon. Admiral Lord Jervis has stated that later he will provide additional ships to comprise a major fighting force. Until then, we must be very circumspect about engaging the enemy. If perchance we find a small number of enemy vessels, we may engage them, but until we have an appropriate number to conduct a major sea battle, our mission is surveillance. Remember also that it will be essential to stay together, never falling out of sight of our other ships."

On the 8 May 1798, we departed Gibraltar for Toulon. On the way we encountered and captured a small French Corvette, the *La Pierre*, which had sailed from Toulon the day before. Interrogating its officers, we discovered that more than ten thousand troops had already been embarked on transports and that many more, perhaps twenty or thirty thousand, had just arrived outside of Toulon. The French fleet of warships would be under command of Admiral François Brueys. I had heard of his reputation as being an experienced and conscientious officer. The officers from *La Pierre* did not know or would not divulge any information concerning when the fleet would sail or what their destination would be. When we arrived at Toulon, we came close enough to confirm our position and then sailed out to a distance of approximately twelve miles to avoid as much as possible being spotted by the French.

The Storm

On 20 May, we encountered a most unfortunate event that seemed always to reflect the temperamental character of the Mediterranean. On this occasion its temperament reflected the full fury of a spurned Italian wife. There arose a monstrous gale from the north-west, which persisted for more than thirty hours with winds so fierce as to shred any sails other than the smallest of small storm trysails hoisted simply to keep our ships in position and into the wind. However, even with the most excellent of seamanship, our ships were tossed about by the sea in waves of more than twenty feet in height. We rolled and pitched and frequently took water over the bow, which raced down the deck in such quantities as to require all hands to go below except those who were absolutely necessary to control the rudder and sails. It was the equal of any storm in the North Sea. During the night the whistling winds rolled *Vanguard* over and snapped off the top of her mizzenmast, which fell to the deck with a thunderous crash, killing two men and injuring several others. Shortly thereafter, the ship rolled again, and this time she lost the top of her foremast, which fell into the sea, remaining tethered to the ship by its rigging lines. As the ship continued to roll and pitch, now being essentially at the mercy of the violent waves, a miracle occurred. With its fury vented, the storm began to abate. Otherwise it is quite possible that I would have lost my flagship.

As *Vanguard* limped ahead with jury-rigged sails and the ship's company full at work repairing the massive damage of the storm, we did have some good fortune. The *Orion* and *Alexander* had escaped serious damage, and on the morning following the storm's abatement *Alexander* took *Vanguard* in tow. We limped toward Oristan Bay in Sardinia. However, our situation became extremely dangerous on the next day because as we approached Sardinia, heavy westerly swells pushed us perilously toward the Sardinian coast. The wind was very light and was unable to provide the sailing force necessary for *Alexander* to keep us clear of shoals along the coastline. In fact, we came so close to disaster for both ships that I shouted to the *Vanguard* captain, *"Berry, hoist a signal to the Alexander to cut the tow lines. While I am willing to lose one ship, I will not lose two! Have all boats ready to be lowered, for I feel it may be necessary to abandon the ship."*

He followed my order, and a great sense of impending disaster and a closeness to death descended upon me. The spectre of having my flagship torn apart on the rocks was something that I would give my life to avoid. However, we were simply subject to the dynamics of nature, and I could not make such a trade.

After what seemed to be an eternity of time, I waited for the tow line to be cast off, dooming the *Vanguard*. However, I believe an angel of deliverance came from the Almighty. Captain Berry raised his looking glass to his eye and said, *"Admiral, Captain Ball has hoisted a signal that* requests permission to stay his course and tend to his action. He wants to continue the tow."

"*Very well, let us continue for the moment,*" I responded, and within the period of not more than ten minutes, I noticed that we were no longer drifting toward the Sardinian coastline but actually making some slow progress toward safety. A relief came over me like a full drink of cool water to one who is dying of thirst. I could do little to contain myself and fought back tears in my eyes. I walked quickly to my stateroom and fell to my knees, thanking almighty God, who had once again saved me. The mission of my life became all the more clear. I must do my duty to the utmost. I knew that God would protect me and that I must never hold back from my destiny to achieve whatever the Lord would place before me. I became His instrument, a David before the Philistines, and any misfortune that would ever beset me would simply be threads in the fabric of His will. He would provide, and I would never question my duty to Him. He would use me as His sword to vanquish the enemy of my country, and His love of our country, a kingdom devoted to Him, would be victorious, no matter what the odds may be, no matter how hard the task might seem. I would find the French, and by His grace I would destroy them. Never would I question that truth.

As the wind freshened, we cleared the coastline and proceeded on to Oristan Bay on a sea as calm as glass. I wrote to Fanny,

> *Figure to yourself a vain man, on a Sunday evening at sunset, walking in his cabin with a squadron about him, who looked upon their chief to lead them to glory … Figure to yourself this proud, conceited man when the sun rose with his ship dismasted, his fleet dispersed and himself in such distress that the meanest frigate out of France would have been a very unwelcome guest … I ought not to call what happened to the Vanguard by the cold name of accident: I believe firmly that it was the Almighty's goodness, to check my consummate vanity. I hope it has made me a better officer, as I feel confident it has made me a better man. I kiss with all humility the cross of salvation.*

Throughout the afternoon when we were saved and into the night, I did little but thank my God and Saviour for continuing my quest in His service. I believe that I also learned in my heart that eager and bold action may be right, but it must be done with humility and conviction. God had consecrated me in this mission, and I swore before Him that I would not fail. When we reached Oristan Bay, I went immediately to the *Alexander* to shake the hand of Captain Ball.

"Alex, I cannot thank you enough for your command decision and outstanding seamanship in our time of great peril. Your name will be mentioned with the highest praise in my next dispatch."

He answered, "Thank you, Admiral. The Royal Navy was today fortunate to have a wind that was ample, even though just barely."

"Sometimes barely being saved is all we need, my dear captain. I stand here as living testimony to the truth of that," I answered, "and today is further evidence. God gives us deliverance, and sometimes it comes with a lesson."

I had known Alexander Ball from our service in the East Indies, when we were both midshipmen. He was very well connected and came from an old Gloucestershire family. In his early days he was known as the "great coxcomb" who fancied expensive uniforms with non-regulation epaulettes. However, I came to find that he was also very reflective, learned, and reasonable.

The Chase

I would learn later that on the very morning of the furious storm, the main body of the French fleet had set out from Toulon with Bonaparte aboard and in company with all of the transports carrying his army. Because they were sailing with the furious gale to their backs, only little damage was occasioned by them as they raced southward, probably passing us in the night. What we did not know was their destination.

In various states of disrepair the ships of our squadron put into Oristan Bay, protected by the islands of San Pietro, where for four days the sounds about the decks of our ships became a symphony of repair. The hammers of our blacksmiths beat constant timpani in company with carpenters' saws of various sizes that murmured slow melodies akin to the sonorous base notes of violas. Supports and stays were affixed to broken masts and cinched tight with encircling iron bucklers. Sails were stitched and double-stitched. New lines and hawsers were brought up from the storerooms and threaded as new shrouds, stays, martingales, and sheets, affixed in complex patterns to yardarms and booms that complete the gossamer rigging of square-rigged fighting ships.

On our second day in Oristan, the governor of San Pietro sent out a very courteous officer with a formal declaration that we could not remain in the harbour for an extended period. Sardinia was occupied by the French, and he feared their reprisals. However, he allowed local merchant boats to supply us with fresh and badly needed provisions. We bought meat, live poultry, fruits, vegetables, flour, and wine much to the delight and considerable profit of the merchants. This indicated to me that although the Sardinians were subject to French control, they had not embraced it. After four days we were repaired, refreshed, and ready to sail. On the evening before we departed, I called the captains of the squadron ships for another conference.

Over a freshly baked goose and bottles of rather good local wines, we discussed the plans for our search. Captain James Saumarez of the *Orion* had ventured out to recover some of our frigates that had been separated during the storm and reported that he had found but one at our prearranged rendezvous point. It seemed that the other two ships had been severely displaced by the storm and had not yet arrived at the rendezvous. However, he reported, "Admiral, we hailed and spoke with the merchantmen who mentioned that he had seen eleven warships on a southerly course south of Corsica. They had assumed the ships to be British, but surely they were not. They must have been a part of the French fleet."

"That is precious news, James, and there's nothing better that I would like to do than to head straightaway after them. However, two things constrain us. First we must recover our lost frigates because they are going to be essential to provide the speed necessary for distant reconnaissance, and secondly we simply have to wait for reinforcements promised by Lord Jervis. To engage our small squadron against the French fleet would be a fool's gamble," I responded. Then I added, "I anticipate that twelve additional warships will be sent, and then we shall have a fleet that is more than strong enough to deal with the French, no matter how many ships they may have."

Saumarez then said, "I am quite impressed, sir, that *Vanguard* is in such good condition, as I thought you might take it to Gibraltar for repairs."

"My good man, I thought you knew me better than that," I replied. I then looked at him and smiled so that he would know I had not taken offence. I then added, "You quite obviously underestimate me and my crew." I was pleased that he smiled back at me.

At the end of our conference it was our consensus that on the morning tide we would proceed to the rendezvous point and gather up our orphan frigates. Then we would sail easterly along the thirty-eight north latitude, which had been designated as the reinforcements' transit course. Then we would look for – and we would find – the French.

At the rendezvous point we found our two small frigates still in excellent condition, and within mere hours of our arrival we sighted the reinforcement force being led by my dear and valued friend Captain Tom Trowbridge in HMS *Culloden*. As the reinforcements back-sailed to join us, I was overcome. I counted eleven additional warships, and at that moment I knew that I had a force that was all I ever would need. They stood beautiful against the azure sky, framed by towering white clouds in the distance. Their sails were pure and white, their sides painted with yellow mustard wash and dotted with glossy black gun ports. The crews of the arriving ships lined the railings, waving their hats, and the men on the ships of our squadron returned their salutes, shouting, "Ahoy, mates! Welcome, lads!"

God and Admiral Jervis had given me my full fleet, consisting of the following:

> My flagship, HMS *Vanguard*, seventy-four guns, under Captain Edward Berry;
> HMS *Goliath*, seventy-four guns, under Captain Thomas Foley;
> HMS *Zealous*, seventy-four guns, under Captain Samuel Hood;
> HMS *Orion*, seventy-four guns, under Captain James Saumarez;
> HMS *Audacious*, seventy-four guns, under Captain Davidge Gould;
> HMS *Theseus*, seventy-four guns, under Captain Ralph Miller;
> HMS *Minotaur*, seventy-four guns, under Captain Thomas Louis;
> HMS *Defence*, seventy-four guns, under Captain John Peyton;

HMS *Bellerophon*, seventy-four guns, under Captain Henry Darby;

HMS *Majestic*, seventy-four guns, under Captain George Westcott;

HMS *Leander*, fifty guns, under Captain Thomas Thompson;

HMS *Alexander*, seventy-four guns, under Captain Alexander Ball;

HMS *Swiftsure,* seventy-four guns, under Captain Benjamin Hallowell;

HMS *Culloden*, seventy-four guns, under Captain Thomas Trowbridge; and

HMS *Mutine*, sixteen guns, under Captain Thomas Hardy.

I walked the deck, from time to time stamping my foot with excitement, and ordered, "Captain Berry, please signal all ships to deploy sea anchors and call a captains' conference at the next six bells." As the signal was hoisted to the first yardarm of the mainmast, I was convinced in my soul of two truths. First a capable fleet of His Majesty's Royal Navy was under my command, and second the days of the French fleet would be numbered to the days it would take us to find them.

As each of the captains was piped aboard, they saluted, and I welcomed each with an embrace. We assembled in my stateroom, and each was given a glass of my best port. I walked to the centre of the gathering, looked at each man's face, and raised my glass, "To God, our beloved country, and to His Majesty."

Each man raised his glass and repeated the toast. I then spoke to the gathering, "Gentlemen, I cannot fully express how happy and proud I am to be in command of such a group. Look about you. Look into the face of each of your colleagues, and you will note that you are in the company of the best officers of any navy in the world. Had I written out the names of the best men I would have go with me into harm's way, that list of names would be the same as the men who sit in this room." I was pleased to see each of my officers look about the room at all of their seated colleagues and smile with a nod. I continued:

"We have the great calling of a mission that will determine the fate of Britain. We must find and destroy the French fleet. Unfortunately we do not know presently where they are located or where they are going. Their destination may be the kingdom of Naples, Malta, the Levant, or Egypt. I suspect they are bound for Egypt. But that is simply a suspicion, and we must act as though the other alternatives are reality. Thus, we will first sail to Italy to find them there, and if they are not, we will investigate the alternatives. In any event, our formation will be a broad fan abreast the flagship in order to provide the widest scope of search. In time we shall find them, and hopefully that will be sooner rather than later. As we go, I commend to you two things. First, please apprise your crew of the vital importance of our mission. Also, as you know, the single thing that most sets the Royal Navy apart from all others is our ability to fire our guns rapidly and with the greatest of accuracy. Therefore, I commend to you the importance of gunnery drills during our search because the effectiveness of our gunnery, ship-upon-ship, will be the matter that gives us victory. The intensity of our gunners in carrying out their duties will obtain two objectives. First, by their focus upon what they have to do, they will become immune to fear of whatever the enemy may be doing. Secondly the excellent fire of our guns will shatter them, and we will win the day."

As our conference progressed, it became a very rich and valuable exchange of ideas among the captains. They spoke of drilling procedures in particular, the effect of which was, I am sure, to improve the drills that would be carried out on each of the ships. I suggested – and they agreed – that a formation abreast with each ship at not less than two thousand yards or more than four thousand yards from its neighbour closer to the flagship would give us the broadest range of search. We discussed at considerable length the strategy to be employed when we discovered the French fleet at sea. At the end of the discussion I told them of my conclusions, "I take from these discussions, as well as our experience at Cape St. Vincent, that our greatest strength is found by engagement of each of our ships upon each of the enemy. The quality of our crews with respect to sailing and gunnery is such that we will win any battle that is fought ship-upon-ship. For an engagement at sea it is my intention to form a single line of battle and to split the enemy forces by sailing through their midst. Then we shall swarm upon one of the sections of their divided forces and fight them ship-to-ship. I believe that we can subdue the divided force before the others can come to their assistance, and when they do, we shall then put upon them in like manner.

"If perchance we find them at anchor, we shall attack straight away, and since they shall be stationary, we shall concentrate upon a portion of their ships as the opportunity presents itself. We shall throw our full force against that portion we shall choose. For this to be carried out successfully, I anticipate that the French will be spaced far enough apart that each of the enemy can be engaged by two of our ships. In such a circumstance, you should be prepared to anchor with both stern and bow anchors attached by mid-ship springs so that you might turn in order to afford yourself the best broadside of fire." I was very pleased that each of my captains understood both the general sense and the particulars of my plan, for each nodded in acquiescence.

I closed the conference by noting that I would not offer them dinner but would have them dine aboard their respective ships, for it was necessary immediately to set a course toward the Straits of Messina. As they rose to leave, I added, "Gentlemen, with due respect to the bard, I want you to know that I have the greatest of confidence in my soul that we will be victorious. I am certain of that because I know that I sail in the company of heroes. Each of you should know that the Almighty has blessed you by placing you in this mission. Officers of the Royal Navy shall each regret that they were not with us and that they were not present when we engage the French. The story of what we do shall become legend, repeated from Englishman to Englishman for all generations to come. That legend will soon be written into history by you, my precious few, my band of brothers."

When I finished speaking, the room remained silent, as each man looked at me and then to one another. After a long while I spoke again, "Now go to your ships, my men, for we have much to do. We have much to do."

We sailed toward Sicily, and during the first night I wrote to Admiral Jervis, "*You may be assured I will fight them the moment I can reach them, be they at anchor or under sail.*" On 14 June, Captain Saumarez discovered from a Genoese merchant that the French fleet had been seen off the west end of Sicily, steering eastward. I ordered the fleet to come about on a course toward Egypt, which I firmly suspected was their destination as a foothold and an operational base that ultimately would be directed toward our holdings in India. Two days later Captain Trowbridge learned from another merchantman that the French fleet was off Malta in preparation for an invasion. Bonaparte's taking of Malta made a great deal of sense to me, as it would provide a place of safety for the French fleet and a provisioning point for stores, supplies, and troops. However, I still felt firmly that Malta would be simply a stepping stone to Egypt, and this conclusion was further buttressed by a letter I received from Sir William Hamilton, who was in Naples, to the effect that he had been apprised of "naturalists, astronomers, and mathematicians" being aboard the French fleet. This fact would be significant only if Bonaparte's objectives were permanent and intended ultimately towards India rather than simply being a strategic military strike at Egypt.

Within a matter of only a few days we discovered from another merchant that Malta had surrendered and that a division of French troops had been left behind while the fleet had departed for another destination. I ordered immediately that our fleet set a course for Alexandria. During the summer, winds in the Mediterranean are rather light and prevail from west to east. Because the French fleet had the better part of a week's head start, I doubted seriously that, even with all sails crowded on, we could catch them before they arrived at Alexandria. On 26 June, more than two hundred miles from Alexandria, I dispatched Captain Hardy in the fast HMS *Mutine* to proceed ahead to discover whether the French fleet was in Alexandria. They were not. On the twenty-eighth, when our ships hove into sight of the city, there were no French ships to be found: only three Turkish ships of the line and several small merchant vessels.

I was disappointed beyond description that we had obviously been on the wrong scent. Nevertheless, I gave orders for the fleet to sail eastward along the coast. Baffled by the whereabouts of the enemy's fleet, I also became anxious that criticism may have been voiced in London about my inability to find them. Letters that I had received contained many references to questions raised in newspapers as to why I could not find such a large body of French ships. My anxiety was also heightened by the fact that officers who were senior to me and who had been critical of the Admiralty for appointing me in command of the Mediterranean fleet would add fuel to the fire of criticism. I voiced this concern to Captain Saumarez, who wisely advised, "Let them say what they want. They are there, and we are here. In due time we shall find them." I thought it advisable to send a lengthy dispatch to the Admiralty as to all the measures which I had deemed prudent to find the French fleet. When I discussed the dispatch in a conference of my captains, Alexander Ball had actually recommended against it, stating, "Admiral, I think it essentially unnecessary to raise a defence of one's actions before one has actually been accused of wrongdoing." In retrospect, I look upon the words of Alex as being wise, but I sent the dispatch anyway.

With some desperation, we continued to sail eastward across the mouth of the Nile, again finding no sight of the enemy. In the belief that their destination might have been the Levant, we sailed northward along the coast of Palestine and found that they were not at the Levant either. We then sailed westward, as I gave in to my fear that instead of having Egypt as their objective, they may have been destined for the Kingdom of Naples. Approaching Syracuse, we were again advised by merchantmen that the French were not at Naples. Anxious and worried beyond measure, I turned my fleet toward Greece. Off the town of Koroni in the Gulf of Messinia, we anchored, and I sent Captain Trowbridge on shore to confer with the Turkish bey. When he returned, he advised excitedly that Turkish warships had recently seen the French fleet sailing on a course toward Egypt. We turned yet again on a course toward Alexandria, and I ordered that full sail be deployed in the vain hope that we would overtake the entire fleet with Bonaparte aboard before it reached Alexandria. Even under full sail, we did not overtake or even sight the enemy.

At one o'clock on the 1 August, I set down to a gloomy lunch, but it was one that became wonderfully delicious when I was advised that the *Orion* had spotted the French merchant convoy in Alexandria Bay. At last the search was over. The French war ships could not be far away. Soon thereafter, their location was confirmed, as I received a message from Captain Saumarez that said, "*The enemy fleet is in Aboukir Bay, moored in the line of battle.*"

Captain Berry would later write, "*The utmost joy seemed to animate every breast on board our fleet at the sight of the enemy, and the pleasure which the admiral himself felt was perhaps more heightened than that of any other man.*" Truer words could not be spoken, and as I rose from lunch, I said to the *Vanguard* officers, "Before this time tomorrow I shall have gained a peerage or a burial place at Westminster Abbey."

The battle that we had sought, the battle we coveted, the battle we had so intensely contemplated was, at last, at hand.

Chapter 11

The Battle of the Nile

Immediately upon coming in sight of the French fleet, I remember ordering with wonderful gusto, "Captain Berry, hoist a general signal to all ships to form a line of battle in positions ahead and astern of the admiral as most convenient."

He responded, "Aye, aye, sir!" And in seconds signal halyards were singing as brightly coloured signal flags were raised, flapping a vibrant song as they rose to the yardarm, telling every one of the ships' captains that our work was about to begin.

This would also be the first naval battle chiefly fought at night.

It did not matter which ship was where in the line. All were equal, and each would be lethal to the French. Throughout the fleet, decks had cleared for action, and the red-coated marines were beating their drums, calling the crews to battle stations. All unfixed partitions were taken down and stowed. Furniture and loose possessions were made fast. Hammocks, hawsers, and loose rigging were bundled inside of the main deck railings as large, round shrapnel buffers. Gun ports were opened. Cannons were loaded, usually with double shot, and run out of their ports. Fortunately the officers and crews had just been fed, and I felt with great assurance that each and every one of my ships was prepared to engage the enemy. I would later find out that Admiral Brueys had sent a large number of his seamen on shore to collect provisions, and on most of his ships, extra stores and equipment had been loaded on their port sides, facing land. This would make effective manning of their portside batteries quite difficult - and impossible on many ships. Brueys had fatefully expected that any engagement would be only toward the open sea. Clearly he did not know me. Nor did he appreciate that I would seize upon this vulnerability.

I was pleased to recall that in my earlier captains' conference, I had ordered that ships should rig horizontal lantern lights on their mainmast yards so that in the night our ships would not fire upon each other. It came to my immediate notice that most of the enemy were anchored with single-line anchors, allowing them to swing with the wind. This suggested strongly that if they had enough deep water to swing at anchor, our ships could proceed to their land side, offering us an ability to bring them to crossfire with some of our ships on their land sides while others attacked from the sea.

The sun was just beginning to set, giving a light golden tint to the horizon and long shadows to the enemy ships ahead, while above in a darkening blue sky seabirds wheeled and darted behind the ships. We were blessed with a moderate sea that was accompanied by a mild but ample wind from the north-east. It filled our sails but allowed all ships to keep an even keel. With a following wind, our attack would be slow and deliberate.

We made our approach in a rough, irregular line. I ordered a signal, *"Prepare for battle; be ready to anchor alongside the enemy; deploy spring lines as necessary."* Cleverly Admiral Brueys attempted to lead us into very shallow water by sending out a brig which then turned and sailed back in water that was too shallow for our warships to navigate. I immediately recognized the gambit and said to Captain Berry, "Look, Berry, he wants us to follow that little brig. Good try, sir, but we shall not. Berry, hoist a general signal, *Sail directly at the enemy line."*

And then I could wait no longer. I shouted, "Berry, let's get to it. Hoist the signal - Engage the enemy closely."

Our van was led by *Goliath* and to its starboard *Culloden* was running abreast and headed directly at the first ship of the enemy van. I saw *Culloden* abruptly slow and then stop. Soon it became apparent that she was aground at the end of a shoal jutting out from Aboukir Point. To the everlasting credit of Captain Trowbridge, he immediately hoisted signals indicating *"I am aground"* and *"Beware."* Recognising *Culloden's* misfortune, the following line of ships followed *Goliath,* sailing clear, and all the following ships passed safely wide of *Culloden.*

At 5:30 p.m., our battle colours, double-sized reds with a breast of the Union Jack, were unfurled. I said to Captain Berry, "I believe Tom Foley can pass on the land side of the van. Signal, *Goliath, you shall engage the enemy to your port side."*

Foley responded immediately, and passed ahead of the bow of the first French ship, the *Guerrière.* At a range of about five hundred yards, *Goliath* was the first ship to fire on the enemy, raking *Guerrière's* bow and then broadsiding a full double shot into her port side. It inflicted enormous damage as double-loaded round shot smashed through her oaken sides, shattered windows, knocked down bulkheads, and showered deadly splinter shrapnel throughout her gunnery decks. Tom Foley later wrote, *"I was not surprised to find the Frenchman unprepared for action on the inner side. As we passed her bow I saw her lower deck guns were not run out, and there was lumber, bags and boxes on the upper deck ports which I noted with no small pleasure. We first fired a broadside into her bow. Not a shot missed at that distance."*

Captain Samuel Hood in *Zealous* followed again on the land side of the French van and raked the *Guerrière* once more with double shot. At this point the *Guerrière's* mizzenmast was snapped and fell across her deck. The chief accomplishment of *Zealous* would be the early engagement and complete destruction of the *Guerrière*.

Captain Saumarez in *Orion* followed again on the inside of the enemy line and anchored opposite the *Peuple Souverain* and the *Aquilon*. His gunners, who were excellently trained and drilled, fired furiously and accurately into both ships. Ralph Miller, the American-born captain of *Theseus*, passed through the French line and came to stop against the *Spartiate*, raking her with broadsides before she could fire a shot.

At this point I was delighted that five of our line had passed to the land side and engaged with relentless fire, which the enemy could not effectively answer.

Our seaside attack followed with Captain Thomas Louis in *Minotaur* and Captain John Peyton in *Defence*, both engaging the *Aquilon* and *Spartiate*. In order to observe the commencement of the action, I had ordered Captain Berry to back-sail the *Vanguard* mizzen so that we stood off and I could see how matters were developing. We had already gained an advantage of eight ships to five in the enemy's van, and the action was developing to our great advantage, as our ships were pouring continued fire into them with only desultory responses.

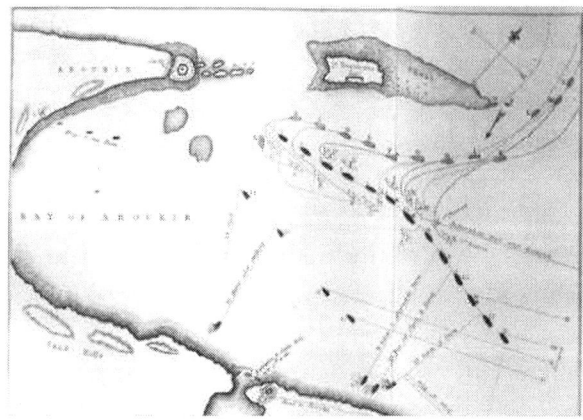

Battle of the Nile

Unfortunately Tom Trowbridge in the grounded *Culloden* was engaged in furious but unsuccessful efforts to free his ship. However, even with our loss of this gallant ship and her expert captain, my plan was working splendidly.

Throughout the first half hour of the engagement, the *Guerrière*, the *Conquerant* and the *Spartiate* were receiving murderous fire from *Theseus, Zealous,* and *Minotaur.* The French van was beginning to crumble under the rain of double-loaded broadsides of round and chain shot being unleashed with a frequency that was at least twice the rate of return fire from the French. Captain Samuel Hood would later write in his journal,

> *I commenced a rapid and well-directed fire into the bow of Guerrière, within pistol shot range, and her foremast went by the board in about seven minutes, just as the sun was closing the horizon. The whole squadron gave three cheers. It happened before the next ship astern of me had fired a shot, and only the Goliath and Zealous had been engaged. In ten minutes more, the main and mizzen masts of the Conquerant went down. At this time also, the mainmast of the second ship was broken, engaged closely by Goliath and Audacious. But, I could not get Guerrière's captain to strike his colours, although I hailed him twenty times, and seeing he was totally cut up and only firing a stern gun now and then. At last being tired of firing and killing people in that way, I sent my boat to board her, and the Lieutenant was allowed to hoist a light and haul it down to show its submission.*

Captain Miller would also later write to his wife,

> *In running along the enemy's line in the wake of Zealous and Goliath, I observed the enemy shot sweep just over us, and knowing well that at such a moment the Frenchmen would not have the coolness enough to change their elevation, I closed them and, running under the arch of their fire, reserved my fire until I had Guerrière's masts in a line, then we opened with such a fire that a second breath could not be drawn before her main and mizzenmast were gone.*

With our ships in full control of the French van, I ordered a signal to *"engage against the enemy centre,"* and as darkness was coming over us, Henry Darby, the courageous and fearless Captain of the seventy-four-gun *Bellerophon*, attacked *L'Orient*, Admiral Brueys's flagship, a massive ship of the line with 120 guns. His courage would, however, be very costly, as under massive fire from the three gun decks of *L'Orient*, I watched as *Bellerophon's* masts came crashing down, killing forty-eight men and injuring more than a hundred others. Darby ordered his anchor cables severed and drifted out of action for the remainder of the battle. Captain George Westcott then took the seventy-four-gun *Majestic* to engage the *Tonnant*, which had eighty guns, as well as the frigate *Heureux*. I had become very anxious about the advantage the French had in the number of guns at their centre. Noting the arrival of Captain Ball, I signalled *Alexander* to engage the enemy flagship, *L'Orient*, and he was soon joined (without the need of signal) by Ben Hallowell in *Swiftsure*, who poured fire not only into *L'Orient* but also into the eighty-gun *Franklin*. Captain Tom Thompson then expertly and on his own initiative positioned his little fifty-gun *Leander* between the *Peuple Souverain* and the *Franklin*. His anchorage was expertly chosen, as it enabled him to rake the *Franklin* down her bow with his portside battery and to fire his starboard guns down the stern of *Peuple Souverain*. Jim Saumarez then brought the *Orion* also alongside the *Franklin*, fighting with the intensity of an angry bulldog.

Seeing our forces fully engaged, I directed that Captain Berry take *Vanguard* against the nearest enemy, the *Spartiate*, which he did very ably by bringing her close aboard and firing effective broadsides down her starboard side. This enabled Captain Miller in *Theseus* to move ahead on the inward side and fire unopposed broadsides into *L'Aquilon* and *Le Conquerant*. The scene all about us was that of great theatre. In the darkening black of night, the constant staccato of flashes from white-gold cannon fire illuminated the entire night. We were able to see quite well the full play acted out with thunderous sounds of cannon fire and the sharp, smashing bangs of shot finding their targets. As each moment passed, it became clearer to me that matters were well in hand. The enemy van had affectively been crushed. The centre was engaged, and the quality of our fighting was taking its toll upon an inferior enemy, even against their larger battleships. We were wearing them down. Steadily and surely we were beating them down.

Then suddenly as I watched the battle unfold, I felt a hard and sharp smack to my head. Everything went black, and I fell to the deck. Although I had feeling, I could see nothing and believed that I was done for. I could sense warm blood pouring down my face, but I could still hear the shouts of men and the booming of cannon fire. However, as those who were nearby came to my assistance, I cried out, "*I am killed. Remember me to my wife.*"

Captain Berry with the help of several others carried me below to the surgery cockpit, where the smell was thick and damp, infused with the acrid stench of cannon smoke mixed with strong aromas of quinine, sweat, and blood. I ordered Berry not to attach any priority to my treatment. I told him, "*Do not identify me to the surgeons. I will wait my turn.*" Whether or not they truly waited for my turn, I cannot say, for after a short while the surgeon came to attend to me. He lifted a large fold of skin that had been stripped away from my skull, covering my good eye. As he lifted the skin and I could see again, I felt the promise of deliverance and cried out, "*Thank God, I can see!*" And then to the greatest of relief, the surgeon said, "*Actually, Admiral, there is good news. Your wound is a little serious, but it will not be fatal.*"

I cried out again, "I thank the Almighty. He has spared me. Yet again He has spared me."

Above decks Captain Berry witnessed a profound and majestic event. Apparently as the *Alexander* had passed close aboard to *L'Orient*, one of Captain Ball's lieutenants had tossed an incendiary grenade onto the *L'Orient's* deck, starting a fire, and the constant gunfire by marines from the rear deck of the *Alexander* had made impossible any effort by *L'Orient's* crew to extinguish it. Therefore, the fire continued unabated, and the broadsides of *Alexander*, which opened gaping holes in the side of the massive *L'Orient*, had provided a strong draft to feed the inferno that quickly engulfed *L'Orient's* entire stern.

As I had become refreshed, realising that my wound was not fatal, I was carried to a quieter place, a nearby bread room. There I sat in some pain, touching gingerly the massive bandages about my head, when Captain Berry appeared with wonderful news, "*Admiral, I have pleasing intelligence. Two more French ships have surrendered and three others, including L'Orient, are completely under our power. It appears, sir, that a victory has declared itself in our favour.*"

With a sense of relief and great exhilaration, it appeared to me that the one positive thing that I could do at the moment would be to begin writing my dispatch of our victory. I sent for my secretary so that I could begin dictating, but when he came to the bread room, I could tell easily that he had been wounded and was in too great a state of shock to be of assistance. The *Vanguard* chaplain was then called to serve as my amanuensis; however, his writing was far too slow, and I decided to write the dispatch myself, scribbling awkwardly with my left hand. It was interesting that – as perhaps a statement of God – in the room next to my bread room, one of the several women who were aboard *Vanguard* gave birth to a son, and I could hear the crying of that child as the herald of a new and glorious moment.

As I was cribbing out my dispatch, Captain Berry appeared again and advised that the enemy flagship was engulfed in flames. I put down my pen and ordered that I be helped on deck. *L'Orient* was a majestic and terrible sight of towering flames against the black night. I could see that on her lower decks, some brave men were still loading and firing their guns, but the flames were growing intense and would soon reach the gunpowder hold. Some French sailors were leaping into the waters and flailing at attempts to swim or desperately holding onto floating debris. I told Berry to launch boats and to save as many as possible. Later I would learn that Admiral Brueys had both of his legs shot off but had bravely ordered that he be placed in a sitting position on deck so that he could continue to command his fleet. However, soon thereafter, he was shot through, and his misery was ended. Captain Ralph Miller witnessed what he later would write as a *"most grand and awful spectacle."* The great *L'Orient* was becoming fully consumed by the fire. Berry and other captains had cut their anchor lines to get clear of what they believed would be a murderous explosion when the fire reached the powder magazine. Most English captains ordered that their decks be soaked with water and that all buckets be filled to be ready for extinguishing any burning debris that might fall.

Soon after ten o'clock the great flagship exploded into an intense and massive ball of fire that reportedly was seen and heard by French soldiers ten miles away. Masts, yardarms, rigging, broken bodies, cannons, and every other part of the ship were hurled into the air, splashing into the sea or crashing down on the decks of nearby ships. For some extended time after the explosion, there was silence. Resolved to finish things off, I ordered that firing be continued until the entire French fleet had surrendered. There actually required only intermittent firing, and by three o'clock in the morning it was over. Captain Miller would later write, *"My people were so extremely jaded that as soon as they had hoved our sheet anchor up, they dropped under the capstan bars and were asleep in a moment in every sort of posture, having been working at their fullest execution of fighting for nearly twelve hours."*

As the battle had worn down, Admiral Villeneuve in his undamaged ship, *Le Guillaume Tell*, at the rear of the French line had apparently concluded that the battle was a complete loss and got underway to leave the bay, ordering *Le Genereux* and *Le Timoleon* to follow him. However, *Le Timoleon* failed to catch the wind and ran herself onto the beach, where the crew set her on fire and escaped to shore in lifeboats. I ordered Captain Hood in *Zealous* to follow Villeneuve, but I soon realised that both he and his crew were totally exhausted and would be vulnerable in an engagement against an overwhelming advantage in the sheer number of French guns. As neither he nor any other ships was fresh enough to pursue the escaping

French, I recalled Hood and let them go. On reflection I could hardly blame them. They were squirrels, fleeing from bulldogs.

In the morning after a brief respite of sleep, I went on deck and laid my eyes upon a terrible scene of carnage. The entire bay was covered with the remains of proud ships, and the water all about was filled with floating debris and the bodies of dead seamen. I asked Captain Berry to make an accounting of all ships in the battle. He later returned with an account that was both magnificent and tragic.

> *Zealous, Orion, Audacious, Minotaur, Defence,* and *Leander* were seriously damaged but remained seaworthy.

> *Vanguard's* mast was shot away and her hull severely damaged.

> *Goliath* had all of her masts shot away, and her hull was damaged.

> The hull of *Theseus* had been severely damaged.

> *Bellerophon* had been dismasted.

> *Majestic* had lost her main and mizzen, and her hull was badly damaged.

> *Alexander* had lost most of her yardarms, and her hull was heavily damaged.

> *Culloden,* although she had been freed from the shoal, where she had spent the entire battle, had suffered serious damage to the hull and had lost her rudder.

My fleet was like a pugilist after a long and furious fight - bloodied, scarred and spent. However, the opponent lay motionless at our feet.

Blessedly only one of our captains had been killed, George Westcott, captain of HMS *Majestic*, which had so bravely engaged two ships of the enemy, the *Tonnant* and the *Heureux*. When told of his death, I felt a pain in my heart, remembering his handsome, smiling, and eager face at our last conference and knowing that the price of victory often comes with a necessary grief in accepting the loss forever of people you deeply respect and love.

With respect to the French ships, I learned the following: *L'Orient* had been destroyed.

Guerrière, Heureux and *Mercure* were severely damaged and later burned as unserviceable.

Conquerant was dismasted and severely damaged. It would become the HMS *Conquerant* but would never see actual service.

Aquilon was dismasted and severely damaged. It would become the HMS *Aboukir* but would never see service.

Peuple Souverain was dismasted and severely damaged. It would become the HMS *Guerrier* but would not see service at sea.

Franklin had lost her main and mizzenmasts but was restored and became the HMS *Canopus*.

Spartiate was dismasted and severely damaged but became the HMS *Spartiate*.

Tonnant was dismasted, grounded, and severely damaged but would later become the HMS *Tonnant*.

Timoleon was grounded and burned by her crew.

Guillaume Tell and *Genereux* had escaped on 2 August with two small frigates.

Our total casualties had been more than two hundred killed and more than six hundred wounded. An accurate total of the French casualties would never be known, but the total number of killed or wounded men would be more than four thousand. Even in great victory the cold arithmetic of war bespoke a tragic price to pay.

Aftermath

In the morning hours before dawn on the day after the battle, I had managed some fitful sleep, which did not bring complete rest but which brought some thankful abatement of the splitting pain that I felt in my head. As I walked slowly about the decks of *Victory*, several of my captains came aboard to salute and extend their hand in congratulations for my great victory. I told them that the victory was not my victory but our victory together, one gained by the blood, sweat, commitment, and fury of every man in our fleet. Almighty God had blessed me with life, but more than life, He had blessed me with men of majesty.

Below decks the ship's physician and his assistants were in constant activity tending to the wounds of seamen and marines who lay sleeping or quietly moaning in the grasp of their injuries. I was also impressed that they were also tending to the needs of more than two hundred French prisoners, almost all of whom were badly suffering. On the main deck and gun decks men who were not badly hurt and who had received some rest were busy tending to repairs of the ship. The stewards' mates had prepared a breakfast of oatmeal with side pieces of cheese and thin slices of oranges or limes. As I returned to the main deck and walked to the quarterdeck railing, I could see boats moving about, collecting men grasping onto floating objects and clinging desperately to life itself. There remained only to gather up spoils and lives remaining in the field of destruction. I called for my secretary, who was recovering well from his minor wound, and dictated a dispatch, which I instructed that he send to the captains of each ship, *"Almighty God, having blessed His Majesty's arms with victory, the Admiral intends returning Public Thanksgiving for the same at two o'clock this day, and he recommends every ship doing the same as soon as convenient. Adm. Horatio Nelson."*

I later dictated an additional general order to be sent to each ship, stating, *"The Admiral desires that the captains, officers, seamen and marines will accept his most sincere and cordial thanks for their very gallant behaviour in this glorious battle."*

Captain Berry later advised me that the assembling of the *Vanguard's* officers and men for the Thanksgiving service strongly impressed not only the ship's company but also the French prisoners who were invited to attend. It had been my hope that our supplication before almighty God within the confined space of a ship with battered sides and blood-stained deck bore witness to the magnitude of peril from which He had saved us.

During the afternoon of 2 August, I dictated my dispatches of our victory. The account of the battle was brief, as I wanted to convey chiefly the results of the enemy's destruction and the consequential isolation of Bonaparte in Egypt. Two copies would be made, one entrusted to Captain Berry, whom I ordered to take command of HMS *Leander*, and the other to Captain Capel in *Mutine*. Berry was to sail at best speed to deliver the news to Admiral Jervis. I did not know until much later that the *Leander* would be captured by the escaped *Genereux* and that Berry would be taken prisoner. In backup, Capel sailed to Naples and then proceeded overland through Austria and Prussia to the Baltic and then proceeded to London. The Capel dispatch would take two months for my official report to reach the Admiralty. In London, the great anxiety concerning my mission had continued with intensity. On 21 August, Lord Spencer wrote to Admiral Jervis, "*I am very anxious to hear from you as we have heard no news of Nelson that can be depended upon.*" On 4 September, more than a month after the battle, he wrote again, "*We still remain in the utmost anxiety about news from Nelson.*" The only real intelligence that had been received in London was that Bonaparte had landed in Egypt, and the following a victory against the relatively small Ottoman forces, he had taken control of the country.

Unofficial news of our victory had been reported from Austrian sources, but the anxiety persisted, as no formal report had been received. First Lord Spencer wrote, "*I do not encourage myself to believe these secondary reports, notwithstanding the quarter from whence it comes which, it should seem, entitle it to some credit, lest I should subject myself to another disappointment.*"

The Great Celebration

On 2 October, Capel arrived in London with my dispatches, and the long period of doubt and anxiety was transformed into a massive eruption of relief, joy, and celebration, which resounded not only in the Admiralty but throughout the entire country. It was reported that Lord Spencer became faint and had to be seated immediately when his secretary announced the news. However, he recovered quickly and danced about the room, embracing all present. He then ordered that the dispatch be given a general delivery to all government offices and to the London newspapers. He then wrote to me,

> *Most sincerely and cordially do I congratulate you on the very brilliant and signal service you have performed to your country and the glorious action on 1 August last, which most certainly has not its parallel in naval history. I have only now time to say this much. In my next, I shall have the pleasing task of acquainting you with the measures which will be taken by government to mark their sense of the merits of yourself and your gallant officers on this memorable occasion. I wrote immediately a line to Lady Nelson to tell her you were safe and what you had achieved. I was happy to hear from Capel that your wound was doing well. God bless you, my dear Sir Horatio.*

A letter written on the next day from Lady Lavinia Spencer, wife of the First Lord of the Admiralty, imparted to me the sense of celebration that was taking place in the nation. She wrote,

> *Captain Capel just arrived! Joy, joy, joy to you, brave, gallant, immortalized Nelson! May that great God, whose cause you so validly supported, protect and bless you to the end of your brilliant career. Such a race surely never was run. My heart is absolutely bursting with different sensations of joy, of gratitude, of pride, of every emotion that ever warmed to the bosom of a British woman on hearing of our country's glory – and all produced by you, my dear, my good friend … at this moment, the guns are firing, illuminations are preparing, your gallant name is echoing from street to street, and every Briton feels his obligation to you weighing him down. But if these strangers feel in this matter, who can express what we in this house feel about you? What incalculable service have you been to my dear Lord Spencer. How gratefully, as First Lord of the Admiralty, does he place on your brow these laurels so gloriously won. In a public, in a private view, what does he not feel at this illustrious achievement of yours, my dear Sir Horatio, and*

*your gallant squadron? What a fair and splendid page have
you and your heroic companions added to the records of his
administration of the Navy! And, as wife of this excellent man,
what do I not feel for you all, as executors of his schemes and
plans? But I am come to the end of my paper, luckily for you,
or I should gallop on forever at this rate. I am half mad and I
fear I have written a strange letter, but you will excuse it. May
Almighty God protect you! Adieu! How anxious we shall be to
hear of your health! Lady Nelson has had an express sent to her.*

The packets delivered to me from London containing letters from
my family and friends as well as people I did not know in the Admiralty
and the government filled satchels. Letters from the dearest of friends,
including principally Admiral Jervis and Captain Locker, contained
warm and personal praise that enveloped my heart and raised my soul.
Newspaper accounts wrote of celebratory bonfires, public speeches,
singing, and special services in cathedrals and churches, giving thanks
to God for our victory.

In Aboukir Bay, the scene was very different, as our ships and the
prizes that could be saved were repaired and refitted for sea. The prizes that
could not be made seaworthy were scavenged for every tool, hoop, fitting,
yardarm, sail, and food that could be made useful. My head was constantly
splitting. Frequently I felt weak and sick, but with the individual driving
figure of my captains, my band of brothers, the work went forward with
great speed. There was also a great incentive to recover the prize money that
was represented by the captured French ships. As always, it was found that
duty and incentive would drive men to accomplishment. Captain Miller
recorded, "*To encourage and enable all my people to do much work in little time,
I venture to make every day a meat day, and to give them an additional half
allowance of wine.*"

By 7 August, we had eight of our own ships ready for service,
and by 14 August, I was able to send Captain Saumarez to Gibraltar with
six French prizes. I took the time also to write a letter to the governor of
Bombay announcing that I believed the general threats to India were over. I
also wrote to my old friend Alexander Davison that he would be appointed
sole agent for negotiating the prizes. I also wrote to my brother Maurice in
the navy office, "*Whatever assistance you may give Davison … I beg that you
may never be considered, directly or indirectly, as having anything to do with the*

agency." I was very sensitive to any claim that I might be self-serving and wanted to be absolutely fair to my captains.

As we were making ready to depart Aboukir Bay, I received instructions from Admiral Jervis concerning an intended conquest of Mallorca. I was ordered to sail immediately to Naples. This provided something of a problem because the captured prizes, *Guerrière*, *Heureux*, and *Mercure*, were not yet seaworthy. Although they represented a sizable sum in prize money, I had no option but to declare them unserviceable and set them afire as we departed.

En route to Naples, I was apprised that Parliament had elevated me to a peerage with the title "Baron of the Nile and Burnham Thorpe," and I cannot but admit that it was pleasing to my spirit that I could take great satisfaction in ascending from a son of a rector in a small village to a status in which I would hereafter be called "Lord Nelson."

With *Culloden*, *Alexander*, and *Bonne Citoyene* in company, we weighed anchor for Naples. Captain Samuel Hood had been given two ships of the line and three fast frigates to blockade the port of Alexandria in an effort to keep Napoleon's army in place and unsupplied. On the trip to Naples we were again treated unmercifully by weather, for as soon as we had passed through the Strait of Messina, a fierce storm struck, and our poor, jury-rigged *Vanguard* lost two of her masts and several seamen overboard in a merciless pounding sea. She had to be towed by HMS *Thalia* for the rest of the journey. Throughout the horrors of the gale I was singularly impressed with the energy and abilities of Captain Hardy, whom I had appointed captain of *Vanguard* in replacement of Captain Berry. Hardy attended excellently to minimise and correct the severe damages inflicted by the storm. On 22 September 1798, the battered *Vanguard* and the remainder of our squadron limped toward the Bay of Naples. Although I would be welcomed as a hero, I arrived exhausted and feeling unwell. One thing, however, raised my spirits. It was a letter I had received during the journey from Lady Emma Hamilton.

> *My dear, dear Sir,*
>
> *How shall I begin, what shall I say to you – 'tis impossible to write, for since last Monday I am delirious with joy and assure you I have a fervour caused by agitation and pleasure. God, what a victory! Never, never has there been*

anything half so glorious, so complete. I fainted when I heard the joyful news, and fell on my side and am hurt, but well of that, I shall feel it a glory to die in such a cause. No, I would not like to die till I see and embrace the Victor of the Nile. How shall I describe to you the transports of Maria Carolina? 'Tis not possible. She fainted and kissed her husband, her children, walked around the room, cried, kissed, and embraced every person near her, exclaiming, Oh Nelson, Nelson, what do we not owe to you. Oh victor, saviour of Italy, both that my swollen heart could now tell him personally what we owe to him! ... How I glory in the honour of my country and my countryman. I walk in shreds ... but with pride, feeling I was born in the same land with the Victor, Nelson ... The Neapolitans are mad with joy and if you were here now, you would be killed with kindness.

We are preparing your apartment for your coming. I hope it will not be long ... and I am so impatient to embrace you. I wish you could have seen our house during the three nights of illumination – 'twas covered with your glorious name. There were three thousand lamps and they should have been three million if we had had time. All the English vie with each other in celebrating this most gallant and ever memorable victory ... For God's sake come to Naples soon.

Lady Emma Hamilton

Chapter 12

Naples

As we made our way slowly into the Bay of Naples, I remember the appearance of our squadron was that of a haggard band of wounded ships making its way with careful and slow steps to deep anchorage in the middle of the bay. On *Vanguard*, Captain Hardy, ever the capable ship's master, had the boatswains rig sufficient boom sails for the ship to be navigated into the harbour on its own, having just that morning cast off the tow lines from *Thalia*. His pride, reflecting my own, refused the sight of our flagship being towed into the bay.

We were unsuspecting of the glorious welcome waiting in the harbour. Captain Capel had earlier arrived with news of the victory at Aboukir Bay, and the grand welcome we received reflected the state of the fitful celebration still being carried on by what was a delirious populace. As we reached the anchorage point, a large number of colourfully decorated boats set out from the dock. King Ferdinand himself was in one of the boats, and in another I recognized Sir William and Lady Emma Hamilton. As Sir William's boat approached, he pointed to the king's boat and loudly cried, *"There is the King whose country you have saved."* Members of our crew cheered and waved their hats, saying, "Let it be so, sir," and, "'T'was our pleasure." A sidewall gangway was quickly lowered, and passengers from the boats ascended its steps. I was impressed and pleased that our visitors would frequently approach the large and impressive figure of Captain Hardy, thinking him to be me, and he would tactfully point his hand to me and say, "The admiral will greet you."

When the king was piped aboard, he walked toward me with his arms outstretched. *"Nostro Liberatore! Nostro Liberatore!* I greet with a full heart the hero who has saved my kingdom. I welcome you to Naples and should rightfully give the city to you, for you have preserved it. You are our saviour and our conquering hero."

I responded, "Thank you, your Majesty. It was simply my duty."

When Sir William and Lady Hamilton arrived at the quarterdeck, it was Lady Hamilton who rushed forward.

"Oh God, is it possible? Can it truly be that you are here?" She opened her arms and embraced me fully, falling almost limp such that I had to sustain her with all the strength of my left arm to keep her from falling on the deck. She recovered her footing and placed her hand upon my face. "Oh, Admiral, there are no words that can truly fit my happiness at this moment, nor suffice to express how I honour you and your ships that have given us new life. How proud it is to be English on this day."

The beauty of her face was wondrous and the touch of her body with my encircling arm seems to bring me to a renewal of life. The wonderful scent that was all about her brought to me a sensation that I had almost forgotten. It was as though I had been introduced anew to the wonderment of why God had made women. Her figure seemed full and robust. Her face had a clear beauty with sparkling brown eyes, all encircled by a full head of lustrous brown hair set with soft curls. I must confess that at that moment I felt a bit out of place, for I knew that I looked pale and exhausted with a red laceration, the remnant of my wound, circling across my forehead. My appearance seemed, however, to be of no matter, for this would be a day of unbounded praise and adulation.

Sir William approached and tactfully offered his left hand, which I was pleased to shake. He said, "Welcome and God bless you, my dear sir. I will not say how glad I am to see you. Indeed, I cannot describe to you my feelings on your being so near to us. This could not be a happier day." As compared with the last time I saw him, almost two years prior, he seemed thinner, almost emaciated, and the deep wrinkles about his eyes indicated that the passage of time was not being good to him. However, his eyes were clear, and his manner was very warm and endearing. I was pleased to shake his hand in true respect for the senior representative of Britain to the Neapolitan court. Later I would learn that he had been very ill during the weeks before my arrival, and whatever the source of his illness, it would remain in various forms of intensity for the rest of his life. He would never again truly be a well man.

Those who had filled the boats in the little armada that greeted us crowded the quarterdeck in their formal dress, impressing greatly the ship's officers and crew. I was pleased to meet the pro-consuls of Austria, Prussia, and various Italian city states whose names were spoken but which I have forgotten, together with wives, children, and various friends of different stature, all of whom smiled broadly in what seemed to be a great event of sincere celebration. It pleased me to no end, and I was touched by the gifts that many of them brought as tokens of their appreciation and esteem. When everyone had come on board, the king requested rather solicitously if he could be granted a tour of the ship. I responded, "Your Majesty, it shall be my delight to walk you about the decks of the ship, for the *Vanguard* is as much a hero as every man is who serves within her. There are still unrepaired parts of her battered sides, and you will see scrapes upon her masts that have been left by the enemy's chain shot. All of her wounds are as true a badge of honour as the cut across my face."

We toured the ship at length, and the king, together with his large entourage, seemed to be awestruck by *Vanguard's* cannons, rigging, stowed sails, hammocks, and galley. He seemed to be particularly interested in the surgeon's operating quarters, and he asked if I had been treated there. I responded that it was so and pointed out to him the adjacent bread room where I had begun to write the dispatches of our engagement. He was enthralled, and remarked, "This is truly wonderful. There is nothing upon the sea that is even near to the power of the British Navy."

I responded, "That is true, your Majesty. No other ships can compare with those of the Royal Navy."

He nodded and said, "Ah, yes. *Si! Si!* It is so."

When we made our way back to the quarterdeck, the king waved his hand toward the docks where two bands in full and colourful regalia played music that was somewhat discordant but that could be recognized as "God save the King" and "See the Conquering Hero Comes". During the anthem my officers and crew stood at attention, saluting. It was a poignant moment that very much lifted my spirits, which at the beginning of the day seemed weary and fatigued. As the bands finished their music, cages at the rear of the dock were opened. Scores of pigeons and doves were released and formed a great soaring flight that encircled our anchored ships and then disappeared from sight toward the smoking Mount Vesuvius.

Sir William

Before he left, the king approached and said that Queen Maria Carolina was ill and could not be present but that she was eager beyond measure to greet me. As Sir William and Lady Hamilton were about to depart, I asked Sir William if he had received the letter in which I requested that he make accommodations for me at a local villa or hotel. He quickly raised his hand and said, "Please, Admiral, I would not hear of it. We have prepared an apartment for you at our quarters, the Palazzo Sessa, which you will find far more accommodating than at any villa or hotel. It is prepared and ready to receive you this evening." I responded with my great thanks, and he invited me to arrive for dinner at 8:00 p.m. if that would be convenient. He added that it would be an easy and casual dinner, as he was certain that after the voyage and the events of the day, I would probably anticipate an early retirement for the evening. I allowed that such was very true, and that I would arrive prior to the dinner hour.

At 7:00 p.m., I was advised that Sir William had sent a carriage. I had just reviewed and completed plans for refitting of the ships, and I looked forward to a restful respite on shore. My bags and personal items were loaded into the carriage, and we set off for the Palazzo Sessa. I had no idea that it would be such a lovely place, and I was awestruck by the sight of it as we approached. The entire building, a small but beautiful Italianate palace, was illuminated in a beautiful orange and gold glow by hundreds of candle lamps placed all around the outside and in every window and balcony. I can hardly describe how warm and welcoming the scene was, as my tired and sick body approached the beautiful candlelit palazzo. Above the general clatter of carriage wheels on the cobblestones, it seemed that a new and desperately needed period of rest could begin.

Emma

Lady Hamilton was waiting at the door with several servants. She rushed out to take my hand as I alighted from the carriage, and she said, "My dear admiral, my heart is ready to burst with happiness to have such a great person as you in our home."

Emma

208

"My lady, I'm obliged and honoured that you and Sir William have invited me to stay at your grand home. I am sure that I shall be very comfortable here."

She instructed her servants to gather up my baggage and follow as she guided me to my apartment. On the way I was introduced to a short and rather stout woman. Lady Hamilton said, "Admiral, please meet my mother, Mrs. Cadogan."

She wore a plain but formal black dress and curtsied, saying, "It is an honour to meet the hero of the Nile, sir. We are happy to have your company and hope to see much of you."

I shook her hand and simply said, "Thank you, madam."

With Lady Hamilton I proceeded to the room, which was resplendent with an enormous adjoining bath. The bedroom was beautifully decorated with a magnificent painting of Mount Vesuvius above the bed. There was also an expansive balcony overlooking the bay where I could see the lights of our ships laying peacefully at anchor.

I asked, "If I might, my lady, I would be content simply to lie down for a few minutes before dinner. What remains of this wrecked body of mine is in need of just a moment of rest before we dine."

"Of course. We shall do whatever is needed, my dear admiral. And I would consider it a great honour if you would allow me to wash the dust of the road from your face," she said.

I was somewhat surprised by her request; however, the prospect of her washing my face seemed most inviting, and I replied, "That would be most welcomed, my dear lady."

As I reclined on pillows set on a large red couch, she ordered a warm bowl of water and sat on a footstool next to the couch, saying, "Simply close your eyes and rest, my dear man." She wet a soft muslin cloth in the warm waters and began gently circling my face in a manner that was soothing and pleasurable. I was reminded of the exquisite relief that could be imparted simply by a gentle touch. She also hummed a quiet tune that I did not recognise but brought back memories from so long ago of the enchanting and quiet song that Cubah had sung when she brought my broken body back to life after the horrors of Nicaragua. The memory was vivid, and the gentle touches of Lady Hamilton on the healing scar that marked my forehead almost brought tears to my eyes. The scent of her, like a bouquet of flowers, overcame me. I could not have imagined a more perfect moment.

"My dear sir, your handsome face is now refreshed, and I shall go and raise Sir William from his bed. Please take a few moments, and when you are ready, come down at your leisure to dine. It will be a small dinner, but I hope you will be pleased," she said softly.

"Thank you, my lady, you have been most kind," I replied. I rested for ten or fifteen minutes longer and then donned my uniform coat and joined the Hamiltons at their grand dining room. The dinner was most pleasant – Italian veal in a mild lemon sauce with Italian pasta that looked very much like the rice of the East Indies. The wine was rich and deep. I refused stronger spirits, being afraid they might upset my system that had been so accustomed to the bland fare served aboard ship for so long. Mrs. Cadogan joined us for dinner but was very quiet. As soon as the sweet course was finished, Lady Hamilton left the room, and Sir William requested that I join him and Mrs. Cadogan in the drawing room, where he offered me a glass of wonderful Portuguese wine that was very dark and rather sweet to the taste.

"Lady Hamilton has indicated to me that she would like to portray several of her 'attitudes' for your enjoyment this evening," Sir William announced.

"I am sure that will be delightful, sir," I responded. When I had earlier visited Naples, someone had described to me that it was a practice of Lady Hamilton to appear in classical dress with certain theatrical objects and to pose in representations of tragic or heroic women of antiquity. After a short while she appeared, accompanied by a very attractive young woman whom I recognized as one of their servants. Both wore sheer dresses in what appeared to be classical Greek style with lovely headbands and long ribbons flowing behind. The two of them, entirely without music, began a slow and graceful dance, pausing from time to time to hold a still pose. When she was in the pose, Lady Hamilton looked at me with a divine expression upon her face. She was quite beautiful. After several stages, they finished their dance and then hurried from the room.

"You might recognise, sir, that they were dancing the Tarantella, which is one of Emma's favourite attitudes," Sir William said. I had not recognised it, but I nodded as though I had.

Lady Hamilton appeared again by herself in a much shorter costume, wearing strap sandals and carrying a bow. She then struck several poses, pausing at length in each. In the first pose she appeared to be looking for something very intently, and then she posed in some excitement with her arm outstretched.

"Diana the Huntress has seen a deer," Sir William advised.

She then ran gracefully from one spot to another and then to another, and then she posed as though she were drawing back an arrow in her bow. Then she ran again to another point and posed over the imaginary deer, having slain it. As she held the pose for some moments, her expression was pensive and quite poignant. She finally stood and bowed gracefully and then quickly ran from the room.

In her final performance Lady Hamilton appeared in a full classical dress with two white flowers in her hair. A servant brought in a Greek column and placed it in the centre of the floor. Lady Hamilton set a pose with both hands on the column, looking into the distance.

"Penelope, awaiting the return of Odysseus," Sir William explained.

She held several dramatic poses. The first showed her with her hands over her heart, slightly bowed and with a look upon her face that was truly mournful. Another featured her arms clasped around her bosom while she looked down with a visage of total grief. The last was a visage of committed stoicism with her hand placed upon her heart. During this pose she looked directly at me, and I was entranced by the melodrama of the presentation and the beauty of her face. She then bowed and walked slowly from the room.

"Well, there you have it – three of my dear wife's famous attitudes from antiquity. I hope you enjoyed it," Sir William said.

"It was a marvellous performance," I answered. "I found all of her performances to be charming and quite frankly, more pleasing than any painting or sculpture could be. It was truly wonderful."

Lady Hamilton soon joined us, still wearing her Penelope dress, and I said, "*Brava! Brava*, my lady. That was a presentation that shall be fixed in my memory. It was truly wonderful."

"To be honest, I must say that I was inspired by my audience and am very pleased that you liked it," she responded.

Sir William and Mrs. Cadogan then excused themselves, as they were quite tired from the events of the day. I sat for some time in the drawing room with Lady Hamilton, finishing my last glass of wine. She asked me questions about the battle of the Nile, evincing a true interest in naval matters, an interest I had never before heard from a woman.

Her praise of my tactics in isolating and overpowering the anchored French ships was intense, as she frequently would comment, "Brilliant," "Wonderful," or "How inventive!" Our conversation was free and easy, much more relaxed and natural than I had enjoyed in years with anyone outside of officers or officials of the Royal Navy. After a while my fatigue registered itself, and I begged to be excused. She replied, "Please rest well, dear Admiral, and if there is anything under the sun or moon that you need, it shall be my duty to provide it, for you deserve everything that your country can give to you. And by the way, sir, I intend to plan a festive celebration of your forthcoming birthday." I retired to my bedroom suite, and after quick evening ablutions I fell into a restful sleep as soon as my head touched the pillow.

The next morning I arose, and after a breakfast of warm bread, jams, and cheese served with honeyed milk, I was taken back to the harbour in the Hamiltons' carriage and witnessed in the morning light the colourful streets and buildings of Naples festooned with ribbons and buntings written in English, "Hail to Admiral Nelson, Our Hero on the Glorious 1 August," and other grand compliments signifying a very profound gratitude of the entire city. In my cabin on *Vanguard*, I reviewed with captains of the ships all matters that were relevant to refitting the squadron and making it again ready for deployment.

When I returned to the Palazzo Sessa in the early afternoon, I read mail from the Admiralty, which recognized that I would spend some weeks in Naples while our ships were repaired. There were also two letters from Fannie that said nothing about the battle or public discourse in England, nothing about me, or any of our ships, or anything having to do with the greatest naval victory the Royal Navy had experienced since the destruction of the Spanish Armada. Instead she wrote of her delight at finding appropriate soft leather gloves, the increasing price of foods in England, the extended period of rain and fog, and her various ailments from the cold drafts at the Burnham Thorpe.

I responded by telling her that I was very much recovered and in better general health than I had been for months. I also mentioned Emma Hamilton, *"I hope one day to have the pleasure of introducing you to Lady Hamilton. She is one of the best women in the world. How few could have made the turn she has. If Josiah was to be under her charge, she would make something of him with all of his bluntness, I am sure he likes Lady Hamilton. She would fashion him much better in six months in spite of himself. The goodness of Sir*

William and Lady Hamilton is beyond everything I could have expected or desired." Actually Josiah had come to betray the early promise that I had seen in him. He had been given the captaincy of a small ship of the line but had not grown in his personal stature to match the new position. His technical knowledge of seamanship and gunnery were modest at best, and he seemed to have no sense whatever for leadership. His personal manner was frequently coarse, and he did not have a personal demeanour that commanded respect.

Lady Hamilton was in a flurry of activity in the planning of my birthday celebration. I had no idea of the extent to which she had planned the affair. Invitations were sent to the captains of all of our ships, who were asked to bring with them all of the officers and midshipman who could be spared from their duties. Also invited and expected to attend were all notable members of the Neapolitan court as well as ranking members of staff in service to the various ambassadors, consuls, and ministers of the allied nations.

When the evening of celebration arrived and I came down to the grand dining room from my apartment, I was overcome with the grandeur that was displayed in bunting, flowers, and streaming ribbons all about the grand room. Formal dinner plates had been set out with silver and ivory cutlery in the midst of great crystal chandeliers and countless candles that almost lit the room to midday. Eighty people would sit and dine with us in the grand dining room that evening, and more than a thousand others would be served in adjoining rooms and upon the garden terrace. I wrote to my brother, "*The dinner was conducted in such a style of elegance as I never saw, or shall again.*" There were probably one thousand people who remained to dance in a ball following the exquisite dinner. Classical bands were situated in the grand ballroom and on the open-air terrace. Their music was excellently played. Having only one arm, I was understandably excused from taking to the dance floor, but I sat in the seat of honour at the head of the king's entourage. I was very pleased to find myself next to Lady Hamilton and Sir William.

Recovered, Somewhat

When I met the queen that evening, her praise was elaborate, and she commented, "My dear admiral, you cannot know the depth and breadth of my joy and comfort to have you in Naples. We must withstand the French horror that is spreading across Europe, threatening our way of life and the sense of proper order and civility that has served our continent for centuries. You are our dear friend and saviour, and if there is anything within my power to increase the bond that we have with you and your country, I shall do it." I responded that I appreciated very much our alliance with the kingdom of Naples and the Two Sicilies in opposing the French menace. I could understand her sentiment, and I remembered that she was indeed the daughter of Queen Maria Theresa of Austria and sister to Marie Antoinette, who had been so brutally murdered by the French revolutionaries. In the queen I believed that I had a true ally.

The celebration of the evening was grand indeed. I enjoyed Lady Hamilton's witty conversation, particularly the comments she would make from time to time about various people on the dance floor. It seemed that she knew everyone and everything in Naples. The colloquy between her and the queen was active, letting me know that the queen considered her to be one of her closest and perhaps dearest associates. It became also clear that Queen Maria Carolina, as a true daughter of royalty, commanded the ability to make her secondary position into one of almost supreme authority. The king was a very animated man but in almost a boyish way. He was known for hunting, field games, and numerous illicit relationships, but he understood only the immediate affairs of his kingdom and was at a loss to appreciate the secondary effects that would happen tomorrow as a result of decisions he would make today. This was not so with the queen, who was both adept and intense in managing not only matters of her court but the international relations of her kingdom as well. She also had a stronger will than the king did, and when they differed, she would more frequently than not control the outcome.

During the evening Lady Hamilton was a delightful companion. She reminded me constantly that all of the celebration was for my glory and honour, and she would not stop in reminding everyone around us that it was I who had secured the safety of Naples. At midpoint of the evening Lady Hamilton had a staff member walk through the grand dining room and terrace, ringing a bell and directing everyone to attend an event in the dining room. When everyone was assembled, Sir William proposed a toast, "To their Majesties, King George, King Ferdinand, to the Royal Navy, and to its glorious leader, Admiral Horatio Nelson." The toast was robustly returned by everyone present, and Sir William announced that a special verse had been written for accompaniment to the melody of the British national anthem. He stated that the verse would be sung by Lady Hamilton. She then strode with immense beauty and grace to the middle of the dance floor and sang the British national anthem in a tremulous and beautiful voice, adding the newly written verse,

> *Join we great Nelson's name,*
> *First on the role of fame,*
> *Let him us sing,*
> *Spread we his fame around,*
> *Honour of Britain's ground,*
> *Who made Nile's shores resound,*
> *God save our King.*

When she finished and as the crowd of guests cheered and applauded with immense vigour, I could only stand and nod to them in all corners of the room and raise my left hand in acknowledgment. Never before had I felt the depth and immensity of such an appreciation for what I had done. Truly and forever any sacrifice and every effort would be worth such a reward.

I could not help but cherish the regard that Lady Hamilton demonstrated, and I enjoyed immensely the attention she focused upon me, when frequently in our conversation she would laugh and touch my arm. At one point she congratulated me on some trifling observation I had made and rewarded me by placing a Swiss chocolate in my mouth. I stayed at the celebration much longer than I had expected, and retired to my room just before midnight with a sense of fulfilment and serenity.

In the harbour the next morning Captain Hardy advised that toward the end of the evening Josiah Nisbet had behaved quite badly. Apparently he was upset at the attention Lady Hamilton was paying to me, and at one point he was said to have remarked, "See there! That is despicable! She is placing her hands all over him, and he is allowing it. Why doesn't she just feed him from her breast?" I made no comment in response to the story. We also discussed news advisories received from the foreign office. They described promising attempts to form a second coalition against France with Portugal, Russia, Turkey, and the Kingdom of the Two Sicilies. This information seemed very fortunate and again reinforced the importance of ensuring that King Ferdinand should remain staunch as an ally. Turkey and Russia had declared war on France, and a Russo-Turkish fleet under Admiral Ushakov had entered the eastern Mediterranean to attack various islands held by the French. It seemed clear to me that if victories could be won in Italy, Austria might also be persuaded to join the coalition.

Before I came to Naples, it had been my intent to have Syracuse as our operational base, as it was situated at a proximity to all of the sailing points throughout the Mediterranean. However, in my morning conference with Captain Hardy, he gave to me a copy of a dispatch which Lord Spencer had sent to Admiral Jervi:.

In every point of view it seems preferable that our headquarters should be in the neighbourhood of the Two Sicilies. They are more secure of supplies and more centrally situated for any

purpose which may occur of employing them: and the great
object of giving courage and support to the Kingdom of Naples,
which from the peculiarity of its present connection with the
court of Vienna stands in a rather higher rank in the scale of
politics than on a superficial view might at first appear, will
be much more effectually obtained by presence of such a naval
force which may at the same time be very usefully employed
in distressing Malta or in intercepting the communication
between France and Egypt.

It thus appeared very clear to me. My orders were to remain
in Naples, and notwithstanding my earlier misgivings concerning
administration of the kingdom of Naples as headquarters of the Kingdom
of the Two Sicilies, I should do my utmost in supporting and encouraging
action at that place. It was also clear that the influence that may be exerted
by Queen Maria Carolina could be essential in bringing Austria back
into war against France. Shortly thereafter, the strategic importance of
Naples became further emphasised when Austria declared war on France,
and it was reported that an army under General Mack von Leiberich
was being assembled to join with the Neapolitans in an effort to liberate
Rome. To me, this meant that I should be engaged in encouraging land
actions of Neapolitan and Austrian armies on the peninsula of Italy while
cooperating actively with the Turkish and Russian squadrons to further
interrupt French influence in the eastern Mediterranean. While I observed
that King Ferdinand's principal concerns were devoted to hunting and
illicit affairs, the queen could be counted on to manage the true affairs
of the kingdom. I also found that in having an influence upon the queen,
I had an invaluable ally. It was Emma, a name she had asked me to call
her, to which I correspondingly requested that she not call me admiral but
Horatio, as now my feelings toward her had become that of a dear friend.

I had found Emma not only to be effective to work with but also
very congenial, intelligent, and understanding. When given a task, whether
in the management of her household or in her relations with the queen,
she was very capable, energetic, and devoted. Sir William had also proved
to be more than a political ally. He was a sincere man who understood
completely the dynamics of political intrigue. He enjoyed a very special
relationship with the king and understood the king's often ineffectual
command abilities. He also accompanied him in his hunts, and even at an

advanced age Sir William was considered the best marksman in the king's hunting groups.

My immediate strategic involvement became twofold: support of the recapture of Malta and of the Admiralty's new plan to recapture Minorca. French forces held both islands; however, our naval domination of the Mediterranean made their resupply impossible, and each of the occupying forces was made to live off the island and defend their positions with only the arms in hand. It seemed appropriate that to best accomplish my mission, a relocation of my main forces to Syracuse would be appropriate. However, when this became known, Emma came to me with an alarming request.

"Horatio, I have just come from a meeting with the queen, who is very alarmed that British ships will leave Naples. She is beside herself with grief over the threat of the French coming down from Rome to attack the kingdom and says that should that happen with no British support, it would be necessary for the kingdom to become neutral and to withdraw from the coalition against the French."

"I can understand that," I replied, "but I can leave one warship here in the Bay of Naples as a gesture of support, and if there is indication of any invasion, I can easily return from Syracuse."

"That is true," she answered, "but to secure Naples as a principal operating base and retain the formal alliance with the kingdom, would it not be wise to maintain your principal force here? We are only a day's sail from Syracuse, and by intelligent planning, your support of British operations can still be carried out." She then added, "Your presence here is essential, and I would hate to see you go."

"If our continued usage of Naples as a principal operating base is a formal request from the king, that would be a strong influence upon me to remain in Naples," I reasoned.

"It may also be," she added, "that your continued presence here may convince the king formally to declare war against France."

I reflected for a moment, smiled, and asked, "Is this something that you are recommending on behalf of the queen?" She did not answer but smiled and tilted her head. I knew the answer was in the positive. At that moment I knew that Emma was one of the most valuable political resources I had, and as I looked upon her face, it had never been more beautiful.

"I shall advise Admiral Jervis that we will remain in Naples at the request of the king and shall condition that recommendation upon a formal declaration of war by the king," I concluded.

"That is wise, my dear Horatio, and I believe you will achieve the results you desire," she answered with another smile.

On the next day I received a note from the queen expressing how delighted she was at the prospect of the British keeping its force in Naples, and within the week the Kingdom of the Two Sicilies formally declared war on France. On October, I ordered Captain Ball in the refitted *Alexander* along with two frigates and a mortar ship to assist in the siege of Malta. Within a month the French garrison at the Maltese island of Gozo capitulated, but the French continued to control the capital of Valetta. In the meantime Admiral Jervis had been succeeded in command by Admiral George Keith, whose reputation was for administrative thoroughness rather than active tactical command. I felt some concern with the loss of strong leadership as had been so successfully demonstrated by Admiral Jervis, and I was distressed that Admiral Keith later had written a formal dispatch to the Admiralty expressing some pointed dissatisfaction with progress in the recapture of Malta.

"How in the name of hell can this man express any dissatisfaction in what we have accomplished when in truth we have carried out completely our isolation of the island and no proper force for its recapture has been sent by the army?" I shouted in a meeting with Captain Hardy.

"Why don't we make that observation a matter of record?" Hardy asked.

"You are damned right, Hardy!" I responded with some anger. "I shall write to the Admiralty and shall send a copy to His Righteousness, Admiral Lord Keith."

I sent a dispatch recounting all of our successful efforts in commanding the waters of the Mediterranean and forcefully recommended that the army supply a sufficient force to recapture Malta. Thereafter the army responded with a brigade of soldiers, and Malta was recaptured. Apparently the word in the Admiralty was that recapture of the island was largely because of my strong recommendation, and comments were glowing about the effectiveness of our blockade. Shortly thereafter, I received two communications that imparted great satisfaction. The first was a letter from Admiral Jervis in which he wrote,

You are as great in the Cabinet as you are on the ocean and your whole conduct fills me with admiration and confidence. I thank God that your health is restored and that the luscious Neapolitan dames have not impaired it. God bless you my dear Admiral and be assured that no man loves or values you more highly than yours truly. Affectionately, St. Vincent.

The other was a copy of the *London Gazette*, which reported that my elevation to a peerage had been formally declared by Parliament. I responded to Admiral Jervis, "*The King of Naples ... declaring war ... is my greatest reward, and I desire no other ... Lady Hamilton is an Angel. She has honoured me by being my Ambassadress to the Queen: therefore she has my complete confidence and is worthy of it.*"

I also wrote to Lord Spencer,

I received your Lordship's letter of 7 October, communicating to me the title his Majesty has graciously conferred upon me, and honour, your Lordship has noted, is the highest that has ever been conferred on an officer of my standing who was not a Commander-in-Chief. I receive it as I ought what the goodness of our Sovereign, has been pleased to bestow ... yet I owe, I feel, this to the Almighty and His unbounded confidence of the King, your Lordship, and the whole world, in my exertions.

Within the same month I received a letter from my friend Alexander Davison describing chiefly the situation with Fanny. He wrote,

I cannot help again repeating my sincere regret in your continuation in the Mediterranean; at the same time I would be grieved that you should quit the station, if it in the smallest degree affecting your feelings. You certainly are, and must be, the best and only judge. Yet you must allow your best friends to express their sensations ... Fanny is in good health but is very uneasy and anxious, which is not to be wondered at. She sets off ... tomorrow for Bath ... She bids me say that unless you return home in a few months, she will join you at Naples. Excuse a woman's tender feelings as they are too acute to be expressed.

As I read Davison's letter in my apartment at the Palazzo Sessa, I whispered to myself, "Oh, why does Fanny complain of my doing my duty at the station where I have been commanded? Please, woman, understand." I then wrote her a letter indicating that it would not be prudent for her to come to Naples but that she should remain at home where I would be as soon as circumstances would allow.

At dinner with the Hamiltons that evening, Sir William indicated that he had received the copy of the *London Gazette*, reporting my elevation to peerage.

"My dear admiral," he said, raising his glass to toast, "I welcome you with the fullest heart to accompany those of us who have the honour of a peerage and want you to know that having you stand beside me as a peer embellishes me greatly by your presence."

"Thank you, my good friend," I replied, "I am humbled to stand with you and am grateful to the Almighty that he has caused me to survive and to receive such an honour."

Emma raised her glass, "How wonderful it is to be in the company of two lords. I am overcome."

Sir William retired to his bedroom early that evening, as was his custom, and after some conversation about goings on in the Neapolitan court, Emma asked, "Would it be pleasing, Lord Horatio, if I accompanied you to your room and bathed your head wound? It seems to be healing nicely, and I would like to see it resolved completely."

I responded, "First, my dear Emma, please do not call me *lord*, and yes, I would be very pleased to have you tend to my wound."

She ordered a servant to bring a bowl of warm water and accompanied me to my room, where I reclined on the red sofa while she again gently washed the diminishing red scar on my forehead.

"Emma, why do you take such pains to care for me?" I asked.

"Because, my dear Horatio, I love you," she answered, putting down the cloth and stroking my face. After a moment she bent down and kissed my forehead and then my cheek and then softly upon my lips.

"I should go now," she whispered and started to leave the room.

"Wait, please," I said as she was walking toward my door. As I approached, I put out my arm. She came to me, and we embraced. I whispered, "My dear Emma, I have to tell you that I return your love in full measure, but I cannot know what kind of love it can be. You are beautiful, and you have captured my heart. But I feel totally restrained by my regard and esteem for Sir William. There is nothing that I want to do to offend him, even though everything about you attracts me so completely. You are a beautiful woman, and touching you at this moment is the dearest and most entrancing thing that I can imagine."

"Sir William loves you, Horatio," she softly responded.

She lifted her head, and I kissed her with a gentle intensity that I had never before known. I was captured by her to the depths of my soul, and the emotion that filled me was as real and undeniable as it was without reason or reflection. It simply was a truth that I could neither deny nor resist.

With her head upon my shoulder, she stroked the back of my neck and said, "I will speak with him. I must." She then left the room. I slept very little during the night, and each time I woke, my thoughts returned to the touch of Emma and the magic of our embrace that renewed in me a vitality of life and an irrepressible longing.

The next morning I ordered an early breakfast in my room. I ate alone, and then I took the Hamiltons' carriage down to the bay to review the refitting progress with Captain Hardy and the other ship commanders. I was very pleased with the vigour and completeness that all of the captains were taking in rendering their ships prepared for sea again. My mind, however, was totally elsewhere, and I felt a great sense of general anxiety. In the middle of the afternoon I returned to the Palazzo Sessa and walked about its surrounding gardens. I thought of Fanny and the often frustrating but sometimes pleasant years we had spent together. She had been an acceptable wife, even though she was frequently neglectful and had never demonstrated any genuine understanding of me or my mission in life. She would be better as a rector's wife, for the objectives of her living the life she desired were never compatible with the demands and constant stress that must be accepted in the life of a commanding officer in the Royal Navy. My thoughts also returned constantly to Emma. She was not only beautiful, but capable of fully appreciating, supporting, and encouraging the man that I was. She was intelligent, vigorous, and accomplished in being a woman who would provide to me a perfect companion. All of my sensations were enraptured by a reverie of her total being – her touch, her care, the constant attentiveness and praise that so often lifted my spirits. I was consumed with the totality of her and truly longed to be with her in every way. There was, however, a great impediment. She was the wife of a minister of His Majesty's government, and he was a man I fully respected and could not dishonour.

I returned to my room and tried to rest, but sleep would not come. In my mind I wrestled with a dilemma that seemed beyond solution. I walked about the room and the balcony, looking down upon my ships at anchor, entirely unsure of the balance of the life that lay ahead. Above all, I had to fulfil my duty, and I would have to bear whatever future the Almighty's providence may declare.

Tria Juncto in Uno

Shortly before the dinner hour a servant knocked at my door and said that Sir William would like to confer with me before dining. I thanked him and donned my formal uniform as was my custom for dinner. I went to the room that was indicated to me as being Sir William's library and for the first time looked upon the small room that was resplendent with filled bookcases, beautiful paintings, and artefacts that reflected the decor and tastes one might expect to be associated with a man of accomplished refinement. Sir William sat writing at his desk, and when I knocked lightly on the side of the door, he smiled broadly.

"Ah, Horatio – or should I say Sir Horatio? – please come in and be comfortable." He indicated a chair next to his desk, and I sat.

"Please, sir, I shall always remain Horatio to you. After all, we are peers together." I returned his smile.

"I shall come to the point, my dear man," he said, leaning back and slightly nodding his head. "I have spoken with Emma, and we should discuss the matter at whatever length may be necessary. She has said that she has very strong feelings of attachment and attraction to you. I cannot say that this surprises me, as you are a man of the highest accomplishment. It may be that you also return that kind of attraction to her as a beautiful and caring woman."

"Indeed, but sir—" I interjected, and he gently raised his hand to stop me speaking.

"You should know she has made exceptional progress in becoming a woman of some refinement, given the challenges she had to overcome by her less-than-sterling upbringing. I also want you to know that I have the greatest admiration and respect for you as a gentleman and commander who is now celebrated by much of the world. I would hope that you are not offended that I consider you to be a confidant, akin to a brother."

"I am deeply honoured to be so considered," I quickly responded.

"Well, splendid. Now, to get to my point, I simply want to say that whatever ... relationship ... may develop between Emma and yourself would not be objectionable to me if we together can maintain and foster the bond that I believe encompasses the three of us. Emma is my wife and must remain with me, and it is my hope that we three might become *tria juncto in uno* – that is, three joined into a single cohesion of love and respect with all of the positives that might come from that. What say you?"

"My dear man, my dear brother, and oh, how I would love to consider you as a brother to me. What you have said raises from me a cloak of despair that has made me miserable. It is quite right that I hold a great attraction for Emma. In truth, I love her, and your acceptance of that is something that pleases me beyond measure. Indeed, it raises my respect and love for you, whom I am more than willing to embrace as akin to a brother, and may it be a brotherhood forever."

"Ah then, let there be no discomfiture in our relationship. We shall be *tria juncto in uno*, and each of us shall be stronger and more comfortable because of it. Now may I offer you a glass of wine? I have several times visited a marvellous vineyard on the River Porto, and they have sent me two new cases of aged claret that I find to be most splendid."

As I toasted with Sir William and sipped his dark, sweet port, there came over me a sense of euphoria and great anticipation of seeing Emma again under circumstances where my attraction for her might be received with no sense of regret. I could not have hoped for a better resolution with Sir William. He was a man of stature and understanding. I would accept a relationship that now would be without restraint or regret. At dinner that evening no mention was made to Emma of our conversation. However, I felt sure that Sir William had communicated his feelings to her. Instead, we spoke of the impending arrival of General Karl Mack from Vienna and the need for effective and immediate joint action of the Austrian and Neapolitan forces against the French to liberate Rome.

I advised Sir William, "With a declaration of war having been made by the kingdom against France and with support from Vienna, a pre-emptive strike against Rome should be immediate. Full support of the Royal Navy will be provided, and I am quite eager to transport perhaps five thousand troops in my ships to augment the land force under the command of General Mack."

"I believe that would be a brilliant move," Sir William responded, "and it is particularly appropriate given the fact that the French are very preoccupied in the eastern Mediterranean, where Russian and Turkish naval units have taken several islands from them in the Adriatic. I also understand that Albanian troops have been aligned with the Turks."

"That is hopefully quite true, although in any action against Rome, major emphasis must be placed upon the Austrians. My confidence in the Army of Naples is not very strong, as I have heard them described as being little more than 'peasants in uniform.' Command must be placed in General Mack, and the primary assaulting force should be with the Austrian Army with only support provided by the Neapolitans."

Sir William nodded in agreement and added, "Do you think a pincer action might be effective, with the Royal Navy landing troops to take Leghorn and then passing south to Rome while General Mack and his Austrian force attack from the south?"

"That is a very workable, even brilliant concept," I replied, "and I will offer it to General Mack when he arrives."

Emma then spoke, "I believe that whatever should or can be done by Naples will be assured by the queen, who is in a fever for revenge against the French for murdering the sister she dearly loved. I believe that she can demand of the king that he do what is necessary."

Sir William chuckled and said, "Of that I am sure, my dear, especially with your encouragement, of course. Now I am somewhat tired and will take my leave. I trust the two of you will have a pleasant evening." He smiled at Emma and me and then nodded and left the room. I looked for a long moment at Emma and said, "I am going to my balcony and hope that you might join me there." She smiled.

My glass of port in hand, I went to my room, removed my uniform jacket, walked to the balcony, and looked out over the bay on a clear night with a sky filled with stars. A soft, cool breeze was blowing, and I heard the door to my room open and then close. After a moment I felt Emma's arms encircle me and felt her place her head upon the back of my shoulder.

"From the time that I saw you when you returned to Naples, standing on the deck of your ship, looking tired and somewhat grey with a battle scar across your forehead, I believe that I fell in love with you. You are the greatest man alive," she said. "I now know that I am hopelessly and irretrievably devoted to you. I will love you forever."

I turned and placed my lips upon hers in a kiss that will forever be etched in my memory. Her lips were soft, and the sweet scent of her, the touch of her, and her very presence next to me fulfilled a longing that had possessed me and now could be released in a rising tide of fulfilment. I moved my mouth to her cheek, kissed it, and whispered in her ear, "You will be mine forever. I thank almighty God for sending you to me and for touching the heart of Sir William to understand."

She stroked the back of my neck and said, "He loves you, Horatio, almost as I do, and he will always be dear to us. Kiss me again, my love."

I did so and then led her to my bed, where we made love that was complete in the joining of two people with a passion that was perfect in tenderness and tumult and with an explosive release that brought tears to my eyes. It was as though I consumed her. The look of her body, white as milk, the touch of her, her eager and unrestrained embrace of me, the feel of her next to me, her welcoming of my entry, her excited breathing and perfect response to my movement within her as I held the back of her head in my hand kissing her deeply, and her urgent gasps as she reached the height of her release that met with my own all conveyed to me that the world would never be the same as before that moment. We embraced in the afterglow, her head resting on my shoulder as she stroked my cheek with the back of her hand, whispering, "Horatio, my Horatio."

When I woke in the morning, she was dressed and sitting on the side of the bed, her hand softly rubbing my chest. She bent down and kissed me and said, "Do not be late for breakfast, my love."

As I entered the dining room, Sir William was shuffling with papers and said, "I have an announcement here from the king advising that General Mack will arrive today and there will be a dinner tonight to greet him." He then looked at me and said, "I trust you had a good evening."

"We had a divine evening, my dear friend," I replied.

"Good," he responded, "then we shall get down to the business at hand."

I looked at Emma. She was the most beautiful thing I had ever seen. She smiled. I smiled back to her and felt within a sense of warmth and excitement that conveyed to me the new and wonderful dimension that had been added to my life.

Chapter 13

Attack upon Rome

I remember the morning when a messenger appeared on the quarterdeck at my usual conference with Captain Hardy, announcing that King Ferdinand requested a conference. I had never before had a private meeting with the king, and I was curious as to what the nature of this meeting might be. I indicated that the messenger should wait, donned my full-dress blue uniform, and rode back to the palace with the messenger. When I arrived, the king was sitting in his formal court in the company of approximately twenty persons, most of whom were women fully dressed in their very best attire and laughing animatedly at the king's remarks.

When he saw me arrive, the king made a sweeping motion, indicating that the assembled entourage should depart. He then descended the five steps from his throne perch and extended a hand to me. He was smiling broadly, and I had to stifle a chuckle, for he was the ugliest and most common-looking man I had ever seen. His head was quite large, and his face was narrow and long rather like that of a draft horse, featuring one of the most protruding noses that God ever made. I understood immediately why many Neapolitans referred to him as *Le Naso Re*, meaning the *Nose King*.

"*Nostro Liberatore!* How good to see you!" he bellowed. "General Mack is supposed to arrive today, but I cannot be here. You see, the duke of my western province is clearing the wild boars from a part of his land and has invited me and Sir Hamilton to assist. I would very much like you to meet with General Mack and plan our assault on Rome. I shall return in three days to review the plans, which I trust will include my riding at the head of the procession as we enter the city gate. You are both brilliant military leaders, and it is my expectation that General Mack will be as successful on land as you have been at sea." I was taken aback that at a time when one of the most momentous military actions in the history of the Kingdom of the Two Sicilies was about to take place, the king would be distracted by the prospect of a hunt for wild pigs. But in a moment, however, it seemed fortuitous, as it would remove him from any important matter having to do with our planned engagement. It was probably better that he would be hunting wild animals.

"Your Majesty, I shall be pleased to do as you have requested," I happily responded with a half bow.

"Well, go now and think of the necessaries for our liberation of Rome from the French menace. It will be a great day for our kingdom, and yet another day for you to add your glorious list of triumphs. While you are planning to hunt down and kill the French, I shall be hunting down and killing boars in the near reaches of Calabria." The king then patted my shoulder, gave a broad smile of misshapen teeth, and walked away with a quick step.

I returned to *Vanguard* and instructed Hardy to send a quartermaster to the palace and to advise me of the moment General Mack arrived. However, the general did not come that day or the next two, but arrived with a great procession on the fourth day immediately before the king returned from his hunting expedition. I went to the palace to inquire whether I might speak with General Mack, and I was told that he was in conference with the king. I was escorted to an ornate chamber where the two sat drinking and talking with great laughter.

As soon as I entered the room, the king rose and walked toward me. "My good admiral, how fortunate it is to have you at this time. The good general has just advised me that he has six battalions of men who will arrive today and take camp north of the city on the Via Roma. I do not think that you have met the general, so please let me introduce him."

General Mack stood, wearing a resplendent uniform and decorations that would make one think him the grand hero of the Austrian Army. He extended his right arm, which I grasped with my left. Embarrassed, he excused himself, saying in quite good English, "Please excuse me, Admiral. I momentarily forgot your wound."

"It is no matter, General, for the rest of me is quite set and ready to undertake our great assault."

"Yes," said the king, "we have been discussing that, and the general has a wonderful plan." We sat, and General Mack spoke.

"It is our intelligence, Admiral, that the French forces in Rome have been depleted by a large withdrawal to Macedonia because they fear an encroachment by the Turks. It will be a good time to attack, and I believe we can make them easy pickings. Before this scare from the Turks, we had been advised in Vienna that the French were planning on the capture of Naples itself. They probably now have information that my forces have passed through the Piedmont and have arrived here. It may even be that upon our assault, they will evacuate the city. We, however, cannot plan on that, and I very much look forward to your support from the sea."

"I assure you all the support I can bring to bear, General," I assured him.

"Splendid," he responded, "and the king tells me that Sir William Hamilton described your plan of landing a force in Leghorn that will attack Rome from the north, and I believe that to be a very brilliant idea."

"I am ready to undertake that plan as soon as you are prepared to move from the south," I replied with some excitement at the acceptance of my plan. I relished the idea of taking Rome with some anticipation of additional recognition that would result from the triumph.

The king clapped his hands and shouted, "*Bello! Molto bello!* We shall win! I know it, and all glory will go to you great men for your service to my kingdom."

I spoke to the general, "I shall draw up an operational plan of four or more frigates and store ships to carry men and supplies for this undertaking. I also think it possible to take Leghorn as an operational base for the army to then proceed to Rome while you attack from the south. Would you agree?"

"I do indeed, and whatever French force may be in Leghorn will be subdued by the troops you land so that there is no counterattack from that direction. I will also draw up my strategic plan and will send a copy to you."

I returned to *Vanguard* and called the captains of my ships together. I outlined and we discussed the general plans for making ready for sea. Each captain assured me that his ship was ready for service, with almost all refitting having been completed. Our action would be a rather simple and straightforward undertaking for the transport of troops in our frigates, and in the store ship, HMS *Alliance*, necessary supplies would be carried. The troops would not have to be permanently berthed, and the estimate was that our squadron could carry approximately five thousand men, horses, and ample supplies that should cover two weeks of operation. The formal plan was completed and sent to General Mack, Sir William, and of course, the king. Fortunately he had no reply.

At the end of the captains' conference I poured each captain a glass of port that had been given to me by Sir William and said, "Gentlemen, we are blessed with an operation which we shall carry out in dispelling the enemy from the great and ancient city of Rome. It is a great undertaking that makes me rest easy and proud, for I know that I have the best ships and the best captains upon the sea."

Each of them smiled and tilted his glass in toast. Captain Trowbridge remarked, "Admiral, you seem to be fit and in the best spirits I have seen since the Nile. I'm sure we are all delighted to have you so fully recovered."

With preparations underway for our operation, I returned in the early evening to the Palazzo Sessa. During the carriage ride, above the clatter of Neapolitan cobblestones I was a contented soul, looking forward to a new mission at sea and dearly anticipating my arrival back at the Palazzo Sessa, where I would be greeted by the dearest and most wonderful woman I had ever known. From the time of our first communion there had been a settled and most exquisite routine. I would return to the Palazzo. I would take my bath. I would make notes regarding my plans for the next day. Emma would help Sir William dress for dinner. She would come to call me for dinner. I would take her in my arms and kiss her. We would hold our embrace and whisper phrases of endearment in each other's ear. She would say that it was time for dinner and would lead me by the hand to the dining room.

Our dinners were always pleasant, entertaining, and helpful. Sir William would discuss his conferences with the king and other ministers of state, or he would describe certain paintings, artefacts, or pieces of sculpture that he hoped to add to his expansive collection. I would share information in dispatches from the foreign office or the Admiralty that I had received if they had not been copied to him. Emma would discuss her conversations with the queen, frequently more substantive and meaningful than conversations Sir William had endured with the king. In total, we would effectively fashion the policy and relationship between Great Britain and the Kingdom of the Two Sicilies. After dinner and sometimes after a brandy, Sir William would excuse himself and retire to his bedroom. Emma and I would sit for a while, usually reviewing matters that had been discussed at dinner and making plans for the next day. I would then stand and take her by the hand and look into her eyes. She would smile, and I would say, "I'm going to stand on the balcony."

And she would answer, "I will join you shortly."

I would go to my room, change into my night clothes, and go to stand on the balcony, looking out over the bay, thinking of things to come. I would hear the door to my bedroom open, but I would not move.

Soon I would feel Emma's arms encircle me and the gentle weight of her head against my shoulder. As with the first night, we would re-enact the same scene from the same play. I would turn. We would embrace and kiss softly and then whisper expressions of love, and then I would take her to my bed to explore the gentle mounds, curves, and valleys of her body. Unabashedly and with a great sense of unrestrained passion, we would make love in an act of physical union that was to me an expression of the fullest commitment and caring that two people could experience. I would then be lost in the deep richness of being with her, being a part of her, and feeling that she had become a part of me.

Success and Debacle

In November, preparations were completed for the attack against Rome. My ships had been refitted and were ready for action. King Ferdinand had mobilized his entire Neapolitan army. More than five thousand of his soldiers would be added to General Mack's army of four divisions. This provided to the general more than thirty thousand troops to move on Rome from the South. Several months earlier Austria had promised to provide sixty thousand troops for a coordinated attack from the east, and a week earlier Russia had agreed to cover Sicily with its Mediterranean fleet. My ships were prepared to depart with more than six thousand Neapolitan soldiers and six thousand cavalry.

Something startling, however, occurred at the final conference with the king and General Mack. It was our final planning conference, where the complete strategic scheme would be once again reviewed. General Mack arrived late and was very sombre in his demeanour, quite unlike the appearance of enthusiasm he had shown before.

"Your Majesty and Admiral, I have been very saddened by news reported to me this morning from Vienna. Apparently the emperor has decided that additional Austrian forces will not be committed to our assault. He advises that the treaty between Austria and your Majesty's kingdom is a defensive treaty only and that because this attack is not defensive, he cannot provide support under the treaty."

I was shocked at this dastardly withdrawal and stood, declaring, "Could they not read the treaty before making the commitment? And if there is a state of war between Austria and France, as I believe the present circumstances to be, why can Austria not attack its enemy? There must be something more to this play!"

King Ferdinand just sat there seemingly in a state of shock, and General Mack replied to me, "I do not know, my good man, what underlying reason there may be. It has been reported that Bonaparte is back in Paris and assembling an army. It may be that our emperor fears a direct attack from Bonaparte's army."

"Fear?" I shouted. "A country at war cannot be motivated by fear. Austria has its own armies, and if they are not ready to confront the French and defeat them, the emperor should declare neutrality and retire to his summer palace for good."

"Please," the general interjected, "do not assume things that we do not know, and I will thank you not to be disrespectful of my emperor. I suspect that he has been influenced by our chancellor, who is a cautious man."

"I mean no disrespect for anyone, but I have great disrespect for the news that I have just heard. They promised support for our operation against their enemy, and now they have said that they will do nothing. I do not understand that. In any event we are here to make war upon the enemy of Britain, Austria, and the Kingdom of the Two Sicilies. Should we dissemble our forces? I say no. We are ready to attack Rome, and we can take it without support of the Austrian Army, offered as a promise and now withdrawn as a breach of that promise. I am ready to attack the enemy, and the question now on the table is this: Are you ready to do likewise? If we are bold and if we attack with a fury, we can achieve great things. Are you ready?"

"It is true that we have more than thirty thousand troops in total, and I believe that Rome can be taken," the general haltingly replied.

"Then let us go. Let us take Rome. And then let us tell the emperor that the enemy has been driven from the city without his promised support," I urged.

The general looked up, and the dour look upon his face changed. What had been a visage of dejection lightened into an appearance of resolve and enthusiasm. He smiled slightly and said, "Then let us go."

The king stood and for the first time spoke, "I'm very pleased that we are together. Let us go and take Rome."

On the ebbing tide of the next morning I departed with *Vanguard*, *Culloden*, and *Minotaur*, carrying three thousand Neapolitan troops and cavalry. The store ship *Alliance* carried another thousand together with supplies. Three Neapolitan ships carried the remaining troops and cavalry. General Mack's army, augmented by the Neapolitan troops and the king, moved northward on the Via Roma.

On the evening before departure I had written to First Admiral Spencer, "*I ventured to tell them directly that one of the following things must happen to the King, and he has had his choice – either to advance, trusting in God for his blessing on a just cause, to die with sword in hand or remain quiet and be kicked out of his Kingdom. Thanks be to God – the King has resolved to act.*"

We proceeded to the landing point north-west of Leghorn and disembarked our forces. The landing was orderly and without opposition. Our forces assembled and marched into Leghorn to find it evacuated of all French troops. Leghorn was taken without a shot. Our forces then reassembled and moved on Rome from the north. At that time I was pleased and confident in our mission. With little more to do, I called my captains to dinner and toasted to a successful undertaking. After dinner I wrote to Emma, "*Last night, I did nothing but dream of you ... I awoke twenty times in the night regretting that I was so far from you.*" The next evening I wrote again:

> *My dearest Emma, I am separated from all that I hold dear in this world and nothing could alleviate this separation from you but the call of my country ... no separation, no time, my beloved Emma, can alter my love and affection for you. It is founded on the truest principles of honour, and it only remains for us to regret which I do with anguish that there are any obstacles to our being united in the closest ties ... I can neither eat nor sleep for thinking of you, my dearest love ... I never made you a promise that I did not strictly keep as if made in the presence of heaven. I have remembered well our union together in these two months afterwards. I shall never forget them and never be sorry for the consequences.*

It was a solid truth to me that I did not fear the consequences of a child being conceived with her, for it was a dear anticipation no matter what the consequences may be. I had become bound to her as the love of my life.

With our forces disembarked and with Leghorn effectively subdued, I decided to return to Naples. There, to my great satisfaction, I received an official report from General Mack that the French had evacuated Rome, and it was taken without opposition. In fact, General Mack stated that the king had led the combined forces through the city's south gate in full dress and glory. For two days all of Naples and I basked in what appeared to be a great victory. After celebratory dinners I enjoyed precious evenings with Emma. Then the scenario of perfection was shattered like a beautiful vase falling from a mantelpiece. At breakfast Captain Hardy arrived in a hurry and announced that messengers had brought a disastrous report from Rome. Apparently the French General Championnet had withdrawn his forces just to the north-east of the city and then launched a counterattack that had sent the forces of the king and General Mack in full retreat. Apparently at the sight of the large French force, the combined army did not defend their positions but simply ran away.

I was thunderstruck with astonishment. "This cannot be, Hardy. Are you telling me that they did not defend the city? They did not fight?"

"I'm afraid so, Admiral," Hardy replied. "They are in full retreat back to Naples."

The next day the king arrived in a panic. He was ashen with fear and exclaimed with total despair that the French Army was moving to attack Naples. He ordered that all members of his court should prepare to quit the city and go to Palermo. General Mack also appeared and announced that he was reassembling his army to return to Austria by way of the eastern coast of the Italian peninsula. However, when he began his withdrawal, his decimated force was intercepted, and at first contact with the French Army he immediately surrendered and was taken as a prisoner of war. I wrote to Lord Spencer that the Neapolitan and Austrian forces had fallen to pieces, "*They have not lost much honour, for God knows, they had but little to lose. They lost all that they had.*"

It quickly appeared that there was no possibility of reorganizing a defensive force with the Neapolitans, as they had demonstrated no ability whatsoever of acting with any commitment or effectiveness. The only thing then to do was to pick up the pieces and assist in the flight of the royal family. I wrote to Lord Spencer,

> *There is an old saying – that when things are at their worst, they must mend. The mind of man cannot fancy things worse than they are here. But, thank God, my health is better; my mind never firmer and my heart is in the right trim to comfort*

and protect those who it is my duty to afford assistance. Pray,
my Lord, assure our gracious sovereign that while I live, I will
support his glory and that if I fall, it shall be in the manner
worthy of your Lordship's faithful and obliged Nelson. I must
not write more. Every word may be a text for a long letter.

My duty then was clear – to move their Majesties, their court, and as many of the English contingent as possible to the safety of Sicily.

Evacuation of the city was carried out in secrecy on the following night. There was a very strong and unruly faction of the Naples population called the "lazzaroni" who were royalists devoted to the king but who would, if they could, object to and even prevent the royal family leaving. In the tumult that existed in Naples, they had roamed through the streets, doing violence to anyone suspected of Jacobin tendencies. They gathered before the Palazzo Reale, where the king and queen addressed them and asked them to disperse. In the dark of the early morning hours, carriages moved people and goods as quietly as possible to the docks where they were carried out to our ships. Word was sent to all members of the English staff that they, too, should evacuate. Sir William, who was quite ill, had to be carried. Emma, however, was a force for organization and comfort to everyone. She emphasized the need for speed and commanded that nothing should be taken except that which was absolutely necessary. She assembled carriages and secured additional carts needed to carry supplies and precious goods, including many of Sir William's prized artefacts. On the dock her words were comforting and encouraging. By first light the king and queen together with a great majority of their court were aboard our ships with almost the entire British contingent. We set sail, leaving Naples to the French.

As soon as we cleared the bay, it seemed that a harsh but just reprimand was handed down by God, who relinquished us to the fury of hell. There arose a gale the likes of which I had seen but once, the time when the Mediterranean almost threw me and my ship against the rocky coast of Sardinia. The wind whistled through our trimmed sales, and our ships lurched and banged constantly into mountainous swells. Everyone aboard was racked with seasickness because of furious and unremitting pitching and rolling of the ships. Sir William was terrified of the ship foundering and sat in his bed with two loaded pistols with which he would kill himself rather than endure what he called the "gurgle, gurgle" of drowning. The king and queen lay in their bed, praying aloud for mercy and redemption. Emma became a remarkable force for compassion and caring throughout the terrible ordeal. With her sleeves rolled up and her hair tied in a bandanna, she went from person to person, comforting and encouraging each one. During the voyage the youngest royal child suffered epileptic fits, and Emma took him in her arms, rocking him and singing a lullaby. She stayed with him for hours upon hours until he died. I watched her with some astonishment but more so with a sense of pride that under such horrible conditions she could be such a strong character of compassion and unerring comfort. Seeing her as she acted throughout the terrible voyage cemented in my heart a love that deepened and would never change. After two days the storm abated, and the seas calmed. After four days we had brought the Neapolitan court safely to Palermo.

In Naples, it became obvious that the flight from the city had been an appropriate move, as the French Army approached in considerable size and camped at Capua. The king's cousin, Prince Pignatelli, had been left behind as viceroy with orders to defend the kingdom. However, he reasoned that defence was useless, as he had no meaningful army, and in order to save the city, he signed an armistice which gave the greater part of the kingdom beyond Naples to French control and sovereignty. What was left of the Neapolitan army disappeared, and many of their number, following their officers, went over to the French. The lazzaroni, however, continued in their allegiance to the king and attacked many of the French positions. Throughout the period of French occupation they remained defiant.

The Austrians, disregarding what should have been a proud heritage, seemed to regard the loss of Rome and Naples with total complacency. They continued to sit idly in Vienna and watch as their allies were subdued. In Sicily, I urgently requested and received a thousand troops for defence of the island. Their number, together with our small fleet that would prevent the transport of any French troops across the Strait of Messina served to give the island effective protection.

In Naples, General Championnet announced disestablishment of the monarchy and the establishment of a new Parthenopean republic. For the time at least, Jacobin principles had been established in the city. In Palermo, the royal entourage had taken up residence in several estates that were unoccupied, and some sense of royal presence had been maintained there. Sir William and Emma had been given a small apartment in one of the estates. I remained aboard *Vanguard*, not seeing Emma, dejected and feeling quite ill. Headaches had begun, and from time to time I felt that my head would split. Rest did not seem to lessen the pain, and I wrote to Lord Spencer, "*My health is at the lowest ebb, and I questioned whether I can go on, feeling that, at times, a final rest may be appropriate simply in the ground, six feet by two.*"

There also came another affront that might have put me down but gave rise within me such an outrage that it worked to my recovery. A young, dandy, and insufferably presumptuous young captain named Sidney Smith arrived in the eighty-gun frigate HMS *Le Tigre* en route to the Levant. The man was a relative of the foreign secretary and brother to the British minister in Constantinople. He also advised me he was an English peer and a Swedish knight of the Order of the Sword of Sweden, a title he carried with great vanity but to my mind provided no basis whatever for placing him in command of a British naval force. However, he carried orders from the first lord of the Admiralty, which he described as giving him the authority to take Samuel Hood and the squadron of ships I had placed under Hood's command for his own operations in the eastern Mediterranean. Because his claim seemed legitimate, as it was supported by the orders he carried, I became inflamed with anger and indignation. Immediately I wrote to Admiral Jervis:

> *My dear Lord, I do not feel, for I am a man, that it is possible for me to serve in the seas with Hood's squadron under a junior officer … And could I have thought it – from Earl Spencer … Smith has told Sir William Hamilton that he shall go east with Hood's squadron under his command. The Knight forgets the respect due to his superior officer. He has no orders from you to take my ships away from my command … Is it to be borne? If so, pray grant me permission to retire.*

Apparently young Smith had made no more positive impression upon Admiral Jervis than he had upon me, for I received an immediate response from the admiral.

> *I'm not surprised at your feelings being outraged, at the bold attempt Sir Sidney Smith is trying to wrest a part of your*

> *squadron from you … I have enclosed orders for you to take him*
> *immediately on your command. I have informed Lord Spencer*
> *of all these proceedings, and send him copies of the letters. The*
> *ascendance this gentleman has over all his Majesty's ministers*
> *is to me as astonishing …"*

Admiral Jervis also wrote a very direct letter to Lord Spencer, one stating, *"An arrogant letter written by Sir Sidney Smith has wounded Admiral Nelson to the quick … And compels me to place the strange man immediately under Admiral Nelson's orders. I experienced a trace of the presumptuous character of this young man during his stay at Gibraltar."* A further letter from Admiral Jervis bound up my wound and set things right.

> *I trust the greatness of your mind will keep up your body so*
> *that you will not think of abandoning the Royal Family of*
> *the Two Sicilies whom you have by your firmness preserved*
> *from the fate of their late Royal relations in France. Employ*
> *Sir Sidney Smith in any manner you think proper. Knowing*
> *your magnanimity, I am sure you will mortify him as little as*
> *possible, consistently with what is due to the great characters*
> *senior to him … God bless you my dear Lord, and be assured*
> *that no man loves and listens to you more truly than your very*
> *affectionate, St. Vincent.*

Thereafter I dispatched Captain Smith to the Levant, giving him the accompaniment of one frigate. Following a spat regarding the upstart Captain Smith, the pain of my head returned, and I felt generally ill throughout my body, having little energy, constantly needing to sleep. I remained on board *Vanguard* and despaired of perhaps never seeing Emma again. A great grey cloud seemed to loom over me, imparting a constant sense of anxiety and uncertainty. Blessedly I received a kind letter from my good friend Alexander Davison and answered to him,

> *Thank you, Alex, most heartily, for your letter. Believe me, my*
> *only wish is to sink with honour into the grave, and when it*
> *shall please God, I shall meet death with a smile. Not that I am*
> *insensible to the honours and riches my King and country have*
> *heaped upon me, so much more than any officer could deserve,*

I am ready to quit this world of trouble and ending only with those of an estate, six feet by two.

During this period of torment I received a direct letter from Lord Spencer that set forth a clear definition of my current duty. He stated that my conduct in the evacuation of Naples was highly approved and that I was expected to stay with the royal family until further notice. Some further good news arrived in the form of General Stuart, who, unannounced, arrived with a thousand more troops to secure the defence of Sicily. This was very comforting to me and allowed the sending of Captain Trowbridge with three frigates to capture the off-shore islands near Naples, which they did with dispatch, taking Procida, Capri, Ischia, and the Ponza islands. Trowbridge then sent word that in Naples, Cardinal Fabrizio Ruffo had assembled a royalist army in Calabria, which, together with the Neapolitans lazzaroni, were ready to attack the fictional Parthenopean republic.

To complicate matters, information arrived to the effect that Admiral Bruix had slipped the blockade at Brest and was joined by five Spanish ships sailing south for the Mediterranean with more than twenty ships of the line. Where they were going and what they were planning to do became a matter of great speculation. The possibilities included evacuation of Bonaparte's stranded army in Egypt, relief of Corfu, recapture of Malta, or perhaps destruction of the British forces scattered in groups of small numbers around the Mediterranean. If Bruix could manage to add to his force additional ships from the Spanish fleet at Cadiz, he would have a very sizable force of more than forty ships of the line. When the French fleet appeared near Cadiz, they did not wait for any of the Spanish ships blockaded there but ran straight for Gibraltar and the Mediterranean. Admiral Vincent opined that an attack on Minorca was probably the enemy's mission and ordered Admiral Keith to concentrate there. At the time Admiral Jervis was quite ill and felt that he had neither the strength nor energy to continue his command. He then ordered Admiral Keith to succeed him in command of British forces in the Mediterranean.

Knowing that the French fleet from Brest was at sea, I concluded that its targets would likely be Minorca or Sicily. I immediately sent three ships to Admiral Duckworth at Minorca and wrote to captains Trowbridge and Ball to send all the ships they could spare to assist me in the defence of Sicily. I assumed that Admiral Keith had sufficient force to deal with the enemy - if Minorca was their objective. One of the ships sent by

Trowbridge was the HMS *Swiftsure*. When it arrived, I received a most unusual present from Ben Hallowell, its captain. The gift was a coffin made from part of *L'Orient's* mast, recovered from Aboukir Bay. I was pleased with the gift but more so by Captain Hallowell's comment, *"Admiral, we believe this is a fitting present for you but hope that it will not be used for a hundred years."*

As the French were entering the Mediterranean with the fleet of more than twenty warships, I felt that my squadron was particular vulnerability, as I had only five frigates under my command at Naples. I expected that Captain Ball would join me from Malta with three more, and I recalled HMS *Lion* from Leghorn. Still the numbers were not totally comforting, and before I learned that he had shifted command to Admiral Keith, I wrote to Admiral Jervis, *"Your Lordship may expect that any squadron under my command shell never fall into the hands of the enemy, and before we are destroyed, I have little doubt that the enemy will have their wings so completely clipped that they may be easily overtaken."*

> After I heard that the admiral was ill. I also wrote,
> *My dear Lord, our St. Vincent, what we have suffered in hearing of your illness … Let me entreat you to comfort us with a force fit to fight. We shall search the French out, and if it be either at Leghorn, Espezia or Naples, we will have at them. We shall have so much pleasure in fighting under the eye of our ever great and good sir. If you are sick, our dear Lady Hamilton will nurse you with the most affectionate attention. Good Sir William will make you laugh with his wit and inexhaustible pleasantry. We all love you. Come then to your sincere friends. Let us get you well and it will be such happiness to us, amongst the foremost of your attached, faithful and affectionate … Nelson.*

His response soon came. *"I have transferred the command to Lord Keith, deeming it for the public good for him to hold a trust which I cannot exercise in person."* My heart sank a bit, but I steadied my determination and resolved that whoever may be in command of us, we must do our duty.

Shortly thereafter, something else occurred that raised my spirits beyond measure. Sir William and Lady Hamilton had taken a house overlooking the Bay of Palermo, and they offered a room to me. Emma wrote, "My dearest, we have finally found the place that will provide us some rest and privacy from the constant racket of the king and queen's court. It is not large, but it is comfortable. And we have a place for you. Please come and stay with us. I have been miserable without you."

I had my personal things packed into a case, and that evening I departed *Vanguard* in high spirits and expectation. When I arrived, Emma showed me to my room, and as soon as we entered and the door was closed, she was in my arms.

"I have been miserable, so very miserable without you," she said.

"My darling woman, I have kept company with you in that misery, and as soon as I received news of your new accommodations, my heart soared higher than a sea eagle," I answered and then kissed her with a renewed passion that came over me like a spring rain upon a parched field.

She then said, "I must go and oversee the preparation of dinner. Tonight I shall sleep next to you, my most favourite place in the world."

At dinner Sir William was full of news. He announced that the Second Coalition had achieved great success in the field against the French. A general named Suvarov with an army of 120,000 men had swept the French out of Piedmont to Verona. They had evacuated much of their army from Naples, leaving only a skeletal force. The remaining Neapolitan army had been reorganised by Cardinal Fabrice Ruffo, whose force was augmented by several Russian and Turkish battalions. Apparently Ruffo had gained control of Calabria and was camped just outside the gates of Naples. Captain Trowbridge, having taken the islands near the city, had control of the city's seaward side. Repossession of Naples then seemed a distinct possibility, and the king and queen had begun to urge a return. In light of my standing orders from the Admiralty to protect and promote the Kingdom of the Two Sicilies, I stated that the prospect of recapture was very inviting and that we should make plans accordingly. Naples must once again become a major facility in service to the Royal Navy. Our dinner that evening was a scenario of high spirits and expectation. Sir William, still suffering from his constant illness, excused himself immediately after dinner.

"Shall I pour you a brandy, my dear," Emma asked me.

"No," I answered, "I do not want a brandy at this point. I want you, my love, only you."

We retired to my room and shared passionate love again, full and unrestrained. I had almost forgotten how beautiful my Emma was and how exquisitely pleasurable her touch could be in responding to the outpouring of my instincts. As we lay together afterward with a cool breeze passing through the window, I whispered, "The Almighty has given me many wonderful things, my dearest, and you are my greatest treasure."

She stroked my hair and answered, "My life is committed to you, my brave hero, my love."

Unexpectedly on the next day I received a newly commissioned ship, the eighty-gun HMS *Foudroyant*, to replace the battered and valiant *Vanguard*. Although I was delighted with the new ship, when I shifted my crew and hoisted my pennant in the *Foudroyant*, there was a distinct sense of loss that I felt as I looked over at my old flagship that had served me so well and had been through so many tribulations with me. It was very much like losing a dear old friend.

I soon received news from Captain Trowbridge, who was standing off Naples. His report stated that merchants bringing supplies from the city had advised that the new French-imposed Parthenopean republic had never been well received by the great majority of the city's population. While it had satisfied the ambitions of some aristocratic cognoscenti and a few opportunistic merchants, there was little popular support. The people of the working classes longed for return of their king, even one such as the vulgar Ferdinand. In addition, people outside of the city gave full support to Cardinal Ruffo and his ragtag army of Neapolitans augmented by some Turks, Russians, and the armed lazzaroni. There also came news that Cardinal Ruffo could not restrain his army from plundering houses and businesses owned by those who had given any allegiance to the French or their fictional republic. Many suspected of having Jacobean tendencies had been cruelly murdered. As Cardinal Ruffo's strength grew, and upon my suggestion relayed through Sir William, King Ferdinand sent the cardinal a formal recognition and commission of command that was subject to further orders from the king. He also gave Ruffo instruction that under no circumstances should he agree to any leniency regarding the supporters of the traitorous republic. Cardinal Ruffo's army soon had Naples surrounded, and with Trowbridge's ships anchored near the seawalls, the city's outlying forts gave up without a fight, the last of the French troops taking refuge in the city's remaining three forts. This allowed Ruffo's army to enter the streets of the city, where again those having shown Parthenopean sympathies were subjected to barbarous revenge. It was reported that scores of dead bodies lay in the streets, and many houses of those who had been in any manner supportive of the French had been set afire. The lazzaroni fully vented their rage and were ready for the appearance of their king and queen.

Meanwhile, news arrived that the French fleet under Admiral Bruix had been battered by a storm and had taken refuge in Toulon. I was a little relieved by this, and given the strength of the newly arrived British troops to defend Sicily, I felt that the time was right to recover Naples. The king and his council requested formally that I embark troops to retake Naples and re-establish royal authority. I rejoined my squadron and set course for Naples with five thousand of the king's troops. In passage, however, I learned that the French troops, as well as the remnants of the Parthenopean forces had been granted a temporary armistice, after which they would be allowed to evacuate the forts and retreat to the north. When Sir William told me of this development, I was beside myself with anger, vented to Sir William:

"The conduct of these peasants pretending to be an army is an outrage. The king's orders have been quite clear that no quarter is to be given to the French or to the rebels."

Sir William responded, "While that may be true, Admiral, it will not be possible to enforce any order until we have troops in the city and the proper command of it."

"The armistice that has been granted by the cardinal is without authority and is revocable. We must restore order and proceed with an orderly process for both the French and the rebels," I answered.

Demonstrating the extent of her control of the kingdom's affairs, a letter issued from the queen, presumably with concurrence of the king, said.

> *The rebels must lay down their arms and surrender to the discretion of the King. Then … an example should be made of some of the leaders with a rigorous severity. The females who have distinguished themselves in the revolution must be treated the same way – and without pity. This is not pleasure but absolutely necessity for, without it, the King could not peacefully govern his people. Finally, I recommend that Lord Nelson treat Naples as if it were an Irish town in a similar state of rebellion … We shall be better off without these rascals … They deserve to be branded that others may not be deceived by them. I recommend … the greatest firmness, vigour, and severity.*

When we arrived at Naples, I disembarked the troops and went ashore to the Palazzo Reale, which seemed almost empty, having been looted by both the rebels and some of the lazzaroni. I summoned Cardinal Ruffo, and when he arrived, I informed him that he had been relieved of command of the king's forces, presenting to him my appointment as commander of the city until the arrival of the royal entourage. I asked about the armistice, and he responded, "*Your Lordship, while matters were proceeding, I did the best that I could and in order to minimize bloodshed and death, agreed to an armistice followed by retreat of the French from our city and amnesty for the rebels who would pledge loyalty to the King.*"

"Cardinal, as you know, the king's orders were very clear. No quarter was to be given to any rebel forces that fought against their king as traitors. The French shall be allowed to surrender and retreat to areas beyond the king's control. As for the rebels, there are many who will be brought to account for their treachery, particularly those who exercised leadership against the king," I announced with the firmest of tone.

"As the king's representative in command, I shall obey any orders you give and recognize that you may countermand anything I have done," Ruffo said.

"Please have your people in authority advise the French that they may surrender and be repatriated. However, tell the rebels that they must surrender unconditionally and face their justice as it shall be handed down by the king," I ordered.

"I will do so, Admiral," he answered.

I chose to avoid any humiliation of Ruffo, as he was a man of high standing in the church and regarded by many in the population with respect. I believe the cardinal's anxiety was eased by the opportunity to come again into the king's good graces. As a gesture of conciliation, I invited him to dinner aboard the *Foudroyant*, and he accepted with some obvious relief.

The Caracciolo Matter

At dinner we discussed the state of one prominent rebel, Commodore Francesco Caracciolo. He had been a revered naval commander in the king's navy and was considered a man of some ability. However, after establishment of the Parthenopean republic he had been prevailed upon by its leaders to take command of the new republican navy and subsequently did something beyond the pale of toleration. He ordered his ships to fire upon both British ships and ships flying Neapolitan flags - ships that remained loyal to the king. He had even fired upon the *Minerva*, which had been his own flagship in the Neapolitan navy. When Captain Trowbridge had taken control of the Bay, Caracciolo fled into the city. At the arrival of our forces, garbed in the clothes of a peasant, he made his way to a rural villa belonging to his uncle. Warned that he had betrayed the king and was in danger of capture, he made his way to one of the boats attempting to flee the city but was recognized and captured. He was brought to the deck of the *Foudroyant* in irons and was described by Sir William as "frail, with a long beard, half dead and with downcast eyes." With compassion Hardy ordered him released from his irons, taken to a cabin, and offered food and drink.

Seizing the opportunity for making an example of a traitor and exacting punishment as I deemed necessary under the circumstances, I convened a court-martial. An Austrian minister in King Ferdinand's service was appointed president of the court, and five senior officers of the Neapolitan navy were appointed to serve with him. Questioning of the prisoner went on for several hours during which Caracciolo testified that he had taken command of the Parthenopean ships under threat of a firing squad had he refused. He also testified that he had not ordered any of the firing upon British or Neapolitan ships and that the real command of the ships had been exercised by French masters-at-arms. The court-martial did not attach great credence to his story, and with a vote of four to two, they handed down a sentence of death by hanging. Announcing the sentence, the president of the court-martial stated, "*You have repaid the high rank and honours conferred upon you by a mild and confiding sovereign with the blackest ingratitude. The sentence of the court is that you shall be hanged by the neck at the yardarm of your own flagship in two hours' time, and may God have mercy upon your soul.*"

Upon receiving the sentence, I confirmed it and ordered the sentence to be carried out by hanging at the yardarm of the *Minerva* on that very evening. He was to hang there until sunset. Then his body would be cut down and thrown into the sea. The president of the court suggested that the execution be delayed for a day in order to give Caracciolo an opportunity to cleanse his soul and prepare for death. However, given the dastardly acts of the man, I felt that within an hour he could make his peace with God and ask for forgiveness for his betrayal. I ordered the execution to proceed and commented to Hardy, "He has been fool enough to quit his master when he thought his cause was desperate, and now he must pay the price." Caracciolo pleaded that he be shot by a firing squad as appropriate to an officer of his rank rather than endure the ignominy of being hanged like a common criminal. When I received the request, I responded, "When he became a traitor, he forfeited his status as an officer and became a common criminal. Carry out the sentence as handed down by the court." That afternoon Caracciolo was handed over to the Neapolitans, who hoisted him by the neck on the foreyard arm of the *Minerva*. At sunset the rope was cut, and Caracciolo's weighted body fell feet first into the waters of the bay.

There followed an unrestrained purge within the city. Executions became a ritual day after day, carrying out the sentences of courts that were hastily organized and ordered to administer their justice with dispatch. Some victims were beheaded while others were hanged in front of unruly crowds. Among them were both men and women of stature, including dukes, titled ladies, bishops, professors, doctors, merchants and lawyers – really anyone who had professed an acceptance of the republican government by statements made, documents signed, or any other evidence, however trifling, which the court found to be an act of rebellion against King Ferdinand.

At dawn one day a fisherman cried an alarm. Admiral Caracciolo had risen from the sea and was returning to Naples. Actually his bloated and very dead body had come bobbing to the surface. His head was clearly above water and facing the city. I was apprised of the event and went to the quarterdeck, where I found the king in great consternation. He had heard the report and rushed to the ship. He looked out at the bay and focused upon a distant object. It was Caracciolo. The king was uttering repeated expressions of horror. He dropped his spyglass on the deck and turned to me, asking, "*Che cosa facciamo?* What shall we do?" There were numerous priests on board as part of the king's retinue, and one of them announced that Caracciolo had risen from the sea floor to beg for the king's forgiveness and a proper Christian burial. The king shouted, "*Fargli avere lo!* Let him have it!" I ordered a boat lowered to retrieve the body and to take it ashore where it was later removed to the church of Santa Maria on the great Piazza and given a Christian burial. It was also reported to me that a great number of his former officers and sailors attended the funeral with tears in their eyes. Within a week the king's authority was re-established fully, and with the exception of ongoing public executions, Naples was returning to its normal state before the revolution. The mess that had been Naples was beginning to abate.

Celebration

On the anniversary date of the Battle of the Nile, my squadron commanders suggested – and I thought it appropriate – that we host an evening's celebration to commemorate the event and to renew the positive spirit of the city. The king and queen were our honoured guests, and invitations were delivered to all of the titled figures of the allied embassies. Separate celebrations were given for the crews on each ship, hosted by its duty watch officer. The captains and all other officers of the squadron attended the festivities on *Foudroyant*. I was impressed and delighted with the arrival of the royal party because the king had ordered the firing of a royal salute of twenty-one guns from all three forts in the city. The salute began when the king arrived and the officer commanding his party's boat fired a red signal gun into the night sky. It was an unexpected honour but one that warmed my heart and reminded me of the regard in which I was held by the Kingdom of the Two Sicilies. I would later discover that the salute had been the original idea of my dearest Emma, an idea embraced by the queen as an honour to me - and as a strong political message. The queen also arranged that a large boat would be decorated as a Roman galley with illuminated lamps, and in the boat's centre there would be a large classical column bearing my name. On the stern two elevated angels held a picture of me. She had also ordered that two thousand candle lamps line the docks, which created a very warm and beautiful environment for the evening. We had hired an orchestra with talented musicians and singers. The orchestral *maestro*, unbeknownst to me and to my great pleasure and surprise, had composed a piece of music that described the fear and anxiety that had beset Naples before the Battle of the Nile and then added, *"But Nelson came, the invincible Nelson, and our city was preserved and again made very happy."*

In a letter written to Fanny I described the evening in detail, hoping that it would again remind her that I was a person of high regard whose accomplishment was valued by the king and queen of one of our important allies. Most of her letters to me had continued to be filled with inconsequential news that I regarded with little interest. She also repeated the constant refrain of anxiety as to when I would return home. To me, the prospect of returning home to a cold house at Burnham Thorpe and to a colder woman with a brittle, tiresome, and unappreciative nature was far from inviting. In Naples, I felt a sense of total commitment to a kingdom that valued me above all that I had expected. My command at Naples fulfilled my duty of protection to an ally of my country that was paramount to a sense of my life's mission and was fulfilled by the support and love of a woman who was now the dearest to me.

Dukedom of Brontë

During the week that followed, I was summoned by King Ferdinand to the Palazzo Reale. Upon arriving, I was escorted to the royal reception room, which by then had been largely refurbished with art returned from the lazzaroni as a result of efforts by Cardinal Ruffo. The king and queen were surrounded by their usual entourage and in the best of spirits. They were sitting in the company of Sir William and Lady Hamilton. The king invited me to sit, and announced, "Admiral Nelson, as you know, I am a man of few words and like to get to the point. If you will accept it, I would have the pleasure to confer upon you a title of Sicilian nobility. I would like to give to you the Sicilian Dukedom of Brontë and would be pleased if you would become a fellow countryman to us as the Duke of Brontë. You are probably not acquainted with it, so I can tell you that it lies on the western slope of Mount Etna. It is an agricultural area where the rents and other income from the estate should provide for you quite nicely. The seat of the estate is called Castello di Maniace. I would also ask that you accept this sword, which once belonged to King Louis XIV, and please wear with pride the decoration for your uniform that signifies your title."

The king then took a jewel-encrusted sword from an enamelled box and held it out to me. It was a beautiful thing indeed.

"Your Majesty, I am overcome," I responded. "It has been and will always be my great honour and pleasure to serve you and your queen on behalf of my king and country."

The queen then spoke, "My good admiral, it is our great pleasure to do this, for we know that you have saved our family and our kingdom. You will always be in our hearts and our prayers. There is no man in the world who has our higher gratitude and esteem. It was very noble of you to refuse the acceptance of any money from us for the considerable expenses you had to bear aboard your flagship when you took us to and from Palermo. It was not so much the expense as it was your act of nobility that impressed us."

"Your Majesty, I shall always be your faithful servant, and I accept this great honour with a heart filled with humility. May God always bless you, your family, and your kingdom. Perhaps I can build an English farmhouse on the estate, and I hope to make all of Sicily bless the day I have now been placed amongst them."

As I held the great sword, my heart was filled with pride. Seated close to the queen, there was Emma. Her head was slightly tilted, and she gave me a familiar, endearing smile that captured my heart. I would never know what part she may have played in that wonderful and magnanimous gesture from the king and queen. I would also be told that the estate would produce approximately £3,000 annually from rents of its land, an income that would provide a handsome and comfortable retirement. Much later I would find that to be an exaggeration. Of greater importance was the fact that thereafter I could be known as the Duke of Bronté, a nobleman. I would also take pride in adding the name of Bronté to my name and signature. Further, I would wear with pride the decoration of the Order of Saint Ferdinand upon the breast of my uniform next to the badge of the Order of Bath and the Order of the Crescent, which I had received from the sultan of Turkey following the Battle of the Nile. It was indeed a proud moment.

Chapter 14

Discord with Keith

On the day following celebration of the Battle of the Nile, I remember receiving a request from Admiral Keith, and although he later would describe it as command orders, it was clearly worded in the form of a request.

After I read Keith's dispatch, I said to Hardy, "He asks that I dispatch as many ships as I can spare to his command in defence of Minorca. Obviously he believes that island to be a crucial element of naval defence in the Mediterranean. To me, his judgment is basically flawed, as it is clear to any astute commander that Naples is the keystone of operations in the Mediterranean."

"What might be the repercussions if you do not respond?" Hardy asked.

"I do not know, and I do not care, Hardy, because it is manifestly more important that we should save the kingdom of Naples and risk Minorca than to risk the kingdom of Naples to save Minorca. For God's sake, Minorca is but a speck compared to Naples, and if Keith wants to act effectively, he should join his forces with those standing off Toulon and challenge the French fleet. That is what I would do. Our ships and our men are far superior and could take them in any battle. That would decide the question, but I fear that Keith is worse than Hotham. He fears battle. Damn it all."

"What will you do, sir?" Hardy asked.

"I shall send a single frigate for his assistance with a message that is all that I can spare in the proper defence of Naples, for it is Naples that is essential. Write out a response to that effect."

"I will do so immediately," Hardy responded.

A frigate was sent to Keith along with my response to his request. He lingered off Minorca, sailing back and forth in fear of the enemy. He would later look upon my response as a disobedience to orders, but that was the measure of the man. He had sent no orders. He had sent only a request, and I responded to that request in my best judgment, which, in the final accounting, was correct. The French did not attack Minorca. They simply stayed at Toulon, and Keith was relieved that he did not have to fight. He was wrong, and I was right. That was the simple truth. Not only did he fail to realize that, but he poured out dispatches of venom against me as well. When I received accounts of the letters he had sent, with a sense of outrage I wrote to Lord Spencer,

> *I have received accounts of criticism against me that have been written by Admiral Keith. This is a rebuke which I received with great pain. My dear Lord, I only wish that I could have been placed in Lord Keith's situation. I would have broken the orders like a piece of glass. The whole fleet of the French would have been annihilated. I regret to say that I do not believe any sea officer knows the sea and land business of the Mediterranean better than myself.*

In the meantime while Keith was dancing around a small and insignificant island, a large number of French ships had slipped out of Toulon and made their way to the Atlantic. Hardy brought a dispatch which stated that Admiral Keith had been ordered to pursue them. He also announced that in Keith's absence I was placed in command of our Mediterranean forces. I was delighted. In the fall and winter of 1799, I separated my forces and disposed them in strategic positions from Constantinople in the east to Gibraltar in the West. Appropriate ships were assigned to guard Minorca, Naples, and Malta. In September, Captain Trowbridge captured the port of Civita Vecchia, which served essentially as the port of Rome, and was offered the surrender of Rome, which could not be accepted for lack of an appropriate occupying force. In fact, my entire fleet in the Mediterranean was sparse, but so were the forces of the enemy. During the period everything seemed relatively quiet, although in writing dispatches to various captains of the forces I had deployed, it was necessary that I remain writing at my desk throughout every day and into the evening. The task was made much easier by the constant thought that my evenings would be spent in the company of Sir William and in the arms of Emma.

Advisories from the Admiralty and the foreign office reported that Bonaparte had left his army in Egypt and was back in France, where he had become the first consul of the republic. It was feared that he was planning very aggressive actions, and the foreign office could only speculate as to where and when those actions might take place. I was ever mindful that there remained a considerable French naval force at Toulon, and it could be sufficient in carrying out Bonaparte's strategies – that is, unless I could intercept and destroy them, which I intended to do.

Take Me As I Am

One morning I received an unanticipated visit from Captain Trowbridge. We discussed pleasantly the general affairs of the Mediterranean fleet within the context of developments in the continent. He then advised me of something that was both unpleasant and surprising.

"Admiral, I know that you feel my esteem for you. You are one of the greatest men I have ever known and by far the greatest naval officer with whom I have ever served. It is my duty, however, as your colleague and friend to advise you of words that are passing among the officers of the fleet. It is said that your affiliation with Lady Hamilton touches upon an excess that distracts from your stature. If you knew what your friends feel for you, I am sure that you would cut out all the nocturnal parties because the gambling at cards within the royal entourage is believed to be excessive to the point of immorality. I beseech your lordship. Do not become involved in those excesses. It is said that Lady Hamilton is an active participant in such gambling. That will damage her character considerably. As you well know, nothing can prevent people from talking, and a gambling woman in the eyes of an Englishman is lost. Please, sir, understand that I am hesitant to make these remarks, but my dedication to you commands me to speak." Trowbridge then looked solemnly at the floor, and there was a long moment of silence between us.

"I know you very well, Tom," I replied. "And I thank you for both your observation and your advice. As for the gambling matter, I am well aware that many fine English ladies, many with high titles, have been found at the gambling tables, and nothing seems to be said about them. However, I have also found that because of Lady Hamilton's common birth and upbringing, she has been made the object of comments that are both churlish and unfair. She is a fine woman and has been of inestimable assistance to Sir William, to me, and to our country in making our dealings with the king and queen at Naples most effective and beneficial to our cause. When you hear the kind of remarks as you have described, I trust that you will defend her because in defending her, you will also defend me."

"My dear commander and friend, I will defend you until my death. And in reflecting that friendship, I believe that you should know everything that is relevant to our circumstances. You should also know that there have been great rumours having to do with your residence with the Hamiltons. There have also been accounts that have arisen from the staff of Sir William that have touched on matters having to do with you and Lady Hamilton, matters that you would mean to keep secret. The accounts, sir, are that she sleeps in your bed," Trowbridge added.

"My residence with the Hamiltons is a residence by invitation of the official British minister to the Kingdom of the Two Sicilies, and private matters are private matters to which no one of good judgment and appropriate upbringing would invade. To the extent that it does not affect my service in the disposition of my forces or the conduct of my ships, what happens in my private life is the business of no one else," I replied.

"Please understand, Admiral, that I have told you matters which I think you should know, and those matters have had no effect upon my allegiance and commitment to your leadership," said Trowbridge.

"Then enough of that," I commented, hoping that it would feel to be a command. Trowbridge smiled and nodded. I then ordered tea, and we spent the balance of a pleasant conversation. It was no surprise to me that accounts and rumours would be made of my relationship with Emma, and I knew that my distracters would use such information against me. However, I believed that the Admiralty and particularly Lord Spencer would dismiss the rumours as idle speculation. To my mind, it made no matter, for my relationship with Emma was something that I treasured and would not give up. I would retire from the service before I would reject the woman who had filled so rich and complete a part of my life. The Admiralty would have to take me or leave me as I am. Should they feel it appropriate that I be discharged, I was comforted by the thought of being the Duke of Brontë and retiring to my estate. In moments of solitude, I made lists of plants and tools that would be needed to run a proper farm in Sicily.

When I received a note from Lord Spencer responding to several of my operational dispatches, he made mention of a report from Lord Keith which averred that I had disobeyed an order in not sending my force to defend Minorca. Hastily and with anger I responded,

I am fully aware of the act I have committed, but sensible of my loyal intentions, I am prepared for any fate which may await

my disobedience … And, do not think, my dear Lord, that my opinion is formed from the arrangements of anyone. No, be it good, be it bad, it is all my own. Much as I approve of strict obedience to orders, although an officer is never, for any object, to alter his orders, he must act with full responsibility. Do not, my dear Lord, write harshly to me. My generous soul cannot bear it. The truth is that it is entirely unmerited.

Early in the new year of 1800, Lord Keith returned as commander of the Mediterranean fleet. He had not found the French. He had not engaged them. He had not been successful in completing his ordered task of destroying them. He had simply sailed about the ocean to no effect. And now he returned as my commander and ordered that I meet him at Leghorn and then return with him to Palermo, where King Ferdinand had taken his court. What Lord Keith wanted in Leghorn was a mystery to me. Nevertheless, I arrived there on the assigned day for my arrival. I was rowed to his flagship, and when I was piped aboard, I was met not by Lord Keith but simply by the officer of the deck who showed me to Keith's quarters, where he was standing erect behind his desk.

"Good afternoon, my lord," I greeted him. "I have brought the dispatches setting forth the employment of our forces with copies of my standing orders to each."

"That is well enough, sir," he responded, "but there is another matter that I want to discuss first. Pursuant to my orders, why did you not send a greater part of your force for the defence of Minorca?"

"Your lordship, I believe that your order specifically stated that I should send those ships that I could spare, and I did that. It was my judgment, pursuant to standing orders I had received from Lord Spencer, to provide full support in the defence of Naples as an essential operating base for the Royal Navy in the Mediterranean Sea. I considered that to be my overarching mission and responded to your request as I thought most prudent."

"Minorca was at risk of an immediate attack that the French could have mounted with their fleet at Toulon, and I needed additional ships that you could have sent from Naples. You should have sent all of your ships with the exception of a small residual force in the Bay of Naples," he responded with a reddened face.

"However, sir, your specific orders left to my judgment the issue of how many ships I could spare and how many I needed for the defence of Naples. Recent history will also show that the French did not leave Toulon. Minorca was not attacked, and I believe that I was right in maintaining the defence of our ally, the Kingdom of the Two Sicilies," I responded with equal fervour.

"Such impudence! How dare you to say that your judgment could eclipse my request, which you should have considered an order," he replied with an even redder face.

"My judgment was, I believe, sound, and I must stand by my actions, however they may be interpreted," I replied in an even tone, believing it best not to contradict a man who had great authority but little history of any effective battle action and in truth no experience of subduing an enemy. However, it then seemed to me best to calm the waters between us, and I added, "Sir, it is my full intention to carry out any action that you may command in this time of peril. All of our forces should act as a coordinated team, and it is my intention to serve you with the best of my ability. I regret any misunderstanding."

My words seemed to dampen his fervour, and his face became more relaxed. He then said, "Well then, let us do what we must. I have issued a force disposition order that should have been delivered to your ship this morning. From here we will go to confer with King Ferdinand at Palermo. We sail on the first tide in the morning."

"Very good, sir. I shall be ready," I responded and saluted him. Then I turned and walked from his cabin. Our entire conversation had occurred while we were standing.

After we arrived at Palermo, the short time that Lord Keith spent there was uneventful and somewhat awkward. There was nothing new or of any significance that was discussed with the king and Sir William. I had previously ordered our Mediterranean forces to missions that were most appropriate in the east and west, given the various positions of enemy forces. When Admiral Keith was honoured with dinners at Palermo, the king seemed both animated and articulate, but the queen commented, "*I have never seen such a stiff man. It is almost as though he was a minor actor in a boring play. Tell me, Admiral Nelson: is he any good as a commanding officer?*"

"Any good?"

I answered, "Why yes, I believe it can be said that he is 'any good.'"

The queen laughed out loud.

After he stayed only a week, the admiral left Palermo, and it was my expectation that he would have little good to say of his visit. This was borne out as correct when I later learned that he described Lady Hamilton and me as *"a silly pair of sentimental fools."* He took his fleet to assist the ships blockading Malta, which was still occupied by the French, and ordered that I accompany with my squadron.

It turned out to be a fortuitous order. On 18 February, as we sailed independently south of Sicily, a lookout atop the mainmast of *Foudroyant* shouted, "French sails on the horizon!" and I ordered my flag captain, Edward Berry, to make a general chase. I also ordered an accompanying frigate HMS *Northumberland* to come with us. It was a wonderful rush to be in the open sea again and to be in chase of the enemy. I shouted to Captain Berry, "Captain, make the *Foudroyant* fly! There is business to do with the French. Make her fly!"

Berry ordered that full sails be set and the decks be cleared. We surged ahead as the marine guards began their drum roll to battle stations. As we drew nearer the enemy ship, Captain Berry said, "Admiral, I believe she is *Le Genereux*." My excitement soared at the opportunity to subdue one of the ships that had slipped out of Aboukir Bay at the Battle of the Nile. However, HMS *Northumberland* was ahead of us and threatened to engage her before we can get at her.

I shouted to Captain Berry, *"This will not do! She is certainly Le Genereux, and to my flagship alone must she surrender. We have to beat the Northumberland to her!"* As I looked back at our wake, I could see that it was not straight, and that would signify that we were not making our best speed. I shouted to the quartermaster at the wheel, *"I'll knock you off your perch, you rascal. Captain Berry, send our best quartermaster to the weather wheel."* He did so, and we closed on the enemy together with the *Northumberland*. Guns of *Le Genereux* opened fire prematurely and fell short, creating high plumes of water. To me, they were a beautiful sight, for another sea battle had begun. Guns of the *Foudroyant* and *Northumberland* began firing simultaneously and with excellent effect. I felt the greatest rush of excitement and saw a young midshipman standing nearby in great apprehension. I walked over and patted him on the head, asking, *"How do you like the music, lad?"* He answered, "Fine, sir."

We smiled at each other, and I welcomed the thought that he was about to embrace an experience that would remain with him until the last day of his life. Gunners of both the *Foudroyant* and *Northumberland* performed their beautiful and orchestrated dance of rapid loading and firing, the best signature of the Royal Navy's battle excellence. We rained a constant and deadly hail of shot into the enemy, and within minutes the sails of *Le Genereux* were shredded and most of her rigging was stripped away. The ship drifted.

Several calls were made entreating the captain of *Le Genereux* to surrender, but no response was received. Then, following several broadsides, her foremast was shattered and fell to the deck. Finally realising that his task was hopeless, the captain of Le Genereux wisely struck his colours. I sent Captain Berry with a boarding party to accept the surrender of the ship, and he returned with the sword of its mortally wounded captain. The next day I met with Lord Keith and delivered my account of the capture of Le Genereux. He seemed rather passive and unresponsive, thanking me coolly and remarking that he had much to do that morning. I expected his account of the incident to the Admiralty to be rather terse, but I was surprised to find that he was generous in giving me a full and praiseworthy credit for the capture. In the report Keith also announced that he was proceeding to Genoa and was leaving me in command of the blockade at Malta.

The subsequent blockade was a boring and tiresome duty, and during the first week after Keith's departure, my health began to fail. My head ached at the point of the wound I had received at Aboukir Bay and pained me incessantly. I also felt frequent pains in my chest, making me fear that I was perhaps suffering from a fatal disease of the heart. In addition, there was a recurrent stinging in my blind eye. I became fatigued, and my whole body simply hurt. I wrote to Lord Keith, "I can no more stay here fourteen days longer than fourteen years … My state of health is such that it is impossible for me to remain, and I must request your permission to go to the care of my friends in Palermo."

Captain Trowbridge urged that I stay on station at Malta, "Admiral, I know that you are suffering, but I also fear that some may believe that your return to Palermo is simply a matter of personal preference. You will be criticized severely."

I replied, "I cannot deny the pressures that my failing body will have upon me and upon my service at this station. It is not a matter that I simply want to go to Palermo. I believe that I must."

"Very well, sir," he answered. "I will command the blockade if that is your pleasure."

"Thank you, Tom," I answered with some relief. "I am sure that you will carry out this mission to the fullest extent that I could."

I set sail for Palermo, and in two days' time I came again under the tender and salutary care of my Emma. Her concern and her affection were comforting and brought a great healing effect to my ravaged body. I believe that she may have saved my life. However, she was very concerned that Sir William had received notice from the foreign office that he was being recalled and that a replacement as minister to the Kingdom of the Two Sicilies had been appointed. This development was shocking. I feared that my effectiveness with the kingdom would be severely curtailed without the services of Sir William and Emma. My concern, however, was short-lived, as I received within the week a letter from Lord Spencer,

It is by no means my wish to call you away from service, but having observed that you have been under the necessity of quitting your station at Malta on account of the state of your health, which I am persuaded you could not have thought of doing without such necessity, it appears to me much more advisable that you come home ... You will be more likely to recover your health and strength in England than in any active situation at a foreign court.

The letter from Lord Spencer was wonderfully fortuitous, as it would allow me to return home with the Hamiltons. Further good news arrived with the reports that the Guillaume Tell, the last remaining French ship to have escaped from Aboukir Bay, had been captured. I ordered a celebration of the capture aboard Foudroyant, and the timing was such that it could be a double celebration, for within the week Emma was celebrating her thirty-fifth birthday. My health was almost fully recovered, and the celebration was joyous. Anchored in the port of Palermo, the main deck of the Foudroyant was draped in silk with colourful ribbons and plumes hanging from the yardarms, moving gently in a breeze that wafted down from the green hills of Sicily. The entire evening was celebrated under light blue skies patterned with beautiful white clouds that, as evening fell, were replaced by a clear black sky and a million bright stars. They, however, counted for little compared to the visage of Emma next to me.

The Holiday Cruise

I had requested of Lord Keith that I be allowed to take the *Foudroyant* for my return to England, but he replied that it could not be spared, thus requiring that we take a land route home through the continent. This disappointed me greatly as the land route would take much longer, but it could not be avoided. Before I left, I decided that we would take *Foudroyant* on a cruise around Sicily with stops at the magnificent Greek ruins at Agrigento and Segesta, something that delighted Sir William and brought some relief from his ill health. The voyage was delightful. I had the ship's carpenter make temporary quarters for Sir William on the port side of my cabin and a separate room for Emma on the starboard side. We were blessed with wonderful weather and gentle seas. Walking tours of the Greek ruins and the Sicilian countryside filled with orange and almond orchards were pleasant, even uplifting. Our evenings were spent with sumptuous dinners of local foods purchased at the Sicilian markets. The local wines, deep red and musty, were excellent. My nights were spent with Emma on the bed in her small makeshift bedroom. The passion we shared was deep, intense, and unbounded.

Returning to Palermo, we discovered an estrangement between the king and queen. Apparently she had discovered and made a great issue regarding one of his infidelities and decided that she would go to stay with her daughter, the empress of Austria. She decided also to take her son, Leopold, and two daughters. The queen requested – and I agreed – that I would take her as far as Leghorn, not knowing what a massive task that would be. Her entourage included almost fifty people with numerous enormous trunks of clothing and crates of personal belongings. It was necessary to convert the captain's cabin and my cabin to accommodate Sir William and the queen.

On the morning before departure as I was gathering my things for leaving the *Foudroyant* at Leghorn, the officer of the deck came to tell me that a visitor had arrived and had asked to see me. I said, "Well, bring him to me."

The officer responded, "I would have done so, Admiral, but it is a woman. She asked that I tell you that Mrs. Cadogan requests a moment of your time." The announcement hit me with a shock, and I wondered if there was something wrong. I went directly to the quarterdeck, where Mrs. Cadogan, with some relief to me, was smiling with her hands folded in a relaxed manner.

"Good morning, madam, I am pleased to see you," I said.

"Good morning to you, sir. Please excuse my interruption, but Lady Hamilton asks that you come to see her. She says there is something important that you should know."

"Everything is all right, I hope," I exclaimed.

"Yes, I believe so, but she asks that you come very soon," she replied.

"I shall," I said and told the officer of the deck to hold the boat. I went to my cabin, took my hat, hurried back to the quarterdeck, and then boarded the boat with Mrs. Cadogan. As we were rowed to the quay, I asked if she knew what Lady Hamilton wanted to tell me, and she answered that she did not. When I arrived at the Hamilton's apartment, I was led to the dining room, where Lady Hamilton was quietly having tea.

"What is this all about?" I asked.

"It's a very small matter, my dearest," was her cryptic response.

"I don't understand. What could be so urgent?" I replied.

She rose from the table and walked to me, kissed me softly, took my hand, placed it on her abdomen, and said, "I am pregnant with your child."

Her statement was earthshaking, but these were the most beautiful words I had ever heard. Immediately I took her in my arms and kissed her. Awkwardly I asked, "Are you certain?"

"Yes, I have been examined by the queen's physician, and he diagnosed my condition as *madre con bambino*. I am a mother with child. Please tell me that you are pleased," she said.

"No, my dearest, I am not pleased. I am ecstatic. I am the happiest man on the earth. How good the Almighty has been to me! And now he has filled my life not only with a woman I adore, but He has blessed me with the promise of a child with her. Oh, my darling, I am above the clouds. Have you told Sir William?

"Yes, I have, and he said that I extend to you his most felicitous congratulations. He also mentioned something about *quatro in uno juncto* and laughed. He is quite pleased," she answered.

We sat for more than an hour and talked about many things, and so many times I would simply lean to her and kiss. I had never had a happier time.

The Long Trip Home

The passage to Leghorn was again very stormy, as though the Mediterranean was repeating to me personally that it was one force I could not defeat. The royal party suffered greatly and wailed as the ship beat against the seas. Sir William was once more in a state of very ill health, and Emma, who was then several weeks pregnant, suffered with a sickness that made it difficult for her to keep nourishment down. When we landed in Leghorn, matters seemed at first to be well in hand. The queen delivered a thankful note citing my efforts in service to her and her family and presented to Emma, Sir William, and me gifts of beautiful jewels. The queen was then taken to the governor's palace, while Sir William and Emma went to stay with the British consul.

News arrived, however, that was very disconcerting. Bonaparte and his army had crossed the Brenner Pass and routed the Austrians at the battle of Marengo. An armistice was then signed that gave to Bonaparte the greater part of northern Italy. His army was reported to be moving toward Leghorn, and it was feared that we would have to retreat to the sea again. Lord Keith sent an order that I send all of my ships to reinforce his fleet at Genoa. Soon Lord Keith himself arrived with fugitives from Genoa and required that all ships at Leghorn depart and be readied for action. He noted that there were three Neapolitan ships available and stated that any sea travel for the queen and her entourage would have to be aboard the Neapolitans. The queen refused, insisting that her party would be taken only on British ships. After much remonstrance Lord Keith remained firm that British warships were not available. It was decided that we would travel over land to Florence, and the queen would take protection under Grand Duke Ferdinand III. The Hamiltons, Mrs. Cadogan, and I would then go to Ancona, and from there, we would take an Austrian ship to Trieste.

The trip to Florence was filled with anxiety. The queen despaired loudly and frequently of being captured by the French, who, she said, would execute her as quickly as they had her sister. Nevertheless, in great haste we made our way to Florence without encountering the French. There the queen decided that she would not stay but would go on to Vienna with us. Arriving in Trieste, it seemed that our entire party, including myself, had taken ill. Sir William could hardly move, and everyone suffered from colds, fever, and swollen eyes. We were, however, in an area controlled by the Austrians and in a city that offered a pleasant rest. By coincidence we also arrived just before the city's celebration of the second anniversary of the Battle of the Nile, and as my throbbing head improved, so did my spirits and those of our entire party. I was both surprised and delighted that the celebration was so colourful and robust. There were lights and streamers placed throughout the streets of the city. The governor and his party received me with great acclaim, and wherever I went, crowds would follow, frequently shouting, "Long live Nelson," and, "Hail to our hero!" It was comforting to be reminded that glorious service would produce glorious rewards – and they had not forgotten.

From Trieste, we went on to Ljubljana, where the reception of the queen and me was equally glorious. The duke arranged our housing in very comfortable apartments and held several dinners in our honour. A symphony was played in tribute to the battle, and toasts were given to the kings of Austria and Britain. Then to my great pleasure, one toast was made to me. Thankfully Emma had largely recovered, and her morning bouts of sickness had lessened. We were provided with a translator to enable us to carry on an easy conversation with our hosts. After a couple of days we were able to take carriages to the countryside for lunches in the open air, where the green hills, the cool soft grass, and gentle winds of the mountains were soothing to our recovering bodies and souls. In the evenings I was again able to sleep with Emma in my arms, and I felt that I was restored to peace with the world.

During the trip to Vienna each town along the way greeted us with gay celebrations and dinners of sumptuous fare, all featuring the best fowl and meat of their countryside. Crowds would gather at our carriage, and many people would come up to touch my uniform. This was something which at first I thought strange, but I was advised that it was the highest of compliments. Thereafter, I looked forward to their touches and would extend my left arm to shake the hands of gentlemen who came up and spoke phrases I could not understand but to which I would smile and respond, "*Danke, grazie*," and would hope that they understood.

When at last we arrived in Vienna, the entourage had become very tired from the long journey. We were greeted again with great ceremony by the royal court. Queen Maria Carolina was overcome with the greetings of her family and was very thoughtful in introducing me to Empress Maria Theresa, saying, "Your Majesty, I am both pleased and honoured to present to you Lord Admiral Horatio Nelson, victor of the Battle of the Nile and protector of the Kingdom of the Two Sicilies. He is the greatest naval hero of our time. The king and I feel that we owe the restoration of our kingdom to him."

The empress responded, "I am pleased to meet you, sir, and will hold you in great esteem for your service to Austria's daughter and her kingdom."

We stayed for three weeks in Vienna. We rested and restored our health, although Sir William remained ill and kept to his bed. The Vienna palace was a grand place with great halls and cool, baroque drawing rooms, the most beautiful that I had ever seen. We were given lavish banquets and receptions. At one, the composer Joseph Haydn attended and played the grand piano while Emma sang from a composition called the "Ode to the Battle of the Nile":

The dire concussion shakes the land,
Earth, air and sea, united groan,
The solid Pyramids confess the shock,
And their firm bases to the centre rock.

During all of our stay entertainment was lavish, and we were escorted by Prince Esterhazy to the mountains, where we observed hunting parties take down stags. We dined *alfresco* amidst the beautiful, snow-capped mountains of Austria. Prior to our final dinner at the royal retreat called Eisenstaedt, the Esterhazy's country estate, I sat for a portrait and endured the taking of a plaster mask of my face, breathing uncomfortably through straws placed in my nose. I found, however, the mask to be a very good likeness of myself, and Emma agreed, "My darling, that is how you look, and a stronger and more handsome man I have never seen[3]."

Back in Vienna, a final banquet was staged, where gracious toasts were offered by George Elliot, Lord Minto, Britain's ambassador to Austria, whom I had never known, but who, I was told, had made a great number of speeches in my support during the uneasy time when I had chased the French before I had found them at Aboukir. Afterward he became a great admirer of our victory and made more speeches to the House of Lords. During the stay he and I became great friends. At the final banquet he introduced me to Joseph Haydn, who had composed a beautiful piece of music that seemed to hold the entire audience in a trance. During the playing it was noted that many in the audience dabbed tears in their eyes, and as the music progressed, lighting in the room was dimmed. Upon completion there was a long and standing ovation, after which Haydn stated, "It is my pleasure to have presented to you, for the first time, a piece that I have named *The Nelson Mass*."

---

[3]   The plaster mask appears on the cover.

I was overcome, and tears filled my eyes. Emma squeezed my hand and said, "You see, my dear, how you are loved so much by these people." I went forward and shook the hand of the composer, whispering my thanks, "*Danke, maestro, danke,*" and then I turned and bowed to the audience as they continued standing and applauding.

We left Vienna and made another arduous, clattering three-day journey to Prague. Another dinner was held at the archduke's palace, a very pleasant affair. Emma seemed to be in the highest of spirits, and at the request of the archduke, she sang "God Save the King" together with a number of songs of her own choosing. She sang beautifully to the appreciation and applause of everyone. Throughout our stay Emma had been the greatest comfort. Our evenings together were spent in warm embrace, and I relished very much not only our precious moments of union but also the stroking of her lower abdomen, noting with pleasure and satisfaction how round it was becoming with the growth of our child inside.

At the end of September, we boarded a riverboat down the Elba to Dresden. I met Lord Minto's younger brother, Hugh, who was serving as British minister and who had arranged for a number of excellent diversions at the theatre, receptions hosted by consuls of allied countries, and formal dinners. At the last the band hired by young Hugh knew a great number of songs which we all sang together. Champagne was served in quantity probably to excess, while we sang and enjoyed the hospitality of our hosts. After Dresden, we continued down the river to Dessau. Sir William seemed to be recovering quite well. He and I spent time playing cribbage, and from time to time we enjoyed the game of faro with Emma and other members of our party.

At Dessau, we were invited to the palace of Prince Franz von Anhalt-Dessau, who announced that he had renamed a local mountain, thereafter to be called "Nelsonberg." The prince was very much taken with Emma and seemed to gaze at her constantly. He once took her aside and asked about the health of Sir William. She recounted to me that she told him that her husband had suffered continuing bouts of illness but that from each one he had recovered and that it was her belief that he would have a very long life. The prince then mused that should Sir William not recover, he, the prince would enjoy entertaining her at his country estate. She replied that she would decline, as she was presently with child. He asked rather impudently how that could have happened with Sir William's advanced age and his bouts of illness. She told me that she responded, "The child is a gift from God, and I shall devote my life to its care." Thereafter, the prince was distant and cool. Our party then continued to Magdeburg, and along the way we were surprised to find that crowds would fill the riverbank, waving their hats and cheering. I enjoyed going on deck in my full uniform to raise my hat and wave back to them. I insisted that Emma join me together with Sir William, who would sit on deck with a brightly coloured blanket on his lap. The blanket had been a present from Prince Franz when he came to see us off.

At Hamburg, there was another great crowd to welcome our barge with a band that played Frisian melodies. Among the crowd was a large contingent of English merchants and students who came to shake my hand with great praise of admiration. One of the merchants named Lee Griffin, who was a shipper of German metals and gears, had arranged for us to be lodged at a very comfortable hotel. He also honoured us with a dinner complete with dancing to lovely music. I did not dance, but Sir William was sufficiently recovered to take a few slow turns up on the dance floor with Emma. I was very pleased to see them together, my good friend and my love, both smiling in a moment of great tenderness. At dinner Mister Griffin voiced his great concern that commerce between Hamburg and England was so threatened by French pressure and overtures to the Baltic countries that they should form an alliance. He was anxious that they would respond positively. I told him that England would have little choice but to ensure that its commerce should be protected, and I would make that known upon my return to London. He responded, "My dear admiral, you are a great blessing not only to the English people but to all those who are dependent upon her. I take great comfort and satisfaction in your assurance."

Also at Hamburg, I met the former French minister of war, General Dumauriez, who had resigned and secretly left France to go over to the Prussians during the terrible period of repression against all who had voiced any support of King Louis. He recounted that he had forged documents from the republican council appointing him as a plenipotentiary to the Holstein court, and it had worked. There were actually a great number of royalist French exiles in the city together with many French poets and artists. Among the English, there happened to be a missionary priest of the Anglican church who approached me with a Bible and asked, "My dear admiral, would you please sign this Bible? And would you sign it here," indicating a spot under which he had inscribed the words, "Saviour of the Christian World."

I looked at the inscription and responded, "I'm glad to sign my name to your Bible, but I fear that this is too great a claim to make."

"Indeed, I think not, Admiral," he responded. "Should Napoleon subjugate England, I fear that he will then be able to take control of the entirety of the civilized continent. However, I believe that it is God's will that you will prevent him from doing so."

I looked at the minister for a long moment and dwelled upon what he had just said. I then responded, "I shall make that my duty, my good man, and I will do my best."

I had hoped that there would be a British frigate in Hamburg to take us home. However, there was none, and I wrote to the Admiralty, requesting that a ship be sent. Waiting for a response, we spent several weeks in Hamburg under gray skies of gloom and drizzle. There was much of melancholy that was on my mind. My correspondence to Fanny had been infrequent and terse. Truly there was not much of endearment that I could express. Fulfilling my needs and as a complement to my life, she had been entirely eclipsed by what Emma had come to mean to me. I had been content with my marriage to Fanny, but in holding to that commitment, there was much dissatisfaction and frustration. I did not truly realize the extent of incompatibility that existed between her and me until Emma came into my life. Fanny seemed to look upon my victories as incidental and never truly expressed in her letters any sincere praise or appreciation of the sacrifices I had made for the triumphs I had achieved. Her letters had been full of comments concerning her delicate health, how cold and uncomfortable the weather was in England, how she had to wear "two suits of flannel" to remain warm, and how the prices of pork had risen. She sometimes asked how Josiah, then a great disappointment to me, was coming along. Over the years of my absence there was an eroding of my affection to the point where I scarcely cared for her at all. On the other hand, there was the exciting, beautiful, and loving woman who had come into my life. Emma had seemed to grasp fully the man that I was and what I must be. Her eyes sparkled when she looked at me. It seems that every minute of her life was spent in concern for me. She had a grasp of history and of my place within the sweep of conflict against the disordered and menacing threat of Bonaparte. Her touch was soothing to my soul, and her embrace excited me more than I have ever known. And with Fanny, despite my full intent and most ardent efforts, I was not able to conceive a child. Now Emma carried my child within her, and that wonder compelled my life. No matter what may happen in the world about me, I would spend my life with Emma.

Waiting in Hamburg, I reflected with great remorse upon what had become of Josiah. He had been such a promising boy, and at Tenerife, he was largely responsible for saving my life. For so many years I had kept him under my tutelage, and as matters turned out, I perhaps should have kept him under full control. However, I used influence with Admiral Jervis to have him appointed captain of the frigate *Thalia*, and that had turned out to be a mistake. His youthful and irresponsible follies soon became incompetence in leadership and command. He was not a good seaman. He had no true appreciation for navigation or piloting, and he was never engaging with his officers. His captaincy became lonely to the point that he did not dine with others in the officers' wardroom but took his meals alone in the gun room. Finally I apologized to Admiral Duckworth for having sent him and his ship under his command. *Thalia* was ill disciplined and ineffective. Two of its officers had requested courts marshal to review the captain's orders and conduct. I wrote quietly and confidentially to the Admiralty that it might be best to have *Thalia* paid off and Josiah separated from the service. His decline had been one of the great disappointments of my life.

After weeks that were near to despair, waiting for an answer from the Admiralty concerning our passage home, I decided to embark our party in the small mail packet ship called the *King George* for a return to Yarmouth. The passage required another week's time, and it was a trip of agony, ploughing through rough seas and squalls. Sir William became severely ill once more, and Emma also suffered but did not complain. Then at last on 6 November 1799, Yarmouth hove into view. At last we were home.

Chapter 15

Back in England

I remember the steady rain that was falling as we approached the dock in Yarmouth. Our little mail ship slowed as it scraped along the sandy bottom but finally came through to rest against the dock, where a very large crowd of people were gathered, covered with a multitude of umbrellas, cheering and waving white kerchiefs. All boats in the harbour were arranged with colourful streamers lying limp in the rain, and all the buildings around were festively decorated with red, blue, and white buntings. A band was present in full dress uniforms that were by then thoroughly soaked with the cold rain. However, it played robustly "See the Conquering Hero Comes". Sir William had told me to expect a welcoming committee, but I never expected such an enormous turnout of broadly smiling people celebrating the moment, celebrating me. I felt a deep gratitude to them. They were the people of England, and looking upon their smiling faces with the lovely town of Yarmouth set in a backdrop under the beautiful rolling green hills of England, it reminded me of why I had fought so furiously against the French during the past three years. I was in England again, and it was, for a time, safe from Bonaparte. The sacrifices I had made and the wounds I carried were but a small price to pay for the glorious recognition that I felt on that morning in the rain.

Sir William and Emma stood with me on the deck as we docked. I wore my full-dress uniform. Sir William had donned a formal morning coat, and Emma stood by my side in a brocade gown with a large sash that bore the words "Nelson and Brontë" surrounded with gold stitching of acorns and oak leaves. The lord mayor of Yarmouth came forward and extended his right hand, which I shook with my left.

He said, "Lord Admiral, it is a great day that we have to welcome you home, and even though there is a rain that falls, in our hearts the sun is shining brightly."

"I thank you, sir, from the bottom of my heart," I responded, and after I shook the lord mayor's hand, I turned to the crowd, lifted my hat, and spoke in the loudest voice that I could muster, "I thank you all with the greatest of personal gratitude for coming during such weather to greet me. Please know that I am a Norfolk man and that I glory in being so."

The crowd erupted in cheers and applause in response to my remarks. I continued, "I have at last come home. God has been good to me."

We hurried into the waiting carriages indicated by the lord mayor and were taken to the Wrestler's Arms, a hotel and public house where rooms had been arranged for our party. We were served eggs and pork with local potatoes and greens. The dining hall was a large room warmed by a crackling fire in an open stone fireplace. There could have been no better place to return home. The lord mayor and the borough council honoured me by swearing me in as a freeman of the borough, and while we ate, the band continued to play patriotic songs that warmed my heart as much as the fire. Before we left, the owner of the Wrestler's Arms made a request. "Admiral, with your permission I would like to change the name of my establishment to Nelson's Arms."

I responded, smiling, "That would be an honour, sir, and I am delighted at your request. However, would it not be a bit absurd since I do not have arms but only one?"

He answered, "It is no matter, sir. I will change it anyway." We both laughed.

We were shown to small but comfortable rooms, and the warmth of the reception by the people of Yarmouth seemed to envelop me as a warm cloak of love and gave me a renewed energy to resolve my private matters and to return in full service to my country. The people of Yarmouth and the very sight of England again cinched up the buckler of my soul and commanded me to go forward. That evening I wrote to Fanny and told her that I would leave for Ipswich the next day and would be with her for dinner on the following evening. She had offered a room for Sir William and Lady Hamilton, and I wrote, "Sir and Lady Hamilton send their best regards and will accept your offer of a bed. I bid my dear father to be assured of my duty and every tender feeling of a son."

The next day our carriage was escorted to Suffolk, very graciously by the Home Guard Cavalry of Norfolk, but when we arrived at the house Fanny had bought, I discovered to my great displeasure that no one was there. The house staff advised that my father had left a few days before to join Lady Nelson in London. Once again she had bungled arrangements, and although my first impulse was to go immediately to London, it seemed fitting that Fanny, having not imparted her plans to me, should wait. I did not stay in the house but took quarters at a Suffolk hotel with the Hamiltons. During the next two days I was received with great honour by officials of the city of Suffolk and took long strolls in mufti around the town square and gardens, enjoying a relaxed sense of being home. The evening before we left for London, I spent another night with Emma in my arms. She told me of things that did not come as a great surprise, but still they did ignite a renewed anxiety.

As we lay together, she said, "Sir William has received numerous and disturbing reports about reactions and rumours within London society concerning the relationship between us, my dearest. The rumours are frank and consistent that I have seduced you into an adulterous affair that will damage your name and career."

I thought for a moment and said, "I do not care, my darling. I shall live my life as it comes, and I shall do my duty. It seems to me that all of London must grant to me a private life that is truly private in all respects. I am an officer of the Royal Navy and will stand before all of London as an officer who has been, to this date, the only military commander who has bloodied the nose of Bonaparte. At the Nile, I gave England control of the Mediterranean and marooned Bonaparte's army in Egypt. Let them judge me for that and let them leave me alone in my private life."

"What will you tell Fanny of us?" she asked in a whisper.

"I will tell her the truth. I can do nothing else," I answered, kissing her forehead.

"She will be hurt," she responded with tears in her eyes.

"I cannot help that. I must tell her the truth. She has a right to know what has happened, and to any protests she might raise, I will not hesitate to recount the many disappointments she has given me. I believe that she has been a faithful wife, but that alone is not enough. She has not understood who I am and what I am. Her letters to me have been filled with drivel and complaints. I am an officer in His Majesty's Royal Navy, but she has wanted me to be something akin to a clerk in some odious place where I would attend to her needs like some footman. She does not understand. She has never understood, and I have never had the support and company of a wife I could love until now. I hold in my arms the woman I have needed for so long and to whom I will give my undying devotion and love. It is you I love, Emma. It is only you." I kissed her again and passed my hand over her abdomen, which was then very round.

I felt a sense of relief in giving voice to feelings that were never before spoken aloud but were so strong and so undeniable. I would go to London and place myself before the Admiralty, ready for service. It was my hope and expectation that they would receive me for what I was, an officer committed totally to doing my duty. If necessary, I would go forth alone against the enemy with sword in hand and would slash Bonaparte into pieces. I believed that there was no other officer in the entirety of the Royal Navy who could command a ship, a squadron, or a fleet as I could. I would offer myself to service, and I did not believe that the Admiralty would turn me away.

The next day, a Sunday, we took our carriage loaded with bags and trunks to London and arrived late afternoon at the hotel on King Street, where Fanny and father were staying. Rain was again falling, and the crowd of people who had come to see me were thoroughly soaked but energetic in cheers of welcome. We were taken to the apartment suite, where Fanny and father were sitting. Fanny had the same look as when I left. Her face was rather plain, and her hair was short and combed down with very little attention to the fashion of the day. Her dress was plain with a collar that covered her neck. As we entered the room, she rose and came forward smiling and embraced me, saying, "Welcome home, my dear husband. It is so good to have you back home."

I gently returned her embrace and simply replied, "Thank you. It is truly good to be home."

I then turned to Sir William and Emma, "Lord and Lady Hamilton, please allow me to present my father and wife, Reverend Edmund Nelson and Frances Nisbet Nelson." There followed comments of greetings and a genteel shaking of hands, everyone smiling and nodding.

Fanny said, "I am sure you are all tired from your journey and would like to freshen yourselves before dinner."

I responded, "That is a capital idea," and asked that the hotel valet show the Hamiltons to their room. I went to the bathroom to wash my hands and face. After I had combed my hair and redone the ribbon holding the sprig off the back of my neck, I emerged, and Fanny said that we should go down to the private dining room she had arranged. There, as we waited for the Hamiltons, Fanny spoke, "Horace, I had expected you sooner."

"I am sorry that I did not come when you expected, my dear. I was also sorry that you were not there to greet me as I expected," I responded. "I was also exhausted when we reached Suffolk and needed some time for rest. I was concerned and still feared that all of the activities in London will require a great deal of strength and time."

"How did you find the house? Is it to your liking?" she asked.

"It seems to be a very fine place, but I took lodging in a hotel," I answered.

"Why did you not stay in our house?" she asked.

"I was not familiar with the rooms or their arrangement and felt that it was simply more convenient to take a room in a hotel," I answered.

"I am sorry for that," she said with a rather doleful face.

"It is no matter," I replied and turned to my father, asking, "Father, how are things at Burnham Thorpe? You look very well, and I hope that you feel as good as you look."

He replied, saying that Burnham Thorpe was in good order and that he had hired a gardener to keep the property planted and trimmed. Fanny added, "But no matter what one can do, it is a cold place, and nothing can be done to stop the drafts that give me terrible colds. Something I truly appreciate in our new house is that it is warm and comfortable, and it is my hope that you will come to love it." I did not respond, but I discussed briefly with my father the recent trips he had taken to Bath. When the Hamiltons arrived, we sat down to our meal. Father and Sir William discussed at length the political goings-on in London and the fracture of Britain's Second Coalition. Toward the end of their discussion, I commented, "I fear that the coalition was an assemblage of countries that were devoid of leaders who would confront Bonaparte. He preys upon weakness, and they were all weak. There wasn't a single general to be found who had the ability or the resolve to beat him in the field. And that is the only way to be rid of him – to meet him in the field and to beat him flat."

"That is a tall order, my boy," Father said.

"With due respect, sir, I do not believe it is that difficult. You see, it has been done at sea. Why can it not be done on land?" I responded.

Sir William spoke up, "Horatio, we are yet to find a fighting general to fight on land as you have fought on sea."

"Well, we must find one … or several," I replied. "I have been sorely disappointed by the Prussian and Austrian commanders. They have gone forth and had him on several occasions with forces equal to his own, and each time he has mastered them. At Marengo, there is no reason why the Austrians could not have beaten him back, but it seemed as though they simply lacked the committed resolve to do so. As you have heard, it is never a matter of how big the dog is in the fight. It is always a question of how big the fight is in the dog, and surely at Marengo, the Austrian dog was big enough but quite obviously lacked the fight."

As the sweet course was served, I noticed that the afternoon was becoming quite late and said, "Please forgive me, but I must present myself to the Admiralty this afternoon," and I departed the dinner.

When I entered the office of the Admiralty and walked through its ornate halls, I was again overcome with a profound sense of attachment to the Royal Navy and its grandeur. The halls were filled with portraits and paintings of battles where we had met the enemy and had taken them down. Those pictures seemed to be great trophies of triumph, and I pledged to myself that one day my portrait would hang there amongst the other great officers so nobly honoured. When I entered the office of the first lord, I was stunned, noticing that on a wall to the left of the reception desk, there was a large drawing captioned at the top, "Officers at the Battle of the Nile," depicting captains of the ships that had been engaged at the battle. I was then overcome as I looked at the top of the picture, for there was a drawing of me and underneath was my name, "Admiral H. Nelson, RN." I stood for a long time looking at the picture and at the depiction of the faces of the men dear to me who had served me so well at Aboukir Bay. I love each one of them with a deep kind of love that was like no other. These were my band of brothers, men who so willingly placed themselves in harm's way and who, through their commitment and their furious willingness to throw themselves at the enemy, were able to achieve the immortality of their depictions placed upon the Admiralty wall, as holy as any place in any cathedral. And when I looked at the drawing of myself, a golden orb of pride glowed within my bosom, and I could not restrain the tears that welled in my eyes. No extent of total sacrifice or absolute commitment could be too great to carry on and to deserve fully the regard of my country in such recognition by His Majesty's Royal Navy. After a moment I wiped my eyes and approached the officer at the reception table.

"Good evening, sir. I am Admiral Horatio Nelson and would like to speak with the first lord of the Admiralty, if he is present, or if not, with any of his senior staff who may remain."

The lieutenant at the desk stood immediately and replied, "Admiral, I'm afraid that the first lord and his entire staff have departed for the day."

"Then please take a message for the first lord and let it read that Admiral Nelson presented himself on the first day of his arrival in London and gives his best regards to the first lord, requesting assignment to active duty."

"I will be very happy to see that he gets that message, sir," the reception officer replied with a broad smile.

"Then I shall depart and return tomorrow. Good night, sir," I said.

"Before you go, Admiral, may I have the high privilege and honour of shaking the hand that you have remaining?" he asked.

I smiled back at this trim and handsome young officer and said, "Certainly you may, sir."

He came around the large oaken desk and extended his left hand, which I firmly shook, asking, "Lieutenant, what is your name?"

"Andrews, sir. It is Jonathan Andrews," he replied.

"Young Andrews, go to sea as soon as you can because the sea is the very front office of the Royal Navy. Your best service will be there, and I bid that you give that service with full commitment to your duty and render it entirely without fear," I told him.

"Yes, sir, I will do that. This night I shall record your command in my diary, and I shall live by your advice," he replied.

"It will serve you well, lad. It will serve you well," I repeated.

When I arrived back at the hotel, Fanny was waiting. She told me that Lord and Lady Hamilton had been given the use of a house by one of Sir William's wealthy cousins, a man named William Beckford, who had absented himself from London in the wake of a scandal that had involved him with a young man and a young married woman. I had been resigned to spend my time in London away from Emma, and I was relieved that she and Sir William had gone to another place. Fanny also said that a number of invitations to receptions and dinners had been received, and they had been "more numerous than there are days in the month." I told her that in the morning I would read them all and decide which ones I would attend.

Fanny then said, "Horace, we must talk. As man and wife, we must talk about things that have been said and what our future will be. I trust that you are now returned as my husband."

"Yes, we must talk, but now is not the time. I am very tired and want only to sleep," I replied.

I went to the bathroom and washed myself for bed and then returned to the bedroom, expecting that she would have laid out my sleeping clothes. However, my trunks were still unpacked, and I had to go through them myself to find my night clothes. Once again her inattentiveness was consistent. I went to bed while she spent time in the bath. When she came out, I lay motionless with my eyes closed, feigning sleep. She got into the bed and took her place next to me, not touching. We slept through the night.

The next day Sir William arrived at breakfast and announced that a levee was being held by the king in the afternoon and that both he and I had been invited to attend. I was delighted at again having the prospect of speaking to His Majesty and asked that Fanny set out my full-dress uniform, indicating to her the trunk where it could be found. Immediately after breakfast, taken largely in silence, I told Fanny that I would be expected at the Admiralty and departed the hotel. At the Admiralty I was disappointed that my new friend, Lieutenant Andrews, was not at the reception desk, but I was soon ushered in to see Lord Spencer.

"Admiral Nelson, how good it is to see you looking so well," he said. "I trust that your long journey across the back side of the continent did not take too much out of you."

"I am healthy, fit, and ready for service, my dear first lord," I answered.

"The message that I received from your visit last night is indeed that you are ready for service. However, given your bouts of illness in the Mediterranean and the long trip to get back home, it is probably advisable that you spend a little time here in London while we decide where best to place your command services," Spencer said.

"The trip was actually restful in many parts, my lord, and I will not need a great deal of rest. I am ready for assignment as soon as it can be made," I responded.

"Well, good then. I shall attend to an appointment forthwith and shall advise you as soon as the decision can be made. In the meantime, please allow your presence to be celebrated here in London," he replied.

"I shall do that, sir, and shall look forward to a speedy decision," I replied. I then stood, and he shook my hand.

As I turned to go, he added, shuffling some papers and not looking up, "While you are in London, I suggest that there should be a good deal of distance between yourself and Lady Hamilton. There has been a great deal of talk, and as with all rumours filtering through London society, no one knows what substance there is or what the truth may be."

"My lord, I can only say that Lady Hamilton was a confidant of the queen of the Two Sicilies and was most invaluable in determining a positive relationship with such an important ally as that kingdom has been," I replied.

"I do not doubt that she was of great service to you," Lord Spencer answered, speaking rather slowly.

I took my leave from the Admiralty and returned to the hotel, where Fanny was absent. I donned my full-dress uniform with all of the formal decorations and medals that had had been awarded to me by England, Turkey, and the Kingdom of the Two Sicilies. The king's levee would be a formal affair, and I thought that my full-dress uniform would be appropriate, including the sword presented to me by King Ferdinand as well as the jewels given by the sultan of Turkey. At lunch Sir William was in the best of moods and spoke quickly, "My dear admiral, you look absolutely resplendent, and I am so delighted that you have recovered your full health, although Emma and I both miss your presence. After all, when any part of a *tria juncto in uno* is absent, that part is missed."

"I must say, my good friend, that I, too, miss very much the company of the two of you," I replied.

The King's Levee

"I am not altogether sure what kind of levee we will have today," Sir William said. "The king has recently been quite ill and was hospitalized for a time for inordinate behaviour. He is said to be recovered, but I am told that his recovery is not complete. He has never liked formal receiving lines, and today's audience may be somewhat disorganized. I should also tell you that I'm advised that he has remarked negatively about the relationship rumours concerning yourself and Emma."

"Has he remarked about the battle of the Nile?" I asked.

"Why yes, he celebrated your victory with great praise," Sir William answered.

"Then I would imagine that he might feel that I deserve some latitude of privacy, something akin to the veil of tolerance that seems so completely to surround the relationships of his sons," I replied.

"You are quite right, my friend. But rumours are rumours, and it has always been a remarkable fact that they seem to be more attractive to London society than are true facts. Heaven knows any rumour seems to be feasted upon with greater relish than the best of cuisine. The rumour mill accords no privacy, and you are now a celebrated person ripe for close inspection," Sir William explained.

"Then let us go and see what the king has to say," I proposed. We were taken by Sir William's carriage, also lent by his rich cousin, to the levee. As a soft rain continued, yet again we waited for some time at the palace while the earlier carriages offloaded their occupants. Upon entering the reception hall, as Sir William had predicted, there was no reception line, and a great murmur of conversational sounds came from the great hall, where an orchestra was also playing. As we entered the hall, I could see the king, dressed in his army commander's dress uniform, laughing and conversing in a very animated fashion with several generals at the great fireplace. Frequently he would extend his hands toward the fire and then rub them together. Soon Charles Greville, Sir William's nephew and attending secretary to the king, came rushing up to us.

"My dear uncle and Admiral Nelson, how wonderful it is to see you," he said, embracing Sir William. He then extended his right hand to me. Then he awkwardly withdrew it and extended his left, which I shook firmly. I was well aware that Mister Greville had been Emma's lover before he passed her on to Sir William.

"Please come, gentlemen. I am sure that the king is looking forward to greeting you." Greville pushed his way through the crowd to the place where the king was continuing a lively conversation with the generals. At a moment of pause during the conversation, Greville said, "Your Majesty, it is my great pleasure to present to you my uncle, Sir William Hamilton, recently your ambassador to the Kingdom of the Two Sicilies, and Admiral Horatio Nelson, our victor of the Nile." The king then turned slowly and looked at me up and down. He chuckled and pointed at the decorations on the breast of my uniform.

"Why, you are gaily decorated, Admiral. How is your health?" he asked.

"My health is excellent, your Majesty, and thank you for asking," I replied.

"Good," he said. He then turned back to the generals and continued his conversation with them. He never looked at Sir William and did not speak to him. After just a moment it became clear that our colloquy with the king was over.

King George III

"Gentlemen, may I offer you a glass of claret?" Greville asked with some apparent embarrassment, and then he led us to a table filled with wines and crystal carafes. Greville added, "You know, it is somewhat ironic that we cannot obtain these wines directly from France, so we import them from New York in America. It is also something interesting that buying the wines from the Americans is a secret closely guarded so that the king does not know that they come from our former colonies. However, one must give the French their due in producing the best vintage in the world. Now please excuse me," Greville said as he went off to gather up other attendees for their greetings from the king, however long or short the greetings may be.

"This morning's meeting with the king – or perhaps I should say our brief audience with the king – does not offend me, as I know that he is not a well man," Sir William spoke with some obvious regret.

"He could have spoken to you," I replied with indignity. "You served him excellently well for the greater part of a decade and preserved the allegiance of a very tenuous ally during very difficult times. It is a pity that he did not, or perhaps was not able to, appreciate that service. It is also a pity that he did not see fit to make any reference to our triumph in Aboukir Bay, a victory that, at least for a time, has preserved his kingdom. I hope he has the capacity to appreciate the fact that the British islands are surrounded by water. Otherwise he would have to depend upon those generals to hold off Bonaparte, and I question that they have ever shown an ability to do that."

With that statement I drained my glass and said to Sir William, "There are things that I have to discuss with Fanny, and I believe that now is probably the best time to do so."

"I bid you good luck with that, my dear friend. I shall stay and find a few old friends whom I have not seen for years," Sir William replied.

Revelation to Fanny

I hired a carriage to take me to the hotel, hoping that Fanny would be there and alone. As I arrived and walked through the hotel's beautifully decorated lobby, I dreaded the conversation that had to be endured with Fanny, still not being sure of the best words I should use. However, the conversation was inevitable, and that afternoon was as good a time as any to have it. In fact, it seemed important that it should take place sooner rather than later.

As I entered, I saw Fanny sitting and reading a book next to the fireplace of our suite.

"My dear, there are things that we must discuss," I said, removing my hat and taking a seat in a chair across from her at the fireplace.

"Of course, Horace, what do you want to discuss?" she asked, closing her book.

I began speaking, not really knowing what I would say. "My dear, you have been a faithful wife to me, and there is nothing under the sun that I would do intentionally to hurt you in any way. However, you have spent years alone while I have been at sea, and I fear that you have suffered greatly in a life that has been a burden to you—"

"I have carried the burden willingly," she interrupted, but I quickly continued, "I have offered my services again to the Admiralty and anticipate that I will again be sent to sea perhaps for additional and continuous years of service in the preservation of these islands against attack. I believe that it would be best for you to have a life of your own and in an estate of your choosing and not to be saddled with a naval officer who is so continuously away from home and so often placed in harm's way, where life or death is committed to the vagaries of battle."

"I know that all you say is true, but Horace, I accept what you must do, for I know that you are a naval officer and I know only so well the inconveniences that the wife of a naval officer must endure," she quietly responded.

"Yes, my dear, but so many of your letters express deep and sincere distress at the dangers that are inevitable in what I must do, and letter after letter expresses anxiety about how long it will be until I can come home. Your distress and the expressions of what seem clearly to be dissatisfaction burden me greatly. I find it difficult to carry your anxieties along with the great pressures and stresses that I must carry as a commander of ships during a war. They simply seem so incompatible," I responded with words that seemed simply to pour out of me, expressing the strongest of feelings that were never spoken until that moment.

"Horace, what exactly are you saying?" she asked.

"I believe, Fanny, that it would be best if we had a divorcement of the marriage," I replied, giving voice to a conclusion that I had felt for so long but then spoke out loud with both regret and relief.

"How can you say that? How can you possibly say that?" she repeated.

She then placed the book on a side table and stood up. She slowly walked to the centre of the room, raising her hands and looking at them for a long moment. She then returned to her chair and sat down.

"Is it that woman?" she asked with a sombre face. "Is it the Hamilton woman? I have heard rumours repeatedly, all told to me in secret whispers that you have taken up with her. Tell me, Horace. Have you taken up with her?"

"Fanny, I think we should have a divorcement because the expectations of each of us are simply incompatible," I replied.

"Horace, have you taken up with her?" she repeated.

"The issue of a divorcement need not turn on rumours, Fanny, but upon our incompatibilities," I answered in avoidance of her question.

"Have you taken up with her?" she repeated again.

"I love her, Fanny. I must admit to you that I love her," I answered in words that I had feared to speak. But then having spoken them, I felt a great release and satisfaction. The admission revealed what was perhaps the strongest and most profound truth of that point in my life.

"How is that possible, Horace? She is the wife of your friend, Sir William Hamilton," she asked, insistently.

"Sir William knows entirely about the nature and extent of our relationship and is not offended by it. In fact, he has encouraged it," I answered.

With an exasperated wave of her hand and an astonished look on her face, she continued, "But how is that possible? All of London is full of stories that she was low born, and for years as a very young woman, she voluntarily submitted herself as a plaything at gentlemen's clubs. She was the mistress of a nobleman who then passed her on to Charles Greville, who passed her on to his uncle, Sir William, as his mistress for years before he married her."

"I have heard those stories, but—" I answered, and she interrupted in a rather loud tone, "Horace, my dear fool, she is ill bred and coarse. She uses language and diction that could only befit a barmaid. And just look at her. She is enormous."

"She is that way because she is pregnant with my child," I announced.

"What! Then it is true. The most notorious rumours are true. You have taken her as your mistress, and you have conceived a child with her.

How could you do that? How could you cuckold someone you call your friend and live with what you have done?" she demanded.

"Cuckold is a defamatory word, and Sir William does not feel defamed by the fact that Emma and I are going to have a child. He knows about our relationship and looks forward to the birth of the child," I explained to her astonishment.

"How can you have any feelings for a woman who would be unfaithful to her husband? Such infidelity cannot even equate with the status of harlot!" Fanny almost shouted. "She is an unfaithful woman who has disgraced her husband, a fine man of high stature, a peer of the realm."

"Fanny, I fear that what you are incapable of understanding is something that cannot be explained to you," I said with exasperation and some anger. "I love her."

She sat in what appeared to be a state of shock and then slowly shook her head.

"I find it difficult truly to believe what I have heard," she finally said. "How could you do this? She cannot marry you as long as Sir William lives, and how could you want to carry on this relationship that is so tawdry and ungodly?"

"Fanny, I cannot deal with what you may think inappropriate or ungodly. I only know that I have found a woman with whom I shall spend the balance of my life, and with things as they are, do you not believe that a divorcement is appropriate to end our marriage? Any continuance of our relationship as husband and wife can never be more than a pretence," I answered. "It is not my intent to hurt you, and I will make a settlement that will care for all of your needs."

She leaned back in her chair and was silent for a very long while. Finally she said, "I took an oath before God to become the wife of a young Captain Horatio Nelson, and I shall remain the wife of Admiral Horatio Nelson for the rest of my life. As God knows, you have no grounds upon which to seek a divorce from me. And although I have grounds, I shall be true to my vow, and I shall not seek a divorce from you. To the extent that you will have me – and even if you choose not to have me – I will continue to serve as your wife."

I was silent as her words battered me like cannon shot. She would not divorce me, and for as long as she would be alive, I could not make Emma my wife. She stood and walked slowly toward her bedroom and then stopped, turned, and spoke coldly to me. "You can sleep in the room where your father has been sleeping, and he can take the suite that had been reserved for the Hamiltons." She went into the bedroom and closed the door.

The Celebration Continues

I knew that Alex Davison had arranged a reception for me that afternoon at his home in Saint James Square. He had said that he would meet me in the lobby of the hotel, so I went down to wait for him. However, as I entered the lobby, I saw him coming in with a beaming smile.

"Horace, my dear friend, it is so good to see you back in London and looking as robust and healthy as you now appear with all of those splendid decorations covering your uniform. In the ways that you have thrown yourself against the enemy to gain the wonderful triumphs you've experienced, I am amazed that you are still alive, but thank God you are here," he exclaimed as he came forward and embraced me.

His words, his smile, and the tenor of his greeting lifted both my spirits and my regard for him as a true and trusted friend.

"I am equally delighted to see you, my dear Alex, and please know that I appreciate without measure all that you have done in accumulating for me the sums that have been achieved in settling my battle prizes," I responded, returning his embrace.

"Well now, it's my pleasure to take you to a reception where we will dine with many of the luminaries of this great city," he said with some apparent sense of pride. "I want you to know that I have just seen something remarkable. There is a rather large crowd of people outside of this hotel who are here simply to get a glimpse of you, but when I told them that I had come to carry you to my house in my carriage, many of the men immediately unhinged my horses and tied them to the back of the carriage. You see, they want to pull it themselves as an honour to you. It may very well be that you are given glorious rewards from heads of state, but having the people of London pull your carriage is an honour that has not been accorded to kings and ministers. I hope you don't mind," he exclaimed.

"Not in the least. In fact, I am overcome that they would want to accord such service to me. I am deeply honoured," I answered.

As we went outside, what Davison had said was true. His horses had been removed from their traces and tethered at the end of the carriage. No fewer than a dozen men were standing ready to pull us. As we came through the door to the hotel, the crowd erupted and gave several cheers of "Hip, hip, hooray." I took off my hat and waved it to them in response, and as we proceeded to the carriage, I was pleased to shake the hands of many of the smiling people who extended theirs. We then started out for Davison's house in St. James's Square, a splendid place designed with Corinthian columns and very large windows. On the way he told me that his guests would include the prime minister, William Pitt, whose father lived next door, several other cabinet members, and the Prince of Wales, whom I had never met but about whom I had heard stories that he was something of an unrestrained spendthrift and lothario. In fact, it was rumoured that my friend from the Caribbean, Prince William, had been sent to sea so that he would not be negatively influenced by his older brother. To my great delight, I was also advised that Sir William and Lady Hamilton had been invited. This raised my spirits to great heights, for I longed so much to see Emma and perhaps to have a private moment with her.

Our carriage moved rather slowly through the streets with the team of Londoners pulling it in great spirit but without the vigour of the horses that were tied behind. My conversation with Davison was delightful as we recounted our earlier days, and I gave to him my thanks again for his great service in factoring the proceeds from the battle prizes. As we approached his house, I looked out the window and saw a small crowd of seamen standing at attention and saluting. Then to my great surprise and delight, I recognized many of them. They had been members of my *Agamemnon* crew. Immediately I shouted, "Stop the carriage! Please stop the carriage now," and I opened the door and bolted into the street toward my old crew members. As I approached, I recognized their faces and remembered many of their names.

"*Agamemnons!* I remember you! You were crew of the *Agamemnon!* Jeffrey Mutchler, my old master gunner, how good to see you! And Christopher Peters, you great navigator and pilot, you look as well as you did on the day we parted. And little Ty Austin, I remember you as a small powder boy carrying more shot and powder than you weighed. I see that you are a young man now, and a fine one you are!"

I believe that the men exulted with pride in the fact that I remembered many of their names. I shook their hands, embraced them, and patted them on their backs. Their faces beamed, as I am sure that mine did as well. We talked and laughed for a brief time, a simple moment in time that to me was sweeter and richer than any fine brandy. But then I told them that I had to leave to attend to important matters. Their responses were thus: "God go with you, sir. We will always be your crew, Admiral!" As I paused before getting back into the carriage, I saluted them, and they stood at attention, returning the salute. As Davison and I went on our way, a warm sense of satisfaction glowed within me. I was yet again reminded that having done my duty, commanding men like those I had just encountered, the best of men who revered me, had been the mission of my life, and in its fulfilment there could be no greater reward. Later I would be advised that my engagement with the former crew members of the *Agamemnon* had been reported in the London newspapers in very praiseworthy stories.

The reception was a resplendent affair. Davison's large entertainment room was hung with glittering chandeliers and large mirrors reflecting the light of innumerable candles. Tables were set with fine china and silver service. Staff scurried about, tending to everyone's desire for champagne or brandy. I was deeply impressed by Davison's thoughtfulness in hanging a banner behind the main table that read, "Honour to the victor of the Nile." Mister Pitt, the prime minister, was in excellent spirits. He stated that every night he slept soundly, knowing that I was ready for service, and as long as my service would be provided, Bonaparte would be held in check. I assured him that it would be so, and we talked at length about the battle in Aboukir Bay and his full appreciation of what he called my "imaginative tactics." His ministers were also knowledgeable of the battle and asked a number of questions that I was pleased to answer.

The Prince of Wales stood to the side, not saying very much. He was a fairly tall fellow who was dressed up in lavender silks with a white ermine collar. He had a rather thin face with long hair combed in broad, looping curls. One could hardly imagine a more foppish and overdone appearance. When Davison introduced him, he thoughtlessly extended his right hand, which I shook with my left. It seemed that he was not aware of the *faux pas*. Nor did he seem to care. He did not speak, and when I asked whether his brother, Prince William, was in London, he only answered that he did not know. After we were introduced, he simply turned away and went to speak with someone else. At that moment I saw Sir William and Emma enter into the room. My heart leapt simply at seeing her again. She was beautiful, as always. She had a lovely headband with a few white feathers and wore a dress that was decorated with a pattern of pink flowers tied high under her bosom, very effectively concealing her pregnancy. I immediately asked Davison if I could have a private moment with Sir William and Lady Hamilton in the library. He said, "Of course," and went to speak with them. After a brief conversation he led them to the adjoining library. I excused myself from the ministers and went to the library.

"How wonderful it is, Admiral, that Mister Davison has been able to honour you with this reception," Sir William said as I entered the room.

"I have appreciated very much what Alex has done," I responded and shook Sir William's hand.

"Perhaps the two of you would like a moment alone," he said. "I have a few friends to greet out there."

As soon as Sir William left the room, Emma came into my arms, and I kissed her with a passion that was warm and deep, fulfilling a need that stretched to the core of my being.

"Oh, how I have missed you, my darling," I whispered in her ear.

"It cannot be more than I have missed you," she answered, and then miraculously as she held herself close to me, I felt a pulse from her abdomen, which Emma also felt.

"Our child has been very actively kicking in the past week," she said with a soft laugh. "I think it knows that you've been gone."

"I have been in misery without you," I said. "It has been a hellish existence."

"I know, my dear," she answered, "and I would give anything to have a place outside of this infernal city where we could be together."

At that moment Sir William re-entered the room and said, "I believe we should re-join the reception. Admiral, you should go first, and then after a brief while Emma and I will join the festivities.

"Yes," I said, "I will go. This moment, however, has been a precious drop of time for me. I have missed you, and I want you to know how much I deeply love you both."

"We know, Admiral. We love you and have missed you as well," Sir William responded.

As soon as I had re-joined the reception, Alex announced that the meal was ready and invited everyone to take their seats. I took my place at the main table next to Alex. Also seated to my right were the prime minister, the Prince of Wales, Emma, and Sir William. To the left were other ministers of the government and Prime Minister Pitt's father. After champagne was poured, Alex rose and announced that the prime minister would offer a toast. Mister Pitt stood, waited for silence, and spoke, "Ladies and gentlemen, I give thanks to my good friend, Alexander Davison, for inviting such an august gathering to this most pleasant reception. It is my honour and pleasure to raise a toast to His Majesty, King George, the king of our nation and our esteemed leader in this time of peril from a great continental threat to our way of life."

Everyone assembled stood and raised their glasses with responses of "To His Majesty" and "To the king." The prime minister continued, "It is also my privilege to toast our honoured guest, Admiral Horatio Nelson, and to give the thanks of a grateful nation for the triumph he achieved at the Battle of the Nile in that momentous defence of our country, and to note not only with gratitude but also with awe and respect, the fact that he sits here not simply as an admiral of the Royal Navy but as a commander who carries the scars of battles as testimony to his great service to our country."

Still standing, the assemblage answered robustly with responses of "To the admiral," "Here, here," and "Well said, sir."

I felt an enormous sense of pride and gratitude for the prime minister's remarks and stood, raising my glass.

"I am deeply grateful for the remarks of the prime minister and for this wonderful gathering arranged by my dear friend, Alexander Davison. I would also like to say that I have no desire that is greater than to serve my country and to defend her at whatever cost may come to me. There is no greater honour than to do my duty to my country. I promise to you all that so long as I shall live, I shall dedicate myself to the service and safety of this great land."

The assemblage responded with shouts of "Yes, yes," "Well said," and "Thank you, Admiral." After we raised our glasses and drank to the toast and my response, everyone was seated again, and the great dinner began. I shook the hand of the prime minister and Alex. Then I sat and began to enjoy the wonderful meal. Conversation at the table was cordial and interesting. Both the prime minister and Alex were very engaged in matters having to do with the strength of the Royal Navy and concern for protection of continental commerce, especially with the Baltic countries. However, I noted something that gave me great concern. The Prince of Wales, who was seated next to Emma, was smiling and leaning near to her in conversation that seemed to suggest that he intended his remarks to be private and personal. I was all too aware that the prince was known to have taken a cavalcade of mistresses, married and unmarried, and could only suspect that he may have intended to include Emma as a new conquest. It gave me great apprehension that this man with a position in life that gave him access to everything he wanted may threaten to take something so precious from me. It did not matter to him what the repercussions may be from the actions he took in his unbounded and irresponsible life. He had the reputation of simply indulging himself in whatever pleased him, and he answered to no one for what results may occur. Throughout the dinner I could hardly take my eyes from his ogling at Emma with a smile that looked somewhat like that of a rodent about to consume a delicate morsel.

As the reception came to its close, I intended to speak very directly with Emma about her conversation with the prince but could not do so, as Sir William and she departed the reception as soon as the meal was over. When I expressed surprise to Alex that they had left so soon, he told me that Lady Hamilton was feeling somewhat unwell. Sir William had expressed apologies that they had to leave. As soon as I could gracefully make my departure, I returned to the hotel, where I immediately wrote a note to Emma, advising her strongly to keep clear of the prince, telling her that any invitations he may offer should be rebuffed, for he was a scoundrel not to be trusted and no good could ever come from any relationship with him, however innocent he may try to make it seem. I feared acutely that he was drawn to Emma's beauty, and his royal stature at the pinnacle of the social order could make his advances almost irresistible. Then and forever afterward I suspected and despised the man.

Fanny returned to our rooms at the hotel shortly after I finished my note to Emma. She stated that at a cost that was less than half of our expense at the hotel, she had arranged that we would take a house on Dover Street. I told her that there is little point in staying together and that I would remain at the hotel. To this she replied that if I remained at the hotel, she would also because as my wife, she would not leave me. To this declaration I responded that if she insisted upon our lodging together, it may as well be at Dover Street, and so we moved. She also stated that we had received an invitation from First Lord of the Admiralty Lord Spencer to dine with them and several officers of the Admiralty staff. Given the fact that I was eager to return to action at sea, such a dinner seemed to be something of a command appearance, and so we went.

The beginning of the dinner was actually a rather pleasant affair, and I had a number of good conversations with Lord Spencer and his subordinates. However, I was somewhat upset when Lady Spencer called me aside.

"Admiral, I feel that I must say to you that during your long absence at sea, the conduct of your dear wife was exemplary. It is not easy to be married to an active naval officer during a time of war for so long as it is necessary for your husband to be away. Fanny has been, nevertheless, a paragon of a naval officer's wife. She has borne up with great dignity and grace, and I trust that you truly appreciate her commitment."

I was somewhat surprised that Lady Spencer felt that she had to say such a thing but responded, "What you have said, my dear lady, is true, and you should know that I fully appreciate her faithful service to me."

At the dinner, however, I was rather put out that Fanny assumed a rather histrionic air of devotion and affection. Whereas she had been cold, silent, and distant following our conversation regarding Emma, at the dinner she gave all appearances of being nothing short of the doting wife, staying by my side, holding my arm and referring to me as "my dearest" and "darling." The entire act on her part seemed to me nothing more than a charade of hypocrisy. My resentment came to a head when during the dinner she shelled a number of walnuts and passed them to me in a wine glass. My response was to push them away. In my anger at her pretence my reaction was more vigorous than I had anticipated, and as I pushed the glass away, it struck a candlestick and shattered. Fanny immediately burst into tears and left the room followed by Lady Spencer. I excused myself from the table and followed them.

When I entered the room, Lady Spencer spoke, "I am very glad that you have come, Admiral. Your wife obviously needs you." I walked to the sofa, where Fanny was sobbing, and sat next to her.

"I did not mean to break the glass, and I apologise for that," I said.

"Why, Horace, do you treat me so badly?" she responded.

"I'm sorry that I broke the glass, but it was simply a reaction to the false and solicitous pretences that you have assumed during this evening," I responded.

"How can you possibly say that?" she blurted between sobs. "I have been a good and faithful wife to you, and everything that I have done for you is now rewarded with ignominy and hatred."

"Fanny, you must know because I have told you sincerely that I do not mean you any discomfort or hurt. Our marriage has been eclipsed, and it is no longer truly a marriage. We should not pretend that it is, and this charade of care and loving that you have displayed this evening does not reflect the truth of how distant, cold, and neglectful you have been to me. I have needed over all these years a wife who was attendant to my needs, but you have negligently failed to pack for me the things that you would know that I needed at sea. Your communications have been little more than letters that I would receive from a sister. You always complain about the weather, the prices of goods, and how cold your accommodations have been. You have never related to me in any meaningful sense of how my victories have been received. Nor have you indicated in your own heart that you have been proud of me. Instead you have prayed that I avoid danger. No true commander can do that. No officer in His Majesty's Navy can avoid going wilfully and constantly into harm's way. It seems that you have failed to come to know the man that I am. And after all of the years of our marriage your embraces have been with little or no passion, and you have given me no children."

She looked at me intently and said, "How in the world can you blame me for that?"

"I only know that you provided a son to Dr. Nisbet, but you have done nothing in the way of providing me with a family," I responded. "And now providence has given to me a woman who will do that."

"Oh, my God, how can you talk to me now of that awful woman?" she blurted.

"I speak of her because she is now a central figure in my future. I did not seek out the relationship. But it was presented to me by fate, and I declare with all seriousness that you should not discount my obligations to her. Had you been to me what she has become, our relationship would be very different. But you have not been what she has become, and I cannot turn away from what I must do. It is clear that our marriage is no longer truly a marriage and should be ended with a sense of mutual civility," I said, intending to defuse what had become a bitter moment.

She looked at me with a hard and tear-streaked face and then said, "I will remain your wife because I am your wife and I shall not divorce you."

"Then let it be so, for I cannot make you," I answered, disheartened again. "Please dry your face. We should re-join our hosts."

I left the room and went back to my place at the table. After a brief time Fanny also returned. The remaining time at dinner was strained, and there were frequent periods of awkward silence. As soon as the final course was completed, I thanked Lord and Lady Spencer for their hospitality, and Fanny accompanied me in leaving. She did not take my arm but again became a cold and insular wife. We returned to separate bedrooms at the Dover Street house.

I was later advised by Alexander Davison that Fanny had told Lady Spencer that her situation was no longer as a true wife to me and that she had been replaced by Lady Hamilton. Alex also said that the actuality of this circumstance had become known within the Admiralty, replacing what previously had been mere rumours. I assumed that the occurrences during the Spencers' dinner would spread through London society like a wildfire in dry grass.

At Dover Street, Fanny and I seldom spoke. We would take meals together, but our small staff seemed to be very mindful of the abyss that separated us. When we did talk, conversations were short and to the point, usually about invitations to various affairs. One such invitation was to a performance of the opera *Pizarro* at the Theatre Royal. The evening began very well, and when we appeared in our seating box, the audience below stood with cheers and applause, to which I gratefully smiled and waved in response. The performance was excellent, and all seemed well until the third act when the tenor sang, *"How well a woman can love ... how she can hate thou hast yet to learn ... Wave that glittering sword to meet and survive an injured woman's fury."* At that moment Fanny let out a very loud cry and fainted, having to be carried from the box. She later returned, and we remained until the end of the performance. However, the incident was reported in several of the London newspapers, obviously giving further credence to the talk of the town.

A Crisis of Emotion

We returned to the house at Dover Street, a warm and comfortable place but one devoid of emotional attachment and severely cold of human sensibility. One evening was particularly silent and strained, and after dinner without comment, Fanny went to her room and I to mine. I tried to sleep but could not. I arose and walked to the main room, where I made a small fire. Looking into the burning logs, I could only feel despair. The fire did not warm me. I was simply too cold inside. Not really knowing why, I walked to the closet and took out a cloak and a plain civilian hat. I put them on and walked to the street outside. I had decided simply to walk and think and to make a plan that would give a meaningful purpose to my life. And so I walked and walked. I pondered my return to the sea and felt some comfort. I had requested a command and would take anything offered by the Admiralty, whether it may be to the Channel Fleet, to the Mediterranean, or to the ends of the earth. My principal concern was, however, the state of my heart and the anguish that seemed to grip it. Emma was now great with our child and near to its birth, but to me she seemed to be the farthest thing on the earth. How I longed to see her. How I longed to hold her and feel the touch of her cheek upon mine. How I missed touching her hair and seeing the gleam of her eyes.

It seemed that I walked down streets without name or number. They were all black and cold. I wandered into Fleet Market and found it empty. I walked down more streets and through parkways, finding no way out of the great pit that seemed to be my endless and meaningless marriage to Fanny. Why could she not have been Emma or more like Emma? Why did I find nothing of value or love in her? Why was it that Emma, however, filled all of my needs? Emma had come into my heart. She held me in a regard that made me feel the greatest value on earth to her. When she spoke to me, her words were always soft and warm and comforting. When I held her, I felt as though I was holding everything that I needed in the world. When I made love to her, it gave to me a delight and fulfilment that was the greatest pleasure I had ever known. My unions with her were greater than the eruptions of a volcano, and afterwards the warm embraces were better than soft spring winds over flowered meadows. They were the very source and essence of happiness. I walked and walked, finding no solution.

I walked across Blackfriars Bridge and down more streets. I found nothing but fatigue and helplessness. My only solution was to escape once again to the sea. The thought of that brought again some solace and my need for duty braced me. However, I found no comfort for my heart and decided out of desperation to go to the house in Grosvenor Square, where Sir William and Emma were living. I mounted the steps and knocked on the door. There was no answer. I knocked again, and after a while a sleepy servant answered and let me in. He seemed shocked when I asked where the Hamiltons' bedroom was located, but then he pointed to its door. I asked for a candle, and he gave it to me. I then knocked on their bedroom door and let myself in, holding the candle high so that they could see my face. I softly sat on the edge of their bed as they awoke.

"My good friend, William, and my dearest Emma, I have been walking the streets of London throughout the night and am desperate in despair," I said as they roused themselves and sat up in bed.

"My dear Horatio, you look a fright. What is the matter?" Sir William asked, rubbing his eyes.

"I feel that everything is the matter, and without your company and the presence of the woman we love, I simply feel lost. I ask that you take me in," I answered. "I feel utterly unhappy without you."

I stood, and they both rose from the bed and draped their night cloaks around their shoulders.

"Well, my dear friend, we shall do what we must do to give you comfort," Sir William answered and gently patted my shoulder.

Emma approached, and Sir William took the candle. I brought her into my arms and stifled sobs that seemed to rise in my chest.

"My darling man, you are safe with us," Emma whispered as a great sense of relief made the anxiety of my heart ease and rise up out of me like the morning mist in a warm sun.

"Thank God for you," I replied. "And you, my dear friend, you are the best friend I have had in life," I said, looking at Sir William.

He smiled and said, "Let us go and make a fire. I'm sure we can find an answer to this puzzle that bedevils us."

We went to the living room, and he gave instructions to the sleepy servant who had been waiting outside the bedroom. The servant made a fire and asked if he could bring some tea.

Emma said, "Yes, that would be nice. Please do. It will help to warm us."

After the fire was kindled, the servant brought and served the tea. Emma sat next to me and took off the hat that had remained on my head. She put her hand on my face and spoke.

"Whatever we decide will be the best for us, my dear. Fear nothing, for you know that we shall always be together." She kissed my cheek, and I was able to smile.

"I am truly sorry for disturbing you, but I did not know what to do," I said. "I have no house that I can call my home, and the woman who pretends to be my wife simply sits as an iceberg on the ocean of my emptiness. She is neither company nor comfort to me. I need you. I need you both."

"Well then, stay with us. That seems to be the answer, and a simple one," Sir William exclaimed.

"Yes, William," Emma said, "that is a simple answer, but I'm afraid that it is a solution that would only serve to fan the fire of rumours that are circling in the city. Not only would it injure you before society, but it may well injure Horatio with the Admiralty. Think of what society in this prudish and hard-faced city would say."

"I do not give a fig for what society or anyone in this city thinks or says. I am frankly done with it all. We are *tria juncto in uno*, and if Horatio is suffering, we all suffer," Sir William said to my great admiration and comfort.

"That may be, my dear, but I do not want to injure you or Horatio. And I am sure that we can find a better solution. We must endure this time, and we should disregard the criticisms that have been made of us. These trials will pass, and however much it pains my heart, Horatio, you should return. Please remember that we love you with a tenderness and strength that cannot be measured. But let us act out our parts as best we can. This time will pass, and soon we will be together again."

The words Emma spoke rang clearly as a bell of truth, and after a moment I said, "You are right, my dearest. Let us do what we must."

I arose and shook the hand of Sir William and then kissed Emma upon her cheek and gently her lips. As I left the Hamiltons' house and walked slowly back to Dover Street, it seemed that the compass within me had been recalibrated, and I knew that as Emma had articulated, this difficult time, like a fitful storm in the Mediterranean Sea, would pass.

Chapter 16

Resolution with Fanny

I remember returning to the Dover Street house, where Fanny had arranged a breakfast with our solicitor, William Hazelwood, for the purpose of arranging the sale of the house she had bought in Suffolk. The meal was rather perfunctory with Hazelwood reviewing various legal terms of sale agency with indescribably dull details of matters relating to what he characterised as "sale of the fee."

"Upon sale of the house, have you given any thought to purchasing another property?" Hazelwood asked.

"We have not," I responded immediately.

"But tell us, Mister Hazelwood, if your agent has any recommendations with respect to attractive properties north of London where we might live," Fanny requested.

I quickly interjected, "My dear, I believe we are not disposed to make any decisions with respect to the purchase of any property at this point."

"We have to live somewhere, husband," she replied, "and it is my impression that you would not want to stay in London.

"Fanny, it seems that I will live at sea," I replied.

We resolved matters relating to the sale of the Suffolk house, and Mister Hazelwood departed. The ensuing conversation with Fanny was strained and focused upon whether or not our asking price for the house had been either sufficient or understated. It really did not matter to me, and after long pause I told her, "William Beckford, who you may recall is the very wealthy cousin to Sir William, has invited us to spend the Christmas season at his newly constructed estate near Wiltshire. The invitation comes through the good graces of Sir William and dear Lady Hamilton."

Fanny slapped her fork on the table and said, looking directly at me, "Dear Lady Hamilton! I am sick of hearing mention of dear Lady Hamilton. In fact, I am resolved that you shall give up either her or me."

"Take care, Fanny," I replied, looking directly back at her, "I will never forget my obligations to Lady Hamilton and shall require that you not speak otherwise of her except with affection and admiration."

"I cannot accept such a direction," she responded in anger and rose from the table, saying, "My mind is made up. I am your wife. Dear Lady Hamilton is not." She stormed from the room.

Feeling a strange sense of relief, I finished what was left of breakfast and went to my room. I gathered and packed all of my clothing and personal things and left the Dover Street house. Fanny and I would never again sleep under the same roof.

Christmas Holiday

Sir William's cousin, William Beckford, had inherited a fortune from his father, who had been a very successful merchant in trade from the West Indies. For several decades most of the sugar, hemp, indigo, and tobacco that originated in the various islands, whether British or not, came through his company. With his considerable inherited wealth, Beckford had built a beautiful estate he named "Fonthill Splendens." It was nestled in the midst of wooded hills and lakes near Wiltshire, and featured an enormous Gothic castle with a tower rising higher than two hundred feet. Actually the place had the look of a monastic cathedral. It was designed for hunting, entertaining, and impressing everyone who had the good fortune of being a guest in its splendour. Red-headed pheasants had been imported from America and walked about the grounds like beautiful chickens.

As my carriage approached the estate, I was greeted by a military escort and a rather large orchestra that played "Rule, Britannia". Beckford's servant staff, more than thirty in number, lined the steps to his enormous door. Beckford himself stood at the centre and rushed forward, announcing, "Admiral, it is a great honour to me that you are my first formal guest at Fonthill Splendens. I have arranged that you shall be treated with my utmost hospitality, and if there is anything that you need or want, you have only to ask." And as we walked through his enormous oaken door, he added, "I have arranged that you shall have the Hamiltons in the next guest room. You see, I know that you have a special arrangement with them, and not only am I mindful of the suggestions that have been made in the newspapers and the general prattle of London, but I find that if they are true, I, for one, believe it to be wonderful. After all, we are people with emotions of attachment that, if honest and not hurtful of others, should be respected and left alone. Whatever relationships you have with Sir William or Lady Hamilton are accepted and welcomed by me."

I responded simply by thanking him for his gracious hospitality and complemented him on the impressive estate he had created. My room was indeed a beautiful place. As was Beckford's habit, no expense had been spared and no item of comfort excluded.

During the remainder of the day, a cavalcade of high-profile guests arrived. They included the writer John Walcott; Benjamin West, the American-born painter and president of the Royal Academy; James Wyatt, the famous architect who had designed the estate; Brigita Banti, the celebrated opera singer; and many members of the artist community, some of whom were Bohemian to say the least. The procession of carriages bringing guests to the estate extended into the evening. Guests were greeted by a great number of torches that flickered along both sides of the roadway, accompanied by the dulcet sounds of an orchestra that played behind hedges, out of sight, creating a very effective scene of magical enchantment.

A welcoming reception had been arranged, and it was the equal of any that could have been enjoyed at any royal event. Crystal candelabras were set out in great numbers, filling the foyer with the most magical, glittering luminescence I had ever seen. Sumptuous foods of every kind were set upon tables of white linen. The tables were filled with food in the great room, ready for guests to enjoy as they arrived. Beckford had imported several vintages of French champagnes from America, and they were poured generously throughout the evening. As each guest arrived, the chief butler would stamp his staff and announce their names as though the evening were taking place at Windsor Castle. I spoke with many of the luminary guests as they arrived, and I was pleased that each greeted me with expressions of honour and admiration. I waited anxiously for the arrival of Sir William and Emma, looking constantly at the great doorway, and finally very late in the evening, they arrived. I rushed forward and shook the hand of my friend, Sir William, who apologised for arriving late, saying that he had not felt well during the recent weeks. He did seem a bit haggard. I then went to Emma and gently kissed her hand in a formal manner. I looked into her beautiful face and whispered softly.

"My darling, I'm going up to my room and must hold you. Please note where I go and do follow me at an appropriate distance." I looked up the grand staircase, and when I walked to the top, I paused and looked behind to see Emma following about twenty steps behind. When I reached my room, I left the door ajar, and after a moment she entered, smiling and beautiful. I immediately took her into my arms and held her close, kissing her neck and cheek. I then looked into her face and kissed her lips. The warmth of her body, the feel of her soft tresses in my hand, and knowing that at least for a few days I would be with her, was enchanting.

"I love you, my dearest," I said, holding her chin in my hand. "I love you more than words can describe, and that this moment there is no man in England who is happier than I."

She softly replied, "I have been in torment without you, and now that we will be together, at least for a while, it brings the greatest pleasure in the world to me."

I continued to hold her and wanted never to let go. Repeatedly I moved my lips from her neck to her cheek and to her mouth. Then I felt her abdomen move, and she laughed.

"There it goes again. It has begun to kick again, probably knowing that you are here next to me," she said.

I knelt and passed my hand over the roundness of her abdomen and felt again a faint movement. With a knee on the floor, I kissed her abdomen and then held my cheek against it.

"Our child, our child, I still find it hard to believe that God has been so good to us to put this child in our lives," I said with a passion that can be felt but never truly described.

"My dearest, we must go back to the crowd of Mister Beckford's guests. Tonight I shall sleep in your arms. Finally I shall again sleep in your arms," she said and added, "Let me be the first to go." She went to the door, turned, and smiled, saying again, "I love you, my dearest. You and the child within me are my world." She then went out and gently closed the door. I remained for some time, simply standing and feeling comfort and satisfaction that consumed me. The only other time I had felt that way was during the service of thanksgiving after the battle in Aboukir Bay. Quietly in that moment after I had held my wonderful woman and felt the movement of the child we had created, a prayer rose from my heart, thanking God for the fortune He had laid in my path.

The holiday at Fonthill Splendens became a respite of perfect comfort and relaxation. Our days were filled with tours of the estate, boating upon its lakes, and for those who desired, hunting the game animals that Beckford had plentifully stocked throughout his lush forests. Sir William seemed to enjoy himself to the utmost, and the activity brought back not only a good colour to his face but also a renewed spring to his step. For me, it was a magical string of days and nights spent with Emma. We also enjoyed our time with the other guests. Their conversations were honest and cordial, accepting what they knew to be our relationship without the razor's edge of judgment and criticism that had been so hurtful in London. We strolled the grounds, talking and laughing in reminiscences of Naples, Palermo, and some of our awful transit times at sea. We dined with Sir William, and I renewed my admiration and love for the man who had become very much like an older brother to me. In the evenings I slept with Emma in my arms. The warmth of her, our whispers of endearment, the touch of my hand upon her body, frequently feeling the stirring of our child within her, and the kisses between us brought a renewed meaning of life.

Dinners orchestrated by Beckford were spectacular. The food, the wine, and the champagne were the best, and everything was presented in an elegant setting of high-ceilinged rooms with Greek pillars, beautiful paintings, and statues in every room. There was also an enormous fireplace that provided a glow of both warmth and comfort. Each evening meal was accompanied by beautiful music. Frequently Madame Banti would sing, sometimes accompanied by Emma. Each seemed to enjoy the other's company, and together they sang wonderful duets. One evening Emma performed one of her attitudes. It was the tragic story of Agrippina in exile, and she performed it with such mastery that at the end many of the guests were in tears. Benjamin West later wrote that at the end of her performance, it was *"as if waking from a dream or freed from the influence of a magic spell."* But the days at Fonthill Splendens were numbered and had to come to an end. As I rode back to London, the parting from Sir William and Emma, and the finale of our wonderful holiday, seemed very much like descending from heaven back into an outer circle of hell that was London.

When I returned to my hotel, I was advised by a note from the solicitor that the house in Suffolk had been sold. Then true to my obligation towards Fanny, I arranged a year's lease for the Dover Street house so that she would have a place to stay until permanent arrangements could be made. I also had Davison arrange with my bank to pay £400 into her account immediately, in addition to a handsome quarterly allowance. Knowing that my separation from her had become a total and irreparable break, I still felt that I nevertheless had to do my duty towards her.

I went immediately to the Admiralty and spoke with Lord Spencer, who advised that I had been promoted to vice admiral and that he had decided to appoint me to command of the *San Joseph*, my first battle prize from the Battle of Cape St. Vincent. I would be second-in-command of the Channel Fleet under Admiral Jervis himself. This appointment brought with it a mixture of feelings. First there had been an issue with respect to prize money for certain ships that had been captured while I was in command of the Mediterranean following the departure of Admiral Jervis and prior to Lord Keith's arrival. Davison had made a request with the Admiralty that I be accorded the commander's prize money for those ships. However, a lower court had held that Admiral Jervis would be awarded the money, as he was still formally the commander of the Mediterranean. However, upon appeal, a higher court held that as I was the actual commander at the time the prizes were taken, the prize money should be awarded to me. I wondered whether Admiral Jervis might feel some resentment as a result of this court case. My second feeling was one of continued deep respect and affection for the admiral, a man who had been an unfailing mentor and supporter. Upon my arrival at Yarmouth, I went straight away to see him, and when I greeted him, he received me warmly.

"Horatio, I'm very pleased that the Admiralty has seen fit to confirm my request that you be given the *San Joseph* and appointed under my command," Jervis exclaimed, extending his left hand.

I shook it and said, "My dear admiral, there is no one under whose command I would prefer to serve. I am delighted again to have a ship with an opportunity once again to engage our enemies with you."

"Yes indeed!" he replied. "I know so well that you are always ready to engage any enemy. I never knew a man in our profession, excepting yourself and Trowbridge, who possessed such a fighting spirit and is so capable of the magic part of infusing the same spirit in others. I know only that your conduct from your first appointment to this very hour has been the subject of my constant admiration."

"Sir," I replied, "I do want you to know that the entire matter of the court case on the Mediterranean prizes was brought by my agent, Alexander Davison, and—"

"Horatio," he interrupted, "I have no feeling about that, and in fact, I never anticipated getting so much as a farthing from those prizes."

To that statement, I felt a relief beyond measure. Then I simply smiled, looked at the ceiling, loudly exhaled, and then said, "Thanks be to God that you feel that way."

We both laughed, and the admiral poured two glasses of port, handing one to me with a faint smile.

"Horatio, please sit down. There is something I want to tell you." I sat. He looked at the floor for a moment and then directly at me. "My dear fellow, there are frequently two kinds of admirals. The first are *shore admirals* who are those men who have acute political acumen and are very successful at promoting their careers by seeming to be successful. They are usually tall, handsome, and well-born. And they can do a good job in promoting the Royal Navy as well as themselves. They say and do the right things, and they never get themselves in trouble. Between us, I would say that Lord Keith is a superb shore admiral." After he paused a moment, he continued, "Then there are *war admirals*. Those are men who are fighters, experts in handling ships at sea and in battle. They are men you can count on to fly at the enemy and shatter them into submission. They have the best of instincts in a fight. They are the men who win our wars. Frequently, however, they are like fish when you put them on shore – out of their element, flapping about – sometimes causing trouble. You, my dear man, are a war admiral. Know this," he said, leaning toward me and looking directly into my eyes, "You are the best war admiral I have ever known. You are the best fighting captain I have ever seen. There is no man on this earth with whom I would rather go into battle. I know that in any fight you will do the best job that could be done, even if it caused your death, and to me as a commander, that is a priceless asset. Having said that, I would observe that you have gotten yourself into trouble by your conduct with Lady Hamilton, and I will not speak of it at length. I am sure you know all the prattle that is going on in London, particularly within the Admiralty, about your affair. I will only say this: Do your job at sea and that is all I shall request of you, but when you go ashore, be circumspect – and manage your private life so that it does not become an object under the glare of society. That is all I have to say about that, and you need not respond."

I remained quiet and nodded, knowing that everything he had said was the stark truth. He filled my wine glass again and lifted his in a toast. I gently clinked my glass with his and smiled.

"My dear admiral," I said, "As you know, I am ready to sail through the gates of hell with you."

"I know, Horatio. I know," he answered.

The Baltic Threat

On several occasions I had visited with First Lord Spencer, insisting that I be given an assignment at sea, and each time we spoke, he assured me that one would be made as soon as an appropriate command could be found. I intensely wanted to escape from London and get back to sea. His appointing me as second to Admiral Jervis was a fulfilment of that promise. In the meantime an alarming situation was developing on the continent. Our former alliances were in tatters. The *Peace of Luneville* had been signed between Austria and France, delivering to the French essential control of puppet states in Lombardy, Liguria, Switzerland, and Holland. Shortly thereafter, a peace was forced upon Naples, which meant that the French would also be in control of the entire Italian peninsula. To make matters worse, it also appeared that Russia, Denmark, Sweden, and Prussia had been in the process of forming what they called an "alliance of armed neutrality." If successful, this would constitute a serious threat to our blockade of France, as the allied nations in a new stance of aggressive neutrality would insist upon an unfettered ability to trade with all nations, including France, and whereas our policy had been to stop and search merchant ships of neutral countries to prevent war supplies from reaching French ports. It appeared that the Baltic States were in the process of adopting a formal policy that would effectively defeat the blockade. If they were successful in renewing trade with France, vital supplies of grain, hemp, and most importantly, timber would again flow into France. Mister Pitt's government decided to respond to this possibility and arranged for the king to give a formal speech from the throne to the House of Lords. In order to give a greater gravamen to the speech, the prime minister requested that Lord Hood and I stand on either side of the king as he spoke. I considered this to be a great honour, and I attended the speech wearing my full-dress uniform with all decorations. During his speech the king read the government's position as opposing, if necessary with force, the policy of any country to insist upon engaging in open trade with France in defiance of our blockade. He made clear that the blockade would include all countries, no matter what the position of their government may be, in armed neutrality or not.

On the day I met with Admiral Jervis and went aboard the *San Joseph*, Admiral Sir Hyde Parker was appointed command of the North

Sea fleet, and Lord Spencer sent to me a request for a conference. I went straight away to the First Lord's chamber.

"My dear admiral," Lord Spencer began, "there is much afoot on continent, and as a result, there is much afoot here in the Admiralty. Something has to be done to break the threatened Baltic pact, and as you probably know, Sir Hyde Parker has been appointed to command of the Baltic Fleet."

"I have heard that, my lord, but with respect, I would ask why that vital command was not given to Admiral Jervis, who has had much greater experience and success in battle?" I asked, fearing some resentment at my temerity. However, this was a very important matter, and the question was appropriate.

Lord Spencer responded in an even tone, "It is believed that with the information Admiral Parker has acquired during the last preparation for a possible war with Russia, his command of our response to matters in the Baltic seemed appropriate."

"I see," I responded, without seeing any wisdom whatever in the decision.

"Admiral, the reason I have asked you to come today is because the Admiralty has decided to name you as second-in-command of the Baltic fleet under Admiral Parker," Lord Spencer added.

"I would be absolutely delighted to accept such an appointment," I immediately responded with great enthusiasm. It had become clear that action in the Baltic was the next great undertaking for the Royal Navy, and command in that undertaking was exactly what I wanted, even if under an admiral whose reputation was for caution. I would make the best of the situation.

After my audience with Lord Spencer I went directly to Admiral Jervis and advised him of the proposed appointment as well as my willingness to accept it, provided he did not object. His response was both positive and robust. He disclosed that he had recommended my command under Parker because, as he put it, "In time of hostility, a shore admiral needs a war admiral to do the fighting work."

I returned to the *San Joseph*, where I found that Fanny had simply thrown my things together and shipped them off in no order and with a number of essential things missing. Yet again, although she had professed her intent to be a good wife, she had failed miserably in being of any assistance to me. I also found a note from Sir William, which, in addition to passing general news, contained something that alarmed me greatly. He wrote that he and Emma intended to give a formal dinner for several ministers of the government and that the guest list included the Prince of Wales. Remembering the man's unfettered ogling at Emma, I was beside myself with an anxiety that overcame me like a storm at sea. Without reflection I immediately wrote to Emma,

> *My dearest, I have received alarming news in a note from Sir William. He tells me that he plans a dinner which will include the Prince of Wales as a guest of honour. The fear of his being in your house and at your table, near you, is overcoming. He will likely put his foot near you and bend to your ear, telling you soft things. If he does so ... turn him out of your house. Do not let him touch you. May God strike him blind if he looks at you. On that day, I shall have no one to dinner. It shall be a fasting day for me. I am gone almost mad. I know his aim is to have you for a mistress. The thought so agitates me that I cannot write. I cannot bear it.*

There was also another matter that troubled me greatly. The king's illness had recurred, and there was constant talk that the prince would be named as Regent Royal to act in all respects on behalf of the king. I knew that Sir William was very mindful of this and was very keen to develop a positive relationship with the scoundrel prince because of the influence he would likely have. I could not question the utility of Sir William having a positive relationship with the Crown, as the issue of his pension was unsettled and the prince could hold the purse strings for that pension. However, my intense fear was that the prince intended to have Emma as another of his mistresses, and I was in torment of any moment when she should be in his presence. However, as matters soon developed, the regency was announced by Parliament, and it came to dominate the prince's time, during which he was said to have attended to his established mistresses, fortunately affording him little opportunity to pursue new ones.

Horatia

To my great relief, I later received a note from Sir William that the dinner had been cancelled. Then in the first week of February, glorious news was sent by Alex Davison. Emma had given birth to a daughter. I requested and received three days' leave from Admiral Jervis and went immediately to London. Arriving at the Hamiltons' house, I was ushered into the bedroom where Sir William was sitting and Emma was nursing our child. I rushed to the bedside and leaned over, kissing Emma gently. I looked upon the child. A more beautiful thing I had never seen, all pale with wisps of blonde hair and features that was the perfect miniature of a beautiful face as she fed slowly from her mother's breast.

"Your daughter is lovely, isn't she?" Sir William asked.

"Yes, she is indeed," I answered, and looking at him, I added, "Please my dear friend, consider her as our daughter, for we remain *tria juncta in uno*."

I looked at Emma and said, "She is beautiful, my dearest, and you are beautiful. My heart could not feel better than at this moment."

I held the child, delighting in holding the slight weight of a new human being that was my child. I brushed her forehead with my lips and said softly, "I shall protect you from Bonaparte. You shall be safe, my child, for I shall do my duty. I promise you that, my dear little thing."

"What shall we name her?" I asked. "Why not name her Emma?

"I fear we cannot do that," Emma responded. "You see, the child I had as a girl was named Emma, so we must call her something else. I would like her name to be Horatia. I would like that very much."

I knew that Emma had given birth to a child when she was very young; however, I did not know that it was a girl, and I did not know that it was named Emma. I also exulted in the proposed name of Horatia.

I looked at Sir William and asked, "Do you favour the name Horatia?"

"I do," he answered. "I do indeed."

"Then we are settled," I responded. "Her name shall be Horatia."

The remaining days of my leave were a peaceful, quiet, and warm time spent with the three people most important to me. We dined wonderfully, and in the evenings I slept with Emma in my arms. During dinners we talked with Sir William for extended periods, warmed in front of the hearth, chiefly about unsettled matters in government and the frequent strains between the Prince Regent, Parliament, and Prime Minister Pitt. There was a continuing and serious problem with the country's finances. The cost of the continuing war had been monumental, and taxes were so high that any increase would suffocate the economy. The financial crisis also underscored the importance of keeping our trade open and continuing the blockade of French ports. When I returned to the *San Joseph*, I immediately penned to Emma,

> *Parting is literally tearing at my flesh but the remembrance of our time together will keep my spirits up until we shall be together again. My affection is, if possible, stronger than ever for you, and I trust it will keep increasing. You know, my dearest Emma, but there is nothing in this world that I would not do for us to live together, and to have our dear child with us. I firmly believe that this campaign will give us peace, and then we will set off for Brontë. In twelve hours, we shall be across the water and freed from all the nonsense of Sir William's friends, or rather pretended ones. Nothing but an event happening to him could prevent my going ... one thousand tongues and slanderous reports would come if I separated from Fannie totally, which I would do with pleasure the moment you and I can be united. I want to see her no more; therefore we must manage until we can quit this country. I love you. I never did love anyone else. I never received a dear pledge of love until you gave me one, and thank you, thank my God that you never gave one to anyone else. You, my beloved Emma, and my country are the two dearest objects of my fond heart. What must be my sensations at the idea of sleeping with you? It sets me on fire, even the thoughts of it. I am sure that my love and my desires are all to you. If any woman naked were to come to me, even as I am at this moment thinking of you, I hope it might rot off if I were to touch her with my hand. Now my heart, person, and mind are in perfect union of love toward my beloved Emma. You are my love, my darling angel, my heaven given wife, the dearest only true wife of my own until death. I know you will never let that fellow or anyone else come near you. Kiss and bless our dear Horatia.*
>
> *Your dearest, Nelson & Brontë*

During the next week I would write to her on each day. I also wrote my last letter to Fanny, responding in part to concerns that she had voiced about her son, Josiah:

> *My dear Fanny, Josiah is to have another ship and to go aboard if the Thalia cannot be ready soon. I have done all for him … To him; I have fully done my duty as a generous man. I neither want nor wish for anybody to care what becomes of me, whether I return or am left dead in the Baltic, seeing I have done all in my power for you. And if dead, you will find that I have done the same, therefore my only wish is to be left to myself and wishing you ever happiness, believe that I am your affectionate Nelson & Brontë.*

My brother Maurice later advised me that Fanny had written across the top of the letter, "This is my Lord Nelson's letter of dismissal." I was saddened that our parting could not have been more civil and less hurtful.

Within the week after my return to Yarmouth, it was announced that Admiral Jervis had replaced Lord Spencer as First Lord of the Admiralty, and while I felt that Lord Spencer had always been a very competent first lord and one of my staunch supporters, I felt that there could have been no better commander in that seat than Admiral Jervis. In conferences with the new first lord, his staff, and Admiral Hyde Parker, there was some question whether I should remain in command of the *San Joseph*, as it had a very deep draft. The Admiralty had concluded that our most likely action would first be against the Danes, and the port of Copenhagen was not very deep. Admiral Parker recommended that I shift my flag to HMS *St. George*. The staff of the Admiralty agreed, and on 12 February 1801, I did so. However, when I arrived and inspected the *St. George*, I found that her draft was almost as great as that of the *San Joseph*. Immediately I made this observation to both Admiral Parker and the Admiralty, recommending that I transfer to a ship with a draft that was at least six feet less than the normal channels of Copenhagen. The Admiralty responded with agreement, and I was given the seventy-four-gun HMS *Elephant*, a newly refitted ship with fresh copper along its bottom. I was also delighted that its Captain was Thomas Foley, one of my band of brothers who had commanded the *Goliath* at Aboukir Bay.

On the continent it appeared that everything was coming to bear against British interests. Tsar Paul of Russia, a mere boy – and a weak and stupid one at that – had been converted entirely from anti-French to pro-French sentiments, largely by his ministers who apparently had concluded that an alliance with France would bring peace with the French and would allow Russia the opportunity to dominate the Baltic. The ensuing Russian aloofness and their eager participation in the formation of a league of armed neutrals made them anything but a British ally. To add flame to the fire, Russia and Sweden had signed a convention undertaking to stop trade in contraband – very narrowly and strictly defined as military goods – and to allow unfettered trade in all other commerce. This had become a very direct rebuke of our French blockade. Soon thereafter, Bonaparte grandly announced that France was at peace with Russia, implying almost directly that they had become allied against Britain.

In Denmark, Crown Prince Frederick had become the effective sovereign of Denmark because of the imbecility of his father, King Christian VII. The Danish fleet, laying in Copenhagen, was considered the most formidable among the Baltic navies, and the foreign office in London made timely overtures to Denmark in order to dissuade them from any alliance with Russia and Sweden. Those overtures were, however, not well received, and the foreign office concluded that Prince Frederick and his government could not be persuaded against a pro-Russian policy. The decision was that a quick action was necessary and that it would first be directed against Denmark.

Immediately after I took command of my squadron, we sailed to join with Admiral Parker at Yarmouth. There I found that the admiral, our commander-in-chief, was not in his flagship, HMS *London*, but was living ashore at the Wrestler's Arms with a young woman he had recently taken as his wife. She was nineteen years old and referred to as "batter pudding" by sailors in the fleet. No significant preparations were being made for a crucial battle that was soon to occur. Admiral Parker had given no order for drills. Nor had he made any plans for an attack. He held no meaningful conferences with his captains, and everyone simply sat at anchor, idle in cold, raw winds blowing down from the North Sea. I spoke to Captain Foley, "Tom, while Admiral Parker takes all of his energy to spend himself in his new wife, we shall prepare for battle. There shall be double gunnery drills every day, and perhaps that will rouse the admiral from his bed sheets. You might advise the ships that they shall be engaged in battle drills every day. Send it as an informal letter so that our absent leader will not think that I have usurped his authority."

"Gladly, Admiral," Foley responded. "It might add some excitement to his endeavours."

Laughing a bit, I replied, "Foley, you know that you should not make whimsical remarks about our commander. Such indiscretions should be mine alone."

Foley smiled and called the gunnery officer. He gave orders for twice daily drills. He also sent my informal letter to the other captains of all ships present, and for the next several days the constant sweep of the North Sea wind was accompanied by the muffled roar of cannon fire not only from my squadron but by all ships present. To my utter amazement, the drills did not have any effect upon Admiral Parker. He remained ensconced at the inn, enjoying his pudding. One morning I decided to go to the Wrestler's Arms with Foley and Colonel Stuart, my commander of marines, for breakfast. I sent a note of compliments to the admiral's room, and he came down to see us.

"Gentlemen, good morning," he said. "What on earth is the cannon fire I constantly hear?"

"They are gunnery drills among the ships in my squadron," I responded. "I have ordered them in order to ensure that we shall fire our guns at least twice as rapidly as the enemy."

What happened next was both astonishing and profoundly disappointing. His response was, "Very well." He then turned and left the dining room.

That afternoon I received news that was even more astonishing. Apparently the new young wife of Admiral Parker had convinced him to plan a ball to celebrate their marriage, and the affair would not occur for another eleven days. This simply was too much for me to bear. My old friend, Thomas Trowbridge, had become an assisting lord of the Admiralty under Lord Jervis, and I wrote to him, confidentially advising of all the circumstances going on at Yarmouth and requesting that sailing orders be sent to the fleet. He apparently conveyed my sentiments to Admiral Jervis, who immediately dispatched a letter to Admiral Parker, a copy of which Trowbridge secretly sent to me. It stated,

> *I have heard by a side wind that you have intention of continuing*
> *at Yarmouth on account of some trifling circumstances. I really*

know not what they are, nor did I give myself the trouble of inquiring into them, supposing it impossible that under the current set of affairs, there could be the smallest foundation for such report. I ... convey to you my opinion, as a private friend, that any delay in your sailing would do you irreparable injury.

Following this broadside of criticism, Parker quickly cancelled the ball and returned to his flagship. Yet we still sat at anchor. As second-in-command of the fleet, I did not know what additional orders, if any, had been handed down from the Admiralty. I had not been invited to any conferences with my commander, and I did not even know whether such conferences had been held. However, I soon came upon an opportunity. In fishing the waters next to our ship, a crewman had caught a large turbot. I knew that the admiral was a gourmand, and hoping that the fish might serve as a vehicle for restoring some measure of communication with him, I had the fresh turbot sent to him with a note expressing my compliments. The gesture seemed to work exceedingly well, and I was invited to the flagship for a conference on the following day.

When I arrived aboard the *London*, Admiral Parker greeted me genially and introduced me to the various ships' captains. Most were unknown to me. Also present was a man named Nicholas Vanisttart, a young man who was a barrister and a Member of Parliament from Hastings. The conference turned out not to be a battle planning conference but one in which Mister Vanisttart described his mission. He announced that the Foreign Office would have us sail to Kattegat Bay, a large body of water north of Copenhagen, and anchor there. He would then go in a cutter under a flag of truce and conduct a diplomatic conference with Prince Frederick. It was his duty to make England's position clear to the Danes in an attempt to dissuade them from further actions as part of the armed neutrality. Whether any battle action might follow would turn up on the Danes' response to Vanisttart's diplomatic mission.

The next morning we set sail for Kattegat Bay. During our transit the North Sea was not its usually turbulent self, and we made the transit in two days, during which I ordered the captains of my squadron to carry out gunnery drills and advised them that I expected their gunnery crews to be able to fire successive rounds in not more than one minute's time. I was pleased to note that even the ships that were not in my squadron followed our example, and it seemed that should Mister Vanisttart not be successful in bringing sense to the Danish prince, our ships would be able to do so. It had been a long time since I had smelled the smoke of gunfire at sea, and it was pleasing watching the feverish and determined work of our gun crews. I had instructed Captain Foley to tell his gunners that their duty was to focus on only one thing - to fire their cannons as quickly as they possibly could, giving no mind whatever to damage inflicted upon our ship. Nothing makes a seaman more effective in battle than to have him concentrate upon one thing and one thing alone – his duty. During the transit I had ample opportunity to study charts of the port of Copenhagen. I assumed that the Danes would be anchored, as the French had been at Aboukir. However, I was sure that they would be arranged in a manner that would coordinate their fire with shore batteries and gunnery towers. Furthermore, the shallow waters of the port would not allow us to navigate on their land side. We would have to fight them on a ship-to-ship basis, simply firing our broadsides against theirs. This prospect gave me a great sense of optimism, as I had great faith in the superiority of our ships and more importantly, the superiority of our gunnery crews.

Diplomatic Failure

Immediately after we anchored in the Kattegat, Mister Vanisttart was taken by a cutter to Copenhagen. He returned the next day, and Admiral Parker hoisted a signal that called all captains to conference. When we arrived, it was apparent that Mister Vansittart's dour demeanour did not signify a success in his mission. His report was very brief. He announced that the prince and his ministers had immediately rejected his overtures. The Danes would not abandon their allies in what the prince called a formal "alliance of armed neutrality." They were determined to exercise what he described as their legitimate rights to free trade, no matter what the effects may be upon British interests. The prince advised that the defences of Copenhagen had been strengthened and warned against any act of aggression from our fleet. Admiral Parker stated that he was inclined to have the fleet remain where it was, in Kattegat Bay, and from there to maintain a blockade of the Baltic. To me, this was an astoundingly incompetent decision. First, it would enable Russia, Sweden, and Denmark to coordinate their forces in much greater numbers than our own, and secondly, it would remove the present opportunity of picking off and subduing one of their allies. Every captain present in Admiral Parker's stateroom seemed to sit in gloomy silence. For the longest while no one spoke, and then restraining the anger and frustration that welled within me, I said, "Admiral, please know that upon your orders, we are ready to stamp out the Danish fleet."

"Thank you, Nelson," he responded. "I am pleased to know that and shall be mindful of it."

He said no more and thanked all of the captains for their attention. They all filed from his stateroom, many looking at me and nodding. I returned to the *Elephant* with an overwhelming sense of disappointment and frustration, which I vented to Tom Foley.

"Here we are, Foley, ready to do what has to be done, and from all indications we shall sit idle at anchor. I despise inaction when valiant measures are called for, especially when we are ready to strike a decisive blow. How I hate such men who are inclined to do only pen and ink things when cannonballs and musket fire are called for. We have talked to the enemy, and it has done no good. A fleet of British ships are the best negotiators in Europe. The persuasion of our diplomat has failed. It is now time for our broadsides to do the talking."

"I agree entirely, Admiral, but is there perhaps a reason for Admiral Parker to wait, reason we do not know?" Foley asked.

"Thomas, I cannot imagine what reason there may be. Right now the Russian fleet is bound up in ice at St. Petersburg and Revel. Very soon that ice will melt, and the Russian fleet will be able to come out and join with the Swedes and the Danes. That will give us a very different and far more difficult kettle of fish to boil. We can take the Danes here and now, and when we destroy their forces, we can then deal with the Russians. It makes no sense whatever to give them more time. If we take down the Danes now, it will demonstrate our force to Sweden. It will clearly show that we are capable of dominating the entire Baltic Sea, and we can give assurances to the Swedes that they will be protected from the Russians. This should peel them away from this armed neutrality business, and when we stomp out the Russian fleet, the Baltic will be ours. For God's sake, Tom, the Baltic can be ours. All we have to do is act now, forcefully and effectively."

"Admiral, how can we convey this to Admiral Parker?" Foley asked.

"I will push him, Tom. I must push him as hard as I can to act and to act now," I declared.

The next morning I decided to put caution aside and wrote to Admiral Parker, intending the letter to be as forceful and as tactful as I could manage. Even if he inferred some asperity in my tone, I did not care.

My dear Admiral,

> *The more I have reflected, the more I am confirmed in my opinion that not a moment should be lost in attacking the enemy. Every day and every hour, they will become stronger. We shall never be so good a match for them as at this moment ... The honour of England is entrusted to you, more than ever yet has fallen to any British officer. On your decision depends whether our country shall be degraded in the eyes of Europe or whether she shall rear her head higher than ever.*

> *Again I repeat, never did our country depend so much on the success of any fleet ... I am of the opinion that the boldest measures are the safest and our country demands a most vigorous exertion of her force ... In supporting you, my dear Sir Hyde, through the arduous and important task you have undertaken, no exertion of head or heart shall be wanting from your most obedient and faithful servant.*

Nelson & Brontë

I do not know whether it was my letter to Admiral Parker or whether it was because of other pressure or considerations, but on the next day he called for a conference of captains and announced that we would proceed with an attack upon the Danish fleet at Copenhagen.

To my great satisfaction and delight, he stated also that I would command the attack squadron.

Chapter 17

The Battle of Copenhagen

I remember the cold April morning following Parker's announcement that we would attack Copenhagen. That morning he and I along with several ship captains went out in a schooner to reconnoitre Copenhagen's main western channel and the Danes' defences. I first noted and advised Parker that my assumption regarding the channel buoys seemed to be correct. The Danes had moved them, and in fact, any ship following the buoys would be led directly aground. In anticipation of this possibility, we had pressed into service pilots out of Edinburg, Northumberland, and Yorkshire who were experienced in the merchant trade and who had frequented the port. I was, however, sceptical of their thorough knowledge, as their experience was based chiefly upon navigating the harbour with accurate buoys. We would have to use sounding rods and lead lines to feel our way, as best we could by piloting with bearings from physical land objects shown on our charts. In any event, it would not be easy because the deep channel was winding and narrow.

As we approached the city itself, we saw a long line of warships and floating batteries that lay beneath a number of additional shore batteries. Hulks of old ships had been fitted out with guns and were placed in line with the warships. At the northern end of their ships, there was the Trekroner Fort, a stout island citadel at the entrance of the inner harbour with more than seventy guns, some of which were large enough to fire shot of forty pounds.

"My God, Vanisttart advised us that the city was well defended, but I did not imagine defences of this magnitude," Parker commented.

"Do not be alarmed, sir. The defences have the look of being redoubtable, but to my judgment, with the ships of the line that I have, I think I can annihilate them," I declared.

"Well then, with what we see before us, I feel it necessary to add two more ships to your squadron. I think you will need them," Admiral Parker added.

"With whatever I am given, Admiral, I will not fail," I responded, but I did honestly feel somewhat grateful for the additional ships. This task would not be easy.

Returning to the fleet, Admiral Parker and I discussed the general disposition of our forces. There was an expanse of water approximately three miles wide to the east of the city. In the middle of that expanse was a great middle shoal with channels on both sides. Admiral Parker would retain his forces in waters north of the city, and I would take my squadron down the outer channel and anchor to the south of the city. It would be from there that I would attack the Danish forces from the south, up the inner channel, called the Royal Channel.

I went immediately to *Elephant* and made notes on my charts, setting out all of my observations regarding the defences. That afternoon I took my squadron down the distant channel. Fortunately this route would be beyond the range of their guns. We anchored south of the city, and that evening I called together the captains of my squadron. The men of note sitting at my table were four of the band of brothers from the Nile: Tom Foley, my captain in *Elephant*; Thomas Thompson, captain of the *Bellona*; Thomas Hardy, captain of the *St. George*; and Thomas Fremantle, who was in command of the *Ganges*. Also present were my second-in-command of the squadron, Admiral Thomas Graves in *Defiance*; Colonel William Stewart, commander of the marines; Colonel Robert Hutchings, who commanded a detachment of the Forty-Ninth Army Regiment; Captain George Murray, captain of the *Edgar*; and a sea officer whom I had just met named Edward Riou commanding the *Amazon*. Riou had gained considerable fame as captain of a ship struck by an iceberg on a journey from Newfoundland to Sydney. Overseeing imaginative repairs to his ship, he then took her, severely crippled, a distance of more than a thousand miles to the Cape of Good Hope. I found him to be a very astute and knowledgeable officer, and I asked him to remain after dinner to discuss his special role in the attack.

During dinner Admiral Graves expressed something of a pessimistic attitude and stated that we would be at a great disadvantage, "attacking stonewalls," as he put it. Tom Fremantle was apprehensive that our attack may be too late now that the Danes had had time to make their defence as he described it, "almost impregnable." Others expressed concern about the shallowness of the channels and the ability of our merchants to pilot our ships effectively. I, too, was apprehensive about relying upon the merchant pilots and ordered that our line of attack should move slowly enough to follow the *Edgar*, who would lead the line of attack. So too, I said that I would send ahead a boat carrying sounding rods. I also ordered that before first light Captain Murray, commander of the *Edgar*, and Captain Hardy should take out a boat to make soundings of our intended passage and to make their soundings as close as he could to the Danish fleet. I also instructed that the oars of their boat should be muffled by wrapping them with sail sheets so as not to make a noise that could be heard by the Danes. I then added, "*If the Danes discover your presence, your oarsman should pull like the devil to get back to the squadron.*" I advised that before first light copies of my final plan of attack would be delivered to each captain, and I then spoke my final message.

"Gentlemen, tomorrow shall be one of the sentinel days of our lives. Each of us has the highest honour and privilege that can be afforded to any ship commander in the Royal Navy. We are called upon to carry out a mission that is crucial to the future of our country, and few men ever have the honour and privilege of that duty. If we do our duty and if we fight our ships in a resolute and gallant fashion, we will win the day. I know in my heart that each of you is a resolute and gallant man, and I know that I can count on every one of you to do your duty to the utmost. You also know that your ships are the best in the world, and you are keenly aware that the positioning of your ship with the quality of your fire will be the key to victory. But most importantly the dedication of our hearts and souls to this task will win the day and will define us for the rest of our lives. We will win this battle because we shall have the determination and resolve to do so. As the commander of the squadron, I know that I shall have a great victory because I have you, the best sea captains in the world. This task will be difficult, but I beg you to remember this - difficulty breaks some men but makes others great. Thank you for coming this evening, and I know that God will be with us all tomorrow."

As soon as they left, I explained my battle plan to the officers who had been asked to remain. "Tomorrow, gentlemen, our plan shall be rather simple and straightforward. In the end every naval battle becomes an issue of how we shall fight, a ship-upon-ship strategy, and therein lies our advantage. I will have the *Edgar* pass the first four anchored Danish ships and then engage the fifth ship of the line. The four ships that follow *Edgar* will in turn anchor and engage each of the first ships in the line. This will prevent the first five Danes from firing upon our entire line as it passes. The balance of our column will then proceed up the channel, and each ship will take its place and engage each enemy ship in the line. Captain Riou, you shall command a group of five ships to follow at the rear. As all the ships preceding you take their place, you shall then go to the end of the Danish line and engage them in order. However, should there be any gap in our line of engagement, order any ship in your group to fill that gap, and then your ship should proceed to the head of the line to engage whatever ships remain. We are fortunate to have twelve mortar boats to assist us, and I shall use the mortar boats simply to lay off and fire at the shore batteries, believing that the shore batteries will answer their fire by aiming their guns at them instead of firing at our ships in the line. When and if I order the marines and soldiers to land and attack the land batteries will depend upon circumstances of the time. After we have subdued the Danish ships, the shore batteries and the city itself can become our targets – that is, if they do not surrender. Admiral Parker will stand off at a distance and will be capable of providing assistance if necessary. I intend that such will not be needed."

There was little discussion concerning the overall battle plan, and when the remaining officers departed, I called for my scriveners and began dictating the plan of attack to be taken by all of the squadron commanders. Because I was obviously tired, my secretary, Tom Allen, suggested that I dictate while I lay down. At first I dismissed the idea, but he nevertheless produced a cot on which I did lie down, dictating my orders and taking hot tea that was brought to keep me fresh. As I finished the orders, my scriveners feverishly made copies that were immediately taken to all ships. I asked about the wind and was told that it was mild and from the west. It would be a favourable wind for our journey up the Royal Channel. As it happened, I was able to get about two hours sleep before I was awakened at first light.

As I walked on deck, I noted that the wind was still favourable. I looked down at the dark waters moving in a helpful tide and saw small pieces of ice floating by. I was reminded that in St. Petersburg, the ice was slowly melting under the balmy temperatures of an approaching spring. The Russian fleet would soon be free to move. Blessedly the Russians could wait. We would take care of the Danes first. As I looked out at the ships in my squadron, I knew that all decks had been cleared and sanded, all loose materials had been secured, surgery stations had been laid out, all men had been fed an early breakfast, all the cannon wheels had been oiled, and all men were readying themselves for the most important day of their lives.

When I found the light of day to be sufficient, I hoisted signals to the *Edgar* to get underway and to proceed as instructed. Once she had weighed anchor, I signalled a column line of battle, as outlined in the battle plan, and then ordered another signal to be hoisted, *"Proceed to engage the enemy."* The wind was fair, and we were riding upon a good flooding tide. On all ships, gun ports were opened. Cannons were loaded and run out of their ports, ready to fire. The *Edgar* proceeded up the Danish line, holding her fire. However, the Danes began to fire as soon as the *Edgar* came into range. As I had suspected, their aim was not well elevated, and most of the shots fell short in plumes of white spray. She proceeded down the line and took her position against the fifth Danish ship, opening with a shattering broadside. The Danes responded with their own, and the battle had begun. The four ships that followed took their positions and began exchanging broadsides with the enemy.

I hoisted a signal to all ships, *"Proceed as directed."* The *Ardent* sailed past the *Edgar* and took action against the next Danish up in line. Then the *Glatton* did likewise. However, to my great disappointment, my dear old ship *Agamemnon* had gone aground on the edge of the great shoal, and there she would remain throughout the battle. I hoisted a signal to the *Polyphemus*, *"Engage the next ship and line,"* and she astutely proceeded ahead of the *Glatton* and took the next Dane under fire. I then saw, however, that *Bellona* and *Russell* had both gone aground, having steered too far to the right of the line of battle. Fortunately there was still enough space to their port sides to allow the remaining ships to pass through, and the two ships aground were also close enough to enemy targets to fire between our ships, and their fire had very good effect. The remaining column passed without incident and took their places next to enemy ships. I ordered the hoisting of my favourite signal, signal sixteen, which directed the entire squadron, *"Engage the enemy more closely."* Captain Riou very astutely ordered ships within his group to fill the spaces made empty by *Bellona* and *Russell*, and took his remaining ships to the top of the Danish line.

By midmorning all of our available ships were in position, and the deafening roar of battle was fully underway. Bursts of yellow-red cannon fire erupted from the sides of all Danish and British ships, and great billows of smoke filled the air. My flagship, *Elephant*, was engaged with the Danish flagship, the *Dannebrog*, and it became apparent to me that our rate of fire was much faster than that of the Danes'. The thing about close action is that once the cannon's aim is made, the fight is determined by

the rate of damage that each ship inflicts upon the other. I was pleased to
see, as I knew would happen, that our fire was tearing at their sides much
more effectively than they could answer, and as I walked the starboard side
of the quarterdeck, I could see the entire line of battle – and was pleased.

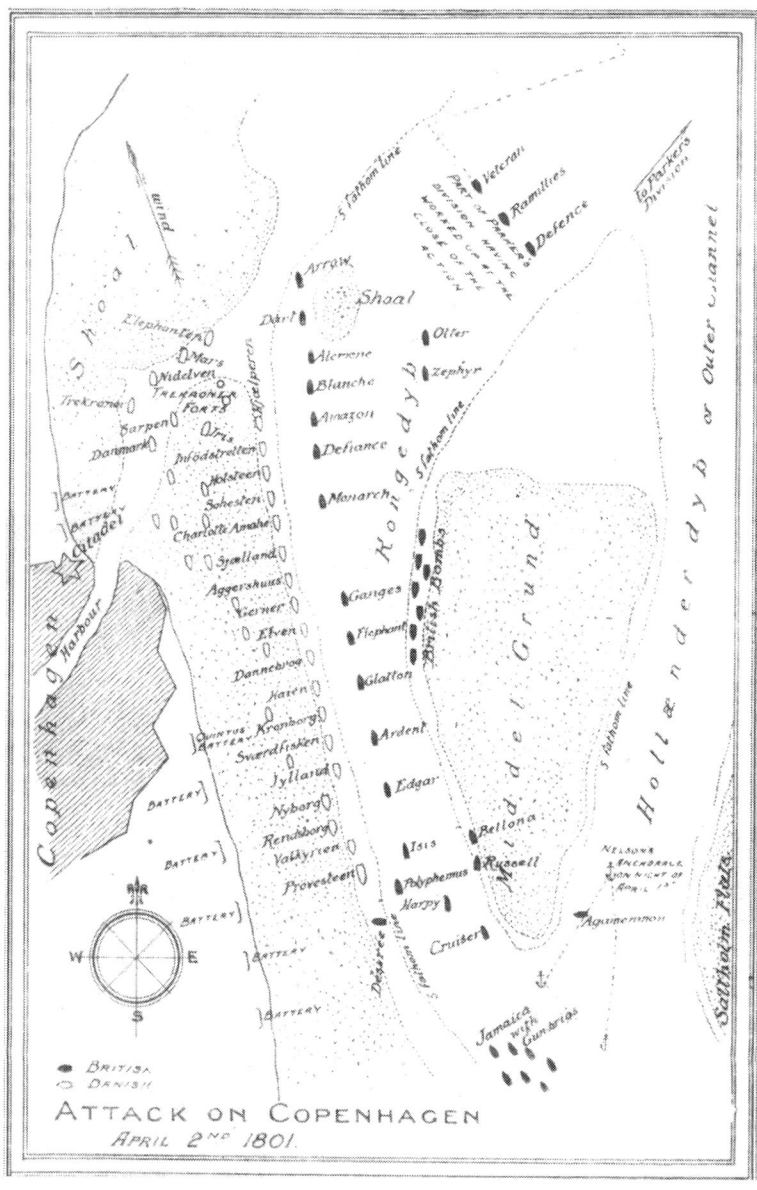

ATTACK ON COPENHAGEN
APRIL 2ND 1801.

318

The British ships were punching them with a much greater fury than the Danes had ever experienced. I knew it would be so. In time we would simply beat them down. However, as the roaring tumult of the battle was at its height and as I walked about the quarterdeck, a shot struck the mainmast of *Elephant*, scattering splinters all about us. Smiling, I then turned to Colonel Stewart and said, *"This is warm work, Stewart, and this day may be the last for any of us at any moment."* I then stood and took a few steps more and then turned to Stewart and quickly added, *"But mind you, Colonel, I would not be elsewhere for thousands."* I was heartened that Stewart also smiled and nodded as the deafening sounds of cannons firing and cannonballs hitting their mark continued. The battle went on, and I had little to do but walk the deck and observe. Each ship was doing its duty, and doing it well. It was clear that British firepower was superior. The great thunderous roar of our guns was more ardent, and it was clear that more damage was being inflicted upon the Danes than in time they would be able to sustain. The battle was going well, as I was confident it would.

Then, the inexplicable happened. I was approached by the signal lieutenant who said, *"Admiral, there is a signal from Admiral Parker's flagship to discontinue the engagement."*

Amazed and incredulous at this perfectly risible order at this time in the battle, I asked, *"Are you sure?"*

"Yes, sir, it is Signal 39, a direction to discontinue the engagement," he answered. *"Sir, should I repeat the signal to our squadron?"* he asked.

"No," I quickly answered, *"Simply acknowledge it."* And then I asked, *"Is Signal 16 still hoisted to our squadron – to engage the enemy more closely?"*

"Yes, sir," he answered.

"Keep it so," I instructed.

Very soon Captain Foley came up from the main deck and asked, "Admiral, do you know what is shown on board of the commander-in-chief's flagship? *It is Signal 39, to leave off action."*

"I shall be damned if I do, Foley," I responded, and then walked to the starboard side of the quarterdeck, raised my glass to my blind eye, and said, *"Really, I do not see the signal. You know, Foley, I have only one eye and I have the right to be blind sometimes."*

"Yes, sir. Very good, sir," Foley responded with a broad smile.

As I walked about the deck with the battle sounding furious all about, I could not imagine how tragic a withdrawal would be at that moment. Parker's signal had been a general signal to all ships present, but if we withdrew at that moment, it would probably be the only way in which we could lose the battle. If we broke off action, surely many of our ships would go aground and become stationary targets. In addition, the attention of our captains would be diverted from fighting to working badly damaged ships that would still be open to fire as they retreated. The signal was mindless, and whatever the price for not obeying it might be, I resolved to be willing to pay that price. My duty to my squadron, fighting like a group of furious bulldogs, was far too great. Just before noon the *Dannebrog* had half of her siding shot away and was on fire as were three other ships in the Danish line, and I could see that the entire line of enemy ships had most of their gun ports disabled while we continued to fire into them with devastating effect. They were done for, and the crews of half their ships had abandoned them, fleeing ashore to land batteries. Some ran to the Trekroner Fort. However, the land batteries continued to fire, as no serious damage had been done to the Trekroner.

What immediately came to mind was how this engagement might be played out. I reckoned that our ships still had probably half of their full complement of powder and shot. And importantly there were Admiral Parker's ships, lying at anchor approximately four miles away, untouched by the battle. They could easily be brought within range of the fort and the city, where my squadron and Parker's ships could engage in a bombardment with little resistance. I knew that the Danish ships simply could not strike their colours because the Danish Navy was not operating as an independent command. It was, in all likelihood, being directed by Prince Frederick from his observation command on shore. I decided to write a message to the prince, giving him an opportunity to cease the hostilities rather than endure the retribution that could be delivered upon his capital city. Intending to be as positive and as engaging as I could make the message, I wrote,

To the Brothers of Englishmen, the Danes,

> *Lord Nelson has directions to spare Denmark, when no longer resisting; but if the firing is continued on the part of the Danish forces, Lord Nelson will be obliged to set on fire all of the floating ships and batteries, without having the power of saving the brave Danes who have defended them so bravely and valiantly.*

Nelson & Brontë

When I finished the note, I instructed that a messenger be sent to get my sealing wax in order to close the message formally. However, I was soon advised that the messenger had been killed by a cannonball. I was also told that sealing wafers were available on the quarterdeck, but I refused to use them. Colonel Stewart asked, *"May I take the liberty of asking, Admiral, why under such hot fire and after so much lamentable destruction, you have attached so much importance to a matter apparently so trifling?"*

I replied, *"Had I made use of the wafer, it would still have been wet when presented to the crown Prince. He would have inferred that the letter was sent off in a hurry, and that we had some very pressing reason for being in a hurry. The wax tells no tales except that we are not in a hurry."*

I then sent Captain Friedrich Thesiger, a man fluent in Danish who had volunteered to accompany my squadron, to deliver the note under a flag of truce. As he made his way onto the quay, all Danish guns ceased firing, and on the Trekroner Fort, a flag of international truce was also hoisted.

A little more than an hour later the Danish adjutant general, Hans Lindholm, arrived at the *Elephant* with a message from the prince, who wanted to know *"the purpose of my note."* I responded my full sentiments to Lindholm, and he suggested that I write them down so that there would be no confusion. I wrote the following,

To His Royal Highness,

Lord Nelson's object in sending the flag of truce was humanity. He therefore consents that hostilities shall cease and that the wounded Danes be taken on shore. Then, Lord Nelson will take his prisoners out of the vessels, and burn and carry off his prizes as he shall think fit. Lord Nelson, with humble duty to his Royal Highness and the Prince of Denmark, will consider this the greatest victory he has ever gained if it may be the cause of happy reconciliation and union between his own most gracious Sovereign, and His Majesty, the King of Denmark.

Nelson & Brontë

Being mindful that Admiral Parker was the commander-in-chief of our fleet, I suggested that Mister Lindholm should go immediately to HMS *London* and apprise the admiral of the exchange of messages with the prince. He agreed, and at the same time as he set off for the *London*, I sent one of my officers to the prince with my second message. As a time of truce was being observed and the battle between ships was clearly over, my chief concern then was to remove my squadron for repairs and treatment of the wounded beyond the guns of the city. The withdrawal was not without some mishaps. Four of our ships went aground. To me, this was an absolute confirmation that any withdrawal under fire would have been disaster, as the grounded ships would have been sitting targets for all of the heavy guns of the shore batteries and Trekroner Fort. With the assistance of the tide, all ships were re-floated in time, and they soon joined the fleet at Admiral Parker's anchorage. One of the grounded ships was *Elephant*, and as Captain Foley worked to free her, I took a boat to confer with Admiral Parker.

I greeted the admiral, "With my compliment, sir, I can report that the Danish ships and floating gunboats have been subdued. A truce is being observed, as I am sure Mister Lindholm has advised you. With our forces present I am sure you will agree that we are in a position to inflict great damage on this great city, and I trust that the Danes are acutely aware of that. Hopefully it will give us the necessary leverage to convince them that withdrawal from the alliance of armed neutrality is in their best interests and that they are better aligned with the British than with Bonaparte."

"I agree with everything that you have said, Admiral. Please also let me extend my appreciation for your discretion in continuing the action as was indicated in my signal," he replied.

"I thank you, sir," I replied, finding somewhat amusing the interpretation of his signal to grant me the discretion to ignore it. However, no further mention was made of the signal.

"Admiral Nelson," Parker continued, "I think it would be wise for you to continue negotiations with the Danes. Our conditions for ending hostilities should be very clear. The Danes must withdraw from the armed neutrality. They must recognize our blockade of French ports with respect to all contraband goods, and hopefully we can gain some degree of rapprochement both politically and economically. And as a positive consideration, the Danish prince will have a free flow of commerce into British ports."

"I shall be more than happy to continue negotiations even though, as you know, sir, politics is not my game," I responded, "and, of course, under the circumstances, our terms shall be inflexible."

"Quite so, and I'm sure that you will carry that message very well," Parker responded.

The next morning, 3 April, I departed *Elephant* to continue the conduct of negotiations with the prince and his ministers. It was quite interesting that when I arrived at the dock, there was a great assemblage of people, including officers, merchants, and others who were seemingly curious to look upon me. Some were smiling and a few even applauded as I walked from the dock to a waiting carriage. In response to the reception, I touched my hat in salute and waved. When I arrived outside the palace, there was another crowd that behaved in much the same way.

I was met at the great door of the palace by Mister Lindholm.

"Good morning, Admiral. On behalf of His Majesty's government, I welcome you, and I very much hope that we might find a suitable accommodation." He then stepped rather close to me and added, "Privately to you, Admiral, I believe that you should know that there has been a very distinct division among various attitudes regarding the truce. Many of the prince's advisers believe that the continued armistice is not advisable, and it may be interpreted by the Russians as surrender. However, many others are of the opinion that observance of your blockade and the continued flow of economic commerce with Britain is in the best interests of Denmark. I simply want you to know that matters are quite unsettled."

"Thank you, sir," I replied. "I am very grateful for this information and want you to know that your services in the quest for peace, as can only be brought about by the armistice, are very wise and very much appreciated by my sovereign's government."

Lindholm led me through the palace and into the king's grand reception hall, where the crown prince was standing, surrounded by a small crowd of ministers and advisers. I removed my hat and walked before the prince. As a gesture of protocol, I momentarily bowed my head in respect, and waited for the crown prince to speak first.

"Admiral Nelson, on behalf of His Majesty, I am pleased that you have come to discuss some resolution of our situation," Prince Frederick stated with an excellent command of the English language.

"Your Majesty," I answered, "it is not simply my duty but my pleasure to play some part in creating the most positive and beneficial relationship between Denmark and Britain. Historically we have been friends, and it is hopeful that in the future of our countries a relationship of prosperous friends will remain."

"What you have said about history is quite true, Admiral. However, we meet this morning because your fleet has arrived and has attacked us. That is hardly a manner in which one friend treats another. It was, in fact, an act of war. It seems only appropriate that we should respond to this aggression with the greatest of resistance."

"Your Majesty, I can only say in the strongest of terms that my sovereign's actions have been taken in a necessary defence of our country's interests at a time when we are locked in a great war with France. We are blockading their ports because we are at war with them, and the terms of that blockade are to prevent them from receiving goods that are necessary to carry on their war against us. Bonaparte has vowed to invade our homeland and enslave our people. We simply cannot allow them to receive from other countries the wherewithal that they could use to destroy Britain. Our blockade is a strategic necessity, an absolute strategic necessity, not something that we choose to do as a matter of mere politics. It is an action we must take as a matter of survival in the very preservation of our country. We do not have a choice. The blockade of France is an absolute necessity."

"The blockade of France is not a necessity for us," the Crown Prince responded. "We are a neutral country, and in our economic interest we must be free to trade with all other countries. We have not taken sides in your war with France, and we stand here on a day that has followed a brutal attack by Britain upon Denmark."

"Please understand, sir," I answered. "I do not desire to engage in any act of war with Denmark—"

"How can you say that," the prince angrily interrupted, "when you have just brought your ships into our harbour without invitation and have caused great destruction and death?"

"Please understand, your Majesty," I immediately responded with an equal ardour. "I have done nothing except that which was necessary in the defence of the vital interests of my king and country. The armed neutrality that has been declared by Russia, Sweden, and Denmark is an act that strikes at the very heart of Britain's security. And it is not truly a neutral action. It is an armed action that, by its very terms, is an intrusion into the conflict between two countries that are at war. It is not possible for us to tolerate actions that will enable France to destroy Britain. I have come here with an armed fleet to counteract the armed neutrality that has been threatened against the very survival of my country. It is my hope that we can agree to an armistice of friendship with Denmark, an armistice that will observe the reasonable terms of war between Britain and France, and one of the most essential of those terms of war shall continue to be the British blockade of French ports. We must prevent their trade in the goods they need for their continued war against us. We have no choice. We cannot endure the French receiving goods that are helpful to their threat of invasion of our island."

At this point several ministers began whispering to the prince. He held up his hand to discontinue his conversation with me while he listened to their comments. After a long moment during which different ministers apparently said very different things, he held up both of his hands, and the ministers stopped speaking. He then turned to me.

"Perhaps we can continue this tomorrow. As perhaps you can infer, I am tugged in different directions," the prince said.

"Certainly, your Highness, I shall be happy to return in the morning. I say in all respect for the Danish crown and the Danish people that what I seek is a restoration of friendship between Denmark and Britain, a friendship of respect and mutual understanding in these trying times," I replied. Then I politely bowed and made my way out of the palace to make my report of the negotiations to Admiral Parker.

When I returned to HMS *London* and recounted to the admiral my conversation with the crown prince, he slammed his fist on the table.

"What!" he exclaimed in anger. "Do they not realize that there is no longer a Danish Navy to enforce any form of armed neutrality? Surely the prince's advisers have heads upon their shoulders and must know that we shall continue to stop and search their ships? What fools are they?"

"I believe, Admiral, that they would depend upon the Russian fleet to protect their merchants. I do not know why there seems to be such a strong bond between Denmark and Tsar Paul, but it seems that some of the Danish advisers feel a strong affinity to the Russians. Apparently I must convince them that we will also destroy the Russian fleet," I replied.

"That is certainly the case," he immediately replied. "Admiral Nelson, I instruct you to return in the morning and to remind them that the Russian fleet is still icebound. Assure the crown prince that unless we can secure an acceptable period of armistice, the cease-fire will not be continued, and after we have subdued the Trekroner Fort and their shore batteries, we shall bombard the city."

"I will do just that, sir," I replied.

Before I went to bed that night, I wrote a short note to Emma. On the envelope I inscribed, *"Lord Nelson to his Guardian Angel."* In the note I wrote, *"It is 2 April 1801 at nine o'clock. I am very tired after a hard-fought battle. Of eighteen sail of the line, large and small, some are taken, some sunk, and some burnt in the good old way. I love you my dearest and miss you every moment."*

At half-past-six in the morning I was up and dressed, ready to return for my discussions with the prince. I had breakfast with Colonel Stewart and our interpreter, Frederick Thesiger, who would accompany me. We boarded our barge amidst the beating of hammers and the singing of sailors' songs as timbers were mended, sails were stitched, and rigging was being restrung on the *Elephant*. We were rowed by barge to the dock, arriving at eight o'clock, where I was again greeted by a smiling crowd of people, some of whom called out in phrases I could not understand. Thesiger leaned toward me and said, "They are wishing you good fortune, Admiral. Some are saying, 'God bless you.'"

I paused on the quay and doffed my hat, saying, "Thesiger, tell them that I love and respect the Danish people and will do my best to establish peace." He translated my words to the crowd, and they cheered. We made our way again to the Palace. In the reception hall the prince, his ministers, and his advisers were waiting. It seemed that each man was standing or seated in the same place where we had left them on the previous day. In keeping with protocol, I bowed and stood, waiting for the prince to speak.

"I am pleased to see that you returned, Admiral," he said. "However, I am advised that we have made a formal agreement with Russia and Sweden. We have specifically agreed that we must insist upon our right of free trade as a neutral country, and any agreement otherwise with your country would be a breach of that agreement."

Disappointed and frustrated by his opening remarks, I replied, "Your Majesty, as I have said before, the interests of my country are absolute, and they are dependent upon our ability to deny the French the goods they need to make war upon us. As undoubtedly you know as a result of the events that occurred yesterday, your navy is presently disabled and incapable of providing escort protection to your merchant ships—"

"I'm very aware, sir," he interrupted, "of what happened yesterday, but we have the commitment of our allies in an armed neutrality that protection will be given to our ships that engage, as is our right to do so, in free trade upon the seas. We are a neutral country, and we have that right by international law that has been observed for centuries by civilized countries," he responded.

"It is also our right to blockade our enemy, and that is also something that has been done by warring countries for centuries. In that blockade we will prevent contraband goods from reaching French ports. That is an absolute," I declared.

At that point I noted that one of the prince's ministers had leaned over, and I heard him say in French to another, "*Vraisamblement, les hostilities reprenderont.*" It seemed to me quite clearly that the minister did not believe that I could understand anything said in French. However, I did understand that comment, and I was outraged that when the Danes were so vulnerable, they would choose to endure a renewal of hostilities.

"*Renew hostilities! I am ready to renew hostilities and to bombard this very night,*" I spoke with an asperity that flouted any concern for protocol or diplomacy. "*I do not want to renew hostilities, but if necessary, I will do so with the greatest of terrible consequences to this great city. Though I have only one eye, I see that all of the city will burn very well.*"

The prince then spoke, "Let us all be quieter please and continue our discussions in a civil manner." The hall became quiet, and then something rather astonishing happened. A man of some obvious rank entered the hall and went directly to the prince, leaned over, and whispered into his ear. The prince evinced some shock and sat up abruptly, but remained silent. After a long pause he said, "I would like to have a recess in these discussions. Admiral, would you please return to your ship and then join us at eight o'clock for dinner. Afterward we will continue our discussion." Surprisingly he did not wait for me to leave, but stood and began walking to another room, motioning that his ministers should follow.

We would learn later that the information whispered into the ear of the Crown Prince was that Tsar Paul had been murdered in his bed by opponents of his alliance with France.

That evening when I returned for dinner, I ascended the staircase to the palace and found the atmosphere far more relaxed than it had been when I departed. The prince seemed far more cordial, almost jovial, and our conversation was amiable. At one point I commented on my admiration of a young Danish officer whose courage, without concern for himself, was remarkable in directing fire aboard the *Dannebrog* at the height of the battle. I suggested that he was worthy of promotion to the rank of admiral. Chuckling, the prince responded, *"If I were to make all of my heroes admirals, there would be no lieutenants or captains left."*

When dinner was finished, we all retired to the conference hall where the prince seated himself and spoke, "Admiral Nelson, my government would be agreeable to an armistice. You have suggested an armistice of sixteen weeks, but I would request that it be fourteen weeks instead. We will observe a cessation of transporting those goods that you deem to be contraband and will request that your detention of our ships in the blockade be as expeditious as possible so as not to hinder their journey."

I was astonished at this turn of events. Later it would become clear that the death of Tsar Paul had caused a distinct reversal in the Danish appraisal of their diplomatic and military situation. Paul had been seriously at odds with the nobility of Russia in many of his policies, particularly his accession to Bonaparte in creation of the alliance of armed neutrality. Now that he was dead, it was strongly assumed that the influence upon his son and successor, Tsar Alexander, who was a very young boy, would end the armed neutrality - and Denmark would be without protection by the Russian fleet.

I was somewhat at a loss to respond to the prince's proposal, but rather quickly realizing that the terms proposed by the prince would have the result of giving to me the great part of my objective in the negotiations, I responded, "Your Majesty, I believe that your proposal is wise, and on the part of my sovereign, I agree to the terms." That evening an armistice was drafted and signed with very little change to the draft proposal we had brought initially. It was a perfect day, spoiled only when a heavy rain soaked my uniform as I was rowed out to make my report.

I returned to the *London* and recounted the armistice agreement to Admiral Parker, who was delighted. He quickly ordered a conference of captains, and we celebrated with toasts of the admiral's best wines. Colonel Stewart was sent to the Foreign Office in London with copies of the armistice. Shortly thereafter, Admiral Parker was abruptly relieved as commander-in-chief, and I was appointed his successor. I was also quickly apprised that news accounts in London reported the battle as a major triumph and identified my actions, particularly the refusal to withdraw my squadron at the height of the battle, as the key to victory. The accounts of my raising my glass to my blind eye and saying that I did not see the signal to withdraw became a story repeated time and again in the Admiralty, the social circles of high society in London, and among the crews in ships throughout the Royal Navy. Emma wrote to me, "*My darling man, all of London celebrates you and regards you as the valiant hero I have always known you to be. The people sing your praises and I have learned that both Houses of Parliament have extended their gratitude and thanks to you for this great victory. But do not tarry. I am miserable without you.*"

Sir William wrote, "*We can only repeat what we knew well and often said before – that Nelson was, is, and to the last will ever be, the first hero of England ... Emma did not know whether she was on her head or heels, in such a hurry to tell your great news that she could utter nothing but tears of joy and tenderness ... Davison cried like a child ... All of London is mad with joy ... I have lived too long to have ecstasies but with calm reflection, I felt for my friend having arrived at the very summit of glory, the "ne plus ultra," that he has had another opportunity of rendering to his country this most important service in manifesting again his judgment, his intrepidity, and his humanity.*"

I was advised in confidence by Tom Trowbridge that Admiral Parker was recalled because the Admiralty considered his withdrawal order to have been ill-conceived and because our ships were saved only by my refusal to obey it at the critical point in the battle. It was rumoured that he would be subjected to a court-martial. I hoped this would not be the case, for his timidity had been no more than I had experienced with Hotham and Keith. I received my appointment as Commander of the Baltic Fleet with very mixed emotions. Matters in the Baltic were not finished, and I wanted to seal them up. By then we knew of the assassination of Tsar Paul and the probable change of Russian policies. However, there had been no formal announcement regarding discontinuance of armed neutrality, and it would be necessary either to confirm a change in Russian policy or to confront and destroy their fleet. That was my duty to carry out, and I accepted it but with some reluctance because I wanted so intensely to return to England for a time of rest with my daughter and my Emma. When Colonel Stewart returned from London, he brought a letter from my old friend Alex Davison.

I am grieved to find that you are not likely to obtain leave of absence as soon as expected. It is said that your service is absolutely required in the Baltic. I have heard that the

329

government will offer you the dignity of Viscount, which you ought to have had long ago and any distinction short of an Earldom in my humble opinion would be degrading. Your last active service deserves every acknowledgment which a grateful country may bestow. The nation would be grateful to see the highest mark of honour conferred upon you.

Disappointed that I was unable to go home and to leave another capable officer, someone like Trowbridge, commanding the Baltic fleet, I nevertheless did what I thought had to be done. I ordered that the fleet weigh anchor and set sail for Ravel. Knowing that the Russian forces were divided between St. Petersburg and Ravel, my intention was to attend to the Ravel forces first, as they were the strongest. Then if necessary, I would give my attention to what remained in St. Petersburg. I gave orders to all of my captains that they should continue to exercise their crews in gunnery, and our transit to Ravel was marked by the usual staccato of cannon fire drills as we made our way to a possible next encounter. Unfortunately in the rain that soaked my uniform following my last discussion with the prince at Copenhagen, I had taken a cold that I feared had developed into pneumonia. I had a constant cough that was so intense that it made my head hurt terribly. Incessantly I brought up phlegm and had great trouble sleeping. I wrote to Admiral Jervis and Alexander Davison, "*It is now sixteen days that I have not been able to get out of my cabin. I am very unwell and if I do not see you soon, probably I never will. Why have I been left here, when for anything which could be known, I ought long since to have been dead, unless indeed the Admiralty thought I had as many lives as a cat or it was a matter of indifference to them whether I lived or died.*"

Nevertheless, it was my duty to press on, and I did so, weary, tired, and bedraggled. At Ravel, my fleet anchored, and I went ashore where I again witnessed that hundreds of people came to see me on the dock. I was told that they commented, "There he is. There he is – the young Suvorov," making reference to their beloved Russian naval commander. At Ravel, I experienced initial disappointment followed quickly by a wonderful success. At first I was not greeted but was simply given an abrasive note stating that the new tsar would not hold any discussions with Britain as long as its warships remained uninvited in Russian waters. My first inclination was immediately to engage the Russians as we had done with the Danes, but then I thought better of it and replied to the caustic note with a gentler message, stating that it was my hope that my presence would simply give rise to a renewed state of friendship between the tsar and my Britannic Majesty. I received a very short response on the next day, which stated only that the armed neutrality had been disbanded. This news came upon me as a great potion to relieve my illness, and my health soon rallied.

With a muted sense of relief and hope, I took the fleet back to Copenhagen, where, to my surprise and delight, I learned that I would be relieved as Commander of the Baltic Fleet and succeeded by Vice-Admiral Charles Pole, whom I had come to know as a good and competent fellow when we were both young captains at Portsmouth. Our exchange of command information was quick. The Baltic was a quiet sea again, and at last I could go home.

Chapter 18

Home Again

I remember the voyage home to Yarmouth as uneventful and filled with pleasant anticipation. I would say that my arrival was also uneventful as I had hoped it would be. I was weary in spirit and exhausted in body. I wanted only to see the ones I had longed for. Throughout my life I had sought and expected the acclaim that would come from a dedication to duty that had taken hold of my life and imparted to me what I confess to be a vain insistence upon recognition of the risks that I had taken willingly in service to God and His ordered structure of my beloved country. I had done my best, my very best in facing the enemy's cannon fire, standing in the open, defiant on my quarterdeck, being with all dedication at the heart of the battle. And by God's grace I had survived. I had brought my enemy to heel, the enemy of my beautiful home country. I was ordered to fight. Fight them I did, and I had subdued them. It was my destiny. In the process I had lost men whom I knew and loved. One in particular stood out in memory: Captain Edward Riou, a shining light which reflected everything I had meant myself to be. In our glorious victory he was cut in half by an enemy shot while he was carrying out a duty he embraced with passion, fearlessly and valiantly, offering himself up to the fateful moment that defined and ended him. No more glorious fate there ever could be. My only regret was that I could not cradle his heroic and beautiful head in my arms and exchange my body and soul for his. In nothing more than a moment I would have made that exchange so that he could go forward to drink deeply and relish the hot, sweet liquor of fame and glory that I had come to know. He had risen as a beautiful spring flower cut early to show magnificently for only a moment and then die. But alas, he was dead, and I lived – exalted, successful, satisfied, and tired, very tired.

There was no crowd on the dock at Yarmouth, but the lord mayor was there with a small entourage. After salutations and introductions we went for lunch at the Wrestler's Inn, and following lunch I asked the mayor if he could provide a carriage for me to go to the Yarmouth Naval Hospital, where many of the wounded from Copenhagen were recuperating. They had been brought by Captain William Bligh, a man who had gained some infamy as a result of his mutinous experience on HMS *Bounty*. However, following the dastard mutiny he had navigated more than a thousand miles in an open sailboat, saving himself and his remaining loyal crew. Afterward, he had provided excellent service in the Royal Navy, including his gallant captaincy of HMS *Glatton* at Copenhagen.

As I entered the hospital, I was overcome by the strong mixed smell of quinine and putrefied flesh. In the aftermath of naval and other military encounters, I had been told that more men died in unsuccessful recuperation from wounds than had died in battle. I asked to be taken to the treatment ward, where the sailors who had survived the battle at Copenhagen were being treated. There I saw more than sixty beds of prostrate men, most with legs, arms, or heads swathed in bandages, some leaking blood. By coincidence, in the first bed I saw a young man who was left with but the stump of an arm, and I thought that a reprise of my fishing story might lift his spirits.

"Well, Jack, what's the matter with you?" I asked.

"Lost my arm, your honour."

I then tapped my empty right sleeve and replied, "Well then, you and I both are spoiled for fishermen. Cheer up my lad. A good life can be lived with but one arm."

I was pleased that he managed a smile and replied, "I see that you have done well, sir."

"Well enough," I answered and patted him on the leg, adding, "We both must buck up and carry on."

I went down the line, chatting with each man and encouraging each to cheer up and overcome his wounds. Everything went well, and I was very satisfied that I had decided to come to the hospital. However, I then came upon a bed where a sailor was unconscious. Around his torso, there were great bandages, and I could see that in some spots blood had seeped through along with other spots of wet brownish fluids. A nurse who accompanied me said, "He has lost some of his internal organs, Admiral, and we fear that he shall not recover." The man was only slightly breathing with faint wheezing sounds. The sight of him and the terrible stench that rose from his abdomen froze me in despair and shock. He could not have been more than twenty years old. He had the handsome face of a bridegroom who would never see a wedding. Never would he know the pleasures of loving a woman and the simple endearments of bouncing a child upon his knee. In that bed he was a wicked personification of the price we paid for victory. After every encounter I had received accounts of our losses in ships and lives, but they always simply seemed to be numbers, only numbers, meaningless numbers with no account for the loss of lives that would have otherwise been filled out with laughter, crying, hope, despair, success, disappointment, and the simple chance to walk down a road on a beautiful spring day. I could do nothing about this man. I simply could do nothing. After a long moment I bent down and gently kissed his forehead and then whispered in his ear, "I know that you will rest in the arms of the Almighty." When I rose up, the nurse tentatively extended her hand to me with a kerchief. I did not know that there were tears upon my face, but I accepted her kindness and wiped dry my cheeks.

I walked to the remaining beds and decided that I should take my time, hearing the name of every sailor with whom I spoke. I shook the hand of each man, where there was a hand to shake, and where there was not, I made a point of pausing and touching their shoulders. As I slowly finished my tour of the ward, I turned and spoke firmly and slowly.

"There is something that I would like each one of you to do. When you go home, I want you to gather your family together and tell them that on this day, 1 July 1801, Admiral Horatio Nelson came and spoke to you and he told you that we together had won the Battle of Copenhagen." I paused. "Tell them that I personally came and told you that, because it is a truth. And to your nurse here, I asked that she give you a note verifying what I have just said. I thank you from my heart for your gallant service and bid that God be with you all."

I left the hospital as rain began to fall from a grey sky.

London Again

With a lingering sense of melancholy but also with it a relief that my return was not encumbered by cheers and backslapping, I hired a single-horse cab and went to London, where I lodged in a hotel on Albemarle Street. Memories of the times aboard my old ship HMS *Albemarle* brought a smile to my face and lifted my spirits. Alex Davison had arranged to meet me for lunch, and we reviewed progress that had been made in settling my battle prizes from the Nile. They were ample but far from a fortune, although the final result of my lawsuit over claims for prize money that had first been accorded to Admiral Jervis was rather handsome. I was disappointed following Copenhagen that Admiral Parker had ordered captured Danish ships to be burned, all except one. We could have saved several others. Davison also gave me other information that was unsettling. My old friend Captain Locker had died, and so had Admiral Howe. My circle of old friends and mentors was beginning to shrink.

He said that he also had heard stories that Fannie had plans to buy a house, saying that it would be a place where she and I could live. I was astounded to hear this news, as I believe that she had no basis upon which to assume that we would ever live together. I expressed my disbelief at this development and gave him rather explicit instructions. *"Alex, will you please advise Lady Nelson that having given her a very liberal allowance for her keeping, I now intend very much to be left alone. I would like to have no inquiries from her and I will send no further communications to her. There was no more unhappy time of my life than when I last came to London. Were I be sentenced to live in such a manner again, I would stay abroad forever. Be clear to her. I want to be left alone."*

Alex indicated that he would make certain that she received and understood my sentiments, and I thanked him. By coincidence, after we finished our meal and I went to my room, a valet delivered a note from her.

My dear Husband,

> *It is some time since I have written to you. This silence you have imposed is more than my affections will allow me. I would very much like to buy a house where we might live. My dear husband, let us live together. I assure you again that I have but one wish in the world and that is to please you. Let everything that has happened since being married pass into oblivion. Let it pass away as a dream. I can now only entreat you to believe that I am most sincerely and affectionately your wife,*

Frances H. Nelson.

Having confidence that Mister Davison would follow my instructions and make clear the message for her that he had been given, I decided to have no exchange of correspondence with Fannie and returned the letter to her marked, *"Opened by mistake by Lord Nelson, but never read."*

Finally everything within me came to life as I went down the hotel stairway and called for a carriage to take me to the house in Piccadilly, where I would again be with Emma. When I arrived, Sir William welcomed me with a beaming smile and an embrace.

"My dear Horatio, how wonderful this day is because it brings you back to us, and as has ever been the case, you return a hero. Of course, I would expect nothing else. Emma is in her bedroom, so let me call for her."

"Please do not, sir, for I shall be happy to go to her. Just tell me where that room is located." He pointed to a door just to the right of the top of the staircase, and I bounded up the stairs with the quick steps of a schoolboy. As I opened the door and saw her combing her hair, I said, "I am returned, my dear love. I am finally returned."

"Oh, Horatio, oh, my darling, darling man, you are here." She beamed as she rose and bounded into my arms. Her embrace, the warmth of her body, the scent of her hair, and the touch of her cheek were all that I had hoped for. I held her tightly, kissed her cheek, took her chin in my hand, and kissed fully upon her lips.

She smiled and said, "My darling, I shall tell Sir William and the household staff that you are tired and desire to nap."

I smiled and nodded and then added, "That may be my intention, but I shall not nap alone."

When she returned, she took me by the hand and led me to her bed, where she said, "Let me help you with this," as she unbuttoned my uniform. We embraced in her bed, and with the greatest pleasure and satisfaction as a man could ever have, I touched her soft flesh and once again explored the wonderful contours of her body that she eagerly gave up to me. Our lovemaking was an exquisite mix of tenderness followed by tumult. Her desire for me was fulfilling and satisfying beyond description, and the pleasure that I took from her in expressing my own love and pleasure within her was a complete definition of love and intimacy of one person with another. I had known for years that she was the only woman of my life and my greatest gift from God beyond all honours and titles. When we lay together, before I dozed into sleep, she stroked my forehead, and I became the most content and complete man the Almighty had ever created.

The weeks that followed were tranquil, restful, and restoring. We first went to an inn called the Fox and Hounds near Walton. Sir William, Emma, and I took long walks and talked of everything and nothing.

The days were calm, dry, and pleasant. I could not have imagined that my homeland could be more peaceful and lovely. We dined on country fare, and every meal was simple and delicious, probably made so because of the warm and delightful people who accompanied me. Sir William's health was much better. His conversations were both informative and entertaining, and his wit was never sharper. My evenings with Emma were perfect. She attended to my every need with a devotion that restored in me a sense of worth and satisfaction that I needed so desperately. Her praise was unending. She would say, "My dearest man, you have done more for this country than any single man has ever done in its history," and, "God has preserved you to carry out your duty, which you have done better than any could ever imagine," and, "I love you more deeply at every moment of every day." I always had a hunger for doing my duty in the midst of risks to my very life, and I had come to know that I needed the recognition and praise that she provided. She filled me with a sense of worth that lifted my resolve to continue the demanding and difficult life that I had chosen. She understood me completely and was everything to me. We made love every night, and every embrace, every kiss, and every union with her became a consummation of all that I needed and everything I wanted.

We travelled on to Surrey and stayed at small but very pleasant places along the Thames, where Emma and I watched and laughed as Sir William fished with a long, flexible rod, often getting his hook caught in trees and bushes. He was very adept at hooking fish but often fumbled awkwardly with them when he brought them to the bank, frequently losing his balance and falling into the edge of the stream. Toward the end of our sojourn he recounted recent articles he had read in the newspapers. They reported serious concerns of the government that Bonaparte seemed once again to be preparing an invasion. He had become the first consul of the French government and was exercising unilateral and complete control of everything in France. The fear was that large numbers of ships and landing craft were being assembled under the command of Admiral Latouche to carry more than forty thousand troops across the channel. The next day Lieutenant Edward Parker arrived and announced that the Admiralty had assigned him as my aide-de-camp. He also carried orders that summoned me back to the Admiralty and informed that I would take command of the Channel Fleet to protect against the renewed fear of invasion.

Boulogne

Returning to the London the following Monday, I met with Admiral Jervis in his ornate chamber as the newly installed First Lord of the Admiralty.

"Horatio, we are confronted with a situation that is absolutely unique in my experience," he exclaimed. "The French do not have a proper invasion fleet, but there are reports that they are assembling an enormous number of smaller ships and landing craft, which they might sail or even row across the channel in twelve hours' time."

"That would be ultimate folly," I answered. "Such a ragtag force can be easily scattered and destroyed. They would meet with the same fate that they've always experienced – utter destruction."

"I agree," he replied. "I have told the government and have included in dispatches to the newspapers the declaration that '*I do not say that the French cannot come. I only say they cannot come by sea.*' But there, they have hundreds of boats and forty thousand troops. They must be intending to do something."

"Very well, sir. I shall make it my duty to ensure that you are a prophet," I promised. During the two days before meeting with Admiral Jervis, I had drawn up a plan for the defence of the channel coast and explained it in detail. I had spent long days as a midshipman along this coast and drew upon my familiarity with everything from the mouth of the Thames to the port of Yarmouth. The plan called for blocking and destroying, if necessary, any enemy vessels of whatever size that may approach any landing beaches where troops could possibly come ashore.

"This is masterful, Horatio," the admiral exclaimed. "I can see clearly that I have picked the best man for the task."

"Thank you, sir," I replied, "The French will not wade onto our shores. You have my guarantee."

The Channel Fleet was clearly the largest force I had ever commanded, consisting of 143 vessels carrying more than two thousand guns with total crews of more than ten thousand men. I hoisted my flag in HMS *Medusa*, and every day Lieutenant Parker became an increasingly valuable assistant. He was extraordinarily astute in learning the disposition of forces and in knowing the names of captains of the ships as well as their organization into various squadrons. I found that I could rely upon him totally for carrying out my instructions and dispersing timely information and orders concerning force composition and disposition. He also had a very natural and positive way about him, showing sternness when it was called for and otherwise being most engaging and cordial. In truth, he was everything that Josiah had not been. In only a short time he became the closest thing to a son that I never had. In fact, I wrote to Emma that, "*Parker sits next to me to cut my meat whenever I want it done, and in all matters having to do with the fleet, he is my right hand man.*" I arranged my standing orders into what I called "my public order book," which was updated daily and contained all standing orders for disposition of the entire fleet. Parker was responsible for maintaining the book, and soon I could rely upon him with complete confidence to clearly and correctly write out orders that I dictated.

As I was able to take command of the fleet in good health and with a profound purpose, I found it to be completely energising of my spirit. I took great joy in orchestrating the entire effort to its best purpose. One of my first orders was a command to all captains that they must exercise their crews in gunnery so that they might be fit for the best of service at any moment's notice. I also instructed that the strictest lookout should be kept by night and by day to prevent any surprise by the enemy. It also seemed crucial to me that there be a spirit among the fleet that worked toward a common purpose, and to that end, I issued the following general order:

> *As much of our success must depend on the cordial unanimity of every person, I strongly recommend that no little jealousy of seniority should be allowed to creep into our minds, but that the directions of the senior officer or the judicious plans of the senior should be adopted with the greatest of cheerfulness. As it is possible that I cannot be at all times in every part of my extensive command, I rely with confidence upon the judgment and support of every individual under my command, and I can assure them of my readiness to represent their service in the strongest point of view to the Admiralty.*

I later discovered that Lieutenant Parker would frequently write letters to Emma, informing her of goings-on in the fleet, and that in one of his letters he had written, "*The Admiral has made everyone pleased, filled them with emulation and set them all on the qui vive.*" This pleased me, even though I never came to know what *qui vive* means.

In August, I took the *Medusa* to reconnoitre French forces at Boulogne and found that Admiral Latouche had moored a line of twenty vessels across the harbour. Three frigates were brought with *Medusa* along with four flat-bottomed bomb vessels. On August 3, the bomb vessels began a bombardment of the French line. I spent the entire day moving from vessel to vessel, encouraging the men and assessing the success of our engagement. As I moved about from ship to vessel to ship, it became apparent that French fire had been directed at my boat, and that evening I wrote to Emma, "*The French have been very attentive to me for they did nothing but fire at the boat and the different vessels I was in. But God is good, and I am safe.*" The shelling of the line had been quite effective, and I was able to report to the Admiralty that ten of the French vessels had been entirely disabled. I was also pleased that, as I wrote to Prince William, who was then the Duke of Clarence, "*The purpose of the operation was to demonstrate to the French that, with impunity, they cannot come outside of their ports.*"

It also became apparent to me that if an invasion were planned, it would not originate in Boulogne, as I counted only fifty or sixty boats inside the harbour. I then decided to make a tour of the other channel ports to discover where an invasion might originate. In all of the lesser ports I was overcome by the paltry number of boats and small sailing craft that were present, and I began to suspect that the entire invasion threat was an empty one. This suspicion was further confirmed by reconnaissance carried out by Captain Richard Hawkins in HMS *Galgo*, who reported that there were no more than sixty boats in the lesser ports, scarcely enough to transport even three thousand men. I reported this information to Admiral Jervis and closed the report with a question, "*Where, my dear Lord, is our invasion to come from?*" It also became clear to me that if we were to erase permanently any fear of an invasion, we should strike at the forces defending the approaches to Boulogne, their major channel port. I wrote a formal dispatch, making this direct recommendation to Admiral Jervis. My recommendation was discussed within the Admiralty and with Mister Pitt, the prime minister, who immediately endorsed it, remarking, "*It is much better to crush the enemy at home and to carry the war from our doorstep to his own.*"

The Admiralty's first preference was for an attack at the mouth of the River Schelde; however, this operation would require significant infantry support, and that was not available. Thus, the best alternative was an attack from the sea against the defences at Boulogne. When I arrived back at London, a great activity had begun in the assemblage of a major flotilla of gunboats and bomb vessels. When preparations were complete, it was planned for the attack to be carried out by fifty-eight gunboats organized into four divisions and supported by twenty-five bomb vessels. I proposed a plan that would feature an attack of all forces acting together in order to overwhelm the French with a massive direct attack that would feature an initial bombardment followed by a boarding force of nine hundred men armed with muskets and pikes. Boats from each section would cut the cables of enemy vessels and commence a boarding action as the enemy boats were towed away. The bomb vessels, many of which were also carrying howitzers, would cover the attack with fire against the French army encampment and shore batteries. Once an enemy boat had been captured, I ordered that only a skeletal holding crew would remain, and the rest of the boarding party would then proceed to the assistance of other boarding parties. The final passage of my orders was that "*division commanders shall have permission to make any additional arrangements in the mode of attack they may think may more easily facilitate it.*" I clearly felt that if I were the commander of an attacking division, I would want the flexibility to do what was necessary to ensure success. Lieutenant Parker requested that I appoint him to command one of the attack divisions, and although I was hesitant to do so, I deeply admired his spirit and the fire in his eye. I agreed.

On 15 August, the attack would begin as soon as night fell, and as with the initial assaults at Tenerife, I would stand off, distant from the battle, and await news while the attacking force carried out my plan. When the attack began, I tried to fill my time by beginning a letter to Emma, and as I heard the sound of battle in the distance, I wrote, "*My mind feels for what is going on forward this night. It is one thing to order and arrange an attack and another to execute it.*" In the distance I could hear the thunder of cannon fire and the muted crackle of small arms. From time to time flashes could be seen at the point of battle. I was beside myself with anxiety and frustration. A fierce battle was going on, and I could only watch from the decks of *Medusa*, far from directing the action with my own hand.

I waited in a fit of anxiety as time slowly seeped by, wanting to know what was happening and yearning so deeply for a victory. Shortly after 2:00 a.m., a barge came alongside with twelve men wounded and eight killed. Nothing besides the sounds in the distance happened for the next hour, and then at 3:00 a.m., a number of other barges returned, filled with more wounded and dead. Reports from the boats were discouraging, and as more boats arrived, it became clear that the attack had simply been a failure. In time it became a disaster. The four attacking divisions became separated in the dark. They had been swept to the south by a strong tide, and as each had identified its objective, the attack became haphazard and piecemeal, not the overwhelming force that I had intended. Lieutenant Parker's division was the first to attack, but the target ship was well prepared. It had rigged an anti-boarding net on booms that jutted ten feet out from the ship's side so that when boarders climbed the nets, they were little more than shooting targets for the French muskets. The attack on one of the French brigs had been successful, but when the boarders tried to cut her cables, they found that the cables had been replaced with heavy chains and could not be cut. The centre division attacked the largest French brig but found that small cannons had been mounted on the ship's gunnels and small two-pound shot could be fired into the boats, killing men and punching large holes in the bottoms of the boats, sinking most of them. However, our chief misfortune had been the tide that flowed out from the harbour far faster than we had calculated, separating our divisions and frustrating any semblance of a single coordinated attack.

It was later reported that Admiral Latouche had speculated correctly that after my initial visit to reconnoitre and fire on Boulogne, I would be back with a large attacking force. Therefore, he prepared for an attack and did so in a manner that honestly I had to admire. He had tightened his defensive line and secured all of the ships and boats firmly with anchor and chain. He also armed every brig and every boat as heavily as possible and added companies of soldiers to add a deadly dimension of heavy musket fire. Watch boats were placed far out from the line to warn of any attack so that the full defensive orchestration of defensive elements would be at their stations, armed and ready.

Terrible news came from one of the returning barges. As the wounded were lifted aboard *Medusa*, among them was young Edward Parker. He had suffered a major gunshot wound in his thigh that had broken the bone. When he was brought aboard, he was unconscious, and I thought him dead. However, I was told that he was still alive, and I ordered that he be taken to the ship's surgeon for immediate attention. As the last of the surviving barges arrived, I went to my stateroom to write my dispatch of defeat. I came immediately to the conclusion, advising that the objective had not been attained, and I accepted sole responsibility for the failure. I then described the redoubtable defences that had been expertly prepared against us, and attributed great misfortune to misunderstanding the strength of the tide. I stated boldly that no derogation whatever should be attached to the conduct of our attacking men or their commanders, as all had shown determined and persevering courage. First Lord Jervis's response was almost immediate. He stated that defeat in some circumstances must simply be accepted as a consequence of war and that the manner in which the enemy's flotilla was made fast to the ground could not have been foreseen. I immediately circulated the first lord's message to the fleet and added a note that was instructed to be read to all of the ships' crews. It stated, "*The moment the enemy has the audacity to cast off the chains which fix their ships to the ground, at that moment Lord Nelson is convinced that the Royal Navy shall overcome them and take them to British ports as prizes – or send them to the bottom. I am convinced of this because the valour and spirit of the men of the Royal Navy cannot be equalled in the entire world.*"

Several of my captains related later that the message was received with cheers by their crews and smiles among the officers. This pleased me, but the momentary pleasure soon passed. I had orchestrated a defeat and could not help but feel that had I been on the scene, leading at the point of battle, things would have been different. At least I could have been relieved of my misery by being listed among the dead. As one final salute to Admiral Latouche, I sent in three howitzer boats to sink or set fire to his flagship; however, after an afternoon of bombardment, the ship would not sink or catch fire, and the boats, having exhausted all of their shot, retreated. I returned home with my fleet still intact but carrying the bodies of forty-five valiant men killed in action. On 18 August, I attended the funeral of two of my young midshipmen, neither of whom had reached his eighteenth year. I then visited the wounded at the naval hospital at Deal on Thames. Lieutenant Parker had been transferred to the hospital, where he could be attended personally by Dr Andrew Baird, an expert surgeon sent down under special orders of Admiral Jervis.

When I first visited young Parker, he seemed to be recovering reasonably well; however, when I prepared to leave, he took hold of my hand and said that he could not bear for me to leave him, and he cried like a child. Efforts to save his leg were unsuccessful, and when it became gangrenous, it was amputated close to the hip. I visited him whenever I possibly could and shared in his promising trends of recovery only to be followed by dispiriting relapses. During the agonising period of his extremis I would sit and talk with him as a father to his son, encouraging him at every moment to dwell upon his future after he recovered. After each visit I would write to Emma and describe his condition. He also wrote to her, and she sent to me one of his letters that swept my heart away. He had written, "*The Admiral is now attending me with the most parental kindness ... he comes to me at six in the morning and at ten at night ... I would lose a dozen limbs to serve him ... he is my dear friend, my nurse, my attendant, my patron, my protector ... The world cannot find words sufficient enough to praise him.*"

Young Parker lingered and suffered through four agonising weeks with a redoubtable spirit that fought death at every stage of recuperation and relapse. Finally on 27 September, he died. When he was buried, I ordered that full military honours be accorded. Throughout the graveside funeral service, conducted in the sound of muffled drums, I stood without emotion. I felt akin to a vessel that had been simply emptied of its contents, all of its contents – every drop and dram. At the end of the service I slowly walked away. Realising with every step that I had left behind a young man who was a bright and warm candle that had illuminated and warmed my life so richly, my resolve would not hold, and fearing that I would fall to the ground, I walked over to a large tree and leaned against it in darkest despair. A flood of grief welled up within me, and I cared not for what any would think who saw me as I bent my head and cried openly and loudly, releasing from my soul an anguish that flowed with a torrent that would not stop. I cried against fate and against the price that had been paid by the dearest and best in being who they were and doing what they had to do so valiantly and selflessly. I do not remember walking away from that tree, and I cannot recall whom I met, what I said, or what I did to return to *Medusa*. I only recall that I sat down at my desk and wrote to Admiral Jervis, "*I really think it would be better to take me from this Command.*" The admiral refused because secret peace negotiations had begun with Bonaparte. He wrote, "*The public mind is so very much tranquillized by your being at your post that it is extremely desirable that you should continue there ... give up, at least for the present, your intention of returning home, which would have the worst possible effect at this critical juncture.*"

I missed Emma desperately and wrote to her almost daily. It was some comfort to know that she was looking for a house where we might live and had found a promising property in Merton village on the Wandle

River between London and Portsmouth. Rampant rumours had begun to the effect that a likely peace was being negotiated with France. As a great relief in September, I was able to see Emma for a brief time when she and Sir William came for a visit at Deal. It lifted my spirits to see and touch and hold my dear woman, if only temporarily, and to converse over dinner with my dear old friend. However, when they left and I returned to *Medusa*, it seemed that I came back to a place of emptiness, and I wrote to her, "*I came back on board but there was no Emma. No, no, my heart will break ... My dearest wife, how can I bear our separation?*"

For another two months as long as the negotiations with France continued, I was kept on my station. Admiral Jervis stated that I should remain as a symbol of Britain's continuing determination to remain ready to engage the enemy in the event the negotiations should fail. In accord with the admiral's expectation and as my duty required, I kept my ships in every respect constantly ready for putting to sea and instructed that gunnery practice should be continued as though we were preparing for battle the next day. When word came that a preliminary peace agreement had been reached, I again requested permission to go ashore, and on 20 October, Admiral Jervis gave his permission but stated formally that I would remain in command of the Channel Fleet until a definitive peace treaty was signed.

With great relief and anticipation, I departed the *Medusa* on 22 October to see my newly purchased home at Merton. My health had returned, and my spirits soared at the prospect of visiting my new home.

Chapter 19

The House at Merton

I remember that as my carriage clattered along the cobblestone streets of London and then down Portsmouth Road toward Merton, my feelings were, as was so often the case, mixed. I relished the anticipation of seeing Emma and the new house she had bought for us, a place where we could live happily and finally together. But I also had serious concern for my finances. The house had cost £9,000 and I had only £3,000 in spendable monies. I had never become rich as compared with those officers who plied the commercial routes during hostilities, taking merchant ships easily and towing them intact and with all their goods to convenient ports, thereby filling their pockets with settlement money from selling the goods and then factoring the ship, converting it to British service. Instead my prize money had come exclusively from battered warships that had been taken by ships under my command. They were not nearly so profitable.

I agreed to buy the Merton house and grounds with an initial payment of £3,000, and the balance to be paid over the next three years. Alexander Davison had offered to provide a loan for whatever I needed, but I had ample faith that providence would provide. And, my years of service were not over. Hopefully more would come, much more. The important thing was that I now owned a house where Emma and Horatia would be with me forever. Before I left the *Medusa*, I received a letter from Sir William.

We have now inhabited your Lordship's premises for some days, and I can now speak with some certainty. I have lived with our dear Emma for many years. I know her merit, have a great opinion of the head and heart that God Almighty has been pleased to give her, but a seaman alone could have given a fine woman full power to choose and fit up a residence for him without seeing it himself. You are in luck, for in my conscience I verily believe that a place so suitable to your views could not have been found, and at such a cheap rate. The proximity to London is but an hour's drive, and it is the perfect retirement place. The house is so comfortable, the furniture is clean and

*good, and I never saw as many conveniences united in so small
a place. You have nothing but to come and enjoy it immediately.
You have a good mile of pleasant dry walk around your farm. It
would make you laugh to see Emma working about the grounds,
setting up hen coops, and already the canal is enlivened with
ducks, and the cock is strutting with his hens about the walks.*

Sir William had always been perceptive as a man of classical tastes. He had been the master of many splendid houses. However, I wrote to Emma that control of the house would be mine and hers alone and that although I fully accepted that Sir William would be our guest for the remainder of his days, I did not want to give up any room for his library of books. Nor did I want him to be accompanied by any of his servants. It was made clear that the house was ours, and he would be our guest.

As the carriage made its way through Merton village, I could not tell the driver where my house was located. Upon inquiry, we found that it would be the third down the road from the second right turn after we left the village. I could hardly wait, and when my eye first glimpsed it, my heart leapt. It was a bit smaller than I had anticipated, but it was truly lovely, a white house that seemed to have been designed as something between a classical house and a farmhouse, perfect to my liking. It had an ample drive that made a circle at the front with an iron bridge over a canal that half-encircled the property. It seemed a marvellous place for Sir William to do his fishing, and I had asked him to stock it with the best fish of his choosing. The property also seemed to have just the right number of trees and open fields.

As the carriage came to its stop, I stepped out and gave instructions for unloading my trunks. Before I finished, Emma burst through the front door with her arms extended. As I embraced her, the warmth and touch of her became my perfect welcome. I kissed her and said, *"You know, the Prime Minister invited me to dinner when I left the Medusa but I refused and told him that I would dine nowhere until I dined with you."*

"Oh, my dear man, how I have longed for this moment. I have been so alone and miserable without you. But you are now here, and I believe we will find nothing but happiness. Please let me show you your house."

I kissed her again and then again, and then she took my hand, leading me through the front door. As I entered, everything she had done was in perfect splendour. The furniture was well arranged, and the walls were hung with portraits, most of her and me. There were maps, mementos, trophies from my victories, and nautical objects placed everywhere. A bust of me looking rather stern stood on a pedestal in the hallway next to a piece of the topmast of *L'Orient.* In the foyer there were drawings of my battles, models of ships, and flags that added wonderful colour. I knew immediately that I could be at home in that place.

"It is far better in looks than I expected. I'm so overcome with joy that I do not know what to do. Believe me when I tell you that my heart races at seeing this place with you in it. I am finally safe on shore again and anchored at my house with the love of my heart," I said, fighting back tears. Sir William came in, and I heartily embraced the dear man.

He said, "I trust you are pleased with your house, my dear friend. I am so happy to be with you, finally returned for a true and well-deserved rest."

My answer was, "I could not be happier, my old friend, my dear friend."

I was also greeted warmly by Mrs. Cadogan and my niece, Charlotte, who was on holiday from a boarding school in Chelsea. We made a quick tour of the house and property. I was entranced by its amenities and the simple fact that it was actually a place I could finally call my own. Charlotte said that she and Sir William had caught some carp out of the canal, and Sir William corrected her, stating that they were pike, *"and very nice fish that provided a lovely dinner."* Charlotte was a delightful young woman, and I wrote to the headmistress of her school, suggesting that the students of her class be granted a holiday to dine with us at Merton. The headmistress accepted the suggestion, and later a number of lovely young girls came with cakes and custard that made for a wonderful dessert following dinner.

One of the most meaningful treats of that first day was holding my daughter, as I had never before held her or watched her toddle about. A great benefit of the Merton house was that Horatia had been retrieved from her nursemaid caretaker and returned to the care of her mother. Emma was totally doting upon her, constantly fussing with her clothes or her hair and speaking to her in the warmest and most endearing manner. She was a beautiful child, and I loved the way she toddled about. When she looked at me, the gleam in her eye and the smile upon her little face, which seemed almost like that of a porcelain doll, was enchanting. Not only had I become the master of my own estate, but I then could be a true father as well.

At dinner on the first night I announced that the property would be called "Merton Place" and that Emma would be "Lady Paramount" of the estate. The entire dinner conversation was pleasant and engaging, exactly the atmosphere I longed for. I was told that there was a nice church at Merton and suggested that we should attend frequently to set an example for all of the parishioners. I also said that I wanted to employ the trades people of the village for all of the services and goods they might provide in preference over any distant purveyors. I exclaimed heartily that I valued all of the stock, particularly the sheep and poultry that walked the grounds. I added that "*none should be killed. They would do good for the land and provide a rich pastoral setting that I admired.*"

Sir William was, as always, full of news. Prime Minister Pitt was being replaced by Mister Addington as a result of some difficulties regarding governance and the granting of rights to Catholics in Ireland. I then suggested that for our dinners we should eat plain but have good wine and that we should provide an open welcome to true friends, especially those of the fleet. Determined that the Prince of Wales should never cross our threshold, I said that no royal blood should come into the house, particularly "*those who have the impudence of the devil.*" The dinner was lovely and finished with a delicious butter cake Mrs. Cadogan had baked.

Not long after dinner I announced that I would retire, as the day had been a long one although a marvellous one as well. As soon as I had washed and was in bed, Emma came into my arms. We enjoyed a wonderful union that lifted my spirits as well as my physical exertion to the height of the man's expression. It also served as a release of all the binding pressures I had endured during my time away from her. Afterward, as I felt the magical warmth of her body next to mine with her head upon my shoulder, I could only whisper, "I love you. I love you so dearly."

The following day I made a more complete tour of the property, counting the livestock and chickens and inspecting the netting that had been put along the side of the canal to prevent Horatia from falling in. I made a number of notes for improving the property and felt with a deep satisfaction that it could be a work that would last over a lifetime. In the late afternoon, however, and even though the temperature was rather mild, I took a chill and had to return to the house. I also was very tired and finally went to the sofa and laid down, telling Emma, "I'm very tired and feel that I am simply worn out." She brought me tea and biscuits, which helped to bring a bit of renewed energy, and as I fell into sleep there on the sofa, she stroked my face much as she had done in Palermo. For the next several days I took things at a slow and easy pace, reading, responding to mail, and simply enjoying the attentive company of Emma, our precious little daughter, and some dear friends.

After a few days my energy was restored, and I decided to take a walk to the village. Rather than wear my uniform, I decided to wear a simple black suit so as not to attract attention. I was happy to walk from shop to shop, talking with the owners rather like nothing more than a neighbour. From time to time I would buy little whatnots for Emma or Horatia. My plain dress worked very well on the first day; however, soon the word was out that I was walking about the town, and small crowds would gather to look at me. Some of the people would ask to shake my hand and say grand things about my service. I was pleased by their reverence and attention, but my anonymity was compromised, and I never could thereafter truly be a simple citizen of the village. I reminded myself that this was another price that I would have to pay. True privacy would never again be granted to me.

We had tried to make it known that we wanted to avoid high entertainment, preferring to lead quiet lives, and after some time we came to know several of the families in the village and enjoyed their company. One was the family of John Pennington, an import merchant who had provided safe passage for many prominent families as they fled the terror in Paris. The Penningtons' company was quite genial. We entertained them, and they reciprocated with quiet, enjoyable dinners at their home on the road to Wimbledon. Another was a Scotsman named James Perry who was a merchant and writer. He owned a part of the *Morning Chronicle*, a Whig newspaper that was gaining popularity. He and Sir William would often exchange very entertaining stories, and I was intrigued by Perry's anecdotes as he would recount his tenure in prison for several months following conviction for libel upon the House of Lords. As a peer having witnessed so much of the pompous posturing that would go on in the lord's chamber, I sympathized with him. I also simply enjoyed his company and that of his wife, as they were interesting and successful people who were not given over to the vapid symbols of pretended high society. In their company we could simply be ourselves and could lead normal lives without having to walk upon the stage of public regard. We also came to know a Jewish man named Goldsmid and his rotund Dutch wife. He had been a financier and broker who had become very rich but lived very simply. They were without pretence, and their dinners were warm and entertaining, although the food was what they called, "kosher," and rather tasteless. From time to time Emma and I would give private dinners for friends, but I asked that we not have more than one or perhaps two each week.

Sir William was a very accommodating guest at Merton. He paid one third of household expenses but still maintained his house in Piccadilly with all of its servants. I suggested that he need not maintain the Piccadilly house, but he responded that it was a valuable convenience when he went to London. I believe it also gave him a continued sense of independence without suggesting a dependence upon me, and I accepted his conclusion although the second house remained a great expense. It was also a *pied-a-terre* when he and I would go to London from time to time. We would frequently attend the House of Lords, and I would visit Admiral Jervis at the Admiralty. As a peer of the realm, I felt it my duty to sit regularly in the House of Lords. I had Mrs. Cadogan alter my formal robe to reflect my new status as a viscount.

I gave my maiden speech to the lords on 30 October 1801. It was a simple speech and rather well received. I seconded a motion of gratitude to my friend James Saumarez, who had been elevated to the rank of admiral. During the speech I also praised the work of Admiral Hood and Admiral Jervis for their efforts toward instilling in Saumarez the talents and dedication that had made him so deserving of his promotion. Shortly thereafter, however, my second speech gave rise to some controversy. The new Prime Minister, Henry Addington, approached Admiral Jervis and me to give speeches that would defend the terms of the Treaty of Amiens with the French. There had been widespread criticism by the former government and some members of the Admiralty who contended that Bonaparte had gotten the best of the bargain, and privately I had shared some of those concerns. However, the treaty was the agreement that we had made, and I felt it my duty to stand with the government. Admiral Jervis and I gave a speech on the same day. His was to emphasize the benefits of the treaty for British commerce and the settlement of peace upon the continent. In my speech I was asked to defend our relinquishment of Malta, Minorca, and the Cape of Good Hope. I described Minorca as "*an island of little value to us, as it was at too great a distance from Toulon to serve as a station to watch the French fleet*" and said that "*Malta was a very foreign state of no* great consequence to Britain." I also noted that *"our ministers had acted with prudence in relinquishing control of the Cape of Good Hope, and it was wise to make it a free port, open to all countries."* Interestingly the presentation by Admiral Jervis was well received, but my speech became the subject of criticism, both by members of the opposition to Addington's government and some senior officers at the Admiralty. It also served to convince me that I should not and would not again speak words that I did not feel to be entirely true.

During this time I continued to be very concerned about the state of my finances. My income, attributed to my special pension for the Nile, together with the normal pension for loss of an arm and an eye and half pay as an admiral during peacetime, provided £3,418. My expenses to Lady Nelson, interest on money borrowed for Merton, and trust accounts for my brother's widow as well as assistance in educating my nephews amounted to £2,650, all of which resulted in less than £800 per year to live on. This presented me with the burden of a practical impossibility. As the government had provided £100,000 to Admiral Jervis and £50,000 to Admiral Duncan at the time of their elevation to vice admirals, compensation to me simply seemed more than unjust. I had always felt in my heart that glory was more important than money, but I had been left without the means with which to live an appropriate style of life. Admittedly I was concerned about the amounts that Emma was spending at Merton Place, but I could not criticize her expenditures, for they were not beyond those which would be defensible for our station in life. I wrote to Addington, laying out the inequities of my problem, but he referred the matter to the exchequer, from which no resolution was forthcoming. While it was true that my assets were greater than my standing debt, I could not spend the soil at Merton to pay for ongoing expenses. Money had always been a burden to me, and the burden would not let up.

At the time, my father had also been very unwell. He was living alone at Burnham Thorpe, where it had been suggested by my brother that Lady Nelson should attend to him. Although she did visit from time to time, she never stayed long. Nor did she really care for him during his frequent illnesses. When in Burnham Thorpe, Fanny would stay at a local hotel and became never more than a temporary visitor. I was concerned for my father, and I spoke to Emma about having him come to stay with us.

"I believe that my father is in crisis, my dear, and is my duty to care for him. At the least we should invite him to come and stay with us until he recovers and is able to take the cures at Bath. If he remains at Burnham, he will die," I said to her.

After a pause, reflecting upon what I had proposed, she responded, "My dear Horatio, I can only admire the care you have for your father. But you know that when he comes, he constantly talks of your wife, and I find that hard to bear. What will you do or what can you say when he suggests that you should see her and, as he puts it, 'tend to her needs?' You know that he will say that."

"If he says such things, I will stop him directly so that he does not continue. As you know, I shall not be in the company of that woman ever again, and I will once again make it clear to him. She is well cared for and in all honesty, better than she needs or deserves. It takes a great part of my income. But she remains my wife, and it is my duty to ensure that she does not suffer for money. I have made a commitment to her, and I must fulfil that commitment, although I will never see her again," I assured her.

"Well then, let him come, and I shall care for him as a true daughter-in-law, even though I am not and even though he frequently speaks ill of me. He is your father, however, and I will not prevent him coming. In fact, I shall care for him better than she ever has and clearly better than she can do, but she refuses," Emma replied.

That morning I wrote,

My dear Father,

> *On 23 October, I shall be at Merton with Sir William and Lady Hamilton. We shall be happy to see you, my beloved father, and I hope that you shall treat our home as your own. My brother and sister will soon be with us, and there is plenty of room.*

Your dutiful son, Nelson & Brontë

Two weeks later Father arrived. He was stooped over, and although he was outwardly more decrepit than ever, his spirits were good. We treated him with kindness and love, and Emma took endearing care of him, to which he responded very positively and affectionately. During the fortnight he spent at Merton Place, it was a pleasant time, but he remained feeble and slept during most of the days. He announced that he believed the cures at Bath would be salutary for him, and I arranged for a carriage to take him there.

Five months later we received news from his physician at Bath that he was dying. This was not at all surprising to me, and I had given up hope that he ever would recover fully. He had written several short notes but never expressed any fear that his days were over. Had he expressed a wish to see me, I would have flown to his side. However, when news came that he had died, I was simply resigned that God's will had been done. His body was taken to Burnham Thorpe for burial. At the funeral I did not want the occasion of seeing Fanny again, and as I had a terrible cold, I wrote a letter advised the funeral rector that I was ill and unable to attend. He responded with a note of thanks and understanding. The funeral was attended by a small crowd which included father's clergy colleagues, parishioners to whom he has preached over the years, and many prominent townspeople. Fanny was there in company with most of the Father's remaining children and grandchildren. I wrote to each, describing my indisposition and my sorrow for not being able to attend.

The Grand Tour

When I recovered my health, Sir William, Emma, and I decided to take a holiday in the West Country, not knowing that at the places we visited, I would again be extolled as a hero. Frankly after I had not received what I believed was deserved accord following the battle at Copenhagen, I thought those days might have been over. We first visited Sir William's properties in Wales, which were being overseen by Charles Greville. From Wales we went to Oxford, where the mayor held a dinner in my honour and made me a freeman of the city. The next day we were entertained by the Dean of Oxford University, where, to my great surprise and satisfaction, Sir William and I were both honoured with honorary doctor of civil law degrees. They were presented to us by none other than Dr. William Blackstone, the most respected and revered jurist of the time. Somewhat snidely the *Morning Post*, always an irreverent newspaper, commented that *"I should have been granted a degree based upon my knowledge of 'cannon laws' rather than civil laws."* Sir William thought that it was an affront, but I did not mind and considered it rather clever.

We went on to Gloucester, where there were cheering crowds and bands that played patriotic tunes. Church bells were pealed upon our arrival. We were taken on a grand tour of the city, and a dinner was held for us under the banner *"Welcome to Noble Visitants and the Gallant Hero of the Nile."* Again I was made a freeman of the city. At dinner I made a speech in which I declared that should hostilities break out again, I was eager to engage the enemy and would assure that no threat of harm should ever reach British shores. At the end of my speech the audience stood and applauded. It again pleased me greatly and served as another reminder that I was revered and respected. It also cinched up in my spirit a great resolve to justify the acclaim and adulation that the British people had accorded me.

We took a boat down the river to Monmouth, and as the boat passed the various villages on the way, crowds had gathered, cheering with local town bands that usually played "See the Conquering Hero Comes". We travelled to Milford Haven, where again the townspeople came to greet us, waving, applauding, and throwing flowers. A dinner was given at which I was again made a freeman of the city. At Milford, I was delighted to be met by my old friend from the Nile, Captain Tom Foley, whose family lived nearby. Again a formal dinner was held and attended by the great number of luminaries, including Lord Kensington and the Earl of Carlisle. The dinner was grand, and I again gave another speech, extolling the history and importance of the town's harbour. I was honoured by being asked to lay the cornerstone of a new cathedral to be called Saint Katherine's. During the ceremony I promised to give to the cathedral the trunk from the mainmast of *L'Orient*, and I did so with great expressions of gratitude from the clergy when it was later delivered. The grand tour would go on for six weeks instead of the original three we had planned. We then went through Swansea and Hereford, where the *Hereford Journal* reported,

The presence of the Hero of Copenhagen and the Nile excited those demonstrations of joy by people of the town to which his transcendent merit duly entitled him. The populace met him at the entrance to the city and, as had earlier occurred in London, they took the horses from the carriage and drew it themselves to their hotel. At dinner that evening, speeches were made and apologies were rendered for the absence of the Bishop whose age and infirmity prevented him from attending. To this Lord Nelson replied that, as the son of a clergyman, and from having been bred up in a sense of the highest veneration for the church and its able ministers . . . The noble visitants, before their

> *departure, remained a considerable time in the great room of the hotel which afforded the inhabitants a better opportunity of gratifying their wish to see their illustrious guests.*

We travelled on to Ludlow, and at the inn where we stayed, a huge crowd of people again gathered to see me. I was obliged to make frequent appearances at the window, waving my hat in acknowledgement to their cheers. We then went to Worcester and to Birmingham, where church bells rang. At the theatre the actor playing the part of Falstaff in *The Merry Wives of Windsor* came to the line and said, *"Before you is the best Lord in the land, I swear it,"* and then he turned ostentatiously to my box and bowed. This brought a roar from the audience. I stood and bowed repeatedly.

Finally we returned to Merton Place. I was excited again to see Horatia, although as exhausted as I had been, I was fulfilled by the adulations paid to me in all of the places we visited. In the weeks that followed, I again went to the House of Lords, where I continued to speak with care on foreign policy issues and matters regarding the Royal Navy. I also joined with Sir William in frequent visits to the Literary Society. At Christmas we entertained with several parties which were festive but exhausting, particularly to Sir William, whose health was becoming a serious concern.

Death of Sir William

Over the next several weeks there was a precipitous decline in Sir William's health and spirit. It was clear that the arduous tour and the bustle of entertainment at Merton Place were taking its toll. When March arrived in the year 1803, it was clear that Sir William did not have long to live. He knew himself that his days were short in number and gave instructions to Greville that no friend, no matter how dear, should be permitted to come to see him and disturb his rest as he prepared to meet his death. On 6 April 1803, he died at age 72. For three days earlier he stayed in his bed, hardly conscious and only remarking in whispers of his thanks to Emma and to me for our love throughout his life. Emma stayed with him constantly, and he died peacefully in her arms with me at the side of the bed, holding his hand.

Emma ordered that mourning clothes be worn by the household staff, and for two weeks I wrote all of my correspondence on mourning paper having a black outline. In his will, Sir William left to Emma an annuity of £800 in addition to the payment of all of their joint debts. To me, he left sporting guns and the miniature painting of Emma. With it, he had inscribed a note of thanks. *"To the most virtuous, loyal and truly brave character I've ever met, and shame to all of those who do not say amen."* I grieved deeply for this gentleman, who had truly been a true friend of my life. But mourning did not last for very long, as I received a request from First Lord Admiral Jervis to confer with him regarding a command to which I would be appointed. All of the Admiralty was anxious that hostilities with France would soon be renewed, and I was unsure what my appointment would be.

War Again

The Peace of Amiens, signed hardly a year earlier, had always been tenuous, and by the early months of 1803, it was becoming plain that war with France would begin again. In anticipation of hostilities, I had met on several occasions at the Admiralty, giving advice with respect to reconstitution of the navy and preparation for the resumption of hostilities. When in London, Emma stayed at Sir William's house in Piccadilly, but for the sake of appearances I took lodging several streets away at 19 Piccadilly. It was a most frustrating time.

However, after I dined one evening at Sir William's house, as I prepared to leave, Emma came close to me to kiss good-bye, but instead she took my hand and placed it upon her abdomen and said, "My dearest man, you should know that I believe that I am carrying another child. You shall be a father again."

I answered, "Oh, Emma, my love, you are the dearest thing in the world to me and there is nothing more wonderful that could be said to me. It makes me the happiest man alive. I love you without measure. I love our beautiful Horatia, and now I shall have another object of my love. How happy you have made me." That evening I broke with our custom of being apart and stayed with her. As we lay together, I stroked her face and whispered, "If the child is a boy child, we should name him William."

She responded, "As you wish."

The next morning I was summoned by Admiral Jervis. Arriving at the offices of the Admiralty, I was escorted quickly to Admiral Jervis's chamber. My meeting with him was somewhat strange, as I had always looked upon him not only as a brilliant commander and mentor but also a friend. However, during this conference his demeanour was very stern and somewhat distant. When I arrived, he greeted me warmly and indicated that I should sit. He then left the chair behind his large cluttered desk and came to sit beside me.

"Admiral," he began, which was unlike the way he usually addressed me as Horatio, "I'm going to appoint you to command of the Mediterranean fleet."

"Sir, I am delighted at the prospect because—" I responded, but he immediately interrupted me.

"You know that your conduct with the wife of Sir William Hamilton has been scandalous. Not only is the Admiralty mindful of it, but so is all of London and for that matter, all of England," he said very directly.

This time I interrupted him and replied, "Admiral, I have been very close with both Sir William and his wife, but our private relationship is something—"

He raised his hand, stopping me, and said, "I know all the stuff of privacy. But you are a very public figure, and the role you play in your life has, because of your very successful service, become a matter of great public regard. Were you a lesser man, you would have been ushered out of the Royal Navy long ago. But you are not a lesser man. You are a great naval leader. You are a brilliant tactician. You have more natural instinct and animal courage than I have seen in any other naval officer. I have decided to appoint you to the Mediterranean command because you are the best man for that post, and I am sure that I will receive criticism in this appointment because there are so many capable and senior officers who are not only available but also very desirous of the command. However, my appointment is what I firmly believe to be in the best interest of our country, and I will stand by it. Besides, it will put you in a place where you belong and will take you away from your detrimental diversions on shore. I want to be honest with you."

"Sir, I will be equally direct with you," I replied, "You shall not regret your decision. I guarantee it."

"I know that, Horatio," he responded more warmly. "You will do the best job possible, and I shall not regret it." We shook hands. I stood and saluted and then turned and began walking away. However, after a few steps, the obloquy of what he had earlier said made me stop. I turned again and walked to his desk.

"Admiral, you should know that I did not design to fall in love with Emma Hamilton," I said. "It is simply that love overcame me as a natural man, and she has provided to me all of the support and love that I have needed so desperately in carrying out my duties. But more than that, the memory of her touch comforts me to sleep, and I hear the sound of her laughter in my dreams. I cannot help it. I love her, and I shall do so for all of my life."

The admiral said nothing but simply shook his head very slowly. I turned again and left his chamber. That evening I wrote to Emma that I would soon be stepping into a boat at Portsmouth to be carried again to a great warship and added, "*I can only pray that the great God of Heaven may bless and preserve you, and that we may meet again in peace and true happiness.*" I went to add my signature, but paused and then added, "*I have no fears.*"

My flagship would be the greatest ship in the Royal Navy, the HMS *Victory*. She had been ordered coincidentally on the day I was born, and in 1765, she was launched, having a magnificent battery of 104 guns. With a full complement of sailors, her crew numbered 850. Their average age was twenty-two years. Slightly more than a hundred of the crew were under the age of twenty, and the youngest was a boy of ten years. I would later be apprised that one of the sailors was actually a woman disguised as a man. On 20 April, I was rowed out from the quay of Portsmouth in the midst of heavy rain and hoisted my pennant in *Victory*.

My quarters were more than ample with nine windows looking out from the stern and two side windows looking each to port and starboard. The cabin was large enough for a dining table that could accommodate twenty persons. I had a separate sleeping cabin on the starboard side with a suspended wooden bed that was later enclosed by curtains embroidered by Emma. Furnishings were of oak, dark and polished to my liking. To all of this lovely space, I added portraits of Emma and Horatia. When I arrived, my quarters still smelled of fresh paint and polish. The entire ship was in a bustle of activity as ammunition and stores were brought aboard and stowed. Tradesmen went about carrying rigging lines, hawsers, blocks and tackle, and various other pieces of equipment manufactured specially for the ship. As I looked upon the bustle carried out on all of *Victory's* decks, a sense of deep satisfaction came over me, and I knew that I had returned to the place of my destiny. I was very pleased that under my command, the captain of *Victory* would be a man in whom I placed complete trust and respect – Thomas Hardy. That evening I wrote to Prime

Minister Addington, *"I am at last afloat and shall sail to Brest. As I arrived at my command, you may rely that my most zealous endeavours shall be used to assist our friends and to distress our enemies, with all in my power. I am sure that Bonaparte is alarmed at our resistance to his will, and I trust that he may have reason to repent his rashness, insolence and folly."*

The Mediterranean Command

During the transit to Gibraltar, I had hoped to meet with my old friend, Admiral William Cornwallis, then in command of the Channel Fleet. I wanted to extend my regards and perhaps to reminisce with him about the care he gave to me at his estate in Jamaica. It had truly saved my life after the pestilence of Nicaragua. However, my search was in vain, and I had to proceed without meeting with him. When I arrived at Gibraltar, I quickly paid respects to the governor and ordered that stores be brought aboard as quickly as possible. After only eleven hours preparations, we made sail eastward into the Mediterranean. On 25 June, we sailed through the Strait of Messina and arrived at a place that brought back a flood of memories, the Bay of Naples. We had aboard the newly appointed ambassador to the Kingdom of the Two Sicilies, and as he was taken from the ship to the dock, in the distance I could see Mount Vesuvius and the buildings of Naples that I knew so well. I wrote to Emma, *"The view I beheld recalled so many circumstances to my mind that it almost overpowered me, for it was here that God delivered you to me."*

I did not stay long at Naples but proceeded quickly to the blockade of Toulon, where I met with Rear Admiral Richard Bickerton, who had been in temporary command of the Mediterranean fleet but who would then serve as my second-in-command. I was unsure of what our relationship would be, fearing that there might be some resentment at my appointment above him. However, our meeting was very cordial, and he told me very distinctly that he wanted to stay at the Mediterranean station. I responded that I would be delighted to have him do so. Fortunately upon the renewal of hostilities Bickerton had landed a force at Malta consisting of several army battalions, and without opposition, he had secured it as a British port and refitting station. It was, however, quite distant, and our most convenient supply ports would be Palermo and Naples. A great concern was several French battalions in Calabria very close to Naples. I was fearful that at any moment they might move against Naples and take it, denying its availability to the fleet. However, for reasons I could never understand, they remained where they were.

In the great overview, Napoleon could move almost as he willed about the continent, but British sea power severely limited his options. The Royal Navy controlled the Mediterranean, the English Channel, and the Atlantic. My mission was to be ever-watchful and to destroy any French fleet that would appear within my scope of command. Bonaparte's greatest naval force was cooped up in Toulon, and I awaited any appearance on the water, perfectly confident that when they did so, I would be able to destroy them. Our effective activity in the Mediterranean was limited to the use of our naval power only. The British Army of Egypt, having defeated the French, returned to Britain the year before for defence of the homeland against the ubiquitously feared invasion across the channel. Therefore, we did not have an ample force of land troops to take meaningful action in any shore campaign. Our task was simply containment of Bonaparte, awaiting any move he might make, and there was a full spectrum of fears as to what he might do next. He could try to retake Corsica or perhaps invade Sardinia. He might send an army to Ireland and invade it as a stepping stone to an invasion of the home islands. And of course, there was the ever-constant fear that he would assemble enough ships at his channel ports to invade Britain directly across the channel. But for that, he would need a major fleet in Boulogne or Brest.

My most pressing task was to keep my fleet as fit and in as good an order as possible, to be ready to counter any move in or from the Mediterranean. Bonaparte's only option in the sea I controlled would be with his fleet at Toulon. For the months that we lay at anchor or patrolled under sail, all maintenance of the ships had to be taken without the benefit of refitting ports. It was a constant battle to manage our stores and provisions, and sending squadrons to Malta for full restoration of provisions proved to be a serious problem. Especially troublesome to me was a possibility that the French might sortie from Toulon while a significant number of ships were away from their battle stations. It then occurred to me that a solution might be available, and I sent a request to the commissioner at Malta that he should send to my operating fleet on a constant and regular basis a transport ship to bring replacement rope, sheets of sail material, fittings, tools, and most importantly, fresh food. He responded very positively to this request, and fittingly, the transport ship was called the *Camel*. This arrangement had never before been done in the fleet, and I sent a special dispatch to the Admiralty, describing the effectiveness of provisioning the fleet at sea with a transport ship rather than taking ships away from their crucial battle stations. The Admiralty quickly took to my suggestion, and as an augment to the *Camel*, the victualing board sent a small fleet of transports, amounting to eighteen by the middle of 1804. They carried out supplies that could be obtained at any available port.

During the months that our fleet sailed back and forth, waiting for the French to show themselves, I sent out my usual orders to all captains that gunnery drills should be run regularly and that they should take special care to ensure that a rapidity of gunfire from all of their armaments must be maintained. I also ordered that special attention be given to exercising the crews and left it to the various captains as to whether this might be accomplished by hornpipe dances, races about the deck and upon the ships' rigging, or however else they might deem appropriate. I always found that exercise of the crew and regular correspondences to home were essential to the maintenance of morale. And of course, obtaining the best available food was essential. In that regard I wrote to my captains,

> *The great thing at this time is health and you will agree with me that it is easier to keep men healthy than for a surgeon to cure them. I find the best thing which we can give to seamen is good mutton for the sick, cattle when we can get it, and plenty of fresh water to complement the daily ration of grog. These things are for me, the commander-in-chief, to look to and, as we are shut out from Spain, getting good food and refreshments from other places has been an arduous task, but one we have done well.*

My concern for likely action in the Mediterranean focused principally on the western areas, as that was where the biggest threat, the major French fleet, was located. To the east I sent a small squadron of fast frigates to monitor occurrences. I was also very careful to tend to our relationship with the Sultan of Turkey. I had always felt a special friendship with him because of the honours he had bestowed upon me following the Nile and because of his intrinsic suspicion of Bonaparte. I wrote, "*I have the pleasure to communicate to Your Highness that one great part of my command is to afford to you the greatest assistance in my power in the event that the restless ambition of the French should menace or again attempt to molest the Ottoman Empire.*"

To this, I was advised by our minister at Constantinople that "*the Turkish government has heard with particular pleasure that your Excellency is the chief commander of the Mediterranean. Your name stands no less here than it does everywhere else.*" I was pleased and somewhat relieved that should there be any mischief to which we had to attend in the eastern part of the Mediterranean, the Ottoman Empire would be ready to assist. I was also fortunate to have what amounted to a useful complex of individuals in various countries who could apprise me of intelligence relating to the goings-on in each of their countries along with the circumstances of French political influence. One was an old friend named James Duff at Cadiz, whom I had known for more than twenty years. Another was James Hunter in Madrid, with whom I kept a steady stream of correspondence. There was Henry Blanckley, the British consul in Minorca, an old friend of my father, and Edward Gayner in Barcelona, who amazingly had access to great information concerning the number and disposition of French naval forces. However, in late 1804, I learned that he had been arrested and imprisoned probably on suspicion that he was supplying such information. Another source of crucial strategic information came from our constant sweep of French vessels at sea. Captain William Layman, who had given me excellent service at Copenhagen, captured a French frigate containing a treasure trove of diplomatic papers along with French tactical documents, including signal codes, shore communication installations, tactical documents, memoranda, and disposition of ships that were not sequestered at Toulon.

Meanwhile, the amount of paperwork that had to be done every day was simply enormous. All of my dispatches to the Admiralty, the Foreign Office, and the numerous commanders and captains of ships throughout the fleet were written out by me in hand or dictated to my invaluable secretary, John Scott. In order to fulfil my duties, work began after breakfast and would go into the night. Whenever an operational matter required that I go on deck, the paperwork would pile up, requiring greater work later. At first I wrote everything out; however, I soon discovered that dictating to Scott was faster, and his handwriting was far more legible than my left-handed scribble. Very often the total of our daily output of dispatches, orders, and letters would fill the mail pouch to the point of bursting. As time went on, I found that my letters became shorter and more to the point with little elucidation. My letters to Emma also became shorter, as frequently there was nothing new to report. My expressions of endearment had to serve as a substitute for having her in my arms. And more important than the scribble scrabble of writing, I found it absolutely necessary to have my commanders and captains at my table for dinner as frequently as possible. This was the essential time when I could personally impart the sense of my instructions and the scope of my directions. They were also times when we could release our anxieties and frustrations rather like brothers having dinner at home, relaxed and with a full appreciation of one another.

We would also have frequent alarms, most of them false and most having to do with reports that the French fleet at Toulon was about to sortie. One occurred in early January 1804 when one of my sloops captured a French merchant ship that carried correspondence from Bonaparte's chief of staff to officials in Corsica, suggesting that he was planning for a division of troops to land on Corsica. This came very close to a time when we had been warned by intelligence in Toulon that the French fleet was very active and preparing to put to sea. However, a sortie did not occur. Nor did the threatened attack on Corsica. However, I sent orders immediately to the fleet to form a battle group, eager to get at any emerging French ships. After it became apparent that no sortie would come, I ordered a return to the regular patrol.

Also in the papers captured from the French merchant, there was information that the new commander of the fleet at Toulon was my old opponent at Boulogne, Admiral Louis Latouche. From time to time I would try to lure him out by ordering ships to sail close to Toulon in numbers that I imagined the French would believe were so few that they could quickly sail out and destroy or capture them. This did not work. Latouche simply stayed put. However, from time to time he would send ships darting out of port only to have them return when an engagement appeared likely. But then on 13 May, two French frigates did come out of the harbour much farther than they had previously. It appeared that the sortie might even be serious, as Latouche himself followed in four battleships. Seeing this, I was elated and formed my blockading force into a line of battle. I also instructed Bickerton to hold the rest of the fleet out of sight over the horizon, ready to pounce when an engagement began. However, as we approached, Latouche turned and returned to port with all of the ships. I wrote to Emma, *"The French sometimes play peek-a-boo with us, coming out of Toulon only to dart back in, like a mouse into its hole."*

Some two months later we intercepted another letter, one from Latouche to Bonaparte in which he arrogantly and falsely stated, "*I took a battle squadron out from Toulon this morning to fight with Nelson, but he ran away. I pursued him until nightfall but he ran to the south-east and would not engage.*"

Furious at this dastard lie, I wrote to my brother William, "*I have read a letter from Latouche to the scoundrel, Bonaparte, contending in a boldfaced lie that he came out to fight me but I ran away. It is my plan to keep this letter close with me and when I capture him, he shall eat it.*"

Unfortunately, however, some two weeks later we learned that Latouche had died, supposedly from a failure of his heart. I again wrote to William, saying that I grieved to think that he died a natural death, for it has deprived me of my revenge for his success against me at Boulogne. And so our regular routine continued – sailing back and forth, extending a constant invitation for battle, an invitation that was never accepted. Dispatch frigates arrived frequently with portfolios of orders and instructions. In one of them there was a most distressing letter from Emma. She had given birth to a daughter, but after only a few days, the child had died. I was devastated but accepted the will of the Almighty and gave thanks that the two most precious things in the world to me remained, my Emma and by Horatia. Soon afterward I contracted a serious chill with a constant cough and pains in my chest. When it would not go away, I wrote to the first lord of the Admiralty, Viscount Melville, who had relieved Admiral Jervis, requesting leave. "*I am very sorry to tell you that my state of health is such that I much fear that before winter, I shall require some months rest. A half-man as I am, I cannot expect to be Hercules.*" I also wrote to Emma, "*I have requested to come home on sick leave and if granted, I shall not stay three minutes in Portsmouth but shall fly to dear Merton where all in this world which is dearest to me resides.*" However, the situation was about to change, and leave would become impossible.

Relations between Britain and Spain had deteriorated throughout 1804. Prime Minister Pitt had also returned to office, replacing Mr. Addington. Pitt was advised that what amounted to tribute payments from Spain to France were in arrears. Those payments had been used by Bonaparte to help fund his military campaigns, and when Pitt was given information that Spanish treasure trips were en route to Cadiz, he decided to force the issue and gave orders to capture the Spanish ships. On 5 October, British ships engaged the treasure ships. In the action one ship exploded, and the other was captured. With this news I knew that war with

Spain would soon follow and decided that no matter what my suffering would be, I could not leave my command. The expected declaration of war by Spain shortly thereafter became reality, and I also soon received word that Admiral Latouche had been replaced as commander of the French fleet at Toulon by none other than Admiral Pierre Villeneuve, the escapee from the Nile.

In Paris, Bonaparte had made himself the emperor of France. In a gloriously arranged ritual with the Pope, he had taken the emperor's crown and put it on his own head so that there would be no interpretation that his authority came from the Pope. And soon thereafter it was clear that his self-possession knew no bounds, and the fear of a British invasion became all the more acute. Prime Minister Pitt moved to arrange a new coalition against Emperor Bonaparte, principally with Russia and Austria. The tsar was understandably fearful, as French proclamations continued to decry all forms of monarchy except, of course, their own in the form of their new emperor. Austria was also ever-suspicious of Bonaparte's desire to absorb them into the French empire as he had done in Spain when he placed his puppet at the head of their government.

Meanwhile, in the Mediterranean all circumstances had remained essentially unchanged, and I had taken the greater part of my fleet to hundred miles southward to bring on provisions at Sardinia. Then in the late afternoon of 19 January 1805, two of my frigates from Toulon approached with a signal, *"Enemy at sea."*

Chapter 20

The First Breakout

I remember the excitement on the quarterdeck of *Victory* in the mid-afternoon of 19 January when the frigates *Seahorse* and *Active*, having signalled a French sortie from Toulon, came near and employed sea anchors. Their young captains, Courtney Boyle and Richard Moubray, were immediately rowed to *Victory*, and they rushed aboard with great excitement to make their report.

"With my great compliments, sir," Boyle blurted out, "I have the pleasure reporting that a French fleet of fourteen warships have sailed from Toulon on a south-south-westerly course."

"Sir, we followed them for approximately four hours, and it seems that this was not intended as a temporary move. They seem at sea to carry out a major mission," Moubray quickly added.

I did not respond to either of the two captains but turned to my flag captain and said, "Hardy, hoist general signal for all ships to weigh anchor and begin clearing the decks for general quarters."

I then turned to the newly arrived young captains and said, "Thank you for your report, gentlemen. It is good news that they do not continue to sulk in Toulon. However, can you tell me where they are going?"

"When we left them, Admiral, they seemed to be on a course west of Sardinia, perhaps to Sicily or to Egypt," Boyle answered.

"I agree that your suspicion is accurate," I answered, "But tell me, why did you both have to come? Why didn't one of you come to make the report while the other stayed with them so that we would know exactly where they are headed? You see, there is now a much greater expanse of sea we have to search. Had one of you stayed and dogged their path while the other made this report, we would know exactly where they are going. Now we have to guess."

"I'm sorry, Admiral. As a senior officer, I should have ordered that the *Active* to remain while I made the report. I apologize," Boyle responded with some obvious embarrassment.

"Let it be a lesson, lad, and now we must find them. Return to your ships and prepare for battle, where I am confident that any mistake will be fully redeemed," I responded as they smiled, saluted, and scurried back to their frigates. I turned to Hardy and said, "Eager and impetuous lads, Hardy. It's not all bad."

Since it was almost a full day from the time the two frigates had left the French fleet, I was concerned that they could have easily altered course. The intelligence I had from our sources in Toulon, such as they were, had speculated that the French objectives would be either Sicily or Naples. If that were the case, I intended to proceed to Cape Carbonara at the southern tip of Sardinia to intercept a projected course that would take them either to Sicily or Naples. My fleet of fourteen ships, four battleships, and eight frigates had been well provisioned. Fortunately we were prepared for however long the search might take. I had also given a general order earlier that whenever we found the enemy, we would attack forthwith, whether it be day or night. Should it be a night engagement, I had given the same orders I had given at the Nile – that blue illuminating lights be rigged on every ship's foremast yardarm so that in the dark we would be able to distinguish our ships from the enemy. In order to discover whether they were headed for Sicily, I sent Captain Moubray in the *Seahorse* to look into Cagliari and Palermo. I also sent Captain Boyle in *Active* to check the port of Naples.

As my fleet approached Cape Carbonara, a gale began to howl as occurred so frequently in the Mediterranean winter. The wind blew fiercely with a heavy, stinging rain for three days. Our ships banged constantly, ploughing headlong into waves that sometimes reached ten or twelve feet. We could make little headway, and simply to preserve ourselves, we could only sail with severely reefed main sails, frequently having to reef all sails except for storm jibs or trysails to give us headway so that we did not founder in the swells. When the storm broke, I received news from Captain Moubray that the French were not to be found at Sicily, and soon after that, Captain Boyle arrived to announce that the port of Naples was empty. I was confounded. Where were they going? When the storm gave out, we made necessary repairs of the gale's damage. I gave a general signal to follow the flagship, intending to move westward in a general search. At the same time I dispatched six of my fast frigates to various points which may have been their objectives – Majorca, Alexandria, Corsica, the Adriatic and the Aegean seas, but as each ship returned over the next week, all reports were negative. The French were nowhere to be found, and finally we were advised that they were back in the port of Toulon, apparently having been savaged by the storm. Our blockade began again, and as before, it was my intention to keep my main fleet near but out of sight, stationing pairs of frigates at various points of direction to intercept another sortie. I also made it clear that at least one of the frigates would remain with any sortie force for two days while the other came immediately to me with news.

The routine of blockade continued as we sailed in lazy circles, my main fleet a hundred miles south of Toulon. I continued tending to regular provisioning and the endless task of dispatching orders and correspondence. And once again there were constant indications that the French were making preparations to leave Toulon. These alerts had some credence because of the fact that all reports indicated that the fleet had not disembarked its troops. Thus, we had to assume that orders would come from Paris to land these troops somewhere in the Mediterranean. So we waited – and waited. During the period of inaction, except for administrative drudgery, I gave a great deal of thought to the options of engagement. Should the enemy appear in an extended line of battle, I favoured the strategy of grouping my attacking force relatively close and splitting the enemy line and then attacking the rear with my entire force so that we might damage or possibly destroy them before the forward van could turn and come to their aid. The greatest comfort to me at all times was my belief that a British ship against any enemy ship would have the advantage with the furious speed with which we could fire our cannons. We had prepared assiduously, and I was confident that we would have the upper hand. I also relished the comment from one of the Danes at Copenhagen who had said, "*I cannot believe the rain of shot we received from the British ships. Only the devil could have fired with a greater speed.*" The period of relative inaction also gave me frequent opportunities to call my captains to dinner for conferences during which we would discuss my options of engagement. It also gave me an opportunity to reinforce the importance of gunnery drills. We had to be ready. The engagement would come.

The Final Breakout

As a gambit to lure the enemy fleet out of Toulon, I decided to take my main fleet to make an appearance at the port of Barcelona, intending that they might suspect that I thought their objective to be the Balearic Islands. After I made the Barcelona show of force, I would immediately return and wait just to the south-west of Sardinia. Because I truly believed that their objective was either to the south or to the east, I hoped this would provide them with an opportunity to come out of port and dash to their objective. I would be waiting along the line of their probable course, and the trap would be sprung. I carried out the plan, making my show at Barcelona, and I then returned to the springing point south of Sardinia. We were ready, whether their objective was Sicily, Naples, Malta, or Egypt.

On 30 March, I received news that Villeneuve had sortied from Toulon with his entire fleet, and it seemed that everything was perfectly prepared. He had been shadowed by two of my fast frigates *Phoebe* and the *Active*. Captain Boyle, in the *Active*, came immediately to report that they were sailing due south. This would be perfect, for I would be waiting and they would be mine. However, perfect circumstance is frequently fouled by happenstance. I would later find out that Villeneuve had learned my true position from a neutral vessel and immediately altered his course to the west. In the meantime great anticipation rose in the fleet. Decks were cleared for action, and we sailed on a north-westward course to intercept. However, Villeneuve would not be coming south. In fact, he would not be going to Malta. Nor was his objective to be Sicily, Naples, or Egypt. His objective was no attack whatever in the Mediterranean. He was proceeding to Cartagena on the southern coast of Spain to join with a Spanish force and then to proceed to a place known only to God and Villeneuve.

As we sailed ignorantly to intercept, hours turned into days before it became apparent that the French would not be coming south. Finally on 16 April, I received definite news of Villeneuve's whereabouts. We learned from another neutral vessel that he was along the southern coast of Spain. I ordered a westward course for Gibraltar. However, westward winds made our progress very difficult, and it took nearly two weeks to get to the straits. In a fury of frustration I wrote to the Admiralty, "*I believe that easterly winds have left the Mediterranean. My fortune seems blown away. I cannot get a fair wind.*"

On 4 May, I took the fleet into the Moroccan port of Tetouan for replenishment. At that point I could only imagine that Villeneuve was on his way to Brest or Boulogne to join with the forces there and to join with Bonaparte's invasion force. Upon learning of Villeneuve's passage through the Strait of Gibraltar, Admiral Orde, who commanded the blockade of Brest, withdrew and joined with Admiral Cornwallis to defend the channel. He doubted – and quite correctly – that he had sufficient ships in his small blockading force to engage successfully with a full French fleet, then swollen with additional Spanish ships. Word later came that Villeneuve had put into Brest, collected the ships that were there, and departed. Reports from land sources as well as merchantmen indicated a startling development. Villeneuve with his combined fleet was headed for the West Indies. That surprise was delivered by a packet schooner as we rested at anchor in Tetouan. I was stunned and furious that our entire network of intelligence sources had been kept totally in the dark for months regarding a major move by a major French fleet.

The Atlantic Chase

As we took aboard additional stores, I pondered my dilemma. My fleet was the Mediterranean fleet; however, our major object of concern was Villeneuve, and he had left the Mediterranean entirely. Clearly the defeat of his fleet was my objective. I had no direct orders from the Admiralty to address the situation regarding Villeneuve, who by then was on his way across the Atlantic. I decided to go to Gibraltar, where orders may have come, but when we arrived and I inquired at the governor's office, there were no orders. I gave instructions to each of my ships' captains to take on all of the stores and as much additional ammunition as possible. I decided that we would chase Villeneuve's fleet across the Atlantic, and wherever we found them, we would destroy them.

After the announcement of my intention was distributed, Hardy came to me somewhat concerned and asked, "Admiral, making this major decision without direction from the Admiralty, do you not think you will be open to criticism?"

"That may be, Hardy, but I cannot wait. Villeneuve has thousands of troops on his ships, and I am sure they plan to disrupt British commerce as extensively as they can throughout our islands in the Caribbean. Reports also demonstrate that they already have a head start of more than two weeks," I responded.

"I agree entirely, Admiral, but the Admiralty is clearly apprised of the situation and will perhaps want you to wait for its command. That should not take long," he replied.

I quickly answered, "My dear man, the reports that confirmed the departure of Villeneuve's fleet also reported that Lord Melville is no longer the First Lord of the Admiralty. He has been replaced by Admiral Charles Middleton, Lord Barham. He is a respected and responsible man, and I trust that he will understand. After all, when Admiral Rooke was many years ago blockading a French fleet also at Toulon, they were ordered to go after them, wherever they went. And more recently I remember that Admiral Byng was ordered to do the same. I will simply be following their precedent. Therefore, I shall immediately apprise them of our action, and perhaps it will relieve the good Lord Barham of some pressure to have made the decision himself. I am going after Villeneuve's fleet. It is my duty to destroy it. I have given instructions to Admiral Bickerton regarding the Mediterranean. He has a sufficient force to tend to matters there because there won't be much going on in that pond for a while."

"Very well, sir. I am with you without reservation," Hardy stated with a smile. "It is always good to have a strong intent and clear directions." I responded to his smile with one of my own.

A short time later I would find out that my judgment found a firm concurrence by the new First Lord. In fact, he had ordered my old friend, Admiral Cuthbert Collingwood, to sail to Madeira with a part of the Channel Fleet. If I had not already passed the island in pursuit of Villeneuve, he was to go himself, and if I had already passed, he was to send a squadron of ships to add to my own. When Collingwood arrived, I had already passed, and he sent a squadron to assist. With great relief I found that the First Lord and I were of the same mind.

On 11 May, my fleet set out for the West Indies under full studded sails and with an ample wind. Given that Villeneuve had departed almost a month before, we drove our ships as fast as we could. However, one of our frigates, *HMS Superb*, had a fouled bottom as a result of being at sea longer than any of the other ships, and she could not make the fleet's best speed. But because I had information that Villeneuve had more than fifteen warships under his command, I could not afford to lose as much as one ship or one cannon, and so we slowed to the best speed that *Superb* could make. Still we made a good progress, and on 29 May, we were close enough to Barbados that I could send one of my fast frigates, *Amazon*, ahead to inquire of information concerning the French whereabouts. The island's governor, Lord Seaforth, had more than two thousand troops on the island, and as soon as he discovered that Villeneuve was in the area, he made them ready for action. He also reported that the commander of British forces in St. Lucia, General Robert Brereton, had sent word that on 28 May, the French fleet and been seen heading south toward Trinidad.

I was sceptical about the accuracy of the Brereton report, as it made little sense that the French would be headed for an objective of little consequence, Trinidad, when so many other islands were larger and more valuable to British commerce. However, it was the only intelligence we had, and if it were true, I could not linger. Notwithstanding my reluctance, I took the fleet and six battalions of troops from Barbados and headed for Trinidad. I wrote to Emma,

> *You will truly appreciate the importance of this communication when I tell you that I shall proceed immediately to Trinidad and have every hope that a battle there will immortalize your Nelson, your fond Nelson, therefore only pray for my success and I shall lay with pleasure my laurels at your feet. A sweet kiss will be ample reward for all of your Nelson's great efforts, forever and ever. I am your faithful, ever faithful, Nelson & Brontë.*

As we proceeded to Trinidad, there came a confirmatory report from sources in Tobago that the French fleet had been seen sailing south toward Trinidad. It was a report that gave us great expectation, but I would later discover that the sources had mistaken my own fleet for that of the French, and when we arrived at Trinidad, the French fleet was nowhere to be found. We turned and sailed north again as quickly as full sails could take us to Barbados, where we learned that all the while Villeneuve's fleet had lingered at Martinique but had recently departed. With no knowledge of their destination, I moved from island to island, searching. I dispatched fast frigates to all points where he might be threatening British targets. All of the scouting ships came back with the same report. Villeneuve was absent. He never appeared at Jamaica, Antigua, Nevis, or any of the other islands where, had he a true intent of damaging British interests, he would have attacked by bombardment, landing troops, or both. I then learned from an American trading vessel that he had put into port at Guadalupe, where he discharged all of the troops. I surmised that this could only mean one thing. He was headed home, an assumption that was confirmed by the captain of another American vessel who reported that he had sighted the French fleet on a north-westerly course some one hundred miles east of the Bahamas. It then became necessary that I warn the Admiralty that the French were returning with a combined fleet that could pose a serious threat of invasion once it joined with the French forces at Brest and Boulogne. To do this, I dispatched the fast-brig HMS *Curieux*. I also sent a formal letter to the Admiralty, one addressing my inability to find Villeneuve and was direct in explaining.

> *I regret very much that I missed the enemy's fleet in the West Indies owing to information given by General Brereton, of which I send you a copy. Otherwise we would have met them, engaged them, and I trust that it would have been a great day for me and I hope a glorious one for our country. Nevertheless, I am returning with my fleet and intend to engage them wherever they may be found. I also would note that in our endeavours, although we never found the French fleet, our presence in these waters prevented them from doing any harm to British interests. I am your respectful Nelson & Brontë.*

I sent copies of the letter to Admiral Bickerton, Alexander Davison, the Duke of Clarence, and others. As the *Curieux* raced ahead, it found the French fleet and quickly passed it, noting carefully its course and speed, enabling the Admiralty to estimate its day of arrival at the continent. As soon as the *Curieux* arrived on 8 July, its swift voyage enabled Lord Barham to take action. On 9 July, he ordered Admiral Cornwallis to dispatch a battle squadron to intercept the returning French. The squadron was under command of Admiral Robert Calder, who sighted Villeneuve's combined fleet off Cape Finisterre. The French ships were widely dispersed, and Calder was unable to make a decisive engagement but was able to capture two Spanish vessels. Villeneuve raced away from any engagement and brought the remainder of his fleet into the Spanish ports of Vigo and La Coruna. I had hoped to overtake Villeneuve during my transit but was unable to do so because several of my ships in company, which I would have needed to engage the larger French and Spanish force, had been again slowed by fouled bottoms.

On 20 July 1805, we put into port at Gibraltar, and I stepped foot on dry land for the first time in almost two years. After five days of rest and the taking on provisions, I took the fleet north and ordered all ships – except *Victory* and *Superb* – to join with Admiral Cornwallis in the Channel Fleet. I then proceeded to Portsmouth after I wrote a short letter to all captains who had accompanied me during the long chase across

I, Horatio

the Atlantic. *"I pray that you will be so good as to express, in the manner best calculated to do justice, the highest sense I have of the merit of the commanding officers and ships' companies who composed the fleet under my command across the Atlantic and back, and I assure my able and zealous commanders that your conduct has met with my warmest approval."*

I was somewhat anxious about the possibility of criticism upon my return, as I had not been able to find the French in the Caribbean. However, to my unbounded delight, I was met by cheering crowds when I went ashore at Portsmouth, and when I went on to London, I was greeted by Lord Minto, who later wrote, *"I met Lord Nelson today in a mob at Piccadilly and got hold of his arm, so that I was mobbed too. It is really quite remarkable to see the wonder and admiration, the love and respect of the whole world for this man. It is actually beyond anything represented in a play or a poem of fame."*

As soon as I had landed, I wrote to Emma, *"My dearest, I am in London for formal reports but at the first moment that is available, I shall fly to you and my dear Horatia. I cannot wait, for my heart pulses at every moment. Please know that my thoughts are never without you."*

I went to the Admiralty to pay my respects to Lord Barham and to discuss the future of operations. The first lord greeted me most warmly and invited me to a conference with his senior staff. As we entered the room, all present stood, and I was introduced to them all. Some I had known, but many were very new. Lord Barham began the conference with a very warm and positive comment, "Admiral Nelson, I want you to know that I appreciate fully the efforts that you have spent over the past two years. You have remained constantly at sea and have maintained your fleet in the best of condition. You have pursued the enemy across the great ocean and back, and your bold and aggressive pursuit of the combined French and Spanish fleet together with very effective actions taken in the Caribbean have preserved our interests there. We owe a great debt of gratitude for your talented services."

I nodded, smiled, and replied, "Thank you, my lord. I have done my best and only desire that you will know that I submit myself to your direction for any service you may ask."

"I know that at this point a period of rest is most appropriate to restore your vigour, but you should also know that as we speak, the French menace is being gathered to threaten our shores. We will need your services, perhaps soon," he replied.

"I shall be at your command, your lordship," I replied, and after some further and small conversations with him and his staff, I took my leave to board a carriage for Merton and instructed the driver to proceed as quickly as his horses would go.

At Merton Place

Going to Merton, I took along John Scott, the warrant officer who had served as my secretary so faithfully and effectively. I learned that he had been born in Birmingham, the son of a printer, and had been selected for naval service upon the recommendation of the rector of his school because his academic accomplishments had placed him at the top of his class. This was no surprise to me, as I had always found him to be not only very intelligent but also very intuitive and circumspect with an uncanny knowledge of what I wanted at various moments. I very much looked forward to his continued service as well as his assistance during my home leave.

I arrived at Merton on the morning of 22 August and found Emma waiting at the door with Horatia in her arms. I kissed them both and held Emma in a long embrace, once again feeling entranced in pleasure with a peace of mind that always came over me at Merton Place. My niece, Charlotte, was also there, and I was delighted to see her, for she was so lovely and so pleasant, a very dear young woman. Emma spoke with great enthusiasm, "Come, my darling man, and let me show you the changes I have made in the house. I hope you will find that they are improvements." She had fitted out the kitchen with a new stove and cabinets and had it repainted entirely in a lovely yellow.

Mrs. Cadogan was in the kitchen, cooking porridge, and asked, "Isn't it just perfect, your lordship?" I replied to her that indeed it was. Three water closets had been installed upstairs, and two dressing rooms had been added. Outside a new Palladian summerhouse had been built. It was all very lovely, but again the expense that came with the new improvements gave me concern, for I was still not a rich man. Emma added, "I would have done more, but Alex Davison has pulled tight on the purse strings."

Quietly I thought, "Good for Davison!" However, everything done was well intentioned, and the expenditures simply had to be accepted. I showed Scott to his bedroom and had one of the tables in the foyer brought up as his work table. After my tour of the new additions, Mrs. Cadogan asked if I would like to have some of her porridge, but I replied that I was not hungry. However, after the trip from London I was a bit tired and in need of a nap. Scott helped take my trunks to the bedroom, where Emma thanked him and asked him to tell everyone downstairs that she would rest with me for a while. As soon as Scott left, I went to Emma and kissed her with a passion that was every bit as equal to that which I felt when we first embraced at Naples. Our passion that followed again brought the exquisite pleasure I had known from nothing else. It was something akin to the perfect excitement of battle, but its intensity was soft and warm, caught up in the approach of my pulsing pleasure and our final realization of a shared release. It was also wonderfully quiet except for the hurried sounds of our breathing toward the end. In the afterglow there was the perfect comfort of having Emma's head on my shoulder as she stroked my chest and whispered endearments that settled upon me complete satisfaction and then perfect rest. Accomplishment and love are the sunlight and air of a man's life. I loved her so completely. Although the Almighty had, in His grace, given to me great accomplishments, I felt certain that they were not over.

The first days at Merton were wonderful. Emma and I would walk around the grounds frequently with Scott and Charlotte and talk about happenings in the family and dinners she had attended with friends at Merton. I would also go often into town to buy gifts for Horatia, Emma, and Charlotte, but I soon found that again whenever I appeared on the streets, even in mufti, crowds would gather about, so much so that it reminded me of Naples after the Nile when the crowds would be so thick that it would be hard for me to make my way. After a while I made a habit of sending Scott into the village shops to arrange private meetings with merchants from whom I intended to buy various things. Still crowds would often gather at the windows, and when I departed, they would crowd around me again. During a single week I must have shaken a thousand hands.

Scott would also bring copies of newspapers, and with some relief I found that their reports were very supportive, frequently referring to me as "Lord of the Main" and "Defender of England's Shores." I had been particularly anxious about how they would treat the chase across the Atlantic since I had never been able to find and engage Villeneuve's fleet. However, all of the reports were actually quite laudatory, depicting me as being "*hot on the chase*" and describing Villeneuve as a cowardly, running scoundrel. One of the papers even ran a caricature showing me with sword in hand charging a mass of Spanish dons and Frenchmen who were drawn to look like monkeys. In the drawing I was shouting, "*Old England, death or victory!*" It made me smile. I was also advised by Alexander Davison that in London shops there were all sorts of porcelain portraits, busts, cups, and other whatnots that carried my likeness. I had mixed emotions about that. It was all well and good that I was admired, but I wasn't sure that it was an appropriate admiration to be featured on inexpensive bric-a-brac.

Frequent dispatches were sent by the Admiralty, but they were usually copies of matters either internal to the Admiralty offices or with other government bureaus. I was pleased to have been sent such information, as it was a sign that the Admiralty wanted to keep me well informed. All the while a pattern of busy correspondence continued, and Scott was of invaluable service. In response to the many admiring letters received from people I did not know, I had Scott simply write the same response to them all, saying, "*I thank you for your recent letter and the warm communication it brought to me. I am pleased to extend my compliments to you for your interest in the affairs of our country. Nelson & Brontë.*" At first I would sign each letter, but after a while I instructed Scott to scribble my name and title as closely as he could and found that he was quite talented at such forgery.

I assumed all the while that I would be given command of the fleet to confront the combined forces of the enemy. I also assumed that I would have strength in numbers that would be approximately equal to that of the enemy. I pondered constantly the issue of strategy. The lessons learned at both Cape St. Vincent and the Nile suggested that if it was possible, the enemy force should be split with concentration on the rear of their forces by a greater number of our own ships that, by a tactical superiority of number as well as a general mastery of gunnery and seamanship, we would be able to severely damage or destroy the engaged rear of the enemy before the van could come to their assistance. Further, it was my firm conviction that under any circumstances, if we could engage them ship upon ship, we would always beat them down.

I requested a conference with First Lord Barham, and he responded almost immediately, suggesting that I come to the Admiralty during the last week of August 1805. In his response he also indicated that the board of the Admiralty had decided that I should command the fleet that would blockade and confront Villeneuve's combined forces. I could not have been more pleased at the honour of being relied upon to carry out that profound duty. The Admiralty's confidence lifted my spirits to the very highest point. They had chosen me to confront the enemy, and with that opportunity an excitement gave fire to my soul. Not only did I relish the prospect, but I knew that I was ready as well.

On the last Monday of August, I made my way to the Admiralty. As I entered Lord Barham's chamber, he came smiling toward me and tactfully extended his left hand. I shook it, and he said, "I am so glad, Admiral, that you are rested and seem to be in the very best of health."

"Indeed I am, sir, and I am eager to do what has to be done," I responded. We spoke for a short while concerning the disposition of the combined enemy forces. He advised that Villeneuve was no longer at Ferrol but had sailed out and had been followed by Admiral Collingwood, who reported that they had put into Cadiz, and there they remained.

I then spoke with some excitement, "My lord, I have given a great deal of thought regarding the strategy of how we should deal with their fleet when it comes out, and I would be most happy to discuss it with you."

"Excellent!" he responded. "I am eager to see any plan you may have."

I then took a large piece of rolled paper from my satchel and spread it out on his conference table.

"My lord, I expect that the enemy will be arranged in a line of battle, or perhaps two lines. That has always been their habit. It is, however, vulnerable and, I believe, provides an opportunity to surprise and confound them." Upon the paper I drew a line that was horizontal, representing the enemy fleet. I then drew two vertical lines below, representing our forces. "Prevailing winds for the next several months are generally from the north, the west, or the north-west. This should give us the windward advantage. However, I would not veer my force to parallel the course of their ships, as probably the enemy would expect. Instead I would order my ships to proceed at their very best speed to break through the enemy line at its centre, and then all of our ships would engage their ships in the rear." I drew a line extending my left column through the enemy and down their starboard side. I then drew a line extending my right column down the port side of the enemy and continued, "This would give us a superiority of number which, with two of our ships to match each one of their ships in the rear and with our greater rate of fire, it will enable us to destroy them quickly. Meanwhile, their leading ships here in the van will have nothing to do but watch as their ships in the rear are destroyed, and when the ships in the enemy van are finally able to turn, we will quit the destroyed ships and put upon the van–ship-to-ship. At that point it will be a battle pell-mell. The orders to each of my captains will be simple and straightforward – put your ship alongside one of the enemy and destroy it."

The first lord looked upon my diagram with a great intensity and commented, "It is certainly not the classical approach but one that impresses me as being bold, aggressive, and probably unanticipated."

"These are the steps that gave us great victories at St. Vincent and the Nile, and I would propose to take steps of the same dance," I responded. "The key, as always, will be the quality of our ships, and I assure you that we will have the best ships upon the water. We will destroy them. I guarantee it."

"I have no doubt in the world that it will be so, my friend and colleague. I have always felt that you would be the man to lead our fleet in what I hope will be the deciding dual with what Bonaparte calls his *Grande Marine Republique*." The First Lord then went to his desk and took from it several sheets of paper and handed them to me. "Admiral, I have made a list of ships and captains who are located either in Portsmouth or in the Channel Fleet. Please take this list and let me know as quickly as you can the names of those you would like to have under your command."

I took the sheets and looked down the list of names. It was a list of men who were rich in ability and dedication. I responded to him, "Admiral, I think I can tell you of those names now without waiting," and I spoke as I read down the list, "Thank God that I shall have Hardy in my flagship. There is no better captain. I would very much treasure the company of Admiral Cuthbert Collingwood as my second-in-command. He has been a friend from my time in the Caribbean and one of the best naval officers I have ever known. I would like to have captains Tom Freemantle, Eli Harvey, Israel Pellew, and Edward Berry, who was a steadfast fighter at St. Vincent. I also think very highly of Charles

Bullen, Edward Codrington, Charles Moore, Philip Durham, Richard Grindall, Henry Digby, Richard Keats, Charles Tyler, John Cooke, Will Rutherford, Tom Dundas, and Tom Bladen. As I have named each of these captains, I have put a mark next to their names. I do not know a great deal about the others on the list, but I have utmost confidence in your choice of whomever else you would appoint. I note, however, that the name of Tom Foley is not on the list. I would very much like to have him."

"I understand that, Admiral, and I would have placed him in the list except that it is reported to me that he is ill and not able for service at this time," Sir Barham responded.

"I am most sorry to hear that, but in the company of the men I have named as well as others you may choose, I will feel most confident. So, choose the others yourself, my lord. The same spirit fills every captain. You cannot choose wrong," I said.

"Excellent!" he responded. "It shall be my purpose to name captains and ships that are the best available, and I hope that you will have in your company thirty-five to forty ships, the best I can find. Our intelligence sources have suggested that the combined enemy fleet will be at least thirty-five warships and frigates."

Lord Barham paused for a long moment and then looked at me very seriously. He said, "Admiral, I trust that you appreciate that the combined fleet now sitting at Cadiz represents the enablement of Bonaparte's dream to invade England. It is reported that he has between seven and ten divisions of his *Grand Armie* on the coast of France. They cannot row themselves or swim across to our shores. They must have the Villeneuve fleet. I have no words that can describe the importance of your task. I also ask that you be ready to embark within ten days."

"My lord, I know exactly what I must do. I will be ready within the week."

I returned to Merton Place, and with every turn of the carriage wheel over the cobblestone road, I felt a great anxiety and an even greater anticipation of commanding a fleet upon which the future of Britain would turn. As I pondered the possibility of difficulties that might be encountered, I reminded myself that difficult times break some men but make others. I also recalled an old lesson and a very true adage that came from it. When I was very young and stood next to an old workman at my father's house, we watched two dogs fighting. Soon the fight was resolved as one of the dogs took flight. The old man chuckled and said, "You know, lad, it is never a matter of the size of the terrier in the fight. It always depends on the size of the fight in the terrier." I never forgot that moment or the truth of his words.

At Merton Place, I told Emma that I would have to leave in a matter of days, as I have been given command of the fleet to confront the combined enemy forces. She drew her hands up to her breast, and I could see them trembling slightly. Tears came to her eyes, and she said, "Once again into the storm. They are sending you into the storm yet again."

"Yes, and I thank the God Almighty that He has made me fit to undertake this task. I would surely like continued rest, but it is entirely out of the question. Duty is the great business of the sea officer, and all private considerations must give way to it, however painful it may be. It is my calling. Would you please begin laying out my things?"

The next three days were spent in relative quiet. I asked that we entertain no one, for I wanted to spend the time with only my dearest family. The day before my departure, I inspected the clothing and accoutrements Emma had laid out on a bed in one of the guest rooms. Everything was there. Emma knew my needs perfectly. The day before my departure I took her to the church at Merton, where we received communion privately and exchanged rings as a sign of our love. I then took her hand and spoke to the small gathering of friends who had come with us. *"Emma and I have taken the sacrament on this day to prove to the world that our friendship is most pure and innocent, and of this, I call Almighty God to be my witness."*

Dinner that evening was plain and simple, after which I took Horatia to her bed and hummed a lullaby as she fell asleep. I prayed beside her bed that the great and merciful God would keep her and my beloved Emma safe from all harm. During the evening I returned several times with Emma simply to watch Horatia sleep. In the early evening I retired to the bedroom and lay for a while with Emma in my arms, treasuring the feel of her warmth. Then in the late evening of Friday, 13 September, I boarded my carriage, and as we rode away, I craned my neck so that I might see the last glimpse of Emma and Merton Place, my treasures. As my carriage clattered back toward Portsmouth, I wrote in my journal:

> *At 10:30, we drove from dear, dear Merton, where I left all I hold dear in this world, to go to serve my King and Country. May the great God whom I adore enable me to fulfil the*

expectations of my Country, and if it is His good pleasure that
I should return, my thanks will never cease being offered up to
the Throne of His mercy. If it is His good providence to cut short
my days on earth, I bow with the greatest submission, relying
that He will protect those so dear to me that I leave behind. His
will be done: Amen, Amen, Amen.

Back in Command

As the first light of day broke, we drove into Portsmouth and went to the house where Tom Hardy was living and took him aboard the carriage. He was dressed out in his full captain's uniform but still a bit groggy from what I suspected was not a full night's sleep.

As he climbed aboard, I greeted, "Good morning to you, Captain Hardy. I trust that you are ready for the final act of this great play."

"I am indeed ready, Admiral," he replied, "but pray, tell me why you think this will be the final act."

"I cannot tell you that with certitude, my good man, but it is my hope that we will meet the French and Spanish devils and end their threat once and for all. It is my great expectation to return to my family and spend the rest of my days at my paradise in Merton."

"I hope with all of my heart, Admiral, that you are correct," he responded, "and please know that I extend to you the promise of all of my efforts to make it so."

"I know you will, Hardy. I know you will," I replied.

It had been my hope that news of my arrival had been kept from the great citizenry of Portsmouth, as I did not want to deal with another crowd of people. However, it was not so, and a great number were already crowded on the dock. Many came forth to shake my hand, and I could see that some were crying. We made our way through the throng with the aid of several marines who tried to hold them back, though unsuccessfully. I shook as many hands as I could as we went through and boarded our barge. As we were rowed away, they cheered and waved their kerchiefs. In acknowledgment, I carefully stood and took off my hat, waving it to them. I said to Hardy, *"You know, Hardy, I had their huzzas before, but now I have their hearts."*

When we returned aboard the *Victory*, the boatswain piped us aboard with his loud and wonderfully shrill sounding pipe. I could see that the entire ship was bustling with activity. I had been away for less than a month, and although departing dear Merton brought pain into my heart, there again on the decks of *Victory*, the scent of hemp lines and tar being spread on the deck greeted me and brought a renewed excitement to my spirit. I was in my second home. I suggested to Hardy that painting not continue beyond the noon hour, as it would be necessary for the paint to dry, and I wanted to get underway with the morning tide.

At dinner that night I invited Hardy and all of the *Victory's* officers and midshipmen to join me at dinner. We had wonderful and friendly conversations, reviewing the ship's readiness. I was very pleased with their reports. Again I emphasized the need for gunnery drills and seamanship in the handling of sails in different winds. The response of all the officers was very positive, and afterwards I was able to begin a good sleep, thinking of Emma, Horatia – and the combined enemy fleet at Cadiz. We weighed anchor at first light, rode a favourable ebbing tide out of the harbour, and began our transit to the blockading fleet at Cadiz. On the way we met the HMS *Constance* with Admiral Bickerton aboard, who was returning home with an illness. I commiserated with Bickerton, who did seem very ill, but I was pleased to learn from the captain of the *Constance* that the French fleet remained at Cadiz. When we joined the fleet, I had Hardy hoist a signal, "Close around the Admiral at seven bells," - 7:30 p.m. In preparation I ordered the stewards to prepare a festive meal, as it also happened to be my forty-seventh birthday. Seventeen captains came aboard and some of them carried gifts, having been advised that it was my birthday. We toasted to the king, to the Royal Navy, and to victory over Bonaparte's fleet. During dinner I spoke generally of my battle plan. Questions were asked and answered, and everyone seemed to think that it would be a master stroke. As we finished the sweet course, a lovely Cheshire pudding with cherries, I spoke, "Gentlemen, before you leave, I have a final toast for the evening." I raised my glass and said, "To our fleet, to all of my captains, and to all the men who serve in our ships – I want you to know that at this moment, before we go to battle, I believe that this engagement will be the final engagement, as I am certain that it will end all of Bonaparte's design to invade our land. It will rest upon our shoulders, and I have the utmost confidence, for I have all of you with me, the most resolute and dedicated officers that any admiral was ever blessed to have. I toast to each of you, You remain my band of brothers."

There was a pause, and then they replied as their glasses were hoisted in response to the toast. "Here, here," "To you, Admiral," "To our fleet, sir," were the various responses, and I could see that there was tearing in some of the captains' eyes as they drained their glasses. One of them – I know not which one – said, "Admiral, we will not fail you." When they left, I felt as confident and as happy as any commanding officer might be. I was sorry that Captains Berry, Conn, and Durham were not there, but I knew that they were on their way. I was sent a copy of a letter regarding the dinner. It said, "*We all dined with his Lordship yesterday and had a very merry dinner. The superiority of Lord Nelson in all the social arrangements which bind us together is a wonderful thing and lifts our spirits to the utmost.*" I was most pleased with the letter complimenting my manner of command, and even more pleased with the fact that it had such an effect upon the captains of my fleet. I knew once again that I had the very best. The dinner also inspired me to continue invitations to several of my captains on every evening when circumstances permitted. The dinners were truly engaging, as I would inquire about their families and their experiences, if I did not know them well. Again I would review the elements of my battle plan. Over time I was certain that every captain knew what our fleet was expected to do, and each appreciated the part he would play.

I was especially attentive to invite Admiral Collingwood as my second-in-command. He would control the second column of our attack, and it was essential that he and I always be on the same page of thought. I found him very attentive and, as always, a most competent commanding officer as well as an endearing man, very much the same as I had known so long ago in Antigua when we both were enthralled by the beauty of Mary Moutray. I also discussed with him, and he agreed, that it was necessary to establish a common identity among our ships. To that extent, I gave a series of orders to the entire fleet in my public order book that the white ensign be flown on each ship's stern line and that the union flag be suspended from the fore topgallant mast. I also instructed that when signal-flag orders were hoisted from the column commander's ship, they should be repeated by all ships, not simply the leading ship. By doing so, I would assure that every quartermaster and every captain would be attentive to all signals and would know exactly the action they conveyed. I also issued written instructions to each captain that he was to follow all orders from the flagship except when I hoisted the signal, "Follow the column commander," which would give Collingwood command of his line of ships.

As I pondered my battle plan, a refinement came to mind – one that would add an element of dynamic flexibility. In addition to the two lines of attack, I thought of adding a third unit, a smaller squadron that would sail to our windward side, giving them a speed advantage and consisting of the fastest frigates, perhaps six or seven in number. It would serve as an element of adjustment, and I could order them to add force where it was needed. Meanwhile, to keep a constant eye on the enemy fleet at Cadiz, I placed five fast frigates – the command frigate in the centre, with two others slightly to the north and two to the south. In the centre and standing farther out to sea, I placed Captain Henry Blackwood in HMS *Euryalus* as the command frigate, to relay information from the other ships concerning the enemy's movement.

Blessedly before sailing, I had been provided with Popham's telegraphic system of signals, an ingenious simplification of our old signalling system. I distributed it to all ships and ordered that it be thoroughly studied and mastered. Over the weeks before the battle we were able to use it effectively and found it to be splendid. In fact, Hardy once commented, "*This is a far better system, because it lets us actually talk to one another.*" I was also glad that I had stationed my watching frigates as I had done, because dispatches of intelligence indicated that Bonaparte's plans for the fleet at Cadiz might not be to move north for an invasion but may be to sail south into the Mediterranean for assistance in a possible invasion of Sicily, Sardinia, or Naples. In either event I would be ready for them. I concluded that the added tactic of a small third division of fast frigates would be helpful, and to all captains I dispatched this addition as a part of my standing battle plan. The plan was now complete, and I added to it the following note, which I described in a letter to Emma as my "Nelson touch."

> *I have made up my mind ... that the order of sailing is to be the order of battle ...*
>
> *The second-in-command, Admiral Collingwood, after my intentions are made to him, shall have the entire direction of his line to make the attack on the enemy and to follow up the blow until they are captured or destroyed.*

The whole impression of ships in the British fleet must
be to overpower from two to three ships … Something must be
left to chance; nothing is sure in a sea fight beyond all others.
Shot will carry away the masts and yards of friends as well as
the enemy, but with confidence I am sure of victory before the
van of the enemy can succour their rear …

The second-in-command will, in all possible things,
direct the movements of his line by keeping them as compact as
the nature of the circumstances will admit. Captains are to look
to their particular line as their rallying point.

In case signals can neither be seen nor perfectly
understood, no Captain can do very wrong if he places his ship
alongside that of an enemy.

On the morning of 19 October 1805, one of the inshore frigates hoisted the signal, "*The enemy ships are getting under sail.*"

Approximately two hours later we received another signal that said, "*The enemy ships are on a course to the south.*"

As the enemy moved, I decided to keep my fleet out of their sight for fear that if they saw my entire force, they might immediately retreat to Cadiz. Above all, I did not want to lose them this time. I gave a signal to Blackwood that he should gather the other frigates, keep a good distance, and constantly report their speed and course. I ordered my fleet on a course and at a speed to keep Blackwood's *Euryalus* in sight, but no closer. After a while it became apparent that their distance from Cadiz would make a retreat back into port impossible. We would have them. Blackwood ordered his frigates in a line, beginning just in sight of the enemy and stretching out toward the *Victory* so that signals of the enemy's exact position, course, and speed could be related by flags or signal lights, and they did this most admirably. At dawn on 21 October 1805, I ordered my fleet on a course to take us directly at the enemy.

I signalled to Blackwood that, as noted earlier in my battle plan, he should assume command of the third division, the frigate squadron, and I signalled to HMS *Pickle* and HMS *Enterprenante* for them to join his squadron. To the fifteen ships that would comprise my line of battle, I signalled, "*Division one, form a column and sail in the wake of the Victory.*" To the twelve ships of Collingwood's group, I signalled, "*Division two, form a column and sail in the wake of Royal Sovereign.*" I then signalled to Blackwood's third division, "*Stand to the north, close aboard, and await instructions.*"

I believe that at that point Villeneuve realized that an engagement was unavoidable. There was no escape. He ordered his fleet on a northerly course and in a single line of battle as I had suspected he would do. The stage was set, and the play was about to begin.

To my entire fleet I signalled, "*Prepare for battle.*"

Chapter 21

The Battle of Trafalgar

I remember when the enemy came into view, its sails being no more than little dots of white on the distant horizon just after the sun rose on 21 October 1805. At this point Villeneuve was approximately twelve miles away with only two choices – to flee or to fight. I had some anxiety that he would move farther to the south, hugging the shoreline and attempting to flee toward the Strait of Gibraltar, but to my great satisfaction, he ordered his ragged column into a line of battle. It was an extended line that stretched across the horizon for seven miles. As we began our approach, my division came into line. Collingwood's division was to my right, a mile away and parallel to my line. I ordered a signal to all ships, *"Deploy full sails for best speed."*

Our course was directly toward the enemy, but the mild wind, barely ample to fill our sails, afforded a closing speed of no more than three knots. I estimated that it would take several hours before an engagement could be made, and with my fleet in order, I decided to return to my quarters so I could attend to personal matters. In my stateroom, all furniture had been packed away or lashed secure, and the men were clearing all loose items. As I saw the portrait of Lady Hamilton being removed from the bulkhead, I said, *"Please take care of my guardian angel."* I then sat upon an ammunition locker next to a cannon that had been brought in and placed to point out from what had been my starboard window and wrote in my diary,

May the Great God, whom I worship, grant to my Country, and for the benefit of Europe in general, a great and glorious victory; and may no misconduct in anyone tarnish it; and may humanity after our victory be predominant in the feature of the British fleet. For myself, individually, I commit my life to Him who made me, and may His blessing light be upon my endeavours for serving my Country faithfully. To Him I resign myself in the just cause which is entrusted to me to defend. Amen, Amen. Amen.

I then wrote out a codicil to my will in which I described the valuable services Lady Hamilton had rendered to our country at Naples, establishing the best relationship with the Kingdom of the Two Sicilies, particularly by inducing its king to declare war on France and later the obtaining of essential supplies for the fleet at Syracuse in 1798. I continued in the most important conclusion,

> *I, leave Emma Lady Hamilton as a Legacy to my King and Country, that they will give her an ample provision to maintain her right rank in life. I also leave to the beneficence of my country my daughter, Horatia ... These are the only favours I ask of my King and the Country at this moment when I am going to fight their Battle. May God bless my King and Country, and all those I hold dear.*

I had earlier summoned Captain Blackwood to come from *Euryalus* to join me in *Victory* so that I might commend him for his outstanding duties in commanding the fast frigate squadron, my watching eyes during the blockade. He had done a truly splendid job. I called for him and Captain Hardy to come to my cabin and witness the codicil. When they did so, I sealed it, and we returned to the quarterdeck. Captain Blackwood asked, *"Admiral, would it not be a good idea to shift your flag to my ship, the Euryalus, and stand off from the battle, observing and being able to direct your fleet as it might be most effectively used?"*

I quickly shook my head as a negative response. No discussion was necessary, and I asked of Blackwood, *"Tell me, Captain, how many prizes do you think would mark our engagement as a great victory?"*

"I believe that fourteen or fifteen would be ample to declare a very resounding victory, Admiral," he responded.

"I will not be satisfied with less than twenty," I retorted.

The wind had dropped off further, and it appeared that we were not able to make more than two or three knots of speed. I then suggested, "Since there are still more than six miles between our leading ships and the enemy, it seems to me that this may be a good time to tour the ship and speak with the men."

Hardy agreed, and he and Blackwood decided to accompany me. Along the main deck, I shook hands with many of the boatswain's mates and praised them for the trimming of the sails, making our best speed. I asked them various questions – their names, where they were from, and how old they were. Most were in their twenties, but many were in their upper teens and the youngest, the powder monkeys, even younger. I was also somewhat surprised to find a number of Americans, Portuguese, Italians, and black natives of the Caribbean among the crew. We went down to the gun decks, where I saw busy preparations being made by gunner's mates laying out their ramming rods, cleaning swabs and retrieval screws, stacking their shot, powder charges, and canisters against the bulkheads, and cleaning the cannon bores and firing locks. Many were stripped to the waist, even in the cool morning of late October. On many, kerchiefs were bound around their heads and over their ears, each packed with cotton to deaden the noise of the cannons. Some men were sharpening swords. Others were adjusting or polishing their gun sights, and some even did little jigs as others played the hornpipe. In one gun crew I came across a man carving a notch in his gun carriage next to a row of similar marks. I asked what it was, and he replied that each mark denoted a previous British victory. He said that he was cutting the notch for today's battle in the event he would be killed in action. I told him, "*You will make notches enough in the enemy's ships,*" and he laughed.

As I made my way from gun to gun, I would pat the men on the shoulder, praise them for their work, and frequently repeat, "Victory always comes from the mouths of our cannons fired quickly and surely." On the orlop deck below the waterline, four decks below the main deck, the surgeon and his assistants were busy arranging their knives, saws, and tourniquets, placing water buckets along the bulkhead, filling medicine jars of laudanum and spirits, and stacking bandages in great heaps, ready for use. The surgeon's deck was sanded, and old sails were laid out where the wounded would be laid. In the galley, the cooks and stewards were busy finishing a full meal of porridge and cold meat to be carried out to the crew at their stations. It was always advisable to feed a crew before battle since we never knew how long it would take. Seamen always perform best after a full meal. Moreover, I always found it comforting and encouraging to the men that before any battle they should see and hear encouragements from their captain, or in this case, their admiral.

We returned to the quarterdeck, where I made a point of shaking the hands of the marines dressed out in their marvellous red coats and black hats. I noted that the wind was still light and that we were making no better headway than we had been when we had gone below. Earlier I asked the officer of the deck, young Lieutenant Cahill, to scan the enemy ships to discover where Admiral Villeneuve's pennant was flying.

"Cahill, have you found Villeneuve?" I asked.

"No, sir, I have been watching for it, but there is no sign of it flying from any ship yet," he replied.

I turned to Captain Hardy and said, "Let us adjust our course one point to port and head for the lead of their van, and then when he shows himself, we will tack to starboard and point our column toward his ship. With this wind there will be plenty of time to adjust, and I want my ship upon his."

"Aye, aye, sir," he responded and ordered the chief quartermaster, "Come to a new course, twelve degrees to port."

I then ordered the signal lieutenant, young John Pasco, to hoist a signal to Collingwood, "*I intend to break through the enemy van at the lead flagship. I confirm that you should break through the enemy line near its centre.*"

As I walked slowly and erect about the quarterdeck, I wanted to exhibit to everyone a figure of calm resolve. I approached a small group of midshipmen and chatted with them. Before I left, I told them, "*Gentlemen, today will be a day that you will recount with pride for the rest of your lives.*" As I walked away, it occurred to me that I might send a signal to the entire fleet, one that might be encouraging and perhaps amusing. I called out, "Pasco, please come. I want to send a signal." He quickly appeared with a writing board in his hand.

"*Hoist the following signal: 'England confides that every man will do his duty.'*"

He wrote down my message and said, "Aye, aye, sir," then bounded off toward his signal bridge. However, after a short while he returned and said, "*Sir, the word 'confides' is not in Popham's dictionary, and I will have to spell it out, which will take an inordinate number of flags. Would the word 'expects' be acceptable?*"

I thought for a moment and replied, "*Yes, let it be 'England expects that every man will do his duty.' That will be fine.*" Off he went, and soon in the quiet of the quarterdeck I could hear the gentle flapping of the signal flags and the rustle of the signal halyard as my message went out to the fleet. Hardy, always attentive, instructed the junior officer of the deck to go and announce the message on each deck of the ship, and as he went from deck to deck, I was delighted to hear rather boisterous cheers. On the main deck I could see men doff their hats and wave them, looking in my direction. There was also much laughing and slapping of backs.

Then Lieutenant Cahill called out with his spyglass to his eye, "Admiral Nelson, sir, the pennant of Admiral Villeneuve has been hoisted in the ninth ship from the head of the enemy line!"

"Thank you, Cahill," I answered, "and now, Captain Hardy, let us point for him. At last I will be able to thank him for running away at the battle at the Nile."

Hardy gave the appropriate orders for a new course, and the pattern of battle was set in place. Captain Blackwood soon approached and said, "Admiral, as much as I have enjoyed your company, I believe it time that I return to the *Euryalus* and reassume command of my squadron. I trust, my lord, that on my return to the *Victory*, which will be as soon as possible, I shall find your lordship well and in possession of twenty prizes."

"Very well, Blackwood. I have enjoyed your company, my young colleague. When you return to *Euryalus*, have your ships come close aboard my column and join in the attack as part of my division. I do not believe that a reserve force will be needed today. You should be part of the attack without delay."

"Yes, sir! Aye, aye, sir! Excellent!" he responded, saluting smartly. Then he turned to go back to his ship.

As he walked away, I added, "*God bless you, Blackwood. I shall never speak to you again.*" He turned and looked at me with a rather astonished look upon his face and then quickly walked away. It occurred to me that I should have said, "I shall never speak to you again – until after the battle," but I dismissed the thought. What was said was said. We could chuckle about it later.

Even under the light wind that pushed our ships ever so slowly, we were drawing near to the enemy. I noticed that the sea, previously calm and flat, was showing swells from the west, and I suspected that it foretold a gathering storm. If such were the case, we should be prepared, so I called for Lieutenant Pasco, and when he arrived, I said, "*Please hoist another signal to all ships that they should be prepared to anchor.*" He acknowledged and quickly hoisted the signal. All ships acknowledged it, and we continued to make our progress slowly toward the enemy's combined fleet. As we did so, in the unnatural quiet that lingered, Captain Hardy approached me and spoke.

"*Admiral, I have taken note that you are dressed in your full uniform, displaying the many decorations. I am concerned that it might make you target for musket gunners in the enemy ship. It would be my recommendation, with respect, that you would be a lesser target in a plain coat."*

"Thank you, Hardy, but this is not a time to be changing coats," I responded. Inwardly I was a little amused. I did not have a plain coat.

As we approached the enemy, I looked about and felt a certain pang of regret. In the great expanse of my sight, there were scores of beautiful ships with brightly painted hulls, and above them there were majestic displays of white sails all set under a wonderful blue sky. It was a perfect and beautiful picture that soon would be transformed into a great shamble of life or death. These ships were about to batter each other in a furious carnage of destruction. Some would be sunk. Most would have their sails and rigging shot away. Some would burn, and so many of the men aboard, young and in the prime of their lives, would be killed or wounded and maimed in the hellish fire and smoke that was about to begin in a massive visitation of hell upon the earth. However, such was the fate of those engaged in war. On the continent the devil Bonaparte, the bastard tyrant, had been waging his war from the Baltic to Africa, attempting to become master of the civilized world. Most personal to me, his dastard intention was ultimately to invade my beautiful homeland and to enslave my people. It was my solemn duty at this time and on this day to make it impossible for him to do so, whatever the cost to my beautiful ships, to my valiant men, or to me.

Battle

As our parallel columns made their final approach, Hardy ordered that the marine drummers again sound the beat to quarters. It was unnecessary, as the entire crews were already at battle stations, but it was a laudable idea to have the crew hear the sharp, rhythmic beat of drums to replace the sepulchral silence that had lasted for so long. Everyone was at his station. Unnecessary personnel were at cover. Sharpshooters made ready on the gunnels and in the rigging as they loaded and primed their muskets. Large battle flags were unfurled and hoisted, making sharp flapping noise in a magnificent display of colour. Gunnery personnel on the main deck were ordered "ready prone," lying flat on the deck to avoid as much as possible cannon shot and shrapnel from the first rounds of cannonballs and chain shot that would be fired by the enemy as we approached. As soon as we could fire a broadside at them, the order would follow, "Station and fire!" And then our gunnery teams would jump to their guns and unleash their practiced dance of fury. But until we crossed the enemy line, we would simply have to endure the enemy fire.

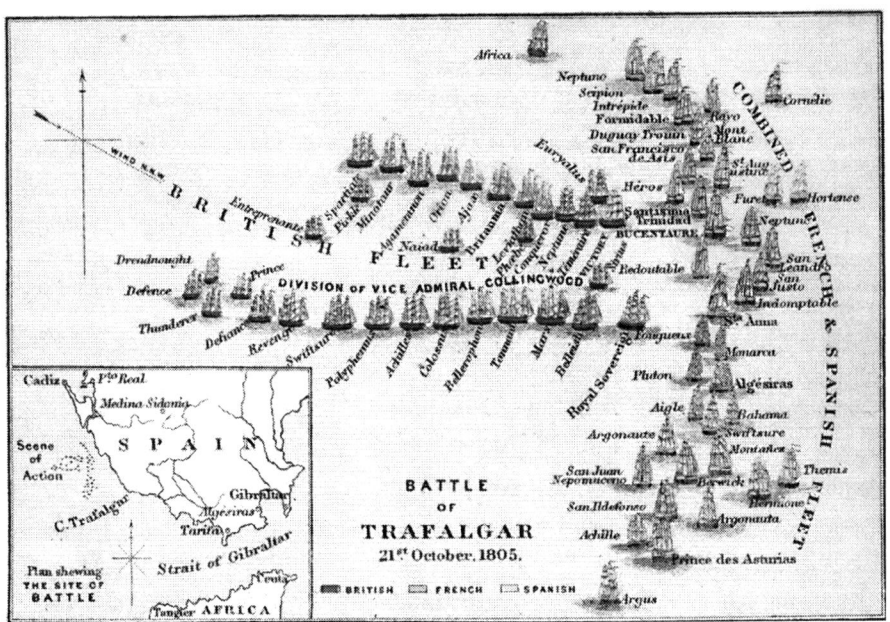

In *Royal Sovereign*, Collingwood made first contact. As he approached just before noon, an opening broadside was fired from the French ship *Fougeux*. The battle thus began. The French and Spanish ships were athwart the sea swells, and their initial fire proved ineffective with most shot hitting the water in familiar tall white sprays or passing overhead – cannonballs making a great *whooshing* sound and chain shot making a distinctive, higher pitched *whizzing* noise. After some minutes *the Royal Sovereign* broke through the enemy line and fired its first broadside down the length of the enemy ships *Fougeux* and *Santa Ana* with great effect. The *Royal Sovereign* was soon joined by HMS *Belleisle*, HMS *Mars*, and HMS *Tonnant*, engaging the next ships in line. As the British crews began to fire their massive response at the enemy, I could watch and hear the rapidity of their fire being much greater than that of either the French or Spanish. I knew always that it would be so and felt confident as Collingwood's column tacked to engage the entire rear of the combined enemy. Ships became joined in a furious and desperate line dance of thunder, fire, and smoke.

My column approached more closely, and we began to receive fire from all enemy ships within range, the *Redoubtable, San Juno, Bucentaire* – Villeneuve's flagship – and the *Santissima Trinidad*, the largest warship in the world, which had been refitted after the Battle of Cape St. Vincent. Their first rounds were not very accurate, but as we drew closer, the broadsides began to find their mark. I could hear chain shot tearing through our sails and breaking our rigging with loud twangs. Round balls and grape shot rained on our bow and down the hull. I also heard the inevitable sounds that followed – the screams and cries of wounded men. Hardy shouted at the top of his lungs, *"Steady on! Steady on!"* and then ordered, *"Relay!"* Then I would hear the sounds of *"Steady on! Steady on!"* being repeated by all officers and petty officers throughout the decks of the ship. It was a very good practice, as it reminded every man waiting at his battle station that our time to reply would soon come. I walked back and forth on the quarterdeck, watching and feeling a terrible anxiety and impatience as we absorbed the first blows of enemy fire. Then I could see a man standing next to Hardy be hit directly by a shot. His body was flung around, and it landed, splayed out on the deck, almost torn in half. Marines ran immediately, gathered it up, and flung it over the port side of the ship. I then remembered that my secretary, John Scott, had been talking to Hardy and asked, *"Was that Scott?"*

Hardy answered, *"Yes, Admiral, it was."*

I replied, *"Poor Scott, poor fellow."* As I continued walking the deck, I put the terrible regret of his death out of my mind. I dismissed it like swallowing a very bitter pill.

What I believed was a canister load of grape shot screamed across the main deck, taking down a half of a dozen marines, shattering their bodies in all directions. As the others in the platoon stood close to one another, I ordered the marine lieutenant to disperse them so that such a loss might not be repeated. We drew ever closer to the enemy, and their batteries continued to take their toll. Our topmast staysail fell to the deck, and was gathered up and thrown overboard. The control lines of our mizzen staysail and main topgallant were stripped away, leaving the sails flapping uselessly in the wind. Great holes appeared in our three forward jibs as well as both the mainsail and mizzen, but they still held some wind. A shot hit the steering wheel at its centre, destroying it completely and sending splinters showering across the deck. Fortunately the chief quartermaster and his second were unhurt, and with a little time and a great display of seamanship, steering was effectively restored with blocks and tackle directly upon the rudder's tiller. Steering instructions were given through a copper tube from the quarterdeck to the new steering station.

Hardy and I continued our pace on the quarterdeck when another shot gouged a great hole in the mainmast, again scattering splinters across the deck. One tore the buckle from Hardy's shoe. Luckily he was unharmed. I approached him and commented, *"Hardy, this is too warm work to last for long."*

In the meantime the *Santissima Trinidad* and another ship of the French line, the *Redoutable*, had come very close to Villeneuve's flagship, the *Bucentaure*. Unsure of what he should do, Hardy asked my advice as to where he should try to penetrate the line, and I responded, *"It doesn't matter, my good man. Go where you please, take your choice."* And then a slight gap opened between the *Bucentaure* and the *Redoubtable*. Hardy tacked to break through between them, and finally as the *Victory* passed between them, our agony of waiting, which had taken the greater part of an hour, came to an end. Hardy gave the order, "Station and fire, port and starboard!" and a great thunder of retribution began as broadside eruptions sounded from both sides of *Victory* with great flashes of light and a roar of thunder that shook the entire ship from mainmast to keel. To port, double shot from all three gun decks smashed the stern of the *Bucentaure*, and to starboard, the broadside shattered the bow of the *Redoutable*. *Victory's* moment of releasing its pent-up fury had arrived. Hardy ordered that sail sheets be let go, bringing us to a complete stop between the targets, and for the next hour, broadsides were repeated, constantly battering both ships. Shots were point-blank with very little gunnery aim necessary. A great billow of acrid smoke covered our ship and rose like a great black storm cloud in the morning air as our gun crews reloaded with a practiced intensity unknown in any other navy.

With successive broadsides, in a matter of minutes it could be seen that the entire stern of *Bucentaire* had been shot away. Successive rounds of ball and canister shot blew away its bulkheads, opening every deck to a murderous repetitions of grape shot. Soon no French sailor could be seen walking upon any of the gun decks of the *Bucentaire*. Meanwhile, the *Redoutable* drifted to our starboard side very close aboard, so close that our yardarms became entangled. Muzzle to muzzle, we exchanged furious fire. I was entranced as I saw our gunnery crews assisted by some boatswains working like maniacal mad men, reloading and firing, reloading and firing. Their furious teamwork was to me nothing less than magnificent. *Victory's* gunners were loading and blasting away at the *Redoutable's* gun ports at a speed more than double that of the French. There was even fear that the flashes of our cannon fire would set the sides of our ships ablaze, and seamen who were no longer working lines dashed with water buckets to splash them on the side of the both ships.

Breaking away from my witness of the destruction of *Bucentaire* and *Redoubtable*, I rushed to a high point on the afterdeck and surveyed the development of other action. Collingwood's column was engaging the entire rear of the French line, and the ships of my division, true to the battle plan, were fully engaged with all of the enemy ships between *Victory* and those of Collingwood's column, fighting side to side with the enemy. It was very apparent that we had taken the measure of the French. We were besting them. I returned to the quarterdeck to advise Hardy that things seem to be going very well, but as I approached him, it felt as though someone slapped me on my shoulder. Then my knees gave way, and I fell to the deck. At first I was able to lean on my left elbow; however, soon it gave way, and I lay prone on the deck at the spot and in the pool of blood where Scott had been killed. The feeling was as though a great hand was squeezing my back, and the pain had a burning sensation, an intense burning pain down the top of my spine. After I was there for only a moment, I could hear a seaman call out to Hardy, "The admiral is down!"

Hardy came immediately. *"Admiral, are you hurt?"* he asked.

"They have done for me at last, Hardy," I responded.

"I hope not," he replied.

Unable to move and with an immense pain across my back, I answered him, *"Yes. My backbone is shot through."*

The seaman, accompanied by a sergeant major of marines and several others, lifted me and began carrying me to the surgeon's station that I had visited on my tour that morning. However, on the way I noticed that one of the lines on the tiller had come loose and called for a midshipman who was standing nearby. *"Lad, please go straightaway to the quarterdeck and tell Captain Hardy that one of the tiller lines has to be replaced,"* I said.

He saluted and said, "Aye, aye, sir," and then scurried on his way to advise Hardy of the problem.

The Last Hours

As the midshipman departed, I took a handkerchief from my pocket and asked the sergeant major if he had another one. He said that he did and produced it. I put one over my decorations and the other over my face so that members of the crew would not see me in my wounded state as I was carried below. I would regret if any members of the crew might become dispirited seeing their wounded admiral being carried away. As we descended into the bowels of the ship, everything became darker, and when we arrived at the orlop deck, where candles flickered in the muffled echoes of broadsides being fired above, I could hear the cries and groans of wounded men. The surgeon, William Beatty, with two others and their assistants were working feverishly with bloodied hands, forearms, and aprons. My ship's chaplain, Alexander Scott, who was of no relation to my secretary, John Scott, accompanied me down. When I was laid on the deck, he asked if there was anything he could do, and I told him that I could think of nothing. When Dr Beatty approached, I told him, *"Mister Beatty, I am afraid that you can do nothing for me. I have but a short time to live. My back is shot through."*

"Sir, let's see what we have," he replied as he and his assistant removed my coat. It caused me great pain, and I cried out. Beatty said, *"I'm sorry, Admiral, but I have to remove your coat."* They rolled up my coat and placed it under the head of a midshipman who was lying beside me and whose head was pulsing spurts of blood. The surgeon inspected my wound, a bleeding hole on the top of my left shoulder, and asked if I was in very much pain.

"I have a great burning pain in the middle of my back, and I have no feeling whatever in the lower part of my body. It is difficult for me to breathe and I feel a gushing in my chest. I am hot and very thirsty."

Soon some water was given to me followed by some lemonade. A fan was soon brought by an assistant who waved it over my face. I could then hear men cheering on the decks above and asked, *"Why are the men cheering?"*

"I don't know, Admiral," he responded.

"Where is Hardy?" I asked. *"Would someone bring him to me? Has he been killed?"*

"I do not believe so, Admiral," Beatty responded.

"*Mister Beatty, please go and attend to those who can be saved. I cannot,*" I told the surgeon.

"*I believe the men are probably cheering because one of the French has struck his colours,*" a voice said to my right. I looked over and saw that it was our signal lieutenant, John Pasco.

"*Pasco, are you hurt badly?*" I asked.

"*Just a musket ball in the leg, Admiral,*" he answered, "*but I cannot stand.*"

"*Good, thank God that you will recover,*" I answered, "*and thank you for your signals. You are very well versed in Popham's new dictionary.*"

A messenger from the quarterdeck arrived and said, "*Captain Hardy is engaged in circumstances that require his presence on the main deck and will avail himself at the most favourable moment to visit you, your Lordship.*"

I recognized the voice of the messenger and asked, "*Who is that who just spoke?*"

"*Sir, my name is Angus Bulkeley. I believe that my father served with you in Nicaragua,*" the young lad said.

"Ah, yes I remember him, a good man," I exclaimed. "Please remember me to your father.

"*I would, sir,*" he answered, "*but he died in Nicaragua.*"

I remained hot, and my thirst would not go away. Frequently I would say, "*Fan, please fan,*" and the surgeon's assistant would wave his fan more rapidly, although it seemed to do no good. I was also given lemonade and watered wine, but it had no effect on my thirst.

I called for the chaplain and told him, "*Mister Scott, I am gone. I am gone. Remember me to Lady Hamilton. Please do that, and remember me to Horatia. Remember me to all my friends. Please remember me also to Mister Rose at the Board of Trade. Tell them I have left a will that has committed Lady Hamilton and Horatia to the care of my country.*"

The ship's purser, Walter Burke, was helping Chaplain Scott to place pillows under my head, and I said to them, "*This is all to naught. I am gone. I am gone.*"

"*I do not believe that is so, Admiral. You will be returning in great triumph to England,*" Burke tried to assure me.

"*It is nonsense, Mister Burke, to suppose that I can live. My sufferings are very great that they will soon be over,*" I told him.

I then saw Captain Hardy approaching and asked, "*Well, Hardy, how goes the battle? How goes the day for us?*"

"*Very well, my Lord, we have twelve or fourteen of the enemy's ships in our possession, but five of their van have tacked and show an intention of bearing down upon the Victory. I have, therefore, called two or three of our fresh ships round to help us, and I have no doubt that will give them a drubbing,*" he answered.

"*I hope none of our ships have struck, Hardy,*" I said.

"*No, my Lord, there is no fear of that,*" he replied.

"*I am a dead man, Hardy,*" I repeated. "*I am going fast. It will soon be all over for me.*"

Then I asked him, "*Please come closer,*" and as he drew near, I added, "*Please let dear Lady Hamilton have my hair and all other things that belong to me.*"

"*I will do that, my good friend and commander,*" he responded. Then he asked, "*Is your pain great?*"

"*Yes, but I believe that I shall last another hour longer,*" I told him.

"*You are a strong man,*" he answered, "*I have faith that you will rally and survive.*"

"*No, no, I cannot,*" I said. "*It is impossible. My back is shot through. The surgeon will tell you, I am gone,*" I said as I saw Mister Beatty arriving.

"*There is Beatty. He will tell you. My back is shot through. Ah, Mister Beatty, all power of motion and feeling below my breast are gone. It is useless, and you should go now and tend to those who can be saved.*"

Hardy said that he had to go to the main deck to attend to the battle but that he would return as soon as he could. I called for the surgeon, and when Beatty appeared again, I told him, "*Mister Beatty, I have sent for you to say, but I forgot to tell you before, that all power of motion and feeling below my breast are now gone.*"

"*My Lord, you told me so before, but let me now inspect those parts of your body,*" he said, and they cut away my leggings, stained with Scott's blood, to inspect my legs.

I quickly answered, "*Scott and Burke have tried that already, but it was to no avail. You know I can live but a short time. Ah, Beatty, I am certain of it. You know I am gone.*"

"*My Lord, unhappily for our country, I fear that nothing can be done for you.*" Beatty responded.

"*I know. I feel something in my breast that is rising, and it tells me that I am gone. God be praised, I have done my duty.*"

Chaplain Scott then asked if the pain was worse, and I answered, "*Ah, the pain; it is terrible. It is awful. It is so bad that I wish I were dead; although I would like to live longer. Death is a fear in life, and life is dear to all men.*"

I heard a repeated muffled of broadsides being fired yet again by the guns of *Victory* and exclaimed, "*Oh, Victory! How you distract my poor brain.*" Then after a while the guns became silent, and I saw Hardy approaching. He bent down to me and said, "*Admiral, it is my pleasure to report to you that you have a great victory. I cannot be sure of how many of the enemy ships we have taken, but they are fourteen or fifteen for sure.*"

"*That is well, my good man,*" I responded, "*but I had bargained for twenty.*"

I then felt a small heave in the ship's movement and remembered the swells that were coming from the west as the battle began. A storm was coming. I felt certain that a storm or perhaps a gale was about to begin.

"*Anchor, Hardy, anchor!*" I spoke as loudly as I could.

Hardy responded, "*I suppose, my Lord, that Admiral Collingwood will now direct the affairs of the fleet.*"

"*Not while I am alive, I hope, Hardy,*" I said with some temper, raising my head from my pillow. "*No, anchor Hardy! Anchor!*"

"*Shall we make a signal, sir?*" he asked.

"*Yes,*" I answered, "*for if I live, I'll anchor.*"

Hardy nodded. Then a very sad and morbid thought came to me, and I said, "*Hardy, don't throw me overboard.*"

"*Certainly not,*" he quickly answered.

"*Then you know what to do. Take care of my dear Lady Hamilton, Hardy. Take care of poor Lady Hamilton.*"

I paused and said, "*Kiss me, Hardy.*"

He knelt down and kissed my cheek.

"*Now I am satisfied. Thank God I have done my duty,*" I murmured, my voice raspy and beginning to fail me.

Some time passed. I do not know how long. Everything was beginning to become faint, a blur. And then without my asking, I think I saw Hardy bend down again, and he kissed me on my forehead. However, I could not be sure whether it was he or another.

"*Who is that?*" I whispered.

"*It is Hardy,*" he answered.

"*God bless you, Hardy,*" I said.

Everything was quiet, and my thirst became acute. I called for drink, and it was brought. A small amount was poured into my mouth, but I had some difficulty swallowing.

The pain continued, and I asked that I be turned on my right side. Someone turned me, but it did not ease the pain. My sight was continuing to dim, and I began to struggle for breath.

I then realized that I could have suffered just as well above deck and spoke faintly and hoarsely, "*I wish I had not left the deck, for I shall soon be gone.*"

For some reason the image of Lady Hamilton holding our daughter came into my mind, and I called, "*Mister Scott.*" When he appeared, I drew him close to me.

"*I have not been a great sinner.*" My strength ebbed away, but I rallied as much as I could and whispered to him, "*Remember that I leave Lady Hamilton and my daughter, Horatia, as a legacy to my country. Remember.*"

Everything became silent, and all became a dark grey blur. I tried to speak one more time, but it was only a whisper, "*Thank God. I have done my duty.*"

I tried to breathe.

Everything faded … and slowly became dark.

Chapter 22 - Epilogue

The Funeral

On the evening following the battle, Nelson's body was placed in a cask of brandy, lashed to the Victory's mainmast. Because of damage to its sails and rigging, Victory was towed to Gibraltar and on arrival the body was transferred to a lead-lined coffin filled with spirits of wine. Collingwood's dispatches about the battle were carried to England aboard HMS Pickle and when the news arrived in London, Captain John Whitby was sent to Merton Place to bring the news of Nelson's death to Emma Hamilton. She later recalled:

> *They brought me word, Mr. Whitby from the Admiralty. "Show him in directly", I said. He came in, and with a pale countenance and faint voice, said, "We have gained a great Victory." – "Never mind your Victory", I said. "My letters, give me my letters." Captain Whitby was unable to speak – tears in his eyes and a deathly paleness over his face made me comprehend him. I believe I gave a scream and fell back, and for ten hours I could neither speak nor shed a tear.*

Nelson's body was unloaded from the Victory at the Nore. It was conveyed upriver in a yacht to Greenwich and placed in a lead coffin and that in another wooden one made from the mast of L'Orient, recovered after the Battle of the Nile. He lay in state in the Painted Hall at Greenwich for three days before being taken upriver aboard a barge, accompanied by Lord Hood, chief mourner, Sir Peter Parker, and, ironically, the Prince of Wales. The Prince at first announced his intention to attend the funeral as chief mourner, but later attended in a private capacity with Prince William Henry when his father, George III, reminded him that it was against protocol for the Heir to the Throne to attend the funeral of anyone except a member of the Royal Family. The coffin was taken into the Admiralty for the night, attended by Victory's chaplain, Alexander Scott. The next day, January 9, 1806, a funeral procession consisting of 32 admirals, over a hundred captains, and an escort of 10,000 soldiers took the coffin from the Admiralty to St Paul's Cathedral. After a four-hour service, he was interred within a sarcophagus originally carved for Cardinal Wolsey.

Nelson's body rests at St. Paul's Cathedral.

Emma

After Nelson's death Emma consistently outspent the small pension Sir William had left her and fell deeply into debt. Nelson had willed his estate to his brother. He gave Merton Place to Emma, but she depleted her finances by trying to maintain it as a monument to him. In spite of Nelson's status as a national hero, the last request he had made of his country to provide for Emma and Horatia was ignored. They showered honours on Nelson's brother instead, and he did nothing to assist Emma. As was her way, she continued to live rather extravagantly at Merton Place, as though money was not a problem. When the little inheritance that she had received from Sir William was exhausted, she sold Merton Place and moved to very modest accommodations in London. From there she moved to a friend's house in Fulham. Economically distraught, she borrowed money where she could.

A friend named Pryse Lockhart spoke with her one day in Greenwich Park and wrote, "*Age and circumstances had made sad ravages in her former splendid countenance … The lovely hair which was wont to hang over her polished forehead was tucked away under a huge cap, or perhaps it had become grey, be that as it may, it no longer served as an ornament … Her eyes, while less brilliant, were still beautiful and that fascinating mouth from which sculptors had modelled still retained its expression.*"

In 1813, desperate, she wrote to the Prince of Wales, then the Prince Regent, "*The slender provision left by Lord Nelson for the bringing up of his daughter comes short of what I deem necessary for the education of one of her descent, the only living blood of that glorious man.*" Her message was ignored. Later she was arrested for debt and spent a year in a debtor's prison, with Horatia, before she moved to France to escape her creditors. Living in poverty in Calais, she became an alcoholic and suffered from jaundice. She died in January 1815 from complications of amoebic dysentery, an illness she likely contracted during her years in Naples. Sir William had also suffered chronically from the disease. She was buried at Calais in the graveyard of the church of St. Pierre.

Napoleon Bonaparte

Nelson's victory at Trafalgar forced Napoleon to terminate all plans to invade England. Instead he set his sights on Austria and Russia and defeated both of their armies at the Battle of Austerlitz. Other victories soon followed, allowing him to expand the French empire over the greater part of Europe.

However, military successes gave way to broader internal political defeats beginning in 1810, when France suffered a string of military losses that tapped the country's military budget. In 1812, France was devastated when its invasion of Russia became a dramatic failure in which entire regiments of soldiers in Napoleon's *Grande Armie* were killed or wounded. Of the original fighting force of six hundred thousand men, only ten thousand soldiers remained ready for service.

News of the defeat in Russia invigorated Napoleon's enemies, both inside and outside of France. A failed coup was attempted while Napoleon lingered in Russia and the British Army advanced into French territories. With international pressure mounting and his government lacking the resources to fight, Napoleon surrendered to allied forces on 30 March 1814. He was taken into exile on the island of Elba. The exile did not last long. In March 1815, he escaped the island and returned to Paris. He again led the country into war, leading his troops into Belgium, where he defeated the Prussians on 16 June 1815. But two days later at Waterloo, his army was defeated by the British Army, led by the Duke of Wellington, with assistance from the Prussian Army. On 22 June 1815, he abdicated. Fearing a repeat of his earlier return from exile, the British government sent him to the remote southern Atlantic island of St. Helena.

On St. Helena, his health steadily began to deteriorate. By early 1821, he was bedridden and growing steadily weaker. He died on 5 May 1821.

Fanny

Fanny Nelson fell ill in 1805 following Nelson's death. She recovered, and for the rest of her life she was in indifferent health. She moved to Paris for a time to live with her son, Josiah, who had become a successful businessman in France. Her eldest grandchild, also named Fanny, recalled her good nature and her devotion to her husband's memory.

She would often kiss a miniature of him, once telling the younger Fanny, *"When you are older little, Fan, you may know what it is to have a broken heart."* Fanny Nelson returned to England and settled at Exmouth. She died 4 May 1831.

Horatia

Before debt set in, Emma took ample care of Horatia, being generous, without budgetary restraints. When Emma died in January 1815, Horatia, who was still living with her in Calais, made the funeral arrangements with the British consul and then returned to England disguised as a boy to escape arrest for the debts Emma had run up in France. On arrival in Dover, she resided with one of Nelson's sisters in Sussex. She was described in her youth as being tall, intelligent, able to speak her mind, and surprisingly well read. She was good at languages, music, and needlework, with a lively temperament. In 1822, she married Rev. Philip Ward, a clergyman. They had ten children. After her husband's death she lived for twenty-two years until her death in 1881.

Prince William

When Prince William Henry returned from service the West Indies under Nelson, he was named the Duke of Clarence and ceased his active service in the Royal Navy When the United Kingdom subsequently declared war on France, he was eager to serve in the Royal Navy and expected a command, but he was not given a ship, perhaps at first because he had broken his arm by falling down some stairs while drunk. However, it was later discovered he was denied a command because he gave a speech in the House of Lords actually opposing the war. The following year he reversed himself and spoke in favour of the war, again expecting a command. None came. The Admiralty did not even reply to his request. He did not lose hope of being appointed to an active post. He was made an admiral, at the insistence of George III, but the rank was purely titular. Despite repeated petitions, he was never given a command throughout the Napoleonic Wars. In 1811, he was appointed to the honorary position of Admiral of the Fleet, a high-sounding but impotent position.

Since his two older brothers died without leaving legitimate issue, he inherited the throne when he was sixty-four years old. During his reign the monarchy and the House of Lords became less important in actual government, and real control of the empire became vested in the House of Commons. At the time of his death William had no surviving legitimate children, although he was survived by eight of the ten illegitimate children he had fathered with an actress named Dorothea Jordan. On his death, the daughter of his younger brother, Edward, became queen - Queen Victoria.

Admiral John Jervis, Lord St. Vincent

In November 1805, Admiral Jervis resumed active service and took command of the Channel Fleet. However, he had long-suffered from poor health, and a change in government led to his resignation in 1807. In his retirement he seldom took his seat in the House of Lords and made his last appearance in 1810. He died on 13 March 1823, and because he had no children, the Barony of Jervis and the Earldom of St. Vincent ended.

King Ferdinand

The French victory at the Battle of Austerlitz on 2 December 1805, enabled Napoleon to dispatch an army into southern Italy. Ferdinand fled to Palermo, and in February 1806, the French again entered Naples. Napoleon declared that the crown was forfeited and proclaimed his brother, Joseph, King of Naples and Sicily. But Ferdinand continued to reign over the latter kingdom, becoming the first King of Sicily, and he continued to reside there under British protection. After the fall of Napoleon, Ferdinand returned to Naples. Parliamentary institutions of a feudal type had long existed in Naples, and the British minister insisted on a reform of the constitution along English lines. The king then practically abdicated his power, appointing his son, Francis, as regent. At additional British insistence, Queen Maria Carolina was exiled to Austria. Ferdinand died in Naples in January 1825.

The Band of Brothers

Thomas Hardy
Hardy carried one of the banners at Nelson's funeral procession on 9 January 1806. He was created a baronet and was given command of the HMS *Triumph* on the North American station in May 1806. In the

War of 1812, he took part in several inconsequential battles before a truce was declared. Promoted to rear admiral in 1825, Hardy escorted British troops to Lisbon, where they helped to quell a revolution. He became First Lord of the Admiralty in the Grey ministry. As First Lord, he encouraged the introduction of steam warships. He resigned in 1834 to become the Governor of Greenwich Hospital and was promoted to vice admiral. He died at Greenwich on 20 September 1839.

Edward Berry

Upon Berry's arrival at Trafalgar in 1805 as Captain of HMS *Agamemnon*, Nelson exclaimed with facetious excitement, *"Here comes that fool Berry! Now we shall have a battle."* Berry had a rich reputation as a fighter. At the battle's close, Berry took to his ship's boat in order to speak to Nelson on the *Victory*, but by the time he arrived, Nelson had died, an unfortunate piece of timing which Berry would regret for the rest of his life. In 1806, Berry fought in the *Agamemnon* at the battle of San Domingo and was highly praised for his actions. That same year he became a baronet and remained in sea service throughout the war. He was made a Knight of the Order of the Bath, and in 1821, he became a rear admiral. During these years, despite constant entreaties to the Admiralty, he never took up further important postings. Following several years of severe illness and extreme disability, he died on 13 February 1831, at his residence in Bath.

Alexander Ball

After HMS *Vanguard* had lost her foremast and topmasts before the Battle of the Nile, Ball towed *Vanguard* to safety, preventing it from destruction on Sardinia's rocky coast. At the Battle of the Nile, his ship, the *Alexander*, was the second British ship to fire on the French admiral's flagship, *L'Orient*, and was chiefly responsible for the fire that caused *L'Orient* to explode during the battle. He was not present at the Battle of Trafalgar, having been assigned by the British government as a minister to Malta, where he served with great distinction for the rest of his life.

Thomas Troubridge

With Nelson at the Battle of Cape St. Vincent, Troubridge was highly commended by Admiral Jervis for his courage and initiative. In July 1797, he assisted Nelson with valour in the unsuccessful attack on Tenerife. However, when getting into position for the attack on the French fleet at the Nile, his ship, the *Culloden*, ran aground and was unable to take any part in the battle. At Nelson's request, however, he was awarded the gold medal commemorating the victory. He then served in the Mediterranean and was created a baronet. From 1801 to 1804, he was an assisting lord of the Admiralty and was made a rear admiral. In 1805, he was appointed to command the East Indies station. When he left in January 1807 for the Cape of Good Hope, his ship foundered in a cyclone off the coast of Madagascar. He and all others on board perished.

Thomas Foley

Tom Foley was truly treasured by Nelson as a member of the band of brothers, having served magnificently at the battle of the Nile and as Nelson's flag captain at the battle of Copenhagen. Ill health, however, obliged Foley to decline Nelson's offer of the post of captain of the *Victory* prior to the Battle of Trafalgar. The position was then offered to Thomas Hardy, who was present at Nelson's death. From 1808 to 1815, Foley commanded HMS *Monmouth*. After peace with France, Foley was promoted to the rank of admiral and made a Knight of the Order of the Bath. He died while he was serving as Commander of the Portsmouth Station in 1833.

James Saumarez

Saumarez was Nelson's second-in-command at the Battle of the Nile, where he distinguished himself by forcing the surrender of the *Peuple Souverain* and the *Franklin*. In 1801, he was raised to the rank of rear admiral. He was created a baronet, and he received the command of a small squadron that was ordered to watch the movements of the Spanish fleet at Cadiz. He performed a brilliant piece of service in which after a first repulse at Algeciras he routed a much superior combined force of French and Spanish ships at the Battle of the Gulf of Gibraltar. For his services Saumarez received the Order of the Bath. After the Battle of the Nile, while in conversation with Nelson on the quarter deck of HMS *Vanguard*, Saumarez suggested that the tactic of doubling the French line had been a dangerous one, as it meant exposing British ships to friendly fire. Before he had a chance to explain, Nelson cut him short and angrily went below. Somewhat irritated, Nelson decided that Saumarez should escort the battle prizes home. The two men never served together again, and an awkwardness remained between them. He was raised to the peerage as Baron de Saumarez in 1831. He died in 1836.

Samuel Hood

In HMS *Zealous*, Captain Samuel Hood played an important part at the Battle of the Nile. His first opponent, the *Guerriere*, was put out of action in twelve minutes. Hood immediately and effectively engaged other ships. When Nelson left the coast of Egypt, Hood commanded the blockading force off Alexandria and Rosetta. Later he re-joined Nelson on the coast of the Kingdom of the Two Sicilies, receiving for his services the order of St Ferdinand. In the seventy-four-gun *Venerable*, Hood was present at the Battle of Algeciras on 8 July 1801, and the action in the Strait of Gibraltar that followed. For these successes he was appointed a Knight of the Order of the Bath. He died without issue in India in 1814.

Josiah Nisbet

After a largely unsuccessful career in the Royal Navy, Josiah became a surprisingly successful businessman in France. He was married in 1819 and had seven children. During much of the time that he was in France, his mother, Fanny, resided with him. He died in his house on the Champs Elysees while on a business trip to Paris in 1830.

Admiral Hood

Admiral Hood was the chief mourner at Nelson's funeral and lived long enough to see Britain triumph in the Napoleonic Wars. He held the post of Governor of Greenwich Hospital until his death in 1816.

The Prince of Wales

From 1811 until his succession to the throne, the prince served as Crown Regent during his father's final mental illness. As George IV, he led an extravagant lifestyle that contributed to the fashions of the regency era. However, for most of his regency and reign, Lord Liverpool controlled the government as Prime Minister. George's governments, with little help from him, presided over victory in the Napoleonic Wars, negotiated the peace settlement, and attempted to deal with the social and economic malaise that followed. George's dissolute way of life earned him the contempt of the people and dimmed the prestige of the monarchy. Taxpayers were angry at his wasteful and seemingly unrestrained personal spending. He did not provide national leadership in time of crisis. Nor did he act as a role model for his people. His ministers found his behaviour selfish, unreliable, and irresponsible. His last years were marked by increasing physical and mental decay and withdrawal from public affairs. Privately one of his senior aides confided in his diary, *"A more contemptible, cowardly, selfish, unfeeling dog does not exist … There have been good and wise kings but not many of them … and this I believe to be one of the worst."* He died in 1830 with no legitimate issue and was succeeded by his brother, Prince William Henry, who assumed the throne as King William IV.

Afterword

May every British child go to the National Maritime Museum at Greenwich and look upon the uniform of Admiral Horatio Nelson, with its bullet hole at the top of its left shoulder and the blood of Mr Scott stained on the leggings when the admiral fell on the spot where Scott had died.

May it be whispered to them that the thousand years of Britain's freedom and the wellspring of innate pride that rests in every British heart has come with sacrifices so freely given and at prices so dearly paid.

CPSIA information can be obtained
at www.ICGtesting.com
Printed in the USA
FSOW01n0616290415
6788FS